ROMANO GUARDINI

November 13, 1997

To Lawrence S. Cunningham

in gratitude for collegial
support, sound advice, and
a wealth of knowledge.

with best wishes,

Robert A. Krieg

ROMANO GUARDINI

A PRECURSOR OF VATICAN II

ROBERT A. KRIEG, CSC

UNIVERSITY OF NOTRE DAME PRESS
NOTRE DAME, INDIANA

Manufactured in the United States of America

Library of Congress Cataloging-in-Publication Data

Krieg, Robert Anthony, 1946–
Romano Guardini : a precursor of Vatican II / Robert A. Krieg.
p. cm.
Includes bibliographical references and index.
ISBN 0-268-01661-5 (paper : alk. paper)
1. Guardini, Romano, 1885–1968. 2. Catholic Church—Doctrines—
History—20th century. I. Title.
BX4705.G6265K75   1997   97-22854
230′.2′092—dc21   CIP

The paper used in this publication meets the minimum requirements of the American
National Standard for Information Sciences—Permanence of Paper for Printed Library
Materials, ANSI Z39.48-1984.

CONTENTS

Acknowledgments   *vii*

Chapter One. From Vatican I to Vatican II   1
The Life of a Theological Precursor   *3*
An Inductive Method of Inquiry   *12*
Seven Theological Themes   *21*

Chapter Two. The Self-Disclosure of God   23
Four Notions of Revelation   *24*
A Conversion, 1905   *26*
Toward a Theology of Revelation   *29*
Toward Vatican II on Revelation   *41*

Chapter Three. The Church: A Light to the Nations   46
The Desire to Belong   *47*
Recovering an Ancient Ecclesiology   *54*
Living a Theology of Church   *59*
Toward Vatican II's *Lumen Gentium* (1964)   *66*

Chapter Four. Liturgy as Play before God   70
Recovering a Sense of Worship   *71*
A Theology of Liturgy   *75*
The Renewal of Worship   *80*

Chapter Five. Christian Faith and Literature   91
Into the Cultural Mainstream   *93*
A "Dialogue" with Rainer Maria Rilke   *99*
The Reception of Guardini's Literary Interpretations   *108*
Toward Vatican II's *Gaudium et Spes* (1965)   112

Chapter Six. Nazism: A Negation of the Person   115
Religion and Politics in the Early 1930s   117
Guardini's View of Nazism   123
What More Could One Theologian Have Done?   133

Chapter Seven. Jesus Christ, Mediator   137
Interpreting the Bible   139
The Living Christ   145
Literary Interpretation and Christology   152
Toward Vatican II's View of Jesus Christ   157

Chapter Eight. A Christian View of the Modern World   161
The Secularization of Germany   162
Coming to Terms with Modernity   165
Personal Existence in the Modern World   169
Toward Vatican II on the Church in the Modern World   177

Chapter Nine. An Interpreter of Truth   183
Waiting on God   184
The Reception of Romano Guardini's Writings   192
Romano Guardini's Legacy Today   202

Appendix 1. Romano Guardini, "Prayer in the Hour of Enduring"   205

Appendix 2. A Chronology of Romano Guardini's Life   207

Abbreviations   211
Works by Romano Guardini   211
Secondary Sources   211

Notes   215

Bibliography
A Chronological List of Selected Writings by Romano
    Guardini   257
A List of Selected Books on Romano Guardini   262
Index   265

ACKNOWLEDGMENTS

I wish to thank colleagues whose academic support made this book possible. Thomas F. O'Meara, O.P., encouraged me in this project from the start and frequently provided wise counsel along with a wealth of pertinent literature. I also tested out ideas with Lawrence S. Cunningham, Richard P. McBrien, and Michael A. Signer. Michael A. Fahey, S.J., and Robert W. Lawrence read the entire manuscript and recommended improvements. Dorothy J. Anderson, Carolyn Drajer, Anne Fearing, and Patricia A. Moorehead worked hard to lighten my administrative duties at the University of Notre Dame while I served as the Theology Department's director of graduate studies. James R. Langford, John McCudden, and Ann Rice gave excellent editorial advice at the University of Notre Dame Press. I benefited from conversations with scholars in Germany: Hanna Barbara Gerl-Falkowitz, Hans J. Mercker, Josef Meyer zu Schlochtern, Hermann J. Pottmeyer, Arno Schilson, and Hermann Josef Schuster (Guardini Stiftung, Berlin). Franz Henrich (director) and Stephan Höpfinger at the Katholische Akademie in Bayern (Munich) and Ludger Bradenbrink at Burg Rothenfels am Main welcomed me to their respective institutes. Heinz R. Kuehn and Regina Kuehn graciously recalled their activities with Romano Guardini in Berlin. Research grants came from the Association of Theological Schools, the Eastern Province of the Congregation of Holy Cross, the Paul M. and Barbara Henkels Fund of the Institute for Scholarship in the Liberal Arts (Notre Dame). Finally, remembering my father, Anthony B. Krieg who died in 1994, I dedicate this book to my mother, Helen Battista Krieg.

FROM VATICAN I TO VATICAN II

We are accustomed to seeing popes stand on the ceremonial balcony of St. Peter's Basilica and give their blessing "Urbi et Orbi" ("To the city and the world") to thousands of people in St. Peter's Square. However, in recent history there was a period of approximately fifty years when popes did not walk onto the loggia. After Italian troops marched into Rome in September, 1870—thereby ending the First Vatican Council—and claimed the city along with the papal lands for the new national government, Pope Pius IX refused to accept the new political order. To show his opposition, the "prisoner of the Vatican" never again appeared on St. Peter's balcony. The next three pontiffs—Leo XIII, Pius X, and Benedict XV—also withheld the "Urbi et Orbi." But this precedent ended with Pius XI, who immediately after his election on February 6, 1921, insisted that the papal staff unlock the balcony's doors. Then he walked out and gave his blessing to the ecstatic multitude in St. Peter's Square. Pius XI's successors have continued to give the "Urbi et Orbi." In fact, beginning with John XXIII, the popes have bestowed their benediction over television and, more recently, on the World Wide Web.[1]

The history of the "Urbi et Orbi" manifests a fundamental shift that has occurred within the Catholic Church during the twentieth century. Amid the intellectual arrogance and political absolutism of the nineteenth century, Pius IX and the First Vatican Council reiterated the tridentine view of the church as the "perfect society," the fortress which safeguards the revealed truth about God and human life in a world that has rebelled against God.[2] But, amid the moral malaise and multicultural "global village" of the twentieth century, John XXIII and the Second Vatican Council presented the church as a "pilgrim people" walking with the human family on a journey to God's kingdom and desiring to share its received wisdom with all people. In other words, the church has undergone a transformation in less than one hundred years. Indeed, it has changed so fast and so significantly that many people still ask, how did we get from Vatican I to Vatican II? What is the path by which Catholicism moved from Pius IX to John XXIII?[3]

The pages that follow shed light on the change in the church by examining the life and thought of a theological pioneer who helped to open the way from Vatican I to Vatican II: Romano Guardini (1885–1968). Born in Italy, he lived all but his first year in Germany and, after the First World War, emerged as one of Germany's most original Catholic minds. Throughout his career, he pursued a twofold commitment: to retrieve the wisdom of the Judeo-Christian tradition and simultaneously to engage in an intellectual exchange with contemporary thought.[4] Although short in stature, soft-spoken, and shy, he attracted hundreds of people to his lectures and sermons.[5] Moreover, he wrote more than one hundred articles and over seventy books, many of which went through numerous printings in German and were translated into other languages. For instance, *Vom Geist der Liturgie* (*The Spirit of the Liturgy*) was reprinted nineteen times, and *Der Herr* (*The Lord*) thirteen times, and both have appeared in four or five languages.[6] Prior to 1950, neoscholastic scholars and church officials saw little of theological merit in Guardini's writings, and yet, since Vatican II, respected theologians such as Karl Rahner, Hans Urs von Balthasar, and Joseph Cardinal Ratzinger have acknowledged their indebtedness to Guardini. Voicing an assessment with which most commentators would now agree, Paul Misner has said of Guardini that "[i]n German-speaking lands there is no one who deserves more to be called a precursor of Vatican Council II."[7]

This book shows that Romano Guardini set the stage for the Second Vatican Council in three ways. First, by his dialogue with modernity he opened a way out of Vatican I's ghetto or self-enclosed Catholicism to Vatican II's "church in the modern world." Second, breaking with neoscholasticism, he employed an experiential or inductive approach to theological reflection that anticipated Vatican II's efforts to read the "signs of the times."[8] Third, he retrieved neglected aspects of the Christian faith's major tenets concerning revelation, Jesus Christ, and the church, and some of the ideas that he promoted were adopted and amplified by the council.

This first chapter treats two of Guardini's three contributions to the renewal of Catholicism. First, it recounts the theologian's journey from an intellectual ghetto into a continuing conversation with twentieth-century culture. In this perspective, Guardini arrived at his most original ideas during his years in Berlin (1923–43) and subsequently developed them during his years in Munich (1948–68).[9] Second, this chapter also explicates Guardini's inductive method in theology. After reviewing these two contributions, I examine seven of Guardini's theological themes in chapters 2 through 8.[10] Finally, chapter 9 highlights the unity of his thought and also its reception.

The Life of a Theological Precursor

THE YOUTH, 1885–1905

Romano Michele Antonio Maria Guardini was an inheritor of Christian humanism, of a wedding of the West's Greco-Roman heritage and Jewish-Christian tradition.[11] Born on February 17, 1885, in Verona, Italy, he lived with his parents not far from the city's Roman amphitheater. At the time, Verona was much the same as it is today. A statue of Dante, who was protected in Verona by Cangrande I, stands in a plaza at the heart of the city—the city of Shakespeare's tragedy of Romeo and Juliet. Across the Adige River, on the hillside, are the Giusti Gardens where Johann Wolfgang Goethe found inspiration for many of his writings. Guardini's parents—Romano Tullo and Paola Maria—were conscious of Verona's rich culture. When Romano was a boy, he received from his father a leather-bound copy of Dante's *Divine Comedy* and cherished it until the end of his life.[12]

When Romano was little more than a year old, he moved with his parents to Mainz, Germany. This city, like Verona, has a rich history of Christian humanism. Founded by the Romans in the first century B.C., Mainz stands at the confluence of the Rhine and the Main rivers and hence is a meeting point of commerce and ideas from north and south, east and west. Also, it has been a locus of Christian faith since the eighth century, when it became the seat of the first German archbishop, St. Boniface. In this international city Romano's father worked in imports and exports, especially of poultry and eggs. (In 1910 his father was appointed a member of the Italian consulate in Mainz.) In Mainz the young Guardini grew up amid museums with artifacts of the Teutons and Romans, the city's Roman fortress, and its churches from the early Middle Ages. Also, he learned of the city's son, Johann Gutenberg, the inventor of the first printing press with movable type. At an early age, then, Guardini came to value both the German and Mediterranean cultures.[13]

In their home on Gonsenheimer Strasse (today Fritz Kohl Strasse) Romano and his younger brothers—Gino, Mario, and Aleardo—lived with their parents as though their home were south of the Alps. They spoke Italian among themselves. Also, they retained their Italian citizenship, for both parents admired the Italian nationalist Benso di Cavour (d. 1861) and looked forward to the day when they would again reside in Italy. In fact, soon after the sudden death of Romano Tullo (b. 1857) in 1919, Paola Maria (b. 1862) moved to Lake Como and then to the family estate at Isola Vicentina, not far from Verona, where she remained until her death in 1957. Throughout his life, Guardini visited Isola Vicentina and found that many of his ideas originated during his stays there.[14]

At school the young Guardini was immersed in Christian humanism. Already fluent in German and Italian, he also learned Latin, Greek, French, and English, and excelled in the study of the classics, reading Dante, Shakespeare, and Stendahl in their original languages. Given his sensitive personality and also the fact that he was a non-German in Wilhelmian Germany, he kept to himself and a few friends. He was especially close to Karl Neundörfer, who died in a hiking accident in 1925. As Guardini was finishing at the Humanistische Gymnasium (today the Rabanus Maurus Gymnasium), he was invited to join other gifted students in discussions on history, the arts, and religious belief at the home of Dr. Wilhelm Schleussner and Frau Josephine Schleussner. This married couple—who were friends of Carl Muth, the founder of the Catholic literary journal *Hochland*—sponsored a study circle in which Mainz's most talented Catholic youth discussed the writings of John Henry Newman, Joris Karl Huysmans, and Léon Bloy as well as those of the medieval mystics. Participating in this group from 1903 until 1913, Guardini forged friendships with Josephine (d. 1913) and Wilhelm (d. 1927) Schleussner.

Soon after his graduation from the gymnasium on August 7, 1903, Romano Guardini entered the most traumatic period of his life. From October 1903 until July 1904, he studied chemistry at the University of Tübingen. However, no matter how hard he worked, he could not fully grasp his courses' subject matter and, as a result, received low grades. This unsatisfactory academic performance fed into the youth's tendency toward melancholy, and he soon found himself struggling with depression—a condition from which his mother also suffered.[15] In July 1904 Guardini withdrew from the study of chemistry in Tübingen and in October embarked on the study of economics with Lujo Brentano at the University of Munich. Although he immediately fell in love with Munich's museums, theaters, and concert halls, he did not relish his studies. Furthermore, as he saw many of his university peers abandon their Christian faith, he questioned his religious beliefs.

In July 1905 Guardini returned to his family's home in Mainz suffering from a crisis of faith. After numerous discussions with Karl Neundörfer, he underwent a religious experience which he later compared to Augustine's conversion. As a result of this event, he recommitted himself to Christian belief and the Catholic Church. Two months later, while studying economics in Berlin, he was praying in the Dominicans' St. Paul Church on Oldenburger Strasse when it dawned on him that he felt called to the priesthood. After discussing the matter with a priest, Johannes Moser, Guardini decided that he should not immediately enter a seminary. Rather, he proposed to officials of the diocese of Mainz that he study theology at the University of Würzburg with Hermann Schell (d. 1906) and other progressive Catholic scholars who were identified with "reform Catholicism." When this proposal was rejected, he opted for the University of Freiburg.[16]

THE STUDENT-PRIEST, 1906–22

The transition to theological studies in March 1906 was difficult for Guardini. During his first weeks in Freiburg he became so depressed that he entertained thoughts of suicide.[17] But, as he heard the lectures of the theologian Carl Braig and the church historian Franz Pfeilschifter, he felt better, for he discovered his love of theology. By June, he decided that, after completing the semester, he should move to the University of Tübingen with its creative theological faculty.

From October 1906 until July 1908 Guardini studied at the University of Tübingen and resided at its seminary, the Wilhelmsstift. Here, he "awoke interiorly" and laid the theological foundation for the remainder of his life.[18] This self-definition occurred as the result of four factors. First, Guardini took courses in theology, scripture, and church history with progressive professors such as W. Koch, J. E. Belser, and F. X. Funk.[19] Second, along with Karl Neundörfer and new friends like Josef Weiger, he formed a literary circle in which everyone read world literature and shared their own writings. He was so inspired by these discussions that he wrote what in 1907 was his first publication: *Michelangelo: Gedichte und Briefe* (Michelangelo: poems and letters).[20] Third, during his year and a half in Tübingen, Guardini found spiritual sustenance at the Abbey of Beuron, especially in its celebration of mass and the divine office. As a result of his retreats at Beuron and his conversations with some of its monks, he became an oblate of St. Benedict, taking the name Odilo. Fourth, Guardini also benefited in Tübingen from the spiritual counseling he received from his priest-professor Wilhelm Koch. In particular, with Koch's help, Guardini overcame the scrupulosity which had afflicted him since childhood.

Although Guardini owed the originality of his thought to no single teacher, he felt a lifelong debt of gratitude to Wilhelm Koch (1874–1955).[21] From Koch, he learned about the development of the church's teachings, and while eventually holding that Koch discussed historical questions to the neglect of the doctrines themselves, he regarded Koch as someone who "witnessed to the truth." For this reason, he was shocked when in 1916 the seminary's rector—"in a not very upright manner"—pressured Koch into withdrawing from the faculty because of his alleged "modernist" tendencies. In his later years, Guardini said that the rector's action was an instance of "the frequent sins of orthodoxy."[22]

In October 1908 Guardini, along with Karl Neundörfer, entered the diocesan seminary in the shadow of Mainz's cathedral and immediately faced difficulties. He studied neoscholastic manuals which he found to be arid and intellectually stifling. Moreover, he chafed under the seminary's regimented daily schedule and authoritarian rule. He could not adjust to an "education which rested on a system of mistrust and surveillance."[23] When he and Neundörfer voiced their dissatisfaction to seminary officials, they were suspected of "modernism" and required to postpone their ordinations for six months. Nevertheless, Guardini was ordained a priest by Bishop Georg Heinrich Kirstein on May 28, 1910, and on the next day celebrated mass with his parents' gifts: a chalice and paten crafted at the Abbey of Beuron.

From the summer of 1910 until the autumn of 1912 the newly ordained priest served in a parish in Heppenheim, a hospital in Darmstadt, the Cathedral of Worms, and Mainz's St. Christopher Church. During this period he made a decision that his parents opposed: in August 1911 he became a German citizen. His action resulted from two considerations. Since he wanted to teach theology, he was required by German law to become a citizen so that he could qualify for civil service to which belonged all teaching positions in Germany. And, having lived twenty-five of his twenty-six years in Germany, he had become German in spirit. In his words: "While I spoke and thought in Italian at home, I grew up intellectually in the German language and culture. . . . I felt that I belonged interiorly to the German essence."[24]

In October 1912, with Bishop Kirstein's approval, Guardini matriculated at the University of Freiburg in order to pursue a doctorate in theology. When it came time to pick a dissertation topic and a director, he displayed his independent spirit by choosing not to study the work of St. Thomas Aquinas under the direction of the highly regarded professor Carl Braig (1853–1923), but to examine the thought of St. Bonaventure with the guidance of the adjunct instructor Engelbert Krebs (1881–1950). He speedily wrote his thesis, entitled *Die Lehre des heiligen Bonaventura von der Erlösung* (The teaching of St. Bonaventure on salvation), and was awarded his Ph.D. on May 15, 1915. During these years, he formed friendships with Martin Heidegger (1889–1976) and also with Josef Frings (1887–1978), who eventually became Cologne's cardinal-archbishop.

In the summer of 1915, Guardini returned to the diocese of Mainz with the expectation that he would teach at the diocesan seminary. However, he soon realized that diocesan officials blocked his way. Since the mid-1800s Mainz's seminary had become a national center for neoscholasticism, and Guardini did not qualify as a neoscholastic theologian because of his studies at Tübingen and Freiburg. Hence, for the next five years he assumed pastoral duties at Mainz's St. Ignatius Church, St. Emmeran Church, and St. Peter Church, and also served as the chaplain to the diocesan youth group called "Iuventus" "youth"). Simultaneously, during the last two years of World War I, he fulfilled his military duty by working part-time as a hospital orderly. In his free time, he wrote a manuscript on the nature of worship, which he submitted to Abbot Ildefons Herwegen for publication in the Abbey of Maria Laach's series *Ecclesia Orans*. Entitled *Vom Geist der Liturgie*, this book quickly attained national recognition in ecclesial and intellectual circles.

In the autumn of 1920, with the permission of Bishop Kirstein, Guardini moved to the University of Bonn in order to write his "Habilitationsschrift," the scholarly monograph required to qualify for a teaching position at a university. Under the direction of Gerhard Esser, he again studied the thought of St. Bonaventure and, in January 1922, completed "Die Lehre vom lumen mentis, von der gradatio entium und von der influentia sensus et motus und ihre Bedeutung für den Aufbau des Systems Bonaventura" (The theory on the illumination of the mind, on the gradations of being and on the influence of the senses and the mind's movement and their meaning for the structure of Bonaventure's system).[25] During his two years in Bonn, he also studied with the moral theologian Fritz Tillmann, became friends with the art historian Paul Clemen, and entered into intellectual exchanges with the phenomenologist Max Scheler (1874–1928) in Cologne and the Jewish philosopher Martin Buber (1878–1965) in Frankfurt am Main. Further, Guardini stayed in touch with the young people in Iuventus and at Easter in 1920 went with them to Burg Rothenfels am Main, near Würzburg, in order to participate in a gathering of the national Catholic youth association, called "Quickborn" (German, "wellspring of life").

The breakthrough for the start of Guardini's teaching career occurred in the summer of 1922 when he lectured on the nature of the church at the national conference of the Catholic Academic Association. In late 1922 these lectures were published as *Vom Sinn der Kirche* (*The Church and the Catholic*) and immediately became a best-seller. They also resulted in Guardini's receiving two academic "calls." The University of Bonn offered him the chair of Practical

Theology and Liturgical Studies, which he declined. Soon afterwards, the University of Berlin invited him to assume its new chair of Philosophy of Religion and Catholic *Weltanschauung* (worldview). As the Weimar Republic staggered under soaring inflation, Guardini accepted this prestigious position and moved to Germany's cosmopolitan capital.

While Guardini's shift in 1905 from the study of economics in Berlin to the study of theology in Freiburg marked the first major transition in his life, his move from Bonn to Berlin in 1923 marked his second major juncture. From this time on, Mainz was no longer his life's geographical center. In Berlin he received a professor's substantial income and hence became independent of the diocese of Mainz. Moreover, since his mother and brothers had returned to Italy, he had no familial ties to Mainz. Having left Mainz in 1920, Guardini did not visit there until 1943.[26]

THE YOUNG PROFESSOR, 1923–44

At Berlin's Wilhelm Friedrich University the thirty-eight-year-old Guardini assumed an academic chair that was surrounded by controversy. Berlin was a predominantly Protestant city, and its few Catholics belonged to the diocese of Breslau. (In 1930 the Vatican established the diocese of Berlin.) The university housed the faculty of Protestant theology (begun in 1810 by Friedrich Schleiermacher) whose professors opposed the creation of a professorship in Catholic theology. However, the Weimar government, which depended on the support of the powerful Catholic Center party, put pressure on the university's administration to institute an academic position for a professor who could teach theology to the school's Catholic students. With the backing of its emeritus professor Adolf Harnack (1851–1930), the administration worked out a compromise whereby the academic chair officially belonged to the University of Breslau's faculty of Catholic theology, but the chairholder served as a visiting professor in Berlin. As a result, Guardini received a cool reception in Berlin from his Protestant colleagues and initially had to rely on the support of the Prussian minister of cult (religious practice) Carl Becker, who had studied with the theologian Ernst Troeltsch (1865–1923), Berlin's professor of the history of philosophy and civilization.[27]

Guardini soon won everyone's respect by his engaging, profound lectures. Teaching three types of courses—systematic theology, revelation in the New Testament (including biblical ethics), and Christian faith and literature—he attracted many students, professors, and members of Berlin's intellectual circles to his lectures. Also, his courses influenced some of Berlin's most outstanding students, among whom were Hannah Arendt (1906–75), Hans Urs von Balthasar (1905–88), and Josef Pieper (1904–), who subsequently observed that "Guardini was an incomparable teacher."[28] On the basis of these lectures, Guardini produced works on Anselm of Canterbury (1923), Kierkegaard (1927), Pascal (1935), Augustine (1935), Dostoyevsky (1939), and Socrates (1943). Because of this success, he retained his academic chair for the next sixteen years— ten years during the Weimar Republic and six during the Third Reich.[29]

Guardini did not, however, confine his professional activity to lecturing and writing. He held informal discussions with students each week on art, literature, and religion. Beginning in 1924, he presided at the Eucharist in the chapel of the Soziale Frauenschule on Wednesdays, and, starting in 1928, he celebrated mass on Sundays in St. Benedict Chapel on Schlüterstrasse. His preaching and spiritual conferences generated such books as *Vom heiligen Zeichen* (*Sacred Signs* [1927]), *Vom Lebendigen Gott* (*The Living God* [1929]), *Vom Leben des Glaubens* (*The Life of Faith* [1935]), and *Der Herr*. Furthermore, in 1923 Guardini emerged as the guiding light of Quickborn at Burg Rothenfels, and in 1924 he became co-editor with Josef Aussem of Quickborn's journal, *Die Schildgenossen* ("the fellowship of the shield"). By the late 1920s Guardini had become a preeminent spiritual and intellectual leader of German Catholic youth.

However, by the mid-1930s Guardini was increasingly viewed with suspicion by Adolf Hitler's Third Reich, and on March 11, 1939, the Reich dismissed Guardini from the University of Berlin. On August 7 Heinrich Himmler's SS seized Quickborn's castle at Rothenfels. In 1941 the Reich banned *Die Schildgenossen* and forbade Guardini to give public addresses. In this vacuum, Guardini concentrated on his writings and produced *Welt und Person* (*The World and the Person* [1939]), *Besinnung vor der Feier der Heiligen Messe* (*Meditations Before Mass* [1939]), *Der Rosenkranz Unserer Lieben Frau* (*The Rosary of Our Lady* [1940]), *Die Offenbarung* (Divine revelation, 1940), *Der Tod von Sokrates* (*The Death of Socrates* [1943]) and *Vorschule des Betens* (*Prayer in Practice* [1943]). Keeping a low profile, he lectured in Berlin's Catholic *Volkshochschule*, offered evening classes in the Jesuits' St. Canisius Church, and presided at masses in St. Benedict Chapel.

By the summer of 1943, Guardini had entered into the third major transition of his life, and, as in the case of the earlier turning points, it resulted in a geographical change. After the Reich advised Germans to leave Berlin because of the round-the-clock bombing by the Allied forces, Guardini packed some of his belongings and moved to St. John the Baptist Church in Mooshausen in the

Allgäu region of southern Germany. Here, he resided with Pastor Josef Weiger until the end of the war. During these two years, he wrote his autobiography, *Berichte über mein Leben* (Reports about my life [1984]).[30] As he awaited his sixtieth birthday and the war's outcome, he had no idea what the future held for him.

THE MATURE PROFESSOR, 1945–68

In the autumn of 1945, through the efforts of Carlo Schmid, a leader in the Social Democratic party, Guardini was invited to the Eberhard Karls University of Tübingen, where he assumed a special academic chair as the professor of the Philosophy of Religion and Christian *Weltanschauung*. He remained for two years, turning down calls to the universities of Göttingen, Munich, and Freiburg, where he was offered Heidegger's position. In 1948, Guardini accepted the University of Munich's new chair in the Philosophy of Religion and Christian *Weltanschauung* within the philosophy department. For the next fifteen years, he filled lecture halls with students, professors, and international guests.[31] During these same years, he preached at mass on Sundays during the academic year at St. Ludwig Church.[32] Moreover, in the postwar years, he offered advice concerning the new direction of the German press, radio, and television to former members of Quickborn such as Walter Dirks, who edited the leftist newspaper *Frankfurter Hefte*, and Clemens Münster, the cultural director of Radio Munich.[33]

Along with his lectures, preaching, and consulting, Guardini continued to write. He gave his analysis of Western society at mid-century in *Das Ende der Neuzeit* (*The End of the Modern World* [1950]) and *Die Macht* (*Power and Responsibility* [1951]), and at the same time completed *Rainer Maria Rilkes Deutung des Daseins* (*Rilke's Duino Elegies* [1953]) and *Über ein Gedicht von Eduard Mörike* (Concerning a poem by Eduard Mörike, 1956). Based on his lectures on Christian ethics in Berlin and Munich, he wrote *Tugenden* (*The Virtues* [1963]). Remaining active in the liturgical renewal, he gave his address on "the liturgy and the spiritual situation of our age" at the First German Liturgical Conference in 1950, served on the Vatican's Preparatory Commission on the Liturgy for the Second Vatican Council, and in 1964 sent the Third German Liturgical Conference a thought-provoking letter on "the cultic act and the present challenge facing liturgical education." Finally, uneasy with some of the emphases of the Second Vatican Council, the eighty-year-old theologian reiterated his ecclesiology in *Die Kirche des Herrn* (*The Church of the Lord* [1965]).

In 1963, at the age of seventy-eight, Guardini retired from the Ludwig Maximilian University of Munich and was succeeded by Karl Rahner.[34] As his health deteriorated, he wrote ten letters to Josef Weiger in which he reflected on God as creator, suffering, and evil. These letters posthumously appeared as *Theologische Briefe an einen Freund* (Theological letters to a friend, 1976).

On October 1, 1968, Guardini died in a Munich hospital of a cerebral hemorrhage. Three days later, Julius Cardinal Döpfner, the archbishop of Munich-Freising, presided at the funeral mass and in his homily praised Guardini's "existential faith": "For him, faith was not a theoretical conviction, rather it became a living experience."[35] Afterwards, Guardini was buried in the Oratorians' small cemetery at Munich's St. Laurence Church.

A PRECURSOR OF VATICAN II

In the postwar years Romano Guardini received numerous awards and honors. In 1952 Pius XII made him a papal prelate (monsignor), and in 1965 Paul VI invited him to become a cardinal—an invitation which the ailing theologian respectfully declined. Along with the church's honors, Guardini was awarded honorary doctorates in philosophy from the universities of Freiburg (1954), Padua (1965), and Bologna (1969). In 1952 the German Book Association bestowed its prestigious Peace Prize upon Guardini, and in 1955 he received Munich's Gold Medal and in 1959 the Federal Republic of Germany's Great Cross of Merit. In 1958 he was welcomed into the Bavarian Order of Merit and also into the Peace Association of the Order "Pour le mérite." In 1962 Prince Bernhard of the Netherlands conferred the Erasmus Prize upon Guardini for his work on behalf of Christian humanism throughout Europe, and in 1965 he was awarded the German Cross of Merit with Star and Munich's Gold Medal of Honor.[36]

These honors and awards confirm that Romano Guardini made an extraordinary journey during his eighty-three years. He overcame his introversion as he lectured and preached to gatherings of hundreds of rapt listeners. Challenging German prejudices, he gained entrance into the nation's top intellectual circles. Further, in a country which prior to 1945 was two-thirds Protestant, he earned the esteem of Protestants as well as Catholics in Berlin, Tübingen, and Munich. Finally, in a church which officially recognized only neoscholasticism, he expressed fresh theological insights in an existential or personalistic language that immediately appealed to Catholics at large and eventually won over bishops, theologians, and philosophers.

Guardini's life was not only important in itself but also as a manifestation of the kind of pilgrimage in which most Catholics have found themselves in the twentieth century. Whereas the Catholicism of the 1800s gained expression in the First Vatican Council's defensive stance against "the world," the Catholicism of the 1900s is manifested in the Second Vatican Council's readiness to enter into a dialogue with modernity. This change in the Catholic Church's posture *ad extra* was anticipated in Guardini's life and came about in part through his efforts.

However, as we will see, Guardini himself had mixed feelings about Vatican II. Throughout his career of teaching, preaching, and writing, he labored to recover the truth of the Judeo-Christian tradition and thus to revive a Catholicism that had become spiritually and intellectually stale. But he did not envision a council and had no idea that he was preparing the ground for the *aggiornamento* which was formally initiated by John XXIII and the Second Vatican Council. When this renewal sprang up and flourished, the elderly theologian recognized that it contained many of the ideas that he himself had communicated so well to Catholics around the world and rejoiced that the church was recovering some of its fundamental insights. Yet, this burst of energy and fresh thought also startled Guardini. As a result, unlike Karl Rahner (1904–84) and Yves Congar (1904–96), who fully committed themselves to Vatican II and its implementation, the aging scholar entered with some hesitation into the conciliar spirit. It is accurate, therefore, to describe Guardini as a precursor of the Second Vatican Council; that is, as a forerunner he helped to bring the church to this moment but did not completely participate in this new phase in the church's life.[37]

An Inductive Method of Inquiry

PHENOMENOLOGY AND THE CHRISTIAN FAITH

Beginning in his youth, Guardini longed for a clear understanding of life's meaning. Because he was not satisfied to know simply one aspect of reality, he was frustrated by his studies in chemistry and economics. As a seminarian at Tübingen's Wilhelmsstift, he clarified his philosophical orientation as he engaged in discussions with his friends Neundörfer and Weiger, his teacher Koch, and the Beuron monks, who encouraged him to study Scheler's works as well as Plato's writings. Out of these conversations in 1907 and 1908, Guardini fashioned four essays that he reworked in 1914 into a monograph of twenty pages, entitled *Gegensatz und die Gegensätze* (Opposition and the opposites). During the next nine years, he labored further on this text and in 1925 produced the revised, enlarged text *Der Gegensatz* (The opposition).[38]

In his theory of opposition Guardini staked out a position distinct from two prevailing philosophies of his day: neo-Kantianism and the antimetaphysical forms of the "philosophy of life" (*Lebensphilosophie*), which we now call existentialism.[39] In the late 1800s and the early 1900s, German scholars like Nicolai Hartmann and Ernst Cassirer revived the philosophy of Kant. However, in Guardini's judgment neo-Kantianism is wrong in that, by accepting the dichotomy between "theoretical reason" and "practical reason," it locates Christian belief within the realm of the knowing subject's feelings and actions and excludes a consideration of belief's objective referent, God. In short, neo-Kantianism reduces Christian belief to a subjective ethics. By adopting a narrow, bifurcated notion of reason, it fails to recognize that Christian belief is a form of knowledge about objective reality and hence about truth.[40]

At the same time, Guardini was also critical of the antimetaphysical forms of *Lebensphilosophie*.[41] He judged that these different philosophies of life, as formulated by Friedrich Nietzsche, Wilhelm Dilthey, and Henri Bergson, are too nonrational. That is, they accentuate the emotive and volitional aspects of personal existence but neglect both our use of reason and the rational order of objective reality. In particular, Guardini criticized Nietzsche's themes of subjectivity, self-realization, and the Promethean will to power.[42] In this vein, he distanced himself from the Catholic theologians Ludwig Klages and Karl Adam because in their neoromantic *Lebenstheologie* they gave too much weight to life's nonrational dimensions and lacked a language by which to discuss adequately the transcendence of God.[43]

Having rejected neo-Kantianism, on the one hand, and the subjective forms of *Lebensphilosophie,* on the other, Guardini located himself within the philosophical trajectory of idealism that formally began with Plato, gained Christian expression in the Johannine writings, and matured into the neo-Platonism of Plotinus and Porphyry. In this regard, on his seventieth birthday, he said that he stood within the lineage "from Plato through Dante and Pascal to Hölderlin, Mörike, and Rilke."[44] And, on his eightieth birthday, he spoke of his indebtedness to Plato.[45] On these occasions, he could also have mentioned his reliance on Socrates, Augustine of Hippo, Anselm of Canterbury, Bonaventure, Nicholas of Cusa, Søren Kierkegaard, Wilhelm Raabe, and Fyodor Dostoyevsky.[46]

Within the neo-Platonic orientation, Guardini found his specific home in the phenomenological movement that was begun in Germany by Edmund Husserl and advanced by Martin Heidegger, among others.[47] Phenomenology—which is itself a form of *Lebensphilosophie*—examines the ontological dimensions of our lives. That is, it analyzes personal existence in such a manner as to go beneath the empirical aspects of reality in order to penetrate to the "essence" (*Wesen*) of human life. Thus, it treats such topics as the reality of being a person and the character of love. While phenomenology draws on history, psychology, and sociology, it seeks to go beyond them by probing into the universal, abiding dimensions of personal existence and love. In short, it intends to inquire into objective reality. This aim is expressed in phenomenology's slogan of the 1920s: we must inquire "into things in themselves," *zu den Sachen selbst*. An echo of this phrase occurs in Guardini's statement: "I was always convinced that it would be only essential to make known the thing or subject matter as it itself wanted to be made known."[48]

Phenomenology depends upon an ontology and epistemology. It assumes that the various aspects of human life are manifestations of abiding realities or essences, and, for this reason, it holds that empirical analysis should not have the last word but should eventually lead to insights into the essence of things and the coherence of reality. Such knowledge frequently depends upon intuition (*Anschauung*), that is, an insight into the way in which all of the pieces of something fit together. At the same time, phenomenology perceives the coincidence of opposites. It accepts that something may be so complex that its elements relate to one another in a dialectical or opposing manner, and, hence, our knowledge of this reality often includes polarities which we discuss by means of concepts or models that are seemingly incompatible with one another.[49]

Guardini found in phenomenology, especially in the work of Scheler, the categories and kind of reasoning that he needed for his inquiries.[50] Tailoring phenomenology to his purposes, he delved into the mystery of revelation, the person of Jesus Christ, the nature of the church, and the principles of the liturgy. As a result, he produced the kind of theology that was subsequently taken up by Hans Urs von Balthasar, Pope John Paul II (Karol Wojtyla), and Cardinal Joseph Ratzinger.[51] In order to understand Guardini's theological method, we must consider his books *Der Gegensatz* and "Die Lehre vom lumen mentis."

DER GEGENSATZ (1925)

At the outset of *Der Gegensatz: Versuche zu einer Philosophie des Lebendig-Konkreten* (The opposition: Toward a philosophy of the living-concrete) Guardini explains that his theory of opposition combines an ontology and epistemology.[52] Thus, his book's aim is to sketch these philosophical components.[53] We will consider one key idea from his understanding of being and also one seminal thought from his view of human knowing.[54]

The starting point for Guardini's ontology is not an idea of being in general but actual or "living-concrete" persons.[55] He posits that the primary reality is the personal existence of the absolute being (God) and, secondarily, the personal existence of human beings. In Guardini's words: "I experience myself as a concrete [being]. And this concrete [being] exists in itself; from the external to the internal [and] from the internal to the external, it forms itself and emerges out of its own origins. This means it is alive."[56] Personal existence occurs in an organic whole, a single coherent being, which is so complex that its unity is not always apparent. In other words, to be a person is to be a being who is constituted by inherent tensions or polarities. For example, every person is at once an individual and a member of a family. Also, a person embodies a tension between "head" and "heart," between the logic of deduction and the logic of intuition. In Guardini's view, the potentially unified though tension-filled being that is called a person is the starting point for considerations of the nature of being in general.

In speaking of the polarities of personal existence, we must however distinguish between the category of opposition (*Gegensatz*) and the category of contradiction (*Widerspruch*).[57] According to Guardini, an opposition is that "peculiar relation, in which two elements exclude each other and are nevertheless bound together, indeed . . . presuppose each other."[58] For example, although the solitary character and communal character of personal existence stand in opposition, they are both essential to a person's life. As a human being moves toward greater individuation, he or she brings these two dimensions into an increasingly harmonious relationship that is possible only because the two dimensions are ontologically one. By contrast, a contradiction or *Widerspruch* occurs when two elements exist not within an inherent unity but with the one always negating the other. Good and evil stand not in opposition but in contradiction to each other. Romanticism errs, therefore, when it locates the conflict between good and evil within the category of opposition. This mistaken acceptance of evil as part and parcel of life is manifest, Guardini notes, in the writings of Hegel, Goethe, Hermann Hesse, Thomas Mann, and Carl Jung.[59]

Corresponding to this ontology is an epistemology that takes for granted our ability to grasp objective reality. In Guardini's judgment, our knowledge of what is real depends upon two cognitive processes which stand in opposition to each other. On the one hand, we perceive the inner unity of something by means of an insight, by a cognitive leap from a comprehension of each part to an apprehension of the whole and the relations of each part within it. This process of insight or intuition involves a perception "which illumines not by means of reasons but by means of interior authenticity and clarity."[60] On the other hand, we often understand the essence of something by means of concepts that we use in opposition to one another. In our effort to make sense of human life "[t]here appears to be a definite fitting together of notions that results in the opposition of notions, to be more precise, in the use of concepts existing within the relationship of opposition."[61] For this reason, we frequently see that our statements about human life are paradoxical. We find ourselves saying that personal existence is simultaneously solitary and communal. In sum, our ability to know the underlying realities of personal existence depends upon both our acceptance of intuition as a legitimate way of knowing and also our readiness to accept potentially creative tensions and paradoxes into our philosophical and religious reflections.

Guardini's theory of opposition is crucial for his writings.[62] This significance is immediately evident in two practical implications for his work. First, because he began his reflections with actual persons, he developed his ideas in response to existential questions which he perceived in his life and others' lives. As a result, he never developed a systematic theology, but pursued particular themes in response to actual situations in his life.[63] Second, given his attentiveness to the underlying tensions or polarities in life, Guardini crafted his thought in a dialectical manner.[64] That is, he frequently juxtaposed ideas within a single text.[65] For example, in *Vom Geist der Liturgie* he points out that authentic worship involves moments of silence as well as moments of communal action. Further, on occasion he treated a topic in one text and then balanced it with a text on an opposite topic. On the one hand, in *Vom Geist der Liturgie* Guardini analyzes the church's worship, and, on the other, in *Der Kreuzweg unseres Herrn und Heilandes* (*The Way of the Cross of Our Lord and Savior Jesus Christ* [1919]) he sheds light on the role of religious devotions within the Christian life. In subsequent chapters, as we examine Guardini's themes, we will note his use of opposition.

"DIE LEHRE VOM LUMEN MENTIS" (1922)

During the first decades of the twentieth century, there occurred a revival of studies on the thought of Bonaventure that sprang from at least two factors.[66] First, from 1882 to 1902 scholars at the Franciscan center of Quarrachi near Florence, Italy, published new critical editions of the medieval theologian's writings, thereby making available texts which had been neglected for centuries.[67] Scholars soon saw that scholasticism possessed more diversity than neoscholasticism assumed.[68] Second, since the Vatican insisted that Catholic philosophers and theologians anchor their scholarship within scholasticism, Catholics who were looking for an alternative to the sixteenth-century Thomistic commentaries of the Dominican Cajetan and the Jesuit Francisco de Suárez saw Bonaventure's writings as a promising resource for another kind of theology.[69]

Guardini had no desire to adopt the scholastic method that was employed both in the Latin manuals of Hermann Dieckmann, Christian Pesch, and Adolphe Tanquerey and the Thomist commentaries of Reginald Garrigou-Lagrange. Rather, he perceived that the Franciscan's theological method provided a valid paradigm for his way of thinking. Setting aside the categories of neoscholasticism, he appealed to this neo-Platonic orientation as he fashioned a synthesis of philosophy, theology, and spirituality. In studying Bonaventure's soteriology and his understanding of the "illumination of the mind," Guardini was, therefore, more concerned about clarifying and legitimating a theological method than about becoming a medievalist.[70]

To be more specific, neoscholasticism was unsatisfactory to Guardini (and others) in part because of its rigid deductive method of inquiry. This way of doing theology took shape during the baroque period. Building on Melchior Cano's designation of the appropriate, authoritative sources of theology, Dionysius Petavius insisted that theology is a science of deduction which requires two major steps. First, scholars should formulate premises of faith out of scripture, the church fathers, conciliar teachings, papal teachings, scholastic texts, and principles of human reason. Second, they should deduce theological conclusions from these premises by means of the deductive logic of the Aristotelian syllogism.[71] These two foundational steps should generate a process of explanation which, in Yves Congar's words, entails this sequence: "thesis, *status quaestionis* (that is, an exposé of opinions), positive proofs from authority, proofs from theological reason, solution of the difficulties, corollaries, and in particular corollaries for life and piety."[72] Beginning in the mid-1800s neoscholastic scholars recovered the baroque method of theology and followed it so closely that they left virtually no room for new theological questions. Moreover, they did not permit new theological ideas, unless these were "conclusions" that they reached by means of Petavius's deductive reasoning.[73]

By contrast, the way in which Bonaventure had reflected on the wisdom of the Christian faith is inductive. That is, it remains grounded in experience, especially in the spiritual life, and allows for the pursuit of new questions. In fact, it begins with the believer's issues. This emphasis on the knowing subject springs from the fact that the tradition of Augustine, Anselm, and Bonaventure emphasizes the heart's restlessness for God and conceives of God as absolute love. It expects, therefore, that the whole person—feelings and will as well as intellect—enter into the believer's quest for new understanding.[74] Bonaventure's holistic approach appealed to Guardini, who was also attracted to the life and thought of Francis of Assisi.[75]

In "Die Lehre vom lumen mentis" Guardini discusses Bonaventure's "theory" concerning our knowledge of God.[76] For our purposes, this monograph conveys two things of importance: Guardini's neo-Platonic ontology and his theological method.

According to Guardini, Bonaventure's ontology is anchored in the view that creation is a unity with gradations of being which, in varying degrees, share in the fullness of existence. This created hierarchy of beings points beyond itself to its divine creator, who is existence itself. On the one hand, the creator remains distinct from creation, and, on the other hand, God has chosen to be creation's source and goal. The aim of human life is, therefore, union with God, and the primary way in which we should relate to creation and to its creator is by means of our whole selves. Further, the created order is an organic whole. Guardini writes: "The theory of the hierarchy [of being] treats the problem of religious unity. And, to be sure, the unity is apprehended not as a juridical-abstract order, but as the living-concrete unity of an organism whose members and organs are the individual parts [of this whole]."[77] Creation's inherent unity is, however, constituted not with uniformity but with diversity, with abiding polarities.

With regard to Bonaventure's epistemology, Guardini highlights the Franciscan's reliance on an inductive method. When one considers only the writings to which neoscholasticism usually refers, it appears that Bonaventure reasoned in a deductive manner. Yet, when one looks at his entire literary corpus, one sees that he frequently reasoned inductively, that is, out of an intuition into an experience. In Guardini's words:

> The doctrine of re-creation, of the hierarchy [of being] is entirely different. Here the starting point is not an abstract principle but a concrete intuition, an image, namely the view of the structural and functional unity of being— which appears as a great organism. The intuition is borne by love to the world in general as also to that which is sublime. The natural world for its part is joined into a supernatural unity of the life of grace.[78]

These two elements of Bonaventure's thought—the unity of being and the role of an inductive or experiential method—bear a striking similarity to the ontology and epistemology that Guardini developed in *Der Gegensatz*. As we previously saw, personal existence, for Guardini, is an organic whole which is characterized by the interplay of opposites, and the starting point for our knowledge of reality is our personal existence, whose essence we can know by means of insight and the dialectical use of concepts.

TOWARD VATICAN II'S INDUCTIVE APPROACH

One year prior to completing "Die Lehre von lumen mentis," Guardini lectured in Bonn on the theological method of Anselm of Canterbury. As he analyzed Anselm's project of "faith seeking understanding," he illumined how this inductive process begins with the heart's reaching out to God and culminates with the person in adoration before God. Guardini then observed that the church and its theology benefit when the church encourages not only the deductive theology of neoscholasticism but also the inductive theology of Augustine, Anselm, and Bonaventure. Although there exists a tension between these theological orientations, this opposition can be a fruitful one for Christians. In Guardini's words, when the church permits these two kinds of theology,

> there emerges a tension between the deductive orientation from the eternal, from dogma, [and] from the church, and the inductive orientation from the concrete, individual reality of events and occurrences. Here beyond ordinary measure lies the process of Catholic theology. The fruitfulness of theology springs out of the tension between the eternal and the temporal, out of the pressure to hold together at the same time both [methods] at least in consciousness.[79]

This statement of 1921 implicitly expresses the theologian's commitment to enrich Catholicism by means of an inductive theological method which would serve as an alternative to the deductive method that predominated in the Catholic Church at the time. Guardini promoted his approach, however, not so much by talking about it as by actually using it as he investigated a wide range of topics. Insofar as he was a prolific and widely read writer, he prepared the way for the various kinds of inductive methods that the Second Vatican Council adopted. To be sure, other scholars also contributed to this shift away from theology as the expression of logically deduced conclusions to theology as inquiry into the life of faith. One need only think of the biblical scholarship of Marie Joseph Lagrange, the theology of proclamation of Josef Jungmann, the *nouvelle théologie* of Henri de Lubac, the historical theology of Yves Congar, and the transcendental Thomism of Joseph Maréchal.[80] Nevertheless, Guardini played a key role in the renewal of Catholic theology because he reached insights by means of his phenomenological method and successfully communicated them to nontheologians as well as to theologians.[81]

The Second Vatican Council implicitly acknowledged the work of Guardini among others by employing inductive approaches in its writings. The council chose to cast its documents not in the categories and language of neoscholasticism but in more existential or personal terms. It also decided to address not the conventional questions of the theological manuals but rather the new questions being asked by Catholics within contemporary society. Further, the council's sixteen documents rely on the findings of modern scholarly investigation concerning the formation of the Bible, the history of theology in the patristic and medieval periods, religious experience outside of Christianity, and the influence of culture upon human life. In choosing to read "the signs of the times," the council demonstrated that its members had learned from the inductive reasoning of creative scholars like Romano Guardini.[82]

In concluding our consideration of Guardini's theological method, a brief assessment is in order. One of the strengths of Guardini's method of inquiry is its attentiveness to the existential basis of Christian faith and theology. Guardini's writings appealed to people because they include astute, limpid descriptions of basic aspects of life such as friendship, loneliness, and our yearning for God. However, his approach has its limitations. One of these is its neglect of historical investigation.[83] Time and again, he sought to shed light on a biblical text's full meaning without engaging in analysis of historical context that shaped an author's intentions and literary genre. To be sure, Guardini steered clear of critical methods and their results in part because from 1907 until 1943 Catholic theologians risked censure by the Vatican when they explicitly relied on historical inquiry. However, even after the Vatican permitted theologians to use critical methods in biblical studies, he did not take them seriously.[84] His uneasiness with Vatican II's teachings likely sprang, at least in part, from the fact that the council's scholarly methods were more inductive than Guardini's.

Finally, Guardini's theological method manifests an important omission: it did not lead him to develop his ideas explicitly in relation to church doctrines. To be sure, Guardini recognized the role of the church's official teachings in critical reflection upon the teachings of the Christian faith.[85] However, he rarely discussed the doctrinal formulation of a basic tenet of Christian belief. In his christological writings he did not grapple with the meaning of the doctrine of Chalcedon, and in his ecclesiological writings he did not discuss Vatican I's Dogmatic Constitution on the Church of Christ, *Pastor Aeternus* (1870), nor Pius XII's encyclical *Mystici Corporis* (1943). Guardini may have opted for silence regarding church doctrines in order to avoid a conflict with Rome, as occurred with his teacher Koch.[86] But, as a result of this avoidance, his theological method is incomplete, which in turn means that his writings are not as rich as they might otherwise have been.[87]

Seven Theological Themes

Romano Guardini did not create a systematic theology. Guided by his pastoral involvements, he developed his thought in response to circumstances and allowed his insights to cluster in theological themes. Commenting on his work in 1955, Guardini noted that he always spoke to concrete situations: "I have never worked on the basis of programs. As often as I tried to do this, I went astray. Almost all of my writings were written in response to opportunities; this term ['opportunities'] could be taken to mean that the writings came about as something in life pressed for linguistic expression."[88] He observed, too, that as he responded to particular circumstances, he found himself returning to certain topics: "By this means, a series of basic thoughts worked themselves out, which also resulted in leading ideas, and were frequently repeated. For the reader who requires always something new, I can only offer the justification that the thoughts in this process became, I hope, more precise and richer."[89]

Guardini's comments provide a key as to how to study his large corpus of writings. Since he kept returning to certain themes throughout his life, we can gain access to his thought by examining some of his major topics. Thus, each of the next seven chapters treats one theme in Guardini's writings: revelation, the church, the liturgy, literature and religious experience, Nazism, Jesus Christ, and the Christian life in the twentieth century.[90] To round out our study, chapter 9 illumines the dynamism which unifies these various themes: Guardini's desire to know the truth and to make it known to his readers.[91]

One last clarification. Each of the following chapters discusses a theme within the context in which it arose in Guardini's life and times in Germany.[92] Since he himself has said that his ideas emerged out of actual circumstances, the surest way to grasp accurately his ideas is to appreciate his texts within their contexts, especially the "movements" that occurred within German Catholicism between the wars.[93] Commentators have rightly observed that some studies have removed Guardini's ideas from their original settings and thus not caught the nuances of his ideas. To be specific, Balthasar and Ratzinger have provided fine insights into Guardini's work, and yet they could have more adequately treated the complexity and critical edges of his thought if they had paid more explicit attention to the circumstances in response to which he articulated his ideas. In other words, each of the remaining chapters is fashioned in light of Heinz Robert Schlette's caution:

> I do not believe that the danger is very great that Guardini could be forgotten. Greater to me appears the danger that the memory of Guardini will be falsified, that his work and his person will be harmonized and stylized in an unhistorical manner and out of context, that one will make too little of the creative initiative and the desire for change which filled Guardini from the start.[94]

The Catholic Church and its theologies have changed in recent decades. Many of us can no longer recall how things were, and why they are no longer the same. Romano Guardini played a major role in leading Catholicism from Pius IX to John XXIII, from the knowing stance of the First Vatican Council to the listening stance of the Second Vatican Council. In this chapter I have reviewed two ways in which Guardini tilled the soil from which sprang Vatican II. First, in his person he anticipated the change which Catholics around the world have made in the twentieth century, for his life was a journey from isolation to dialogue with modernity. Second, he sketched out and employed an inductive method in theology that was an acceptable alternative to the deductive approach of neoscholasticism. The third way in which Guardini served as a precursor of Vatican II was to develop themes on the church's central teachings, the first of which for our consideration is the notion of revelation.

THE SELF-DISCLOSURE OF GOD

ON APRIL 24, 1870, the First Vatican Council approved its Dogmatic Constitution on the Catholic Faith, *Dei Filius,* in which for the first time the church formulated an official statement on revelation. According to the council, God's communication consists of a set of truths or "laws." In the council's words, along with God's "natural" revelation through creation, "[i]t was, however, pleasing to his wisdom and goodness to reveal himself and the eternal laws of his will to the human race" in a "supernatural" way.[1] Although this statement mentions that revelation includes the communication of God's self, this aspect remains undeveloped in the constitution. Instead, the document associates "the eternal laws" with the "deposit of truth" which God has entrusted to the church. In this view, Christian faith entails cognition of God's teachings.

Almost one hundred years after the First Vatican Council, the Second Vatican Council spoke its mind on the mystery of God's word. On November 18, 1965, the council in its Dogmatic Constitution on Divine Revelation, *Dei Verbum,* declared that revelation primarily consists of God's self-manifestation. In a statement clearly patterned after Vatican I's formulation, Vatican II stated: "It pleased God, in his goodness and wisdom, to reveal himself and to make known the mystery of his will (see Eph 1:9)."[2] Here we see that while Vatican I used the expression "the eternal laws of his will," Vatican II spoke of "the mystery of his will." This linguistic change conveys the understanding that at the center of God's word stands not a body of teachings but a divine person. This view is enhanced as the document goes on to speak about the revelation of God's "self" and "intimate truth." In other words, by contrast to Vatican I's notion of revelation as a set of "laws" which we grasp with our minds, Vatican II adopted the notion of revelation as the disclosure of a person whom we know with our whole selves.

This shift in the church's notions or paradigms of God's word indicates the spiritual and theological fermentation that occurred in Catholicism from 1870 to 1965. One of the scholars who contributed to this rethinking of the church's basic tenets was Romano Guardini. At the University of Berlin, he regularly lectured on God's communication in the New Testament, and in 1940 published his *Die Offenbarung* (Revelation). In this seminal book, he conceived of revelation as God's self-disclosure. Whereas the neoscholastic theologians who were Guardini's contemporaries used the metaphors of laws and truths in their presentations on God's word to us, he adopted the language of person. Thus, he supplied what Vatican I had not explicitly stated in *Dei Filius*.

This second chapter explains Guardini's understanding of revelation. It provides this explanation after first reviewing the theological options that were available in the early 1900s and, second, clarifying how Guardini's religious transformation of 1905 contributed to his understanding of God's word. The chapter concludes by showing that his view prepared the way for Vatican II's *Dei Verbum* and also its Pastoral Constitution on the Church in the Modern World, *Gaudium et Spes*. Further, it calls attention to a shortcoming in Guardini's theology of revelation, namely, its ahistorical, positivistic character—a shortcoming which meant that his work was surpassed by the council.

Four Notions of Revelation

Since the Enlightenment, the topic of revelation has surfaced as crucial in Christian belief. The Enlightenment's conviction that human reason had come of age resulted in scholars' judgments that talk of God's word had fallen by the wayside, along with superstition and magic. One of the outspoken representatives of the extension of rationalism to religious matters was G. E. Lessing, who in 1777 maintained that "the accidental truths of history can never become the necessary proofs of reason."[3] On the basis of this axiom, he held that the teachings of Christian faith had to stand independent of Jesus and his disciples. The church's so-called divine truths had to be shown to be universal ideas and norms which human reason could apprehend apart from their first proponents. As Christians struggled to respond to this intellectual challenge, there emerged at least four models of God's special communication to human beings: revelation as ethics, revelation as a set of truths, revelation as human consciousness, and revelation as interpersonal encounter.[4] I will briefly review each of these notions.

One way of conceiving of God's revelation is to view it primarily as a matter of ethics. Drawing on the philosophical system of Immanuel Kant, liberal theologians have held that the teachings of the Bible belong within the realm of "practical reason." They see that Jesus was a teacher of the moral life who instructed his followers on the basis of his example, his explicit ethical teachings concerning love of neighbor (e.g., the Beatitudes), and his radical trust in God as a loving parent. The University of Berlin's preeminent church historian,

Adolf Harnack, brilliantly presented this position in *Das Wesen des Christentums* (*What Is Christianity?* [1900]). According to Harnack, Jesus

> desired no other belief in his person and no other attachment to it than is contained in the keeping of his commandments. Even in the fourth Gospel, in which Jesus' person often seems to be raised above the contents of the Gospel, the idea is still clearly formulated: "If you love me, keep my commandments." . . . To lay down any "doctrine" about his person and his dignity independently of the Gospel was, then, quite outside his sphere of ideas.[5]

According to a second notion, revelation consists of the set of truths that Jesus Christ gave to his followers and that the church now safeguards. In this view, to speak of God's word is to present a body of teachings that the human mind can grasp but to which it could not reason on its own. Since this is the model of the First Vatican Council and neoscholasticism, it operated in the Latin manuals that governed Catholic theology for over a century.[6] For instance, in his *Brevior Synopsis Theologiae Dogmaticae* (*A Manual of Dogmatic Theology* [1911]), Adolphe Tanquerey states: "*Divine revelation* properly called is the manifestation to us of some truth by God through the supernatural illumination of our mind." As used by Tanquerey, the phrase "some truth" expresses the sense of a specific teaching or law that God imparts to our intellects. This understanding becomes clearer when Tanquerey links God's "truth" with "divine concepts." In Tanquerey's words: "This illumination of our mind is called the *speaking* of *God* because divine concepts are really and properly manifested to man who hears."[7] For Tanquerey, as for all neoscholastic theologians, a theology of revelation must give priority to a "cognitive-informational model" of God's word.[8]

A third notion is that revelation is, at least in part, a form of human consciousness. Recognizing the role of the knowing subject in every act of knowledge, this view sees that the believing community's efforts to express in words who and what is known in God's word are always colored by the culture and thought-world in which the community lives. In its extreme form, as evident in Hegel's *Phenomenology of Mind* (1806), this notion of revelation neglects the objective reality of God's communication and focuses on the development of our self-awareness in various epochs. In 1907 the Catholic Church condemned the notion of revelation as a form of human consciousness, and in 1908 the Holy Office excommunicated Alfred Loisy (1857–1940) for promoting this view. In the early 1900s, German Catholics who were identified with reform Catholicism held a moderate understanding of revelation as a mode of human awareness.[9] Among these scholars stood Hermann Schell and Wilhelm Koch, both of whom influenced Romano Guardini.[10]

A fourth model is anchored in the view that God's word comes to us as an interpersonal encounter in which God has chosen to reveal God's self to us and to which we respond in trust, commitment, and dialogue with God. This notion came to prominence in the nineteenth century. In his *Philosophical Fragments* (1844) Søren Kierkegaard tells the story of the king and the maiden in order to convey his insight that, in choosing to enter into relationship with us, God has bridged the "infinite qualitative difference" between God and ourselves and approached us as a lover would reach out to the beloved. In the early twentieth century, other expressions of this view occurred within Protestant dialectical theology. In his commentary on Paul's letter to the Romans (*Der Römerbrief* [1919]) Karl Barth claims that a chasm exists between God and the human family but that God has overcome this gap in Jesus Christ. Similarly, in their writings on God, Ferdinand Ebner and Martin Buber employed the philosophy of personalism, as did Emil Brunner, who held that, because of God's grace, human beings are disposed for an "encounter" with God.[11]

During his studies, Romano Guardini came into contact with representatives of the four views outlined above. He learned about revelation as a form of consciousness during his conversations with Johann Moser in Berlin, who had studied with Schell, and also during his classes with Wilhelm Koch in Tübingen. At Mainz's seminary, he heard lectures on the neoscholastic view of God's word as a set of truths. At the University of Berlin, he lectured side by side with members of Harnack's theological circle who presented the notion of revelation as ethics. Finally, he learned about God's communication as self-disclosure when he read Martin Buber's *I-Thou* (1923) and felt at home within this theological orientation.

A Conversion, 1905

Guardini's model of God's word originated, in part, out of the religious conversion that he underwent in 1905. After recounting this event, I will consider how it led to Guardini's reflections on the transformation of St. Augustine and also to Guardini's writings on revelation.

In his *Berichte über mein Leben* Guardini comments that a number of factors brought about his personal "encounter" (*Begegnung*) with the living God. As noted in chapter 1, after graduating from Mainz's Humanistische Gymnasium in 1903, Guardini failed in his chemistry studies and did not fare much better in courses on economics. Moreover, in Tübingen, Munich, and Berlin, he interacted with atheist and agnostic students. By 1905, he had begun to doubt God's existence. In his words: "My religious convictions began specifically to waver. I cannot name a special occasion for this. Not even the one which pedagogical wisdom accepts gladly as the rule, that I had come into some kind of erotic relationship, for this did not occur."[12] He pursued his questions with a priest at Munich's St. Boniface Abbey but without a satisfactory resolution. "In the evening if I wanted to say a prayer, I did not know to whom I should address it and—a grotesque thing—frequently recapitulated a proof of God's existence in order to know that there is a God to whom I could pray" (p. 68). One evening, he spoke at length with an art student whose use of Kantian thought to refute Christian faith left Guardini disoriented and speechless.

In August 1905, as he was ending his stay in Munich and preparing to move to Berlin, Guardini and his friend Karl Neundörfer rested for a few days at the Starnberger See in the Bavarian Alps. As they discussed their religious beliefs, Guardini realized that Neundörfer had come to a new understanding of his Christian faith. During these same days, he read Houston Stuart Chamberlain's *The Foundations of the Nineteenth Century* (1899) and was struck by the author's belief that God acts within history. With this thought, a feeling of God's nearness awoke in Guardini: "The sense of a supreme presence remained with me, a presence weaving behind everything and caring [for us]—a presence about which however one can say nothing" (p. 70).

After these pleasant days, Guardini and Neundörfer returned to Mainz to stay with their families. One afternoon they met at Romano's home and again discussed belief in God. At one point, when they were reading in separate rooms, Guardini had a religious awakening, which he subsequently described as follows:

> I remember, as though it had been yesterday, the hour at which my decision occurred. It was in the small attic room in my parents' home on Gonsenheimer Strasse. Karl Neundörfer and I had spoken about the questions which concerned both of us, and my last words were: "Something will come from the verse: 'Those who find their life will lose it, and those who lose their life for my sake will find it.'" The literal meaning of this verse, Matthew 10:39, says what occurred to me. It became clear to me that there exists a law according to which persons who "find their life," that is, remain in themselves and accept as valid only what immediately enlightens them, lose their individuality.

If they want to reach the truth and attain the truth in their very selves, then they must abandon themselves. This insight had surely had its preparation, however it had escaped me. After my statement, Karl Neundörfer had gone into the adjoining room from which a door leads to a balcony. I sat at my desk and thought: "To relinquish my life, however to whom? . . . Not simply to God, for if a person means only God, then he can say 'God' and mean himself. There must be an objective reference. . . . There is however only one: the Catholic Church in its authority and certainty. . . . The question of finding or relinquishing one's life is ultimately decided not in relation to God but in relation to the church. . . . I can abandon my life, or I can maintain it." . . . At that moment everything became completely still. . . . Then I went to my friend and spoke to him. Something similar must have occurred to him. . . . For him the question had been, where is the way of love, and the answer had come: in the church. During the following days I was very happy, [filled with] a peaceful and calm happiness.[13]

Guardini's recollection of his religious experience of 1905 is enlightening in both its content and its form. After recounting the above, it goes on to tell how this experience led to his decision to study theology in Freiburg, enter Mainz's seminary, and be ordained a priest. In other words, it makes clear that this moment was the foundational event of Guardini's adult life. Furthermore, as recollected by Guardini, the form of his conversion is similar to the form of Augustine's transformation as recounted in the *Confessions.* Just as Augustine was speaking of faith with his friend Alypius at the time of his conversion, Guardini was discussing belief with Neundörfer. Also, both events occurred in secure settings, a garden and an attic room, and during a period outside of the ordinary routines. Augustine's breakthrough stemmed in part from his new knowledge of neo-Platonism, and Guardini's insight came from his dissatisfaction with neo-Kantianism and his reading of Chamberlain's book—a problematic book in German nationalism, as we will see in chapter 6. Moreover, biblical texts were the catalysts of both transformations. Augustine read Romans 13:13–14, and Guardini reflected on Matthew 10:39. Finally, immediately after their respective breakthroughs, both men felt a new sense of peace and a release of creative energy. These similarities between Augustine's conversion and Guardini's, as conveyed in *Berichte über mein Leben,* indicate that in Guardini's judgment he had experienced what Augustine described in his *Confessions.*[14]

In light of Guardini's view, it is not surprising that he subsequently prized the *Confessions.* During his first year of teaching at the University of Berlin, he lectured on Augustine's life and thought. Out of these lectures he wrote in 1929 an essay entitled "Das Gebet" (Prayer) on Augustine. In 1931 he again lectured on Augustine, and, in 1935, after the appearance of his books on Pascal and Dostoyevsky, he completed *Die Bekehrung des Aurelius Augustinus* (*The Conversion of St. Augustine*).

In this book Guardini shows how Augustine's life and thought make sense only in relation to his religious transformation in August, 386. By its very nature, Guardini notes, conversion is an event which requires the response of the whole person. It "can only be something that seizes a man with a life-or-death grip: total orientation to the all-demanding God, to Jesus Christ." The self-involving character of this event results from the fact that what occurs in this moment is God's self-disclosure to the individual and God's call for the individual to give his or her entire self over to God. In Guardini's words: "This is the God who 'arises,' enters into history, there to act; this is the God who selects an individual and draws him into history." From this moment on, a person sees himself or herself as well as other men and women primarily in light of revelation. According to Guardini, *Confessions* displays how Augustine reordered his life and thought on the basis of his encounter with God. However, this book is so profound that readers may benefit from "a usable guide" to it, an introduction that explains Augustine's spiritual journey and the Christian *Weltanschauung* to which this journey led. Such is the intent of *Die Bekehrung des Aurelius Augustinus:* "What it does try to show is what Augustine's thought is like at the root, there where he would never dream of a 'purely natural' standpoint stripped of all Christian elements. His thought is anchored in the world and its truth as it breaks in on him through revelation—'the' world, hence, in the logic of faith, the only true conception of the world."[15]

Guardini's account of Augustine's conversion is indirectly also an analysis of Guardini's own transformation and simultaneously a consideration of the kind of event which in his judgment is constitutive of mature Christian faith. In this view, Christian belief rests upon an experience, more specifically, an interpersonal encounter between God and ourselves, in relation to which the communication of a set of teachings or laws is secondary. This conviction is the cornerstone of Guardini's theology of revelation.

Toward a Theology of Revelation

GUARDINI'S SOURCES

Guardini's religious experience served as a primary source for his thoughts on God's word and indeed for his entire theology. For him, his turning point of 1905 stood as an analogy for God's self-communication within history.[16] Just as God can encounter one person and establish a new relationship with him or her, so God has acted within human affairs in order to turn the hearts and minds of the entire human family. Having come to this insight, Guardini needed a suitable language in which to express it, and for this he turned to the philosophy of personalism. In particular, he drew on four sources: Rudolf Otto's phenomenology of religious experience, Søren Kierkegaard's view of God's otherness, Wilhelm Dilthey's notion of *Weltanschauung,* and Martin Buber's language of "I-you."

One source for Guardini's thought was the work of Rudolph Otto (1869–1937) in the phenomenology of religion. As professor of Protestant theology at Breslau (1904–17) and then at Marburg (1917–29), Otto studied world religions with the aim of uncovering their common ground. A fruit of his labor was *The Idea of the Holy* (1917) in which he argues that at the heart of every religion is the experience of the "numinous," the "holy," that which is "wholly other." This reality is an "absolutely primary and elementary datum" and therefore cannot be reduced to something else, for example, to ethical principles as occurs in Kantianism. Every religion expresses, to some extent, this fundamental, irreducible reality. In Otto's words: "There is no religion in which it does not live as the innermost core, and without it no religion would be worthy of the name." [17] Every authentic religious experience consists of a sense of the numinous, of the *mysterium tremendum.* That is, in the presence of this reality human beings are filled with a sense of "awe" and even "dread," for they are overwhelmed by this reality's "majesty" and "energy." [18]

Otto's analysis made a lasting impression upon Guardini, for it provided him with a language in which to convey the insight that religious belief originates not in ideas but in experiences—experiences in which we encounter objective reality, the living God. [19] In his essay "Religiöse Erfahrung und Glaube" (Religious experience and faith [1934]), Guardini builds on *The Idea of the Holy* when he observes that human beings come to an awareness of the wholly other as they sense the mystery which surrounds their lives, that is, as they undergo phenomena such as the birth of a child, the death of a loved one, or a severe thunderstorm. However, according to Guardini, we must distinguish between natural religious experience and the Judeo-Christian faith, for whereas the former is caused by ordinary events within the created order, the latter comes about in response God's specific acts within history. Guardini states: "This faith is something essentially different from 'every religious experience.' What originates from it, the life of faith with its order, is something essentially different from every 'religion'—so much so that, to take an extreme case, faith without experience appears possible in the sense of a tumultuous life: the naked faith of obedience."[20] As we will soon see, however, in Guardini's judgment, the distinction between natural religious experience and the Judeo-Christian faith must not be pushed to a radical separation.

A second source to which Guardini appealed was the work of Søren Kierkegaard (d. 1855).[21] Alarmed by the way in which Hegel and other German idealists spoke of God as the "idea" within their philosophical systems, Kierkegaard argued for the distinction between what we can apprehend by human reason and what can be known only by the "leap of faith." In books such as *Philosophical Fragments* and *The Sickness unto Death* (1849) the Lutheran religious thinker sought to demonstrate that authentic faith rests on only one reality, God's word, which is addressed to us today as it was to Abraham and Sarah and also to Jesus' followers. For this reason, God's communication is "contemporaneous" with every generation. Further, it is brought to us not by a brilliant teacher like Socrates but by a unique individual, Jesus Christ, our savior.

Guardini reiterated Kierkegaard's conviction concerning the singular character of revelation as known within the Judeo-Christian scriptures and tradition.[22] In his essay "Der Ausgangpunkt der Denkbewegung Sören Kierkegaards" (The starting point of Søren Kierkegaard's movement of thought [1927]) Guardini carefully explicates Kierkegaard's analysis of authentic personal existence in *Sickness unto Death*. It is with approval that he presents Kierkegaard's claim that the act of faith involves the self relating to God as the ground of one's existence. In Guardini's words: "That required relationship exists in that I must relate to myself 'before God.' This 'before God' stands at the heart of Kierkegaard's notion of person. A person exists only as something which is 'before God.'"[23] At one point, Guardini even implicitly links Kierkegaard's reflections with his own conversion. In a statement which echoes Matthew 10:39 as well as Kierkegaard's thought, Guardini writes: "If I do not accept myself as I am, if I turn away from myself and seek to be what I am not, then I relate falsely to myself. Then I destroy myself."[24] In other words, only those who lose themselves by giving themselves to God will find themselves.

While accepting Kierkegaard's understanding of personal existence in relation to God, Guardini did not adopt a hard distinction between religion and Christian faith. In "Religiöse Erfahrung und Glaube," he observes that Protestant dialectical theologians in general and Kierkegaard in particular have spoken of a radical discontinuity (*Widerspruch*) between natural religious experience and Christian belief, when in fact the two, though distinct, relate to each other as opposites (*Gegensätze*). In other words, although natural religious experience and the Christian encounter with God are distinct, they are interconnected. Indeed, the former can prepare the way for the latter:

> The "either/or" in this form—presented so powerfully by Kierkegaard—is not Christian. . . . It is not true that the human family and the world are "sin," and that every [natural] religious experience is not true and contrary to God. There is truth about God and in relation to God in every moment of [natural] religious experience; however, in every such moment there is also ambiguity and, for this reason, the risk of no truth and rebellion. . . . Between [the numinous] and the holy God [who is] manifest in revelation [there] exists a similarity, if not a connection![25]

A third source for Guardini's reflections on revelation was the writing on the notion of worldview by Wilhelm Dilthey (1833–1911), who was a professor at the University of Berlin from 1882 to 1906.[26] According to Dilthey, human beings search for the coherence of their lives. They desire a sense of the unity of their view of the natural order, their understanding of human life, and their set of moral values and religious beliefs. This understanding of the whole is one's *Weltanschauung*. As Dilthey defined it, "a worldview is the frame of reference in which, on the basis of a perception of the world, questions concerning the meaning and significance of the world are resolved and the ideal, the good, and the most important standards by which one conducts one's life are derived."[27] Dilthey judged that, prior to the Enlightenment, most people found their worldview within their church. However, since the 1700s, many people in the West have formed their philosophy of life apart from any explicit religious belief. At best, they now regard their religion as simply one element within their horizon of understanding. Further, since Western society no longer agrees upon a universal, transcendent point of reference, each worldview is itself subjective and relative.[28]

After the First World War, German scholars took an intense interest in the category of worldview. Between 1918 and 1924 Ernst Troeltsch, Karl Jaspers, and Max Scheler wrote thorough studies on this topic.[29] During this time, too, Guardini assumed his academic chair for the Philosophy of Religion and Catholic *Weltanschauung* at the University of Berlin and entitled his inaugural lecture of 1923 "Vom Wesen katholischer Weltanschauung" (On the essence of the Catholic worldview). In this address he introduced some of his foundational ideas on revelation.

According to Guardini, a *Weltanschauung* is the point of view from which a person describes the whole of reality as well as each of its elements and their interconnectedness.[30] It involves both the perspective of seeing and also what is seen. The knower seeks to bring into congruence his or her vantage point and the deepest dimensions of life so that what results is not the knower's subjective apprehension but the knower's conformity of heart and mind to objective reality, the truth. The knower undertakes this kind of observation for the sake of understanding in itself, not primarily for the sake of action (e.g., ethics). This kind of viewing involves insight, including "intuition" (*Anschauung*), which permits the knower to detect inner relationships and the heart of reality. A *Weltanschauung* requires, therefore, both proximity to the subject matter and also critical distance, or, as Guardini puts it, "the viewer must grasp the world, indeed penetrate it, and at the same time be free of it."[31]

How can one attain a perspective that springs from a close relationship to reality and yet provides a critical distance on it? One must see reality in the light of God's word in Jesus Christ. In this effort, it does not suffice to rely primarily on God's "natural revelation." For the freedom required for the most accurate understanding of life's meaning, for the objectively true *Weltanschauung*, one must depend upon God's "historical, supernatural revelation."[32] One must build a worldview on the basis of God's self-communication in Jesus Christ. Such an understanding of life presupposes Christian faith, for "[f]aith means stepping to Christ, to the standpoint where he stands [and] to see out of his eyes." Further, this Christian belief should be Catholicism, for when a person enters into the Catholic Church, he or she moves into the community whose worldview expresses the whole of reality and its essence. To put this idea another way: "The church is the historical bearer of the full view of Christ for the world."[33] Once a person adopts the Christian *Weltanschauung* as known within Catholicism, the person stands not within a subjective and relative framework of other worldviews but within the horizon of meaning which is objective and absolute.[34]

Interestingly, after 1923 Guardini stated time and again that Christian faith is a special kind of *Weltanschauung*. However, he never developed his thought on this topic into a full account of faith and theology.[35]

A fourth source to which Guardini turned was the dialogical personalism of Martin Buber. Guardini's strong attraction to personalist thought was enhanced by his early contacts with Buber himself. As already noted, Buber contacted Guardini shortly after the publication of *Vom Geist der Liturgie* (*The Spirit of the Liturgy*) in 1918.[36] In the autumn of 1922, the two scholars met for the first time in Bonn, and afterwards Buber wrote to the Protestant theologian

Friedrich Gogarten: "I have also met Guardini at the lecture which I heard. In our conversation he drew close to me, however subsequently withdrew to the distance of [an] assured sense of church."[37] Buber followed up on the meeting by inviting Guardini in the spring of 1923 to attend a Jewish-Christian conference in Frankfurt am Main. Guardini replied in writing that he would be honored to attend. In his letter to Buber, Guardini commented on *Ich und Du* (*I-Thou*) which had appeared a few months earlier: "For a long time I have been reading your book. I am filled with respect, for it is well done. Perhaps I will come [to the conference in order] to say to you what I have questions about. However, these are entirely within my positive regard [for your book]."[38] Guardini surely respected *I-Thou*, for his reflections on personal existence and revelation bear a family resemblance to Buber's. Moreover, as we will see in later chapters, Buber and Guardini remained in personal contact until the end of their lives.

In *I-Thou* Buber develops three ideas that are crucial to Guardini's reflections. First, the Jewish philosopher observes that a person is not an isolated self but a relation, one who enters into relationships with other persons and the world. In Buber's words: "In the beginning is the relation—as the category of being, as readiness, as a form that reaches out to be filled, as a model of the soul."[39] Further: "Whoever says You [Thou] . . . stands in relation" (p. 55). And, "the world of relation" consists of three "spheres": relations with the natural world, with other human beings, and with God (pp. 57, 150). Second, distinguishing between a relationship of I-you and a relationship of I-it, Buber holds that the I-you relationship constitutes personal existence. If we are to mature into full persons, we must enter into interpersonal relationships. Buber writes: "The basic word I-you can be spoken only with one's whole being. The concentration and fusion into a whole being can never be accomplished by me, can never be accomplished without me. I require a You to become; becoming I, I say You. All actual life is encounter" (p. 62). Third, according to Buber, the primary relationship at the heart of personal existence is one's relationship with God, who as the absolute person always relates to us as the "eternal you." Buber writes: "Extended, the lines of relationships intersect in the eternal You. Every single You is a glimpse of that. Through every single You the basic word addresses the eternal You" (p. 123). And finally: "By its very nature the eternal You cannot become an It; because by its very nature it cannot be placed within measure and limit, . . . " (p. 160).

Buber's ideas fell like seeds into the fertile soil of Guardini's mind where they germinated and then sprang up in his theological anthropology.[40] In *Welt und Person* (*The World and the Person* [1939]) Guardini develops the theme that "man does not exist as an enclosed block of reality or a self-sufficient figure evolving from within, but rather exists for that which he encounters from without."[41] This understanding of personal existence originated, Guardini says, in the Bible and has developed within the Judeo-Christian tradition, especially in the writings of Augustine of Hippo. It embraces two notions of person. One is that a person is a "perceiving and acting subject" (p. 127). That is, personal existence is characterized in part by the ability to relate to oneself as an "I." At the same time, there is a second, complementary notion of person: a person is a being-in-relation to other persons. Personal existence consists in part in relating as an "I" to another who is a "you," and conversely in being a "you" to another who is an "I." In other words, a person is one who participates in relationships of mutual self-disclosure. "When I glance at another as 'I,' I become open and 'show' myself. But the relation remains incomplete unless the same movement begins from the other side and the other lets me become his 'you'" (p. 128).

Having introduced two concepts—person as subject and person as relation—Guardini extends his use of these two notions to the mystery of God, as he makes three points. First, the personal existence of human beings is derived from and is analogous to the personal existence of God (p. 156). God is both personal subject and being-in-relation within the divine life itself. In Guardini's words: "From all eternity God is the prime reality and ultimate mystery, but also the one who expresses himself" (p. 135). Second, the triune God freely chose to communicate God's self not only within the divine life but also outwardly, and, as a result, creation came about. Creation is the fruit of God's word and possesses within itself, in a derivative manner, the character of the "you" in relation to God. God calls each human being to the realization that: "My being 'I' consists essentially in this, that God is my 'you'" (p. 141). Third, human beings can enter into the "I-you" relationship with God only through their union with Christ in the Holy Spirit. Paradigmatic of the transformation that is required of all people is the conversion of St. Paul who, in the presence of the risen Christ, realized that he could not be united with God on the basis of the Law but only by means of his union with Christ. For this reason, Paul declares: "If anyone is in Christ, there is a new creation" (2 Cor 5:17).

Much more could be said, of course, about Otto's phenomenology of religious experience, Kierkegaard's analysis of the self in relation to God, Dilthey's category of worldview, and Buber's view of the "I-you" relationship. However, it suffices that we have a basic grasp of these ideas so that we can see how

Guardini brought them together in his theology of revelation—which is best classified as a kerygmatic theology, that is, as a theology which sees revelation as God's self-disclosure in Jesus Christ, who seeks to enter into an "I-you" relationship with all human beings.[42]

DIE OFFENBARUNG (1940)

In 1940, one year after the publication of *Welt und Person,* Guardini completed *Die Offenbarung: Ihr Wesen und Ihre Formen* (Revelation: Its essence and its forms). Although this book is only 155 pages in length, it presents a wealth of insight into the mystery of God's word. According to Guardini, revelation involves a personal encounter between God and human beings.[43] It is an event in which God's words and actions are properly interpreted by those persons to whom God freely and intentionally directs them. Guardini states: "Revelation shows itself never as an abstract system, but always as an acting life. At the end of the history of revelation stands the figure of the incarnate Son of God. Everything is fulfilled in him."[44] In order to explicate this understanding of God's self-communication, I will follow Guardini's threefold presentation of (1) God as revealer, (2) natural religious experience, and (3) the witness of the Bible.[45]

First, according to Guardini, revelation is God's freely given self-disclosure that occurs as a singular event or meeting. At the start of *Die Offenbarung,* Guardini writes:

> The first sentence of any theory of revelation [should] read: what revelation is, only revelation itself can say. It is not a moment in a series of natural disclosures of human existence, but comes from a pure, divine initiative. It is also not a necessary self-communication of the supreme being, but a free act of the God who is person. [It is] an event therefore which we can understand only by going to the teaching of the Bible and preferably taking the risk of understanding God too "humanly" rather than too "philosophically." "God reveals" means above all, "God acts." This action encounters human beings as they are and places them with their shortcomings and good qualities under (divine) judgment. It demands that they be converted and raises them, when they obey, to a new beginning. Indeed, their obedience is already this beginning, for the fact that they are able to obey is itself a gift of the same God who calls them. Thus we cannot derive revelation from the natural order but must accept it on the basis of itself alone. (p. 1)

Guardini immediately adds that God's word comes from the same God who created the natural order and who can be known in creation. God's act of creation and God's act of revelation are related, and yet they are also distinct. They are connected to each other in a relationship which is not one of contradiction or dualism but of opposition or polarity. As a result, the knowledge of God that we can attain from the natural world remains distinct from the knowledge which comes to us as a result of God's historical revelation. Whereas the former depends on our desire to know God, the latter originates from God's decision to disclose God's very self to us. This distinction between our natural religious knowledge and the knowledge of historical revelation within the Judeo-Christian faith is analogous, Guardini says, to the distinction between our comprehension of an inanimate object, for example, a crystal, and our understanding of another person. Natural religious experience is similar to our knowledge of a crystal's chemical composition—a knowledge which depends upon our initiative and use of an empirical method. The revelation offered in Judeo-Christian faith is comparable to our knowledge of another person as a person—a knowledge which depends on our self-disclosure and also on the other person's response to us. This distinction between ordinary religious knowledge and the Judeo-Christian faith determines the next two major points.

Guardini's second topic is ordinary knowledge of God or what is conventionally called natural revelation. Drawing on Otto's *The Idea of the Holy*, Guardini describes a natural religious experience as that moment in which something more breaks through the everyday elements of a situation so that a person receives a sense of something "holy" or "numinous" before which one should be reverent and obedient. Such moments may occur, Guardini notes, when we find ourselves close to the earth, as when camping, or when we live through a situation of joy (the birth of a child) or grief (the death of a loved one), or when we are struggling to make a major decision. In situations like these we often sense that we are in the presence of the "numinous." Guardini writes: "With the expression 'the holy,' we mean therefore that before which there arises in healthy persons the desire to bow down—to bow down in a manner they could not do before something which is only earthly" (p. 8). Further, at such moments we realize the inadequacy of our conventional use of words to speak about what has occurred at this moment and must resort to using symbols and figurative discourse.

The sense of having had a religious experience raises questions, however, for twentieth-century persons which Guardini notes while alluding to the critiques of religion by Ludwig Feuerbach and Sigmund Freud. One of these questions concerns the referent of a natural religious experience. Is there an independent reality to which such a moment refers, or is the moment solely something subjective? Also, if there exists a numinous reality or realities, how do we decide whether we are in the presence of something truly good or in the presence of something harmful to us and perhaps even "demonic"? Questions like these require, Guardini points out, that we have criteria by which to assess transcendent experiences (pp. 16–25).

In Guardini's judgment, a natural religious experience points beyond itself to an even fuller encounter with "the holy." Indeed, it ultimately points to Judeo-Christian faith. Natural revelation confirms its positive character and its orientation to historical revelation by exhibiting certain features, among which are the following. First, it whets our appetite for understanding the source and goal of our lives and creation, and it disposes us to intuit that this ultimate referent itself transcends the created order. Second, as evident in the thought of ancient philosophers such as Plato, natural revelation strengthens our innate drive to know the truth and inspires us to reach for the "absolute truth," the true God. Third, it heightens our awareness of our longing for a personal fulfillment which this world itself cannot give. Fourth, an authentic religious experience awakens us to the fact that we become full persons only as we enter into mutual relationships with other persons and ultimately with the absolute person, the transcendent and yet personal God. Implicitly appealing to Buber's *I-Thou* as well as Guardini's own *Welt und Person,* Guardini writes:

> I become foremost my whole self, my "I," when I come upon the "you" who is directed to me. This is, therefore, the person whom I love. However, this person's summons reaches through and beyond him. My proper "you" must be an absolute "you," and the most significant service of the person whom I love is to point me to that absolute "you" [God]. (p. 34)

Finally, we turn to the third topic: historical revelation as presented in the Bible. According to Guardini, the difference between natural revelation and historical revelation is comparable to our knowledge of a family's home and our knowledge of the family itself. Natural religious experience is similar to knowing about a family by walking through its home, while everyone is away, and observing each room's photographs, furnishings, arrangement, colors, and art. By contrast, the historical revelation of the Judeo-Christian faith is similar to knowing the family itself within its home. God's specific acts in human affairs disclose God with a directness and clarity unattainable in natural revelation. In Guardini's words:

> This activity is itself the primary and abiding foundational revelation: that God is the one who can act and really does act [in history]. His act brings

history into a direction, operates in history, leads and interprets it, admonishes and reprimands. As a result, [historical] revelation further realizes itself in this history and through it and in all forms which emerge in such a process. (pp. 53–54)

This understanding of historical revelation manifests itself, Guardini observes, in the Hebrew scriptures which recount how God chose time and again to speak and act for the good of Israel. God even went so far as to make covenants which commit God to the well-being of the Jewish people and simultaneously commit Israel to God. Moreover, the Bible attests that "revelation itself has a history" (p. 58). God made the initial covenant with Abraham (Gen 15:1–21) and then deepened it in his covenant with Moses in which God revealed the divine name and called Israel out of slavery into freedom (Ex 3:1–20). God reiterated this covenant with David (2 Sam 7:1–16). Further, God spoke through the prophets and the psalmists. As a result, Israel witnessed to the fact "that God really enters into the world with divine communication, that God really acts and speaks" [in human affairs]" (p. 66). But it is also clear that, throughout this history, God has respected human freedom and, as a consequence, God's intentions for people have been frustrated at times by human weakness and evil (pp. 60, 73–74). Since God's covenant was not fully realized, God sent Jesus Christ into our situation of incompleteness.

God's intention for the coming of the kingdom, for the fulfillment of the covenants between God and the human family, is realized in Jesus Christ who inaugurated his mission by declaring that "the time is fulfilled, and the kingdom of God has come near" (Mk 1:15). Jesus spoke and acted on God's behalf. Indeed, "what he does, God does; what opposes him, opposes God. Now God's destiny becomes complete and proper" (p. 75). Whereas human resistance and failure and also evil had previously hindered God's words and deeds, Jesus Christ enacted God's intention within human affairs and brought it to completion. Moreover, it has become evident that God's self-communication is primarily not a body of teachings but a person: "the authentic revealer, redeemer, renewer is the person of Christ himself" (p. 77).

What then is the "content of the revelation of Christ"? Guardini mentions six aspects. First, Christ brings the ancient covenants to fulfillment in "the new covenant of love and grace." In this new intimacy, Christ shows that the true God is not the "greatest essence, or basis of the world, or the absolute spirit, but is the one who speaks through the existence of Christ." Second, Jesus Christ reveals that the one God is triune: Father, Son, and Spirit. In Guardini's words:

"God reveals God's self in a form of existence which surpasses all human persons: as that one who bears in God's self the differentiations of a threefold I-you relationship and thus has community within God's self" (p. 80). Third, Jesus Christ discloses that the living God transcends the notions of God that we fashion for ourselves. Hence, we cannot derive the true God from human presuppositions, nor can we demand that the true God conform to our ideas of what God should be. Fourth, Jesus Christ makes known God's view of human life, namely, that human beings "are something before God and are absolutely important for God" (p. 81). Fifth, he sheds light on what God expects of human beings. He clarifies "the determination of the human task, the understanding of Christian values and obligations" (p. 82). It becomes clear that this ethical order is not opposed to the natural order but is in fact a further specification of it. Sixth, Jesus Christ has revealed "the coming of the new creation and the last things." God is drawing the world and human history to a transcendent future which fulfills and surpasses our deepest desires and aspirations. "The world and human beings with their work and destiny—in the form of salvation or abandonment—will be eternally sustained in the earnestness and in the love of God" (p. 84).

Guardini concludes *Die Offenbarung* with a consideration of the contemporaneity of Jesus Christ through the life of the church in the Holy Spirit. Referring to the work of Kierkegaard on this topic, he develops the Danish philosopher's view that the living Christ continues to invite men and women to encounter him in a manner not unlike the ways in which the first disciples came to know Christ in the Spirit after his resurrection (p. 134). Unlike Kierkegaard, however, who views faith as a private act, Guardini insists that this meeting with Christ occurs within the church by means of preaching, the sacraments, worship, and prayer. To make this point, he reiterates the insight with which we began our review of *Die Offenbarung*: historical revelation is the event of God's self-disclosure that has culminated in the incarnation. Guardini writes: "God reveals God's self fundamentally not in the form of doctrines but in the form of action; it is this action which then bears God's teaching" (p. 118). In light of this understanding, how can women and men come to know God? Not first of all in the church's teachings, as important as these are, but in an encounter with Christ alive in the Spirit through the church. Alluding to the conversion of St. Paul, Guardini observes that Jesus Christ

can reveal himself to everyone, and when and how he chooses. The encounter of Damascus can recur in every era. As a rule, [God] has entrusted this to the church, which proclaims him and his message, explicates what is situated in this person and message, bears this person and message into the world, interprets on this basis personal existence, and draws again what abides in personal existence into the realm of Christ. (p. 125)

This statement conveys two further elements in Guardini's view of revelation. First, it highlights the importance of conversion.[46] As previously mentioned, Guardini brought his own religious breakthrough of 1905 to his reflections on the divine word. In light of this experience, he took his bearings from the testimonies of Paul and Augustine to their respective religious transformations. Crucial in this perspective is that God's self-disclosure first of all involves God's action towards us and our encounter with God in Jesus Christ. Anything else that may be said about revelation, for example, concerning specific "truths" about God, must be situated in light of this experiential basis: if we want to communicate God's revelation to others, we must provide them with opportunities to meet the living Christ, for instance, in the church's liturgy and prayer.

Guardini's statement above makes a second point that I can only note here and then treat in the next chapter. His comment accentuates the church's essential role of witnessing to God's historical revelation, so that people may know in their lives the kind of transformation which Paul and Augustine underwent. In spite of its unworthiness, the church is called by God to assume "the function of contemporaneity." It must be the community in which "the faith of the teacher helps the hearer. Faith inflames faith. What comes forth [from God] is no naked word but a believed-in word—a word which is at least in some measure believed in" (p. 154).

Toward Vatican II on Revelation

ANTICIPATING *DEI VERBUM* (1965)

In twentieth-century theology *Die Offenbarung* was a major stepping stone from the First Vatican Council to the Second Vatican Council. It was such because it does not sustain the paradigm of God's word as the communication of a body of teachings. In other words, Guardini did not primarily use such terms as "laws" and "deposit of truth" which characterize neoscholastic tracts on revelation as well as Vatican I's *Dei Filius*. Instead, he relied on an interpersonal model of revelation with its language of "I-you" that permitted him to illumine God's self-disclosure, especially in Jesus Christ. Given this understanding of God's word to us, *Die Offenbarung* helped to open the way to Vatican II's discussion in *Dei Verbum* of God's "mystery" and "intimate truth." For this reason, according to Wolfgang Beinert, Guardini made an "essential contribution" to Vatican II's understanding revelation.[47] Yet, *Die Offenbarung* is a pre-Vatican II document, for it remains silent on an aspect of revelation which receives attention in *Dei Verbum*, namely, the subjective or historical dimension of God's word.[48]

There are two important ways in which Vatican II's Dogmatic Constitution on Divine Revelation acknowledges the role of the human subject in receiving God's word to us. First, the document calls attention to the fact that the church's understanding of God's communication has changed. It states: "There is a growth in insight into the realities and words that are being passed on." And: "Thus, as the centuries go by, the church is always advancing towards the plenitude of divine truth, until eventually the words of God are fulfilled in it" (n. 8). Second, building on Pius XII's encyclical *Divino afflante Spiritu* (1943), *Dei Verbum* recognizes the role of critical methods within biblical hermeneutics. It declares: "Seeing that, in sacred scripture, God speaks through human beings in human fashion, it follows that the interpreter of sacred scriptures . . . should carefully search out the meaning which the sacred writers really had in mind, that meaning which God had thought well to manifest through the medium of their words." In this regard, the constitution recommends the use of critical methods in the interpretation of scripture. It states: "Hence the exegete must look for that meaning which the sacred writers, in given situations and granted the circumstances of their time and culture, intended to express and did in fact express, through the medium of a contemporary literary form" (n. 12).

In contrast to *Dei Verbum*, *Die Offenbarung* gives little attention to the role of the human subject in the reception of God's word to us. It avoids talk about the place of human consciousness in our apprehension of God's self-disclosure and thus steers clear of statements that, in the light of Pius X's condemnation of modernism in 1907, could be construed as jeopardizing the objectivity of God's word. As a result, *Die Offenbarung* implicitly conveys a positivistic view of revelation. Guardini's statements imply that when we encounter God's word to us, we are confronted with an empirical reality which is almost as unavoidable as the rock of Gibraltar. Making this point, Hans Mercker has written: "Guardini seems to have the view that revelation is an island, a measured block, which stands in itself untouched by the progress of the history of the [human] spirit, at the same time without determination by its context."[49]

Furthermore, *Die Offenbarung*, which was written three years prior to

Divino afflante Spiritu, makes no mention of the role of biblical interpretation in discerning God's word within scripture. It conveys a view which prevailed after the condemnation of modernism, namely, that scripture must be read with no consideration of the situation and intention of specific authors, as explained by critical methods of interpretation, and with a disregard for the literary genre of biblical texts.[50] Guardini does not treat this topic in *Die Offenbarung,* in part because he had already formulated his views on biblical interpretation in an earlier essay titled "Heilige Schrift und Glaubenswissenschaft" (Sacred scripture and scholarly inquiry into the faith [1928]).[51] Since I discuss this text in chapter 7, I need only note here that, according to Guardini, theologians have little use for the results of higher criticism.

Another expression of Guardini's dismissal of historical investigation is found in his autobiographical reflections of 1944. Commenting on a shortcoming in Koch's lectures of 1907, he notes that Koch "had too much respect for 'critical scholarship,' as it was understood at that time; for this reason [he had] too little consciousness of revelation as the given fact and power from which to build up with confidence that image of the new creation which theology should treat." In his study of the Bible, Koch saw the "historical-biblical data," but "lacked the power to penetrate to the essence and wealth of these connections." This deficiency did not trouble Guardini because, as he reports, his conversion enabled him to delve into the Bible's meaning. In his study of scripture and tradition he "experienced that by means of this 'Copernican turn' of the believing mind the depth and fullness of the sacred truth discloses itself to us."[52] Thus, while Guardini did not question Koch's orthodoxy and respected him as a Catholic theologian, he also resolved to adopt a theology whose subject matter would be God's self-disclosure, as ascertained in the Bible without historical investigation.

In light of the Dogmatic Constitution on Divine Revelation, we can now see that by employing the notion of revelation as an interpersonal encounter, *Die Offenbarung* added to the theological fermentation which produced *Dei Verbum.* Also, *Die Offenbarung* is a pre-Vatican II statement for it makes too little of the human dimensions in the biblical reception of God's word to us. That is, it presents a positivistic view of revelation and neglects the role of critical methods in biblical interpretation.

ANTICIPATING *GAUDIUM ET SPES* (1965)

In 1958 Guardini turned again to the topic of revelation in his *Religion und Offenbarung* (Religion and revelation) in which he presents his thought on natural religious experience, as he discusses "the experience of the holy," "the symbolic character of things," and "the mythical character of religion."[53] Guardini intended *Religion und Offenbarung* to be the first of two volumes, the second of which would examine historical revelation. However, the second volume never appeared.

The fact that Guardini did not finish the second volume of *Religion und Offenbarung* indicates that he was not primarily concerned about formulating a complete theology of revelation. Rather, he wanted his thoughts on God's self-communication to serve as the cornerstone of a Christian worldview that provided a fresh perspective on Christian doctrine and also on modern thought.[54] Thus, instead of working on the second volume of *Religion und Offenbarung*, Guardini wrote such texts as "Zur Theologie der Welt" (Toward a theology of the world [1960]) and *Tugenden* (*The Virtues* [1963]).

Early in this chapter, we noted that *Die Bekehrung des Aurelius Augustinus* was meant to highlight how, after his religious transformation, Augustine ordered his life and thought in relation to God's word. Guardini wanted to show that "[Augustine's] thought is anchored in the world and its truth as it breaks in on him through revelation—'the' world, hence, in the logic of faith, the only true conception of the world."[55] In other words, in his study on Augustine, he was intent upon explicating Augustine's Christian worldview. This aim coincides with Guardini's lifelong effort to bring his understanding of revelation into dialogue with modernity so as to construct an encompassing view of the church and the contemporary world. An undertaking of such breadth meant, as he knew, that he would not become a specialist in any one academic field and would run the risk of being a "dilettante."[56]

In 1955, on his seventieth birthday, Guardini spoke about his persistent concern to do for our time what Augustine had accomplished for his age, that is, to lay out a Christian worldview. He explained that since the start of his career he had pursued one goal: "the knowledge of that which becomes clear in the encounter of the Christian faith, or, to be more precise, of the believing person with the real world."[57] In his lectures in Berlin, Tübingen, and Munich, he discussed the Christian understanding of the meaning of life. In some ways, his endeavor was similar to that of others like Wilhelm Dilthey, Karl Jaspers, and Eduard Spranger, each of whom had written on the category of *Weltanschauung* and also expounded their respective worldviews. But, unlike these scholars, Guardini committed himself in particular to expounding the Christian view of life. Thus, in his many diverse writings he engaged in "the consistent, that is to say methodical, encounter between [Christian] faith and the world. And not only the world in general, for [neoscholastic] theology also does this in its distinct questions, but in the concrete: in culture and its appearances, history, society and so forth. Especially important for me has been poetry." [58]

This statement is significant in two ways. First, it clarifies why Guardini did not push himself to finish his theology of revelation but instead pursued a wide range of themes, including a theology of the church and also an analysis of contemporary life. Second, it manifests another way in which this theologian set the stage for the Second Vatican Council. As we have already seen, *Die Offenbarung* put forth an understanding of God's word that came to maturity in the Dogmatic Constitution on Divine Revelation.

Now we must add that Guardini's intention to bring his understanding of God's word to bear upon modernity anticipated the council's aim in its Pastoral Constitution on the Church in the Modern World, *Gaudium et Spes*. In its preface to this astounding document, the council states that "it wishes to set down how it understands the presence and function of the church in the world of today." Then, in reference to the complex issues facing society, the council adds that it wishes "to enter into dialogue with [society] about these various problems, throwing the light of the Gospel on them and supplying humanity with the saving resources which the church has received from its founder under the prompting of the Holy Spirit." [59] Surely, this goal is similar to the one that shaped Guardini's life. In later chapters we return to *Gaudium et Spes,* but at this point we are ready to see what Guardini's view of revelation meant for his understanding of the church.

THE CHURCH
A Light to the Nations

ON JULY 18, 1870, the First Vatican Council adopted its second and last formal teaching, its Dogmatic Constitution on the Church of Christ, *Pastor Aeternus.* Originally included as one chapter within the council's long schema on the church, this document—which contains the statement on papal infallibility— was separated from the entire draft at the request of Pope Pius IX and then passed by the council. The constitution presupposes what the original schema spelled out: the church is first and foremost an institution. The constitution conveys this understanding in its frequent use of such terms as "governance," "office," "primacy," and "jurisdiction." At the same time, it works with the metaphors of "foundation," "temple," and "rock," all of which express the sense of the church as an unchanging, fixed reality.[1] These features in the constitution fit within the ecclesiology that the schema made explicit: "The Church has all the qualities of a true society. . . . [I]t is so perfect in itself that, although it is distinct from all other human societies, it is nevertheless far superior to them."[2]

Almost one hundred years after Vatican I, on November 21, 1964, the Second Vatican Council approved its Dogmatic Constitution on the Church, *Lumen Gentium,* in which it subordinates the notion of church as institution to other views or models of the church. The constitution's first chapter presents the church as a "mystery" which shares in the ineffable life of the triune God, and then it speaks of the church as the mystical body of Christ (e.g., 1 Cor 12). The constitution's second chapter describes the church as the people of God (e.g., Jer 31:31–34; 1 Pet 2:9–10). It is not until the constitution's third chapter that the council presents the church as an institution. This order of chapters conveys the council's mind: the church is a complex reality which expresses itself first of all as a community, a "communio," and secondarily as an organization.[3]

From 1870 to 1965 many people labored to change the Catholic Church's official self-understanding. Beginning in the late 1800s biblical scholars shed light on the various notions of church that are found within the New Testament, especially the metaphor of the body of Christ, and patristic scholars did the same with the writings of Irenaeus and Augustine. Also, during the 1920s, in the youth movement and the liturgical movement, Catholics throughout Europe experienced the church as a community, and they came to know their commonality with Protestants as they endured with them the two world wars, the horror and shame of the Shoah, and the rebuilding of postwar Europe. This ecclesiology of communion gained official support, albeit with a hierarchical interpretation, in Pope Pius XII's encyclical *Mystici Corporis* of June 29, 1943. In formulating this view of the church, Pius XII relied primarily on Emile Mersch's *Le Corps mystique du Christ* (1933) and Sebastian Tromp's *Corpus Christi quod est Ecclesia* (1937).[4] However, another scholar who contributed both by his writings and his pastoral leadership to this ecclesiological renewal was Romano Guardini.

As a theology student, Guardini became aware that while the church is an institution, it is in fact much more than this. It is also a community committed to God's revelation in Jesus Christ.[5] In 1922 Guardini formulated his ecclesiology in *Vom Sinn der Kirche* (*The Church and the Catholic*). Further, between the wars he communicated his understanding of the church to thousands of young Catholics at Burg Rothenfels. In 1964 when Vatican II adopted its Dogmatic Constitution on the Church, it gave official approval to an ecclesiology that Guardini had promoted for at least forty years.[6]

This third chapter illuminates Guardini's ecclesiology in four steps. First, it describes how Guardini came to his insight regarding the church within the context of Germany's longing for community after the First World War. Second, it reviews and evaluates *Vom Sinn der Kirche*.[7] Third, the chapter recounts how, in light of his ecclesiology, Guardini shaped the life of Quickborn at Burg Rothenfels and occasionally came into conflict with German bishops. Finally, it discusses his view of the Second Vatican Council.

The Desire to Belong

GERMANY'S LONGING FOR COMMUNITY

In 1915 Max Scheler predicted that when the Great War came to an end, Germans would desire a stronger sense of themselves as a people (*Volk*) and that they would act on this desire by seeking guidance from Catholicism. In an essay entitled "The New Sociological Orientation and the Task of German Catholicism After the War," the phenomenologist wrote that after the rapid industrialization in the late 1800s Germans felt isolated from one another and their existential roots. In part because of the war, they were increasingly aware of their longing to enter anew into close human relationships and also to recover life's basic experiences. As soon as the war was behind them, they would turn to their past, specifically to their *Volk* heritage with its emphasis on their communal bonds and ties to the earth. At the same time, they would look for a transcendent point of reference, hence, to religion, especially to Catholicism with its powerful sense of community. According to Scheler, German Catholics had strengthened their solidarity during the *Kulturkampf* and retained "the *corpus Christi* understanding of the church" amid the trend toward "the atomized society of political democracy." In this vein, Scheler observed:

> A chief element of the Catholic strength lies precisely in this. The ethos of the believing *Volk*-association recognizes as its basis the immediate feeling of a primary mutual responsibility of one person for another. Such a feeling is not founded first of all on [individual] consent. Rather, this ethos recognizes the idea of an organic and invisible interweaving of all parts of the ethical world in time and space, and this ethical world remains defective until the coming of the kingdom of God.[8]

In hindsight we know that Scheler's prediction proved fairly accurate. Throughout the 1920s and 1930s Germans tried to overcome the trend toward individualism by entering into vibrant groups and movements. In the extreme, Nazism on the political right and Bolshevism on the political left exploited this widespread yearning to belong to a corporate reality.[9] Since this longing for community influenced Guardini's ecclesiology, its manifestations require a brief review.

As World War I dragged on and then officially ended on November 11, 1918, Germans' desire for a greater sense of togetherness became linked with neoromanticism. Similar to the romanticism of the early nineteenth century to which had belonged Ludwig van Beethoven, J. W. Goethe, and Friedrich Schlegel, the neoromanticism of the first half of the twentieth century sought to move beyond the polarities between heart and mind, and subject and object, by appealing to the nonrational dimensions of human life.[10] This romantic orientation showed itself in the widespread appeal of the writings of Friedrich Nietzsche, Rainer Maria Rilke, and Henri Bergson. In their respective ways, each of these writers drew on feelings as well as ideas in order to convey a sense of the whole of reality, and each of them contributed to the emergence of various forms of *Lebensphilosophie* or existentialism.[11]

After the Great War Germans recovered the distinction between society (*Gesellschaft*) and community (*Gemeinschaft*) that Ferdinand Tönnies had proposed in *Gemeinschaft und Gesellschaft* (1887), and they employed it to make sense of their relationship to the Weimar Republic. Most Germans were not well prepared for democracy in general and were not enthusiastic about the Weimar Republic in particular. They had not rebelled against Kaiser Wilhelm II nor against Bavaria's King Ludwig III. Rather, they had watched Germany's monarchical rule collapse on November 9, 1918, as a consequence of Germany's defeat, and they did not have strong ties to the founders of the Weimar Republic: Friedrich Ebert, Matthias Erzberger, and Hugo Preuss. Also, their confidence in the Republic wavered as they endured severe food and fuel shortages and the economic effects of the war debts and reparations, to which their new leaders were constrained to agree in the Treaty of Versailles. Spiraling inflation meant that in Berlin the loaf of bread which cost .63 Marks in 1918 was priced at 163.15 Marks in 1922, at 3,465 Marks in July 1923, and at 201,000,000,000 Marks in November 1923.[12] Given this absurd situation, Germans regarded their new government as a form of *Gesellschaft* and directed their desire for *Gemeinschaft* to their churches and clubs.[13]

Germans expressed their sense of *Gemeinschaft* in ways that were both exhilarating and ominous. In their churches they joined with new vigor in worship, retreats, and pilgrimages; in their sport clubs they gathered for soccer games and contests in marksmanship; and in their villages they celebrated local festivals. They spoke of themselves as a *Volk*, a people united by race, history, and culture, and some Germans went so far as to take seriously the racial writings of Paul de Lagarde (1827–91). Although most Germans viewed their *Volk* revival as nonpolitical, this movement embodied a conservatism that distrusted democracy and favored some form of authoritarian rule. For this reason, Friedrich Meinecke observed in 1924 that "the need itself for identity, the deep craving for the inner unity and harmony of all laws of life and events in life remains nevertheless powerfully preserved in the German spirit."[14]

Germans' yearning to renew themselves as a *Volk* also manifested itself in a national youth movement. In 1901 a group of friends, while gathered in a tavern at Steglitz near Berlin, formed the *Wandervögel* ("wandering birds") with the aim of renewing their ties to nature and the Teutonic culture. Within twelve years, the *Wandervögel* had become a loose national confederation of groups of predominantly Protestant young men who joined in camping trips during which they would retell German legends and sing folk songs. In October 1913 thousands of *Wandervögel*, representing thirteen youth associations, camped on the Hohen Meissner, a mountain near Kassel. Amid their hiking and singing, they formulated a credal statement, the "Meissner Formel," on the value of freedom and the renewal of the German spirit by means of a return to nature and the *Volk* heritage. By the late 1920s, hundreds of thousands of youth belonged to the *Wandervögel.*[15]

In literature and the arts the yearning for *Gemeinschaft* produced the turn to the mystical or inner elements of life in which one could sense the whole of reality. In their expressionist art Wassily Kandinsky, Franz Marc, and the other members of Der Blaue Reiter exposed the hidden dimensions of personal and social existence. In 1912 Marc articulated this aim in his essay "Die 'Wilden' Deutschland," which includes a statement that Romano Guardini paraphrased ten years later in reference to the church. Marc observed that "*[m]ystical reality* has awakened in human hearts and with it the primal elements of art."[16] In architecture Walter Gropius and his associates in the Bauhaus school designed buildings and furniture that were meant to express and encourage the "organic" character of human life.[17] Moreover, in literature, novels like *Siddhartha* (1922) by Hermann Hesse and *The Magic Mountain* (1924) by Thomas Mann highlighted the nonrational drives at work in personal existence and society.

As Scheler had predicted in 1915, Germans' desire for organic relationships brought positive results for the Catholic Church. German Catholicism clearly benefited from the neoromanticism of the early 1900s, just as it had previously thrived within the romanticism of the early 1800s.[18] Respected intellectuals converted to Catholicism; among them were Scheler himself, Dietrich von Hildebrand, and Edith Stein. Catholic theologians and spiritual writers expressed their religious vision in the language of the *Lebensphilosophie,* as evident in Karl Adam's *Das Wesen des Katholizismus* (1924), Engelbert Krebs's *Dogma und Leben* (two volumes, 1921–25), and Peter Lippert's *Das Wesen des katholischen Menschen* (1923). Catholics became more active in their parishes and joined in processions on feast days.[19] Instead of joining the *Wandervögel,* young Catholics became members of Catholic youth organizations such as Quickborn and Neudeutschland. In August 1922 representatives of these Catholic organizations gathered in Munich for three days, during which they formulated a credal statement, the "Münchener Formel," comparable to the "Meissner Formel" of 1913. However, unlike the earlier statement, this one was explicitly Christian. It stressed that Catholic youth were dedicated to Jesus Christ within the Catholic Church.[20] By 1933 there were 1.5 million young Catholics involved in thirty-three organizations, affiliated within the umbrella organization Katholische Jugend Deutschlands.[21]

Representative of the Catholic youth associations was Quickborn. Begun in 1909 by three priests in Silesia—Hermann Hoffmann (d. 1972), Klemens Neumann (d. 1928), and Bernhard Strehler (d. 1945)—it required that its members abstain from alcoholic beverages and frequently attend Mass and receive the sacraments. By 1919 it numbered approximately 6,000 members from all parts of Germany. Wanting to establish a centrally located national center, Quickborn's leaders purchased the castle (*Burg*) at Rothenfels near Würzburg in February 1919. In the summer of that year, they held their first *Tagung* (national conference) at Burg Rothenfels. In August 1920 they attracted 1,500 young men and women to their second *Tagung*, which had as its theme "Christus unser Führer," and they also inaugurated their journal *Die Schildgenossen*.[22]

In 1915, when Scheler predicted the awakening of Germans' longing for community, he was not yet a Catholic. Nevertheless, his discussion of the church as the *corpus Christi* fueled Catholic theologians' interest in this ancient ecclesiology.[23] In 1919 Scheler initiated correspondence with a young theologian who was also conscious of Germans' desire for community and simultaneously familiar with the ecclesiology of the body of Christ. This theologian was Romano Guardini. In 1920 Scheler entered the Catholic Church, but within four years he had renounced his Christian belief.

GUARDINI'S REFLECTIONS ON COMMUNITY

In his autobiographical reflections of 1944, *Berichte über mein Leben*, Guardini recalls that the seed of his ecclesiology germinated in 1907 at Tübingen. At that time, in conversations with Karl Neundörfer, he came to see that the church is "the mysterious reality which is immersed in history and nevertheless is the guarantee of eternity."[24] In short, the church is a complex reality which we cannot fully understand. What then should we say about it? The church is "the community of action and suffering"; it is the "organic" association of women and men united with Jesus Christ through the power of the Holy Spirit. As such, it possesses at least three further "aspects." First, it has a "sociological-juridical" dimension. That is, it is an institution. Second, "as the unity of contemplative, reflective, prayful activity," the church consists of a "liturgical" element. Through its rituals, sacraments, and symbols, it manifests God's love in the world. And "through both [of these aspects] there is realized the third aspect of the church as the guardian of the divine truth which is always endangered by human willing and human loss of will." In short, the church is the herald or prophet of God's word.

This view of the church as a mystery that embodies distinct, though complementary, qualities or traits is one with which we are now familiar, for it is presented in Vatican II's *Lumen Gentium* and in post-Vatican II presentations of "models" of the church.[25] But in 1907 this kind of ecclesiology was not widely known, for the church's formal teachings and Latin manuals emphasized that the church is an institution. How was it then that by the age of twenty-two, Guardini had already arrived at his sophisticated ecclesiology? He was influenced by two major sources.

In courses with Wilhelm Koch and others at the University of Tübingen, Guardini and his friends studied the ecclesiology of Johann Adam Möhler (1796–1838) of the Catholic Tübingen School. In his seminal book of 1825, *Die Einheit in der Kirche* (The unity of the church), Möhler writes that the church is a spiritual or mystical communion in Jesus Christ which assumes tangible expression in institutional structures and doctrines. Drawing on the romanticism of his day, Möhler contends that the church consists of the "organic" association of its members in a unity which the Holy Spirit effects. In Möhler's words:

> The communication of the Holy Spirit is the condition for the acceptance of Christian faith within us. The Spirit unites all of the faithful in a spiritual community, through which the Spirit is communicated to those people who are not yet believers. Christ is imparted through love, which is witnessed to in the church through the life in it [which is] at work in us. We become conscious of Christ only in the community of the faithful. . . . Therefore, all of the faithful form the body of Christ and among themselves a spiritual unity. As the higher principle, by which this unity is produced and formed, Christ is only one and the same.[26]

In 1832 Möhler complemented his early pneumatic view of the church with the christological understanding of his *Symbolik* (*Symbolism*) in which he analyzes the doctrinal differences between Catholicism and Protestantism by means of a study of their "symbols," their formal confessions. Möhler again conceives of the church as a *Gemeinschaft* in the Holy Spirit, but he stresses that the church remains united with its objective referent, Jesus Christ, and that it witnesses to Christ through its institutional form. In other words, the church is the body of Christ, as expounded in Romans 12, 1 Corinthians 12, Colossians 1, and Ephesians 1. Möhler writes:

> And as in the world nothing can attain to greatness but in society: so Christ established a community; and his divine word, his living will, and the love emanating from him exerted an internal, binding power upon his followers; so that an inclination implanted by him in the hearts of believers, corresponded to his outward institution. And thus a living, well-connected, visible association of the faithful sprang up, whereof it might be said—there they are, there is his Church, his institution wherein he continues to love, his spirit continues

to work, and the word uttered by him eternally resounds. Thus, the visible Church, from the point of view here taken is the Son of God himself, everlastingly manifesting himself among men in a human form, perpetually renovated, and eternally young—the permanent incarnation of the same, as in Holy Writ, even the faithful are called "body of Christ."[27]

Although from *Die Einheit* to *Symbolik* there is a shift in emphasis from the Holy Spirit to Jesus Christ, both books stress that the church is a community and that since the church is a living reality it continually embodies creative tensions, the interplay of opposites (*Gegensätze*). According to Möhler, there exist the polarities between the individual believer and the whole assembly of the faithful; between the church's inner reality and its outer manifestations, its institutions and rituals; between sin and grace; and between the eternal Jesus Christ and the association of women and men engaged in their everyday activities.[28]

Möhler's ideas are evident in Guardini's ecclesiology. Like Möhler, Guardini speaks of the church as a "mysterious reality" which is first of all a "community of action and suffering." Also, with Möhler, Guardini insists that the church is united in Jesus Christ and possesses various "aspects" that stand in tension with each other: the church is a community and also an institution; it gives thanks and praise to God through its worship and prayer and simultaneously attests to the truth in a world not always eager for it.

While Möhler's ecclesiology was one source for Guardini's work on the church, there was a second as well: his positive experiences of community. The longing for *Gemeinschaft* that surfaced among Germans at the *fin de siècle* also stirred in Guardini. With his friends, he felt the isolating effect of the rapid industrialization under Kaiser Wilhelm II. But for him two factors heightened this desire to belong. First, as an Italian living amid Germany's rising nationalism, Guardini was an outsider. Second, by disposition he was a shy and sensitive person who, although friendly with his peers, was a relatively private person.[29]

What were Guardini's positive experiences of community? The first one that he mentions in *Berichte über mein Leben* is the study group of Wilhelm and Renate Josefine Schleussner to which he belonged from 1903 until 1913. As already mentioned in chapter 1, the Schleussners gathered around them Catholic youth with intellectual promise and discussed with them church history, literature and art, and the writings of the mystics. Guardini valued the meetings with the Schleussners and sought out opportunities to speak alone with Frau Schleussner, in whom he was able to confide.[30] In fact, in the autumn of

1905 he told the Schleussners of his decision to enter the seminary, even before he said anything to his parents.[31] When Frau Schleussner suddenly died in 1913, Guardini was saddened and tried to aid Herr Schleussner by making a trip with him to Silesia.

There was a direct link between Guardini's participation in the Schleussner circle beginning in 1903 and his acceptance of Möhler's ecclesiology four years later. Möhler's view of church as *Gemeinschaft* rang true for Guardini, in part because he had discovered with the Schleussners the kind of Christian communion of which Möhler had written in *Die Einheit in der Kirche* and *Symbolik*. Guardini's friend Adam Gottron has noted that with the Schleussners they had a foretaste of the ecclesiology that emerged in Germany between the wars. In Gottron's words:

> One can say in summary that we experienced much of what came to blossom and fruition after 1918 in Germany, already ten years previously in the home of the Schleussners: the encounter again of church and culture, the liturgical movement, the critique of the "unrefined acquisition of empire," to which Germany at the time had fallen.[32]

This experience of church affected Guardini so deeply that in subsequent years he recreated it in whatever circumstances he found himself. The Schleussners's circle consisted of a group of talented, committed Catholics who deliberately came together in order to mine the wisdom of the Judeo-Christian tradition and also to appreciate art, literature, and culture. These same ingredients are found in the literary circle that Guardini and his friends formed in the Wilhelmsstift at Tübingen from 1906 through 1907 and humorously called "Schönfurzia" ("sweet gas"). Also, these same ingredients came together when, as chaplain to Iuventus from 1915 until 1919, Guardini shaped the group's activities to include not only social events, prayer, and retreats but also discussions of art, literature, and culture. Finally, as Guardini became involved with Quickborn beginning in 1920, he guided that association so that it too eventually possessed the traits which had characterized the Schleussners's circle. In sum, Guardini's vision of the church matured as he brought together Möhler's ecclesiology and his communal activities at the Schleussners's home.

Recovering an Ancient Ecclesiology

VOM SINN DER KIRCHE (1922)

Soon after completing his "Habilitationsschrift," Guardini gave his lectures "on the meaning of the church" (*Vom Sinn der Kirche*) in the summer of 1922 at a conference of the Catholic Academic Association.[33] At each of his lectures, he filled the auditorium to capacity with members of Iuventus and Quickborn as well as with conference-goers who had heard about the articulate priest from Mainz.[34] These lectures were so well received that they immediately appeared as a book entitled *Vom Sinn der Kirche.*

At the outset of *Vom Sinn der Kirche* Guardini declares that "the church is awakening in souls," thereby paraphrasing Franz Marc's statement of 1912 that "*[m]ystical reality* has awakened in human hearts."[35] The "awakening" of the church has come about, Guardini asserts, as people have moved beyond neo-Kantianism with its emphasis upon the individual person and subjectivity to the recognition both of the communal nature of human life and the objective character of reality. In this regard, Germans are discovering themselves as a *Volk* and, during their severe economic hardship, are making sacrifices for the common good. At the same time, they are coming to a new awareness of life's breadth and depth, for they are increasingly conscious that life is not primarily a matter of doing but a matter of being and sharing in a reality greater than one's self.

Among Catholics this shift in consciousness is showing itself, Guardini avers, in their recovery of the ancient sense of the church as the mystical body of Christ (Rom 12; 1 Cor 12). The church is a community as well as an institution. Indeed, it is the *Gemeinschaft* united in Christ, who as its head sends the Spirit to draw all individuals into solidarity as they participate in the coming of God's kingdom (Col 1; Eph 1). This new awareness has surfaced in the liturgical movement with its seminal insight that worship is a communal activity with an objective referent, God.

It has become clear, Guardini says, that the church consists of two distinct though interdependent elements: the community and the individual believers. On the one hand, it is constituted by human solidarity in Christ. This aspect is "the kingdom of God as church," as community. On the other hand, it is made up of individual men and women who mature into full persons by means of their union with Christ. This element is "the kingdom of God as personality" (p. 38). Both aspects, the communal and the individual—which constitute a polarity—are essential to the one reality, the church. For this reason, the church must preserve this creative tension within its life. With this commitment, the church stands apart, on the one extreme, from the "one-sided conceptions" of "Communism" and the "totalitarian state" and, on the other extreme, from the ideology of "individualism."

According to Guardini, the church is in fact "the way to personality," to full human individuation. Within the church, a person can discover the proper "hierarchy of values" in relation to which she or he can grow into a whole self before God. To be sure, the church does not consistently live up to its vocation as the bearer of what is genuinely human: "Christ lives in the church, but Christ crucified" (p. 55). Nevertheless, the church offers the path to human development, for it reveals "the Absolute," the eternal point of reference that is necessary for authentic human maturation. Modernity's attentiveness to change within history and culture has produced an ideology of "relativism" that the church challenges as it "confronts man with the Reality in the Absolute." In particular, the church witnesses to God through its teaching, its "moral and social system," and its worship—three elements that guide people to their self-realization in Jesus Christ.

Although some would say that the church deprives people of their free choice, such is not the case. In negative terms, freedom is "the absence of external constraint." And, in positive terms we should say that a person is "free when he recognizes honestly the hierarchy of objects, and their values" (p. 71). The greatest good of human choice is God. Thus freedom concerns the possibility of choosing to live for God; "the man who is truly free is open to God and plunged in Him." Opting for God requires, however, that a person be capable of severing "bonds" that keep one from moving toward the greatest good. One such bond is the "intellectual" constraint of misleading ideas such as the ideologies of individualism and relativism. A second possible hindrance to freedom are the "cultural and national bonds" that direct someone toward such idols as nationalism. A third possible obstacle is a person's "character." A human being tends to rely on the strengths of her or his kind of personality while ignoring its limitations, and, as a result, the person does not move toward wholeness. The church can correct this tendency toward one-sidedness. "The church is the whole reality, seen, valued, and experienced by the entire man" (p. 86). As we participate in the church, we receive the guidance and strength to become fully individuated in relation to God.

In Guardini's judgment, the church is the *Gemeinschaft* for which human beings long. For many years, each German "felt himself to be a self-contained microcosm" (p. 92). But this attitude has changed, and now Germans want to belong to a community, as evident in the attraction of many young people to youth groups such as Quickborn. Noting the rise of fascism in Germany, Guardini prophetically adds that in the extreme the desire for togetherness is dangerous, for an overbearing form of belonging to a group is "capable of destroying personality" (p. 95).

The church possesses the resources to maintain the right balance between the community and the individual person. As it pursues knowledge for its own sake, the church "effects a community of truth" (p. 96). Also, in its deliberate participation in the mystical body of Christ and its celebration of the sacraments, the church is "a community of life." Further, it reveals "the community of the saints" and also shows itself to be "the community of suffering," the human solidarity of all those who share in the passion of Jesus Christ (p. 102). Finally, the church points beyond itself to the perfect community, the triune God. In the church, people are brought not only into communion with one another but also into union with the God who is Father, Son, and Holy Spirit.

In conclusion, "the sphere of Catholic faith—the church—is not merely one alternative among many, but [is] religious truth, pure and simple, the kingdom of God" (p. 114). Recognizing that this claim may seem naive when one thinks of the church's shortcomings, Guardini notes that it makes sense when one distinguishes between the church's "real inner form" and its outer manifestations, between its primary reality and its secondary expressions in human affairs. Since the institutional church is not always true to its essence, all Christians should publicly express the church's inner reality, namely, their participation in the living Christ.

THE RENEWAL OF ECCLESIOLOGY

In 1922 Guardini formulated in *Vom Sinn der Kirche* the ecclesiology that he had initially thought about in 1907. As he himself subsequently noted, it is a multifaceted notion of church. To express it, he had to use such words as "mysterious reality," "community," "liturgical," "sociological-juridical," and "guardian of divine truth." At the time, *Vom Sinn der Kirche* came as a breath of fresh air and appealed to thousands of Catholics who were attracted to the book's view of the church as the mystical body of Christ and its engaging, nontechnical language.

To appreciate the warm reception of *Vom Sinn der Kirche* in the 1920s we must recall two types of ecclesiology to which this book presented an alternative. One was the then dominant neoscholastic ecclesiology as expressed in a Latin manual such as Adolphe Tanquerey's *Brevior Synopsis Theologiae Dogmaticae* (1911).[36] Tanquerey's tract on the church declares that the church is an institution in which there are the officeholders, on the one hand, and the rank and file, on the other. It asserts the "thesis" that "Christ established the Church as a hierarchical society by bestowing on the Apostles the threefold power of teaching, of ruling and of sanctifying the faithful."[37] It supports this claim by listing propositions that cite "proof-texts" from the Bible and appeal to the church's history as seen without the help of modern historiography. The text is clear and precise, but since it is cast in scholastic categories, it is also intellectually dry and abstract. Further, it appears irrelevant, since it answers only the questions of medieval scholasticism.

A second type of ecclesiology that *Vom Sinn der Kirche* challenged was the understanding of church offered by liberal Protestantism. In Guardini's judgment, some theologians had become so enthralled by historical study that they had lost sight of the church as the mystical body of Christ that witnesses to God's revelation. He conveyed this assessment in his book review of Friedrich Heiler's *Das Wesen des Katholizismus* (1920). This book presents a "mechanistic" view of the church, in contrast to the "organic" model proposed by Guardini. *Das Wesen des Katholizismus* describes the church as an assembly of individuals held together by an implicit social contract, and it wrongly implies that Christians could live isolated lives and still remain Christian. According to Guardini, the ideology of individualism has eroded Heiler's understanding of church as community. Moreover, there is little sense that the church serves an objective reality, God's word. Rather, this ecclesiology holds that our knowledge of revelation is subjective. Guardini concludes that "Heiler's book stands as a sign of a dying time, a time which was relativistic in thought and absolute only in its prejudices."[38]

By contrast to neoscholasticism's institutional notion of church and liberal Protestantism's social-contract view of church, *Vom Sinn der Kirche* presents a complex ecclesiology, anchored in an appreciation of the church as a "mysterious" reality. This book's merits and shortcomings deserve mention. Its strengths spring from its recovery of the ancient model of the church as the mystical body of Christ. This understanding recognizes that the living Christ stands at the center of the believing community and that the source of unity is the Holy Spirit. Another merit of the book is its personalist, nontechnical language. However, this language bears the stamp of the neoromanticism of the day, as is evident in the book's idyllic description of the church and its avoidance of the thorny issues inherent in the church as an institution, for example, the authority of the pope and the tension between the church's monarchical and collegial tendencies.

One other strength of the book is its description of the church's distinct and opposing "aspects."[39] By starting with the claim that the church is a mysterious reality, Guardini is able to lay out its distinct, even opposing dimensions: it is "communal," "sociological-juridical," and "liturgical" as well as "the guardian of divine truth," hence prophetic. It is unfortunate, however, that the book fails to note that the church is the advocate or servant of social justice, of the coming of the kingdom of God within history.[40] This omission is somewhat surprising, since Guardini knew of the extraordinary work of Wilhelm Emmanuel Baron von Ketteler (1811–77), bishop of Mainz from 1860 to 1877, who laid the foundation for Pope Leo XIII's social encyclical *Rerum Novarum* (1891).[41] Also, Guardini was familiar with the efforts of the priest Carl Sonnenschein (1876–1929) for adequate housing, a just wage, and social assistance for workers and their families in Berlin. He had studied with Sonnenschein at Tübingen's Wilhelmsstift and subsequently stayed in contact with him.[42] Nonetheless, Guardini remained silent on the church's call to serve the poor (Mt 25:31–46), and this omission is regrettable, since as we will see in chapter 6, it had consequences for Guardini's ways of resisting Nazism.

In any case, *Vom Sinn der Kirche* had a lasting impact on Catholic thought, for it gave the "programmatic formulations" of the ecclesiology that in 1943 gained the Catholic Church's official acceptance in Pius XII's *Mystici Corporis*.[43] As early as 1940, the Jesuit theologian Erich Przywara noted that this book served as an important building block in the bridge from Möhler's *Die Einheit* and *Symbolik* to the twentieth century's revival of the ecclesiology of the body of Christ.[44] Roger Aubert reiterated this same point in 1946, hence three years after *Mystici Corporis*.[45] In short, one cannot adequately map the path from Vatican I's ecclesiology to Vatican II's understanding of church without mentioning *Vom Sinn der Kirche*.[46]

Living a Theology of Church

QUICKBORN AS CHURCH

Many theologians express their ecclesiologies in their deeds as well as their words. Romano Guardini himself engaged in this twofold form of expression, for not only did he articulate his view of church in his lectures and books, he also communicated it in his pastoral leadership. Therefore, we must review his involvement at Burg Rothenfels and afterwards his conflicts with the official church.

The castle at Rothenfels stands on a high palisade overlooking the Main River. Since its primary building was erected in 1148, it has grown as new sections were added over the centuries, so that the entire complex now forms a large rectangle with an inner courtyard which one enters through a gatehouse. On three of its corners are towers with peaked roofs on which stand crosses that are visible from many miles away. Since 1919, when Quickborn purchased

Burg Rothenfels, youthful voices have radiated out into the countryside from the castle's chapel, refectory, and meeting room, the Knights' Hall. Beneath the castle, nestled between the palisade and the Main River is the village of Rothenfels with its yellow sandstone buildings, typical for this region of Lower Franconia. In Rothenfels, the road that spirals down from the *Burg* connects with the main road, which runs north toward Fulda and south toward Würzburg. Of course, Burg Rothenfels is tied, too, to the outside world by the Main River, which winds from east to west until it flows into the Rhine River. The road and river permit travelers to make their way to Burg Rothenfels, where even today they are welcomed with food, lodging, and companionship, for the castle is now a hostel and conference center.[47]

Romano Guardini initially came in contact with Quickborn in 1917 when Iuventus joined in some activities with Mainz's chapter of Quickborn.[48] Three years later, his visit to Burg Rothenfels for Easter changed his life, for, as he later said, it "became more important for my pastoral ministry than almost anything else."[49] He was so impressed by what he found at Burg Rothenfels that in August 1920 he attended the second annual *Quickborntag* (national conference) and was inspired to write an essay on Quickborn.[50] During the next three years, as he studied in Bonn and then moved to Berlin, he returned on numerous occasions to Burg Rothenfels in order to give spiritual conferences, preside and preach at mass, and lead religious devotions. By the summer of 1923, Guardini had decided that he wanted to remain involved with Quickborn at Burg Rothenfels, even if it meant less time for his academic life.[51]

For Guardini, Burg Rothenfels became an experimental laboratory in which he tested out his insights regarding community, worship, and education. Following the paradigm of the Benedictine monasteries, he stressed that life at the castle should include daily mass and common meals. In the chapel he gradually introduced the use of the German missal and the celebration of the mass with the priest facing the people. Apart from explicitly religious activities, he encouraged folk dancing, hiking and sports, and, at the same time, directed the young men and women to have public readings of poetry and literature, hold concerts, stage plays either of their own making or by the masters such as Shakespeare, and even put on puppet shows.[52]

In effect, Guardini brought to life at Burg Rothenfels the vision of church that he articulated in *Vom Sinn der Kirche*. Here, German youth discovered the church as the living body of Christ, in which each of them made singular contributions as they deliberately committed themselves to Jesus Christ. Guardini himself expressed this view in 1949: "It has always belonged to the spirit of Rothenfels to live not on the basis of programs but out of the will for the truth and in response to the challenges of the day—trusting in the power of the inner form that was real at Rothenfels."[53]

Many people who participated in Quickborn have attested that they lived Guardini's ecclesiology at Burg Rothenfels. One former member, Ernst Michel, has written:

> Here Catholics were given an opportunity to examine the testimony of the reality of the church and therein to prove that they themselves—the people in this time—really live out of the church—not only that the church lives in them, but that they have reached its subject matter. Not the institutions of the church but the witness of the faithful came to words here. The church itself is bound to the world. The church—if it is, what it [truly] is—is not laws but grace, not the religious ghetto but the kingdom of freedom of the children of God. In relation to the world this means that the church is always and throughout open without limits, that no condition of the world can intimidate the church to abandon its faithfulness.[54]

The philosopher Joseph Pieper has written that at the castle in the early 1920s he delighted in the search for the truth and in the sense of closeness with God and his peers. In Pieper's words:

> Most influential and formative were the weeks we spent at Burg Rothenfels, in lower Franconia, at the beginning of the twenties. . . . [P]rimarily through getting to know Romano Guardini, we encountered a hitherto unsuspected dimension of spiritual reality and proceeded to seize hold of it with passionate intensity. We came to understand what a "sacred sign" is in reality, and that, beyond all the stifling crassness of moralistic and doctrinaire talk, something real takes place in the sacramental-cultic celebration of the mysteries, something that, otherwise, can only be spoken about. We came to realize that this is the core of all intellectual and spiritual life, and not only in Christianity but in all pre-Christian and non-Christian religions. Moreover, we learned these things in a relaxed atmosphere of unrestricted openness to the world.[55]

The theologian Karl Rahner was also deeply affected by life at Burg Rothenfels. In August 1920 Rahner accompanied his sister Anna to Rothenfels and, along with hundreds of other young people, joined in the second *Quickborntag*. Here, he met Romano Guardini, who led everyone in "spiritual exercises." Afterwards, Rahner remained active in Quickborn in Freiburg as well as at Burg Rothenfels and thus discovered that the church could be a vibrant community of prayer and intellectual pursuits.[56] Subsequently, he drew on this experience as he formulated his ecclesiology. In 1963, when Rahner moved from Innsbruck to Munich in order to assume Romano Guardini's academic chair at the University of Munich, he was motivated in part by his desire to follow in the footsteps of the theologian who had made a lasting impact on him in his youth.[57] Recalling his activity in Quickborn and his ties with Guardini, Rahner stated near the end of his life:

> Yes, I belonged to an organization called "Fountain of Youth" [Quickborn]. It was more of a grass-roots than a church-directed affair. But it was still Catholic, religious, extremely active and intense. There too I received many positive influences that affected my future life, especially since that was when I first met Romano Guardini at Castle Rothenfels.[58]

Michel's, Pieper's, and Rahner's statements describe well the ecclesial life that Guardini nurtured among German youth. In realizing his vision at Burg Rothenfels, however, Guardini came into conflict with the founders of Quickborn. In 1924 he assumed the role of Quickborn's spiritual leader, and, although the founders were committed to requiring Quickborn's members to abstain from alcoholic beverages, he pressed for a lessening of a concern about drink and for greater emphasis upon the intellectual life and culture. As friction increased, Bernhard Strehler relinquished control of Burg Rothenfels in 1927, and Guardini became its leader.[59]

Guardini also came into conflict with the editorial board of the journal *Die Schildgenossen*. Klemens Neumann and others held that the journal should serve as a spiritual journal addressed to former members of Quickborn who had withdrawn because of age. Guardini argued, however, that the journal should treat such themes as Christian life, literature, and culture for a wide audience of adult Catholics. At Easter in May 1924, Guardini and an associate Josef Aussem became co-editors of *Die Schildgenossen*.[60]

Romano Guardini labored from 1920 to 1939 to shape Quickborn at Burg Rothenfels into a community in which young Catholics could experience the church as the living body of Christ. From one perspective, it was pure chance that Guardini served as the spiritual leader at Burg Rothenfels between the wars. If he had not labored here, he would have undoubtedly assisted youth elsewhere. But from another perspective, it was seemingly meant to happen that he worked here, for by its design and location Burg Rothenfels exhibited Guardini's view that the church abides "in" the world but is not "of" the world (Jn 17:16–19). For Guardini, as for Vatican II, the church, like Burg Rothenfels, is the city on a mountain to which all peoples are invited to feast at the table of the Lord (Is 2:1–3). In this vision, Quickborn at Burg Rothenfels was the *lumen gentium,* the light of the nations (Is 42:6; 49:6).[61]

GUARDINI AND THE CATHOLIC HIERARCHY

In 1952 Romano Guardini wrote a letter to Pius XII's undersecretary of state, Monsignor Giovanni Battista Montini, the future Paul VI, in which he thanked the pope and Montini for naming him a papal prelate (monsignor). Also, he shared his conviction that the act of faith in Jesus Christ requires one's commitment to the church. He stated that

> the acknowledgment of the church has been the controlling insight of my life. When I was still a student of political theory [in 1905], it became clear to me that the specifically Christian decision occurred not in relation to the notion of God, also not in relation to the figure of Christ, but in relation to the church. From then on, I knew that a genuine effectiveness is only possible in unity with the church.[62]

This statement conveys a thought which, as we have already noted, Guardini had previously articulated in his autobiographical reflections of 1944: in his religious experience of 1905 he realized that if he were to make an act of faith in Jesus Christ, he must commit himself to the church. In practice, however, this commitment did not keep him from criticizing the hierarchical church. In 1937 in *Der Herr* he noted "the limitations of the Church": "indolence, intolerance, tyranny, narrowness."[63] Moreover, we best appreciate Guardini's statement when we read it in relation to the theologian's activities, for in this context we see that for him obedience to the church included opposition (*Gegensatz*). This loyal dissent is evident in four of Guardini's conflicts with ecclesiastical officials.

The first of these conflicts occurred between Guardini and officials of the diocese of Mainz. As noted in chapter 1, the friction began in 1908 when Guardini entered the seminary in Mainz and questioned the neoscholastic course of studies and the emphasis upon strict obedience in the program of spiritual formation. As a result, he was delayed from ordination for six months. During this time, he developed a stomach ailment that he attributed to seminary life.[64] The tension between Guardini and the diocesan officials grew after the young priest was awarded his Ph.D. from the University of Freiburg in 1915 but was not invited to teach at Mainz's seminary. At the time, he judged that Dr. Ludwig Bendix, the pastor of Mainz's cathedral and the diocese's general vicar, was blocking his appointment to the seminary faculty.[65] With the success of *Vom Geist der Liturgie* in 1918 and his move to the University of Bonn in 1920, Guardini distanced himself from his diocese. He was eventually reconciled to the diocese through the efforts of Mainz's Bishop Albert Stohr.[66]

A second conflict arose as some bishops questioned the activities and organization of Quickborn, especially at Burg Rothenfels. In the early 1920s the Fulda Conference of Bishops discussed a formal ban against Quickborn because young men and women simultaneously resided at Burg Rothenfels for conferences and retreats. Some bishops also voiced alarm because Quickborn had no formal affiliation to the Catholic Church and was, therefore, not accountable to a specific bishop. They were troubled, too, by the liturgical experimentation that occurred at Burg Rothenfels. Further, some officials charged that Quickborn was elitist, since under Guardini's leadership the association attracted to Burg Rothenfels many youth who were interested in intellectual and cultural topics. When the critics of Quickborn brought their concerns before the bishops' conference, they did not succeed in having it take formal action because Quickborn and Guardini had earned the respect of Munich's Archbishop Michael Faulhaber and also the bishops of Würzburg, Rottenburg-Stuttgart, and Breslau.[67] Interestingly, in the mid-1930s when Quickborn became formally linked with the Fulda Conference of Bishops in order to be legally protected against the Third Reich's interference, Guardini distanced himself from Quickborn while remaining active at Burg Rothenfels.[68]

Commenting in 1944 on the relationship between the German bishops and himself, Guardini wrote: "In fact the official church has stood with distrust at a distance from me for a long time, if not in relation to all of my endeavors, at least in relation to [Burg] Rothenfels. Those in positions of ecclesiastical authority have given me no help of any kind and until recently had drawn me into nothing."[69] He immediately added that he received support from lay leaders and then eventually from some bishops. In his words:

> Thus something occurred which upon reflection has filled me with gratitude: the lay people immediately accepted my work and with increasing enthusiasm in recent years the ecclesiastical authorities have also begun to trust me. I perceive this as a confirmation that makes me happy and hope with my heart it will remain this way until the end.[70]

A third conflict took place in Berlin. From the outset at the University of Berlin, Guardini felt estranged from diocesan officials. He recalled: "The situation was such that the official embodiments of Catholic academic life ignored my lectures. From the outset all official supports failed me—so that I was however also free from all concern for not belonging to the cause."[71] Also, he found himself increasingly at odds with Monsignor Carl Sonnenschein, who criticized Quickborn for neglecting service of the poor.[72] It appears, too, that Guardini experienced some friction with Berlin's Bishop Konrad von Preysing, because he engaged in pastoral ministry for Berlin's Catholic students, especially at St. Benedict Chapel, without being directly accountable to a specific pastor or diocesan office.[73]

A fourth conflict arose with regard to the liturgical movement. Since I will review this conflict in the next chapter, I need only note here that in 1940, amid the war, there developed a controversy concerning liturgical experimentation. Some officials charged that the changes in the liturgy were contrary to church teachings and were confusing the people. In particular, Archbishop Conrad Gröber of Freiburg opposed the liturgical movement and questioned Guardini's leadership. At the invitation of Bishop Stohr, Guardini wrote an open letter to the German bishops in which he criticized extremist tendencies in the liturgical movement and called for moderate renewal. This letter made a favorable impression upon many bishops and helped to defuse the controversy.[74]

These points of disagreement between Guardini and bishops show how in his judgment loyalty to the church did not entail blind submission to ecclesiastical authorities. Guardini was obviously convinced that a Catholic theologian could disagree with bishops and at the same time claim fidelity to the church. This conviction rested on his ecclesiology, in which the church as the body of Christ is primarily a living community and, like all living realities, possesses polarities that are potentially creative. This point is made in *Berichte über mein Leben:* "Of course the church is not identical with a single unit within its hierarchy or with a theological school or with a conventional way of doing things. It is more than this, and in every single instance the process of renewal is open to the church's totality and its essence." To be sure, Guardini added, we must respect those in authority within the church. "Nevertheless, there is also the immediate relationship to the church in the fullness of its essence, and because of this relationship it is possible to proceed [in a conflict], as Paul says, 'in confidence' when insight and inner authority warrants it."[75] In his letter to Monsignor Montini in 1952, Guardini mentioned that he had deliberately lived in obedience to the church. What he neglected to say, however, was that out of "inner authority" he had at times promoted ideas and practices that went contrary to some bishops' policies and theologies.

Toward Vatican II's *Lumen Gentium* (1964)

Today, Catholics accept the teachings of both the First Vatican Council and the Second Vatican Council. They uphold *Pastor Aeternus* and also embrace *Lumen Gentium* and *Gaudium et Spes*. In affirming both documents, Catholics may assume that the earlier council led of necessity to the later council. However, such was not the case. The way from the assembly of October 1870 to the assembly of October 1962 came about because of a spontaneous spiritual and theological fermentation among Christians.[76] At the center of this renewal was the rediscovery of the church as community and the fresh reflections on the ecclesial mystery in light of scripture—a process that occurred among Protestants as well as Catholics. Studying this phenomenon in 1927, the Protestant theologian Otto Dibelius entitled his book "the century of the church."[77] Since 1965, commentators have often said that Vatican II was the council on the church.[78]

Romano Guardini surely played an important role in nourishing the thought that grew into Vatican II's teaching on the church. Otto Pesch has rightly observed that the seed from which sprang the renewed understanding of the church was the ecclesiology of the body of Christ which Möhler had recovered in the early 1800s, and that Guardini was among the first theologians in the early 1900s to foster the growth of this neglected ecclesiology. In Pesch's words: "With this [recovery], a new theology of church could emerge in the twentieth century. Romano Guardini formulated the motto in *Vom Sinn der Kirche:* 'The church is awakening in human hearts.'"[79] Pesch's use of Guardini's sentence is apt, since in 1922 it became the clarion call for the church's revival in Germany. Also referring to *Vom Sinn der Kirche,* Arno Schilson has stated: "According to most [scholars] the tangible beginning of a [Catholic] 'church movement' in Germany is dateable to this publication; with it there began the 'century of the church' (Otto Dibelius)."[80]

Recognition of Guardini's significant role in the renewal of ecclesiology prompts three questions. First, how did Guardini's writings contribute to Vatican II's understanding of the church? Second, how did Vatican II's teachings surpass Guardini's ecclesiology? And third, how did Guardini himself view Vatican II's documents on the church?

First, although we cannot see direct lines of influence from Guardini's ecclesiology to Vatican II's documents, we can observe how the ideas that Guardini expressed beginning in 1922 came to fruition in the Dogmatic Constitution on the Church and the Pastoral Constitution on the Church in the

Modern World. He promoted the insight that the church is the community of believers united in Christ, and Vatican II worked this understanding into *Lumen Gentium*'s metaphors of the church as the people of God, the pilgrim people, the new Israel, and the body of Christ. Common to these metaphors is, as Walter Kasper has highlighted, the notion of church as *communio* that is rooted in the ecclesiology of the body of Christ.[81] Further, Guardini's work also had an impact on the council's way of speaking about the church. That is, the council, like Guardini, recognized that since the church is a mystery, we require more than one image or notion when speaking about it. In 1907 Guardini discussed with Karl Neundörfer the church's various "aspects," and fifty-five years later the council used an array of metaphors and ideas in the Dogmatic Constitution on the Church. With regard to the church's structure, he saw that the church is not primarily its officeholders but the entire community, most of whom are laity.[82] In this way, Guardini's ecclesiology differed from Pius XII's *Mystici corporis* which stresses the hierarchy within the body of Christ. With regard to the church's mission, he insisted that the church is not meant to serve itself but is called to remain "in" the world; similarly, in the Pastoral Constitution on the Church in the Modern World the church and the world are viewed as complementary realities. Finally, Guardini's emphasis on the church's "liturgical" dimension and its prophetic dimension as "witness to the truth" contributed to the unfolding of Vatican II's recognition that the church is the "universal sacrament" of God's presence in human affairs.[83]

Second, while Guardini prepared the way for the Second Vatican Council, he was surpassed by its ecclesiology at a number of points.[84] Whereas he did not explicitly discuss change within the church, Vatican II valued the church's historicity. In describing the church as the people of God and the pilgrim people in *Lumen Gentium,* the council implicitly recognized that the church itself changes as it enters into different eras and cultures, without however losing its gift of God's unchanging revelation in Jesus Christ.[85] Another point of difference is that, applying the language of the two "natures" of Christ to church, Guardini spoke of the church's divine character and its human character. However, Vatican II did not adopt this terminology in reference to the church.[86] Further, Guardini neglected a consideration of the church as an advocate or servant of justice, but in *Gaudium et Spes* the council insisted that the church is called to speak on behalf of universal human dignity and rights, thereby welcoming the kingdom of God into history.[87] In this vein, whereas Guardini tended to stress the differences between what the church cherishes and what society values, Vatican II acknowledged the truths that the church and the world hold in common—without, however, overlooking the distinctiveness of Christian belief. Finally, he remained silent on ecumenism, and yet Vatican II accentuated the unity of the Christian churches and urged better communications among them.[88]

Third, Guardini conveyed an ambivalence about Vatican II's teachings on the church.[89] The very fact that he did not speak in public about the council indicated his uneasiness with it. Further, in 1965 the seventy-nine-year-old theologian communicated his mixed feelings concerning the council's ecclesiology in *Die Kirche des Herrn* (*The Church of the Lord*).[90]

Die Kirche des Herrn consists largely of material that Guardini presented in 1955.[91] With a slightly different emphasis, it treats the themes of *Vom Sinn der Kirche*, as is evident in the chapters' titles: "Revelation and Mystery," "The Church and Contemporaneity with Jesus Christ," "The Guardian and Dispenser of the Truth," and "The Visibility of the Church." The book's last chapter treats a new theme for Guardini. Entitled "The Eschatological Character of the Church," it discusses the church as witness to "the last days," that is, to life after death and the new creation.

Woven into *Die Kirche des Herrn* are some of Guardini's thoughts on the council. On the one hand, the book's overall tone conveys a positive view of the council's *aggiornamento*, and this stance is made explicit in that the book is "dedicated to the memory of His Holiness Pope John XXIII in Reverence." On the other hand, the book cautions that since the church is a complex reality, we should not adopt one model of the church to the neglect of other, opposing notions. Guardini acknowledges the validity of the metaphor of the church as the people of God, and yet he immediately adds that the church is also "the rock" (Mt 16:18), a metaphor found in Vatican I's *Pastor Aeternus*. He points out that the metaphor of the pilgrim people expresses well the mystery of the church as a community making its way in history to God, but that this view must be filled out by the metaphor of the rock which captures the sense of the church's responsibility to represent God's unchanging revelation. In his words: "The Church is also the unflinching one, guarding the yea and nay of the truth, so that Scripture could make a very severe statement, that he who does not listen to [the church], knowing what he does, should be regarded as a 'heathen and a public sinner.'"[92]

One year after the publication of *Die Kirche des Herrn* Guardini, in a letter to Paul VI, mentioned his understanding of the church as the bearer and guardian of revelation. On the occasion of the theologian's eightieth birthday, when the pope invited Guardini to become a cardinal, the octogenarian wrote to the pontiff (Montini) that the church must witness to the truth about God and human life. As we already noted, in 1952, after being named a papal monsignor, Guardini had written in a letter to Montini that Christian faith includes belief in the church. In the letter of 1965, Guardini returned to his earlier idea:

> At the time of my first theological studies something became clear to me that, since then, has determined my entire work: what can convince modern people is not a historical or a psychological or a continually ever modernizing Christianity but only the unrestricted and uninterrupted message of revelation. Of course, it is then the task of the teacher to position this message in relation to the problems and needs of our time. I have sought to do this in different settings, including Berlin for twenty years amid little Christian air. The experience was always the same. What a contemporary person wants to hear is the full and pure Christian message. Perhaps he will then say no to it; however, such a person knows little about its source. This insight has always proven to be true.[93]

Guardini's emphasis upon the church as the herald of God's word in both *Die Kirche des Herrn* and his letter of 1965 to Paul VI points to the center of his ecclesiology in general and also to his ambiguity toward Vatican II's teaching on the church. For Guardini, the church is the community of truth. It is constituted by its vertical relationship to the living Christ and at the same time by the horizontal relationships among its members.[94] A theology of the church is sound, therefore, only so long as it maintains the polarity between the church's vertical and horizontal aspects. Given this view, Guardini seemingly feared that Vatican II's emphasis upon the church's horizontal axis, for example, by means of the metaphor of people of God, had caught the eye of Catholics and had eclipsed the council's account upon the church's vertical relationship with God by means of the metaphor of body of Christ.

For Guardini, the church is the "mysterious reality" that manifests itself primarily in its communal form of life.[95] It is the people who are united in the body of Christ and, simultaneously, it is the rock, the protector of God's revelation. In Guardini's life, these metaphors were united in Burg Rothenfels, for this castle is the locus of a community and, at the same time, it stands upon a palisade. As he rightly observed, one of the major aspects of the church is its liturgical activity, and, since he wrote extensively on this topic, chapter 4 reviews some of these writings.

LITURGY AS PLAY BEFORE GOD

IN THE 1930s, at most Roman Catholic masses around the world, the priest faced the altar with his back to the congregation. There were, however, a handful of exceptions to this almost universal form, one of which was the mass for students at Berlin's St. Benedict Chapel where Romano Guardini regularly presided at the Eucharist. Regina Kuehn, who frequented this mass, has described it:

> The Students' Chapel was a large basement room made suitable for celebrating Sunday liturgies. There was a sizable figure of Christ, a metal repoussé, in back of the freestanding, simple altar surrounded by wooden cubes for seating. The presider's cube closed the circle. Most of us, however, stood, because [Guardini's] *Sacred Signs* had taught us the significance of this noble gesture. . . . [When mass began], [w]e became absolutely quiet, and in complete stillness and composure we stood to witness a cosmic event of world-wide consequence in which all of us—each one individually and all of us together—played a part. . . . The *missa recitata* was the manner of celebration. All of us were familiar with Latin.[1]

Heinz Kuehn, who was also a member of this student congregation, has amplified Regina Kuehn's description by recounting how everyone joined in the mass: "The impact of the sacred action was all the more profound because Guardini celebrated the mass *versus populi*; it was a *missa recitata*, something still new in those days, and we, the congregation, were the altar boys and girls responding [in Latin] to his invitations to pray."[2]

The Kuehns' recollections of the masses at St. Benedict Chapel disclose an underlying principle in Guardini's understanding of liturgy: worship requires the assembly's active participation. Although there are different roles within worship, everyone should somehow share in the ritual if it is to be liturgy. For this reason, the priest should face the people and the entire congregation should respond to the presider's prayers.

Romano Guardini was not the first modern proponent of the principle of active participation in the liturgy. Beginning in the mid-1880s many people worked at retrieving this sense of worship as found within the early church. Nevertheless, from 1918 into the 1960s, Guardini played a major role in the liturgical renewal by means of his writings and pastoral leadership. In texts like *Vom Geist der Liturgie* he illumined the underlying principles of authentic worship and also the value of private prayer and religious devotions. Simultaneously, in his pastoral leadership he demonstrated what liturgy could become as he presided in St. Benedict Chapel and at Burg Rothenfels am Main. Because of his contributions in word and deed, he was one of the foremost leaders in the movement that led to Pope Pius XII's encyclical on worship, *Mediator Dei* (November 20, 1947), and also to the Second Vatican Council's Constitution on the Sacred Liturgy, *Sacrosanctum concilium* (December 4, 1963).[3]

This fourth chapter presents Guardini's understanding of liturgy and also describes how he implemented this view within the life of the church. This account unfolds in four steps. First, I recall some of the key people and ideas of the liturgical movement from the mid-1800s until the end of World War I. Second, I recount how Guardini discovered the nature of liturgy. Third, there is a review of the book which emerged from Guardini's discovery: *Vom Geist der Liturgie*. Fourth, I highlight his contributions to the liturgical movement from 1918 to 1968.[4] In particular, I consider his letter of 1940 to the German bishops on some dangers in liturgical renewal, his contribution to Vatican II's Constitution on the Sacred Liturgy, and his open letter of 1964 on our capability for the cultic act.[5]

Recovering a Sense of Worship

THE LITURGICAL MOVEMENT PRIOR TO 1918

In recent years, changes in the liturgy have brought the church beyond the baroque form that had shaped Catholic worship from the 1600s into the mid-1900s. For three centuries, the mass was similar to a performance in which the priest acted out a drama at the altar, while each member of the congregation passively watched or prayed private devotions. Responses to the priest's prayers came in whispers from the acolytes or, on Sundays and at funerals, perhaps from an organist or choir. For most weekday masses, the priest ignored the feast of the saint and, vested in black, said a requiem mass. If it were a "high mass," the priest sang the prayers and was answered in song only by the organist or choir. Since there existed no missal with the prayers and readings of the day, most people had only a vague idea of what the priest was whispering in Latin at the altar. Also, the people rarely shared in "Holy Communion," and, when they did, they usually did so before or after mass.[6]

This form of the Eucharist is now alien to most Catholics because of the movement that began in France in 1833 when the Benedictine monk Prosper Louis Pascal Guéranger (1805–75) reestablished the Abbey of St. Peter at Solesmes, not far from Le Mans. Soon after his ordination in 1827, Guéranger promoted an ultramontane theology against the Gallicanism of his day. In this spirit, he and a small circle of associates recovered the monastic liturgy, especially the Roman rite of mass. Further, Guéranger spearheaded the retrieval of ancient liturgical practices by writing his three-volume *Institutions liturgiques* (1840–51) on the mass and his nine-volume *L'année liturgique* (1841–66) on the major feasts of the liturgical year.[7]

The vision of the Abbey of Solesmes took root in Germany in 1863 when two monks from Solesmes, Maurus Wolter and Placidus Wolter, refounded the Abbey of Beuron and dedicated its Benedictine community to the ancient liturgical life. In 1884 one of its monks, Anselm Schott, published the first German and Latin missal, *Messebuch der heiligen Kirche*, which allowed the congregation to follow the readings and prayers at mass. Nine years later, Schott published the *Vesperbuch*, thereby making the divine office accessible to the laity. As the monastery at Beuron flourished, it sent some of its members to reestablish other abbeys. Among them was the Abbey of Maria Laach in 1892, not far from Coblenz, and the Abbey of Mont-César in 1899, near Louvain.[8]

Through the efforts of the Benedictine abbeys, the renewal of the liturgy gained momentum and then official recognition from Pope Pius X (1903–14), who saw that improved worship would strengthen his commitment to the "restoration of all things in Christ." Soon after his papal election, Pius X issued his first *motu proprio*, entitled *Tra le sollecitudini* (November 22, 1903), in which he promoted the "active participation" of the faithful in the mass. In his words:

> It being our ardent desire to see the true Christian spirit restored in every respect and be preserved by all the faithful, we deem it necessary to provide before everything else for the sanctity and dignity of the temple, in which the faithful assemble for the object of acquiring this spirit from its foremost and indispensable fount, which is the *active participation* [my emphasis] in the holy mysteries and in the public and solemn prayer of the Church.[9]

Pius X's goal of bringing "the true Christian spirit" into modern life had its problematic side in his support for integralism, the French ultraconservative movement in opposition to new methods and ideas in theology and biblical studies.[10] Nevertheless, the pope's acknowledgment that the laity should participate in the mass gave institutional backing to the reform of the liturgy, and, adding to this support, the pontiff issued *Sacra Tridentina Synodus* (December 22, 1905) on the value of daily reception of Holy Communion and then *Quam singulari* (August 10, 1910) on permitting children to receive their "first Holy Communion" at the "age of reason."[11] Also, to Pius X is credited a slogan for the renewal of the Eucharist: "Do not pray at mass, pray the mass."[12]

The Benedictine monk Lambert Beauduin (1873–1960) of the Abbey of Mont-César also worked for the updating of the liturgy. On September 23, 1909, at the Catholic Conference in Mechlin, Beauduin gave a paper entitled "The Proper Prayer of the Church," in which he called for a shift from the restoration of the ancient liturgy to a renewal of the liturgy for contemporary life. Emphasizing Pius X's notion of active participation, he observed that the faithful needed to understand anew the texts and rites of their worship. In 1914 Beauduin shared his insights concerning worship in his book *La piété de l'Eglise* which was immediately received as the liturgical movement's "manifesto."[13]

Abbot Ildefons Herwegen (1874–1946) at the Abbey of Maria Laach promoted the study of the history of worship. After being elected abbot in 1913, he inaugurated the "academic circle" which included Kunibert Mohlberg, Odo Casel, and Anton Baumstark. To make known the findings of this group's research, the abbot instituted in 1918 the series of books entitled *Ecclesia Orans,* whose first text was Guardini's *Vom Geist der Liturgie,* and in 1921 he founded the journal *Das Jahrbuch für Liturgiewissenschaft.* Herwegen also approved of experimental liturgies, such as Albert Hammenstede's "dialogue" mass (*missa recitatio*) in the abbey's crypt chapel.[14]

By 1918 the reform of the liturgy had spread to most of Europe's Benedictine monasteries and was beginning to reach into the parishes. As Europeans reflected on the war's horrors, they looked for a transcendent point of reference— God—in relation to whom they could reknit their personal and communal lives. Although fascinated by the fatalism of Oswald Spengler's two-volume *Decline of the West* (1918, 1922), most people wanted their hope restored. As a result, they desired to deepen their prayer and worship.[15] One of the pastoral leaders who addressed this desire was Pius Parsch (1884–1954) at the Austrian Abbey of Klosterneuburg. By means of his preaching, conferences, devotional literature, and writings on the early church, Parsch undertook what he called his *Volksliturgisches Apostolat,* his apostolate for a liturgy of the people.[16] Independent of Parsch, another creative leader in the liturgical movement was Romano Guardini.

GUARDINI'S RECOVERY OF WORSHIP

For the first twenty years of his life, Guardini knew only one kind of prayer: private prayer. At home, his mother set the example, for she was "pious in a very interior and austere manner."[17] At the gymnasium, Guardini began each day in the chapel.[18] Later, as a student suffering a crisis of faith at the University of Munich, he sought solace and guidance through private prayer at St. Ludwig Church.[19] In the autumn of 1905 in Berlin, he became aware of his vocation as he prayed at St. Paul Church.[20] In the spring of 1906, when he began to study theology at the University of Freiburg, he made his way through a period of depression by attending mass, praying the rosary, and making the stations of the cross.[21] Through these years, Guardini developed a strong habit of prayer in private, even when at mass. However, shortly after moving to Tübingen for theology studies, he learned another way to pray.

In late 1906 Romano Guardini and Karl Neundörfer accompanied their friend Josef Weiger on a visit to the Benedictine Abbey of Beuron where Guardini discovered communal prayer, the church's liturgy. In 1944, in his autobiographical reflections, Guardini recalled his arrival at the abbey:

> My first visit there remains vivid in my memory. It was evening. We went from the train station immediately into the monastery and received our rooms not in the guest wing, which was not yet built, but in the cloister itself. Staying in the cloister made our visit warm and living. In their simplicity the rooms were like home, with a great deal of dark wood and an indescribable element which made one feel a deep sense of well-being. We received something to eat and then went to Compline. The church was already dark with only a few candles in the choir. The monks stood in their places and prayed by heart the beautiful psalms of Compline which was then monotonal. Through the whole church moved mystery, sacred and simultaneously soothing. I eventually saw that the liturgy has a great deal of power and glory. At the beginning it was the simple door of Compline rather than the portals of majestic liturgical action [at mass] that led [me] more intimately into the heart of the liturgy's holy world.[22]

In 1966, again recounting this visit of 1906 to the Abbey of Beuron, Guardini linked it with his writing of *Vom Geist der Liturgie:*

> My first encounter with the liturgy occurred during my student years in Tübingen, 1906 to 1908, at the Abbey of Beuron. Pater Odilo Wolff and others gave the encounter a personal touch. I resided with my friend Karl Neundörfer (who died prematurely) in the cloister. My first impressions have operated through my entire life.
>
> At the time my friend Karl and I adopted the plan to present the essence of the church through its two fundamental elements. Neundörfer would treat the legal dimension in a book entitled *Vom Geist des kanonischen Rechts* [On the spirit of canon law], a book inspired by [Rudolf] von Ihering's classic *Der Geist*

des römischen Rechts [The spirit of Roman law]. He died in the mountains of Sils-Maria [in 1925] before he could complete this project. I wrote *Vom Geist der Liturgie.* Herwegen and my friend Mohlberg published it as the first book in the series *Ecclesia orans.*[23]

In sum, the first stay at the Abbey of Beuron introduced Guardini to a new world. In subsequent visits to the abbey, Guardini discussed his discovery not only with Neundörfer and Weiger but also with the monks themselves.[24] Moreover, during these visits and afterwards, he wrote down his thoughts on the nature of the liturgy.

As a young priest, Guardini thought further about the character of the Eucharist and divine office and took note of the inadequacy of the mass as celebrated in the parishes. Serving as a curate at Mainz's St. Christopher's Church (1912) and St. Ignatius Church (1915), he observed that, while he presided at a mass, the faithful would pray the rosary and their private devotions. Many years later, commenting on the practice of private prayers during mass, he wrote: "The senselessness of this activity was unbearable, and I was able to avoid inner harm [only] by making myself insensitive to it."[25] What Guardini himself had done for many years at mass had become highly problematic for him. This painful contrast fueled the reflections which generated *Vom Geist der Liturgie.*[26]

A Theology of Liturgy

VOM GEIST DER LITURGIE (1918)

At the outset of *Vom Geist der Liturgie* Guardini distinguishes between worship and private prayer and then introduces the book's major themes. The liturgy is the church's objective form of worship. It is "the Church's public and lawful act of worship, and it is performed and conducted by the officials whom the Church herself has designated for the post—the priests."[27] Liturgy or worship (e.g., the mass and the divine office) is distinct from "popular devotions" (e.g., the stations of the cross and the rosary) in that the former is a communal activity while the latter is an individual activity, even when done in common. Moreover, unlike religious devotions, worship possesses abiding "laws" or principles that assure its universality and objective character (p. 124). These include the following. First, true worship springs from a healthy emotional life. Second, it relies on reason as it seeks to communicate the truth about God and our personal existence. Third, it expresses human emotions, albeit in a focused manner (p. 129). Fourth, authentic liturgy requires the congregation's active participation. Fifth, it is rooted in the natural world and culture (p. 137). These five basic principles assure that liturgy will truly be "the entirely objective and impersonal prayer practiced by the Church as a whole" (pp. 122–23). In subsequent chapters, Guardini delves into aspects of these five norms.

Reflecting on the principle concerning the congregation's active participation in worship, he observes that the mass does not involve a gathering of individual believers, each of whom is praying in private to God. Rather, the Eucharist is a communal activity that concretely manifests the worship of the entire church in union with Christ. Liturgy expresses the church as the body of Christ. In Guardini's words: "The Church is self-contained, a structure-system of intricate and invisible vital principles, of means and ends, of activity and production, of people, organization, and laws" (p. 142). It is united not primarily by human effort but by Christ in the Holy Spirit. "The faithful are actively united by a vital and fundamental principle common to them all. That principle is Christ." Further, the Holy Spirit "governs this living unity, grafting the individual on to it, granting him a share in its fellowship and preserving this right for him" (p. 142).

The church's worship has developed over the centuries so that its design reaches across cultures, not unlike a Greek temple, and expresses "great vigor and intensity." The liturgy's form is "clear in language, measured in movement, severe in its modelling of space, materials, colors and sounds; its ideas, languages, ceremonies and imagery fashioned out of the simple elements of spiritual life" (p. 154). This structure conveys "an inner world of immeasurable breadth and depth." At the same time, because the liturgy's form is almost timeless, worship must be complemented by religious devotions which provide what people may find lacking in liturgy. This polarity between worship and devotion is similar to the complementarity between the liturgy's images of Christ and the gospels' representations of Christ. That is, the mass presents "the Sovereign Mediator," "the mystic Christ," while scripture introduces a human being who is "entirely one of us, a real person—Jesus, 'the Carpenter's Son'" (p. 158). Since the church is "Catholic," that is, "actual and universal," it must encourage this reciprocity between the liturgy and popular devotion, between the Christ of the mass and the Jesus of the New Testament.

Active participation in the liturgy requires our bodies (e.g., in processions) as well as our minds, and, therefore, we must employ symbols as well as ideas. On the one hand, this principle grates on rationalists, for they cling to an implicit dualism between mind and body, and, on the other hand, it annoys romantics for they cannot tolerate the claim that some religious symbols are more valid than others. In any case, we must recognize that human beings generate symbols to convey their deepest perceptions of reality. "A symbol may be said to originate when that which is internal and spiritual finds expression in that which is external and material" (p. 167). The liturgy's symbolic activity builds on the "fundamental rules" that shape the symbolic gestures in our ordinary lives, for example, embracing and sharing a meal. The church depends on believers with a rational disposition to help in the "discrimination" among symbols, and, simultaneously, it relies on believers who possess a romantic disposition to foster the "cohesion" of material elements into religious symbols.

This consideration of the role of symbols in worship leads to the insight that liturgy is similar to art and play. Liturgy is not the type of activity which is intended to accomplish something; it is not functional. Rather, worship is the kind of activity which expresses significance or meaning; it is purposeful, as are art and games. Like painting and playing, liturgy is undertaken for its own sake and brings about a disclosure of a reality which we would otherwise miss. The believer at worship is like the artist "who merely wants to give life to his being and its longings, to give external form to the inner truth" (p. 180). So too believers rely on the liturgy to manifest the deepest truth at the heart of creation, the mystery of the triune God. Believers at worship are also like children at play. "To be at play, or to fashion a work of art in God's sight—not to create, but to exist—such is the essence of liturgy" (p. 181). In this vein, biblical images of worship are Ezekiel's vision of the seraphim before the throne of God (Ezek 1:4) and wisdom's hymn: "I was daily his delight, rejoicing before him always" (Prov 8:30).

Building on his comparison of liturgy to art, Guardini points out that worship like art must respect the relationship between beauty and truth. Scholastic philosophy has rightly observed that "beauty is the splendor of truth" (p. 190). As applied to liturgy, this principle means that everything in a mass must serve God's self-communication. For this reason, it is not the "connoisseur" who discovers the "essence of the liturgy," but "[t]he careworn man who seeks nothing at mass but the fulfillment of the service which he owes to his God" and also "the busy woman who comes to be a little lightened of her burden." People err, therefore, when they are interested in worship "merely for its aesthetic value" (p. 185). Liturgists with an "aesthetic mentality" fail to respect the necessity of restraint in art and hence in worship. Since liturgy like art is meant to express an inner reality, it must possess a degree of "modesty," for "all true inwardness still shrinks from self-revelation, just because it is full of all goodness" (p. 193).

Thus, liturgists should heed the words of Plato who warned that those who are excessively devoted to beauty will distort the truth. In fact, worship becomes truly beautiful when all of its elements function in order to reveal God's word become flesh.

This consideration of liturgy in the service of truth leads to the conclusion that liturgy gives witness and praise to objective reality. This view of worship calls into question the Enlightenment's relativism and its functional view of truth. In their respective ways, Kant, Fichte, Schopenhauer, Hartmann, and Nietzsche have emphasized the priority of the will over the intellect. This Enlightenment mentality produces modernity's zeal for "success" and "power" and its disinterest in the truth, in orthodoxy. The result of this tendency is that "[r]eligion becomes increasingly turned towards the world, and cheerfully secular" (p. 205).

According to Guardini, Catholicism rejects the claim of Goethe's Faust that "in the beginning was the deed," and, on the contrary, it witnesses to the truth of John's Gospel: "[i]n the beginning was the Word" (Jn 1:1). If there is to be right action, there must first be right thought. "No matter how great the energy of the volition and action and striving may be, it must rest on the tranquil contemplation of eternal, unchangeable truth" (p. 209). When properly pursued, this commitment to the Logos leads to a life not of "frigid majesty" but of "truth in love," and it is concretely realized in worship where "the Logos has been assigned its fitting precedence over the will." When Christians join in the liturgy, they find that they receive "peace to the depths of their being" and that, with this inner tranquility and direction, they are able to act with "courage" in the world (p. 211). What then is the essence or spirit (*Geist*) of the liturgy? It is the word made flesh, who lives now as the head of the mystical body, the church, and in the liturgy the church joins with Christ in giving thanks and praise in the Holy Spirit to God, the Father.

A CLASSIC TEXT

Vom Geist der Liturgie was a seminal work in the unfolding of Guardini's thought. Its ideas subsequently blossomed into articles and books on worship and prayer as well as into *Vom Sinn der Kirche* (*The Church and the Catholic* [1922]). It also played a key role in the liturgical renewal. Soon after its publication, Max Scheler praised the book, and Berlin's leader of Catholic social action, Carl Sonnenschein, ordered 1,000 copies.[28] Tens of thousands of Catholics were soon reading the book, which became a handbook in Catholic youth groups and within five years underwent twelve printings.[29] In light of the book's success, Hans Maier has described it as "the foundational book of the liturgical movement."[30] Further, transcending its original situation, *Vom Geist der Liturgie* has become a classic in liturgical theology.[31] As such, it still offers insights of importance, of which I will note three.[32]

First, *Vom Geist der Liturgie* reminds us that a Christian community should not "pray at the mass" but rather "pray the Mass."[33] What then is active participation in worship? It involves a coincidence of opposites (*Gegensätze*).[34] True liturgy pulls people together while it also keeps them apart. At some moments, it asks for a communal response (e.g., in song), and, at other moments, it directs each person inward as it requires silence, listening, and reflection. Also, active participation entails a dynamism which is both internal and external; the stirring of our hearts and minds should come to expression as we stand, make the sign of the cross, sit, and kneel. Moreover, basic elements in human life such as bread and wine, oil and water, should disclose and effect God's outreach to us and our response to God.

Second, *Vom Geist der Liturgie* insists that our worship should focus on its objective referent, the living Christ. This transcendent and yet immanent person has called the community into existence, and in worship the assembly should disclose its unity with Christ. Challenging the epistemological assumptions of Descartes and Kant, this book employs a phenomenological method in order to shed light not only on our human lives but also on the source and goal of life. *Vom Geist der Liturgie* accentuates the solidarity of all people, the sacredness of creation, and the objectivity of truth. Presupposing the ecclesiology of the body of Christ, it shows that in its Eucharist a parish should express and strengthen its very self, its communal life in Christ.[35]

Third, the book offers insights into both modern society and also Catholicism. On the one hand, it takes issue with today's emphasis on individualism and self-realization. In this regard, it points out that the form of a mass is not a matter of a priest's personal taste. Further, it confronts modernity's relativism and functionalism by warning that these tendencies may result in tyranny. In other words, fifteen years before Adolf Hitler's Third Reich, this book alerted its readers to the danger of fascism.[36] On the other hand, *Vom Geist der Liturgie* passes judgment on the church's tendency to freeze one specific form of worship and directs attention to the principles in relation to which worship can change. While warning against Christian faith being subsumed into the culture of the day, the book also directs its readers to discover God's grace as mediated through the material world, contemporary symbols, and the human body. In short, this little book calls the church to engage in the renewal of its forms of worship.[37]

Vom Geist der Liturgie is surely a seed from which has sprung ideas which still speak to us today. For this reason, Kathleen Hughes has pointed out that "[m]any of Guardini's liturgical preoccupations remain central to the agenda of renewal. While the reform of the liturgy is virtually complete, the renewal that it promises has barely begun."[38] As we will now see, many of this book's ideas blossomed in Guardini's later writings.

The Renewal of Worship

TOWARD PIUS XII'S *MEDIATOR DEI* (1947)

After the success of *Vom Geist der Liturgie,* Guardini set out to bring the reform of the liturgy from the Benedictine monasteries to the parishes. As much as he loved the Abbey of Beuron's liturgy, he saw himself called as a diocesan priest to help the entire church improve its worship and prayer. For the next five decades, he gave himself to this effort and met with positive results. In this regard, Franz Henrich has written that, beginning in 1918, Guardini "opened the way for the liturgical renewal, which until then was stamped by the monastic ideal and the life of the cloister, [to move] into the parishes, and he gave a much wider frame of reference to the renewal."[39] Hans Maier has reiterated this point: "What [Guardini] wanted [and] what he also realized in the course of his life was twofold: to bring the liturgical movement out of its monastic and academic settings into the parishes among the people, and hand in hand with this [effort] to form the faithful for liturgy through theology and pastoral [leadership]."[40] In order to appreciate Guardini's leadership in the liturgical movement, I will review his pastoral work with German youth and also some of his writings on worship and prayer.

In Berlin and at Burg Rothenfels Guardini labored to give young men and women rich experiences of the Eucharist. At this chapter's start, I cited the accounts of Regina and Heinz Kuehn of the masses at St. Benedict Chapel. Similar descriptions could be given of Guardini's masses at Burg Rothenfels. Expanding upon Schott's *Messebuch,* Guardini translated more parts of the mass into German. The people at a mass eventually also sang German hymns. Moreover, beginning in late 1923, Guardini worked with the architect Rudolf Schwarz in renovating the chapel, and, as a result, this large room became a "flexible space" in which the presider could move the altar, the ambo, and chairs in order to adjust for the type of liturgy. With a free-standing altar, the priest at mass faced the congregation, which was gathered in a semicircle around the altar. Further, Guardini established the use of an offertory procession in the mass, and in the late 1920s he modified the celebration of the Triduum. Lectors read the scriptural texts for Holy Saturday in German, and the Easter vigil was moved from Saturday dawn to Saturday evening. By 1930, the congregation was walking in a candlelight procession after the lighting of the Easter candle.[41]

Guardini did not focus, however, solely on worship. Along with his daily recitation of the divine office, he was also faithful to the rosary.[42] In *Vom Geist der Liturgie* he states: "There could be no greater mistake than that of discarding the valuable elements in the spiritual life of the people for the sake of the liturgy, or than the desire of assimilating them to it."[43] Acting on this conviction in retreats at Burg Rothenfels and spiritual conferences in Berlin, Guardini insisted upon times of silence for meditation and led retreatants in meditations as he instructed them in the importance of posture, breathing, recollecting one's mind, and quieting one's emotions. For these spiritual exercises, he drew on the Christian mystics such as Jan von Ruysbroeck and eventually on Buddhism.[44]

In sum, the young people who prayed with Guardini discovered the riches of the liturgy and religious devotions.[45] Out of this experience, Walter Dirks has written: "We were Catholic students who knew how to use Schott's missal and also knew Pius X's instruction that 'you should pray the mass.' However, we were touched by [cultural] influences which were both in part complementary and also in part contradictory; it was not only our youthful immaturity but also the spirit of the time which made us insecure."[46] But, according to Dirks, Guardini led him and thousands of others like him to a vision of their lives within the mystical body of Christ.

Along with his pastoral leadership, Guardini enriched the liturgical renewal by means of his writings. In 1919, he wrote *Der Kreuzweg unseres Herrn und Heilands.* In an effort to clarify the role of material things in worship, he wrote a series of articles, entitled "Liturgie im Alltag" (Liturgy in the weekday) for Quickborn's newsletter, and in 1922 he put these reflections together in *Von heiligen Zeichen,* which explains the church's use of kneeling, the sign of the cross, the use of holy water, candles, and incense. Also, he gave conferences at Burg Rothenfels on the principles of worship, which he published in 1923 as *Liturgische Bildung* (Liturgical education). Here, he explains that in worship "the invisible" reveals itself in "the visible," in the use of material elements (e.g., bread) and by means of physical movements (e.g., kneeling and standing). Another text which emerged from Guardini's pastoral leadership was *Besinnung vor der Feier der heilige Messe* (*Meditations before Mass* [1939]), which consists of meditations on the meaning of the Eucharist. Further, *Der heilige Franziskus* (*The Focus of Freedom* [1927]) sheds light on the life and spirituality of St. Francis of Assisi. *Der Rosenkranz Unserer Lieben Frau* (*The Rosary of Our Lady* [1940]) discusses the mystery of God's presence in the life of Mary and the church. Guardini's talks at the Jesuits' St. Canisius Church in Berlin generated *Die letzten Dinge* (*The Last Things* [1940]). His other writings on the spiritual life during his years in Berlin include *Vom lebendigen Gott* (*The Living God* [1929]), *Das Gebet des Herrn* (*The Lord's Prayer* [1932]), and *Vorschule des Betens* (*Prayer in Practice* [1943]).

It is noteworthy, however, that Guardini's efforts to bring the liturgical renewal into the parishes resulted in two conflicts. The first run-in occurred between Guardini and Odo Casel (1886–1948) who wrote *Die Liturgie als Mysterienfeier* (*The Mystery of Christian Worship* [1922]) and other texts on the history of Christian worship.[47] In 1919 Guardini began to collaborate with Casel and others at Maria Laach Abbey in the study of the liturgy, and, beginning in 1921, he served as an associate editor of the abbey's *Das Jahrbuch für Liturgiewissenschaft*. After his essay on the value of popular devotions appeared in the journal, Casel criticized it in the journal's next issue.[48] This criticism upset Guardini, who judged that Casel had little desire to promote the liturgical renewal outside the monasteries. As *Der Kreuzweg unseres Herrn* and *Von heiligen Zeichen* became best-sellers among Catholic laity, Guardini distanced himself from the Abbey of Maria Laach and withdrew from the editorial board of *Das Jahrbuch für Liturgiewissenschaft*.[49]

A second conflict, which I briefly discussed in chapter 3, unfolded in the late 1930s and early 1940s as conservative Catholics complained about the changes at mass in some parishes and gained the support of Archbishop Conrad Gröber of Freiburg. One critic was Max Kassiepe, O.M.I., who became alarmed not only by some liturgical practices but also by articles in popular journals such as *Liturgisches Leben*, which was edited by Johannes Pinsk, a chaplain to Berlin's students and Guardini's close friend and colleague. In 1939 in *Irrwege und Umwege im Frömmigkeitsleben der Gegenwart* (False paths and detours in today's spiritual life), Kassiepe charged that the church was being hurt by "liturgism," that is, by emotional and irresponsible forms of worship. He cited variations in the Confiteor and Agnus Dei and also the celebration of the Easter vigil on Saturday evening. He alleged that, without ecclesiastical approval, an elite group of liturgists were making changes in the mass and discouraging people from praying the rosary and the stations of the cross. He charged, too, that priests were taking the liberty of using German instead of Latin in the church's songs and prayers.[50] Kassiepe's book struck a chord among influential Catholic conservatives who charged that some priests were shaping the mass into a form of political protest against the Third Reich.[51]

As conservatives pressed their criticism, German bishops tried to remedy the situation. Bishop Albert Stohr of Mainz asked Romano Guardini to write him a letter on the liturgical renewal. In "Ein Wort zur liturgischen Frage" ("Some Dangers of the Liturgical Renewal" [1940]), Guardini requested that the bishops avoid "a short circuit of authority" that disregards the living reality of the church's worship. It would be better that they continue to support the liturgical renewal while at the same time advising its leaders to avoid four destructive tendencies: "liturgicism," "dilettantism," "pragmatism," and "conservatism." "Liturgicism" rightly recognizes the necessity of recovering the primary intentions and forms of the liturgy, but it fails to learn from parishes' actual worship. "Dilettantism" adopts the appropriate aim of bringing the liturgy nearer to everyday life, for example, by promoting the use of German at mass. Yet, it is intolerant of practices that do not fit its narrow views of worship. "Pragmatism" is validly concerned about what is feasible today. However, it fails to respect the liturgy as an activity undertaken for its own sake. "Conservatism" correctly wants to preserve the tradition's truths. But, since it has an inadequate grasp of history, it gives primacy to practices that are secondary within the history of the liturgy. In conclusion, Guardini recommended that the bishops encourage genuine renewal while discouraging the four extreme positions.[52]

Judging that Guardini's letter shed light on the situation, Bishop Stohr distributed it to all German bishops and eventually published it. Twenty years later, he explained that the letter made a significant impact upon the Fulda Bishops' Conference: "With this letter of brilliant intelligence and masterful skill, Guardini showed a way between [doing] too much and [doing] too little, between rigid resistance and too rapid progress, and accomplished for his friends and associates a service hardly overshadowed."[53]

In another constructive step, Bishop Simon Konrad Landersdorfer of Passau formed a task force, which included Romano Guardini, to study the liturgical renewal in Germany. Following this initiative, the Fulda Bishops' Conference established a liturgical commission, charged with overseeing liturgical renewal in the parishes, and appointed Guardini to this commission. In 1942 the commission issued its "Guidelines for the Liturgical Structure of the Parochial Liturgy."[54]

Although many bishops agreed with the views which Guardini had expressed in his letter of 1940, Archbishop Gröber sustained Kassiepe's grievances and also those of August Dörner in *Sentire cum Ecclesia* (1941). He disapproved of the liturgical movement in general and of Guardini's ideas in particular.[55] On January 18, 1943, Gröber wrote an open letter to the Curia and the German-speaking bishops in which he criticized new theological and liturgical ideas. Although this letter implicitly attacked Guardini's work, Guardini himself did not respond. However, at the request of Vienna's Cardinal Theodor Innitzer, Karl Rahner wrote a public statement in which he clarified that scholars were engaged in a responsible recovery of the church's forgotten riches in theology and liturgy.[56] In April 1943, Cardinal Adolf Bertram of Breslau petitioned the Vatican to allow the German church to implement further changes in the mass, the divine office, and the singing of German hymns.[57]

The Vatican responded to the controversy in ways that pleased the theological progressives, including Guardini. On June 29, 1943, Pius XII issued his encyclical *Mystici Corporis* in which he acknowledges the validity of the theology of the body of Christ when it is cast within a hierarchical framework. Three months later, on September 30, 1943, the pope released his encyclical *Divino afflante Spiritu* in which he gives permission for the limited use of critical methods within biblical studies. Moreover, on December 24, 1943, the Vatican's Secretary of State Cardinal Maglione sent word to Cardinal Bertram that the Vatican would permit the changes in worship that Bertram had proposed.[58]

Official approbation of some liturgical modifications did not end here, however. Four years later, on November 20, 1947, Pius XII issued his encyclical *Mediator Dei*, which many see as the liturgical movement's Magna Carta.[59] While speaking primarily about worship throughout the church, the pope addressed the German controversy by warning against abuses from enthusiasts of liturgical change.[60] But this caution is a minor theme. The major theme is the importance of improving the church's worship and the validity of the principle of active participation in the liturgy. *Mediator Dei* states:

> The sacred liturgy is, consequently, the public worship which our Redeemer as Head of the Church renders to the Father, as well as the worship which the community of the faithful renders to its Founder and through Him to the heavenly Father. It is, in short, the worship rendered by the Mystical Body of Christ in the entirety of its Head and members.[61] ·

This statement sums up well much of what Romano Guardini had put into words and action at Burg Rothenfels and St. Benedict Chapel in Berlin. Further, *Mediator Dei* gave an official basis for further renewal of the liturgy, as envisioned by Guardini and others. Of course, change could only come slowly and in small steps, especially after Pius XII tried to restrict new ideas in theology by issuing his encyclical *Humani generis* (October 12, 1950).

TOWARD VATICAN II'S *SACROSANCTUM CONCILIUM* (1963)

After the Second World War, Romano Guardini continued to participate in the liturgical movement. Choosing not to return to Burg Rothenfels, he limited his ministry primarily to Munich's St. Ludwig Church. Also, he frequently spoke at conferences, for he judged that renewal now required Catholics' education concerning worship and prayer. In 1950 he gave the paper "Die liturgische Erfahrung und die Epiphanie" (The liturgical experience and manifestation) at the First Liturgical Conference in Frankfurt am Main.[62] Fourteen years later, when illness kept the seventy-nine-year-old theologian from attending the Third Liturgical Conference in Mainz, he sent a letter titled "Der Kultakt und die gegenwärtige Aufgabe der Liturgie" (The cultic act and the present challenge of the liturgy).[63] In 1957, acting on his commitment to the laity's theological education, he assisted in the founding of Munich's Katholische Akademie in Bayern.[64] Along with these activities, Guardini continued to write on worship and prayer. At the request of the German Liturgical Commission, he translated with Johannes Wagner and Heinrich Kahlefeld the Hebrew Psalms into literary German for the new *Deutscher Psalter* (1950).[65] Thirteen years later, he supplemented the psalter by writing *Weisheit der Psalmen* (*The Wisdom of the Psalms*), a collection of meditations on thirteen psalms. Guardini's other writings on liturgy and prayer from the postwar period include *Theologische Gebete* (*Prayers From Theology* [1948]), *Drei Schriftauslegungen* (*The Word of God on Faith, Hope and Charity* [1949]), and *Die Sinne und die religiöse Erkenntnis* (The senses and religious knowledge [1950]).

On July 25, 1959, Pope John XXIII announced his intention to convoke the Second Vatican Council, which would begin on October 11, 1962. Soon afterwards, Guardini was invited to be a member of the Preparatory Conciliar Commission on the Liturgy.[66] He accepted this honor but was not able to give himself to this task because of his declining health.[67]

In promulgating *Sacrosanctum concilium* on December 4, 1963, the Second Vatican Council affirmed the movement that began with Prosper Guéranger in 1833, spread to other Benedictine monasteries, and then matured among German Catholics through the efforts of leaders like Odo Casel, Balthasar Fischer, Romano Guardini, Ildefons Herwegen, Josef Jungmann, and Pius Parsch. The Constitution on the Sacred Liturgy reiterates theological principles and ideas which Guardini had promoted in *Vom Geist der Liturgie* and afterwards. It states that in the liturgy "complete and definitive public worship is performed by the Mystical Body of Jesus Christ, that is, by the Head and his members."[68] Then it upholds the principle of active participation when it declares that

> all the faithful should be led to that full, conscious, and *active participation* [my emphasis] in liturgical celebrations which is demanded by the very nature of the liturgy, and to which the Christian people, "a chosen race, a royal priesthood, a holy nation, a redeemed people" (1 Pet 2:9, 4–5) have a right and obligation. In the restoration and promotion of the sacred liturgy the full and *active participation* [my emphasis] by all the people is the paramount concern, for it is the primary, indeed the indispensable source from which the faithful are to derive the true Christian spirit.[69]

Sacrosanctum concilium is clearly the fruit of the labor of many leaders, among whom stands Romano Guardini.[70] There is no doubt that the council's Preparatory Commission on the Liturgy at least implicitly drew on Guardini's writings in its drafting of the constitution.[71] Also, the postconciliar commission for the implementation of the Constitution on the Sacred Liturgy honored Guardini by proposing that selections of his writings be included in the new readings of the divine office. However, the Vatican did not approve this recommendation, for it decided that the new divine office should include few contemporary texts.[72] Reflecting on Guardini's influence upon *Sacrosanctum concilium* and its implementation, Arno Schilson has written:

> The postconciliar reform of the liturgy which is now already twenty-five years old—above all, the acceptance in Germany which was prepared for and celebrated—cannot be understood apart from the untiring preparatory work of Romano Guardini. Also, Vatican II's Constitution on the Liturgy, which is the mature fruit of the liturgical movement, presupposes and at the same time crowns Guardini's commitment to the renewal of the liturgy and the retrieval of our capability for liturgy and symbols.[73]

In conclusion, we should note that while Guardini prepared the way for the Constitution on the Sacred Liturgy, he did not speak to some of the challenges in the postconciliar church. For example, he did not comment on the ways in which Catholicism's renewal of worship should learn from other Christian churches, Judaism, and the world religions.[74] Also, he did not foresee how changes in the liturgy should proceed within non-Western cultures.[75]

"DER KULTAKT" (1964)

In April 1964 church leaders, liturgists, and theologians gathered in Mainz for the Third Liturgical Conference amid a celebratory spirit as a result of the council's promulgation of *Sacrosanctum concilium* four months earlier on December 4, 1963. Some of them became puzzled, however, when they heard Johannes Wagner read Guardini's letter at a plenary session; they wondered whether Guardini had lost his enthusiasm for the renewal of the liturgy.[76] Therefore, we must ask, what was the message in "Der Kultakt und die gegenwärtige Aufgabe der Liturgie," and how did this message fit into his life's work?[77]

In his letter, Guardini observes that, with Vatican II's approval of the Constitution on the Sacred Liturgy, the liturgical movement had entered into its fourth major phase. In his view, Guéranger had initiated the first phase at the Abbey of Solesmes in 1833 by directing a "restoration" of the Roman rite.[78] Beauduin at the Abbey of Mont-César led the movement into its second stage beginning in 1909 when he called for scholarly research into the history of liturgy. The third stage began after the First World War when Pius Parsch at the Abbey of Klosterneuburg and the leaders of the Catholic youth movement (including Guardini) brought liturgical reform to the parishes and the youth movement. Finally, in its constitution on the liturgy, Vatican II confirmed all three stages of the movement and "laid the foundation for the future." As a consequence, the renewal had reached a new juncture: "Now, as a result of the impulse given by the Council, a fourth phase must begin, one infusing new life into the liturgy" (p. 26).

According to Guardini, postconciliar liturgists would face two issues. First, they would need to answer, "What is the nature of the genuine cultic or liturgical act as opposed to the religious act, such as individual devotions or the loose communal act of popular devotions?" The leaders of worship would need to move the church beyond the mentality that regards liturgical actions as somehow secondary to a believer's interior prayer. They must teach that when the congregation stands, walks in procession, sits, and kneels, it is in fact praying. Christians must recover the sense of the ancient church which held that "the external action is itself a 'prayer', a religious act; the times, places, and things included in the action are not merely external decorations, but elements of the whole act and would have to be practiced as such, and so forth" (p. 24).

Moreover, the recovery of the sense of the liturgical act would depend on a second issue. Liturgists would need to consider the impact of our technological culture upon people's ability to engage in communal activity. In a society which values self-autonomy and the intellect at the expense of interpersonal relationships and a sense of the whole person, Christians may lack the potential of joining in the church's worship. Hence, Guardini provocatively asks:

> Is not the liturgical act and, with it, all that goes under the name of "liturgy" so bound up with the historical background—antique or medieval or baroque—that it would be more honest to give it up altogether? Would it not be better to admit that man in this industrial and scientific age, with its new sociological structure, is no longer capable of a liturgical act? (p. 26)

Guardini's questions are still jarring. They seemingly convey a skepticism about the contemporary church's potential for worship. Further, they gain force from the criticism of liturgists for being so preoccupied about the details of a ritual as to neglect underlying issues. Guardini points out, for instance, that ministers of worship should concern themselves not with how they "must organize a procession better," but with how "the act of walking [can] become a religious act, a retinue of the Lord processing through his land, so that an 'epiphany' may take place" (p. 25).

Today, Guardini's letter of 1964 prompts three observations. First, he did not mean to cast doubt on the liturgical movement, the Constitution on the Sacred Liturgy, and its implementation. Rather, he was playing out the coincidence of opposites (*Gegensätze*) that had characterized his work. Prior to Vatican II, Guardini questioned the prevailing view of things, and he continued to do so after the council. As he explained to Bishop Tewes, he was delighted with the new form of the mass which Vatican II had introduced.[79] Guardini reiterated this point in the second edition of *Liturgie und liturgische Bildung* (Liturgy and liturgical education [1966]). Here he recalls that, as a newly ordained priest, he hoped that the day would come, when presiding at mass, he would be able to say aloud in German, "The Lord be with you," and hear the entire congregation respond, "And also with you." Thanks to Vatican II, the day that he envisioned had arrived.[80]

Second, in 1964 Guardini raised the question of our potential to engage in liturgy not as a new question but as one which he had discussed as early as 1918.[81] In *Vom Geist der Liturgie,* he points out that culture can help or hinder our ability to participate in worship. In his words: "The lack of fruitful and lofty culture causes spiritual life to grow numb and narrow; the lack of the subsoil of healthy nature makes it develop on mawkish, perverted, and unlaw-ful lines."[82] After Vatican II Guardini did not stumble upon a new question about the liturgy and culture. Rather, he wanted the church to engage in a li-turgical renewal that would not be hindered by the limitations of a highly tech-nological society.

Third and finally, Guardini's letter arose in part from his anxieties about modernity. In the 1960s, the aged theologian found himself unable to under-stand Germany's emerging culture.[83] In a letter to Josef Weiger—a letter writ-ten shortly after his letter to the Third Liturgical Conference—Guardini said that he could not fathom recent art, literature, and music, and hence felt alien-ated from contemporary society.[84] In particular, he feared that the emphasis upon individualism and self-sufficiency would make it difficult for people to worship appropriately.[85]

To be sure, Guardini's letter of 1964 stands in continuity with his previous writings and simultaneously conveys the seventy-nine-year-old theologian's uneasiness with the 1960s. Also, it is his attempt to establish a creative tension out of which the next generation of liturgists might discover what active par-ticipation in worship may entail in the late twentieth century. Referring to the letter and the issues it mentions, Burkhard Neunheuser of Maria Laach Abbey has written: "Guardini is, in this regard, basically an optimist—on condition, however, that we honestly confront these problems, and that we work seriously for an education that corresponds to the facts."[86] Regina Kuehn, who studied with Guardini in Berlin, has confirmed that he never lost confidence in the li-turgical movement. In her judgment, he was concerned, however, that insofar as the faithful could not participate in liturgy, then they would fail to worship as members of the mystical body of Christ. In her words:

Guardini's approach was born out of a pastoral concern. In his era, an age of highly developed individualism, it was no longer considered 'proper, useful or fashionable' to express one's personal or communal faith. . . . Guardini feared that the parish—the place where faith is made real—would consequently be-come an impoverished collection of individuals instead of the embodiment of the living and acting Christ.[87]

In his last years, Guardini held firmly to his vision of the renewal of the church's worship. To the extent that he was confused by contemporary trends in art, literature, and music, his bewilderment troubled him because—as we will see in chapter 5—throughout his life he had possessed an unusual facility in interpreting literature. In any case, at the end of his life, he did not regret his labors' fruit in the postconciliar church. The Vatican's liturgical commission for the implementation of *Sacrosanctum concilium* acted rightly when, upon learning of Guardini's death, it prayed at its eleventh general meeting (October 17, 1968) in gratitude for this theologian's life in service of the church's liturgical renewal.[88]

❖ 5 ❖

CHRISTIAN FAITH AND LITERATURE

IN EARLY 1923, after accepting the call to Berlin's Friedrich Wilhelm University, Guardini considered what he should teach as the professor for the philosophy of religion and Catholic *Weltanschauung*. Seeking the advice of seasoned professors, he turned to the phenomenologist Max Scheler. At a meeting with Scheler in Cologne, Guardini received a suggestion that shaped his entire career. Forty years later, Guardini recalled this moment:

> In a conversation which was very momentous for me [Scheler] said to me: "You must do what is meant by the word '*Weltanschauung*' [worldview]: as a responsible, conscious Christian observe the world, things, people, [and their] actions, and then say in a scholarly way what you see." And, I still recall how he made this [advice] more specific: "Investigate, for example, the novels of Dostoyevsky and study their outlook [on life] from your Christian standpoint, in order to illuminate, on the one hand, the works under consideration and, on the other hand, [your] standpoint itself."[1]

Guardini acted on Scheler's advice. He gave his inaugural address in Berlin on "the essence of the Catholic worldview" and taught courses in which he sustained an explicit dialogue between his Catholic *Weltanschauung* and contemporary thought. Such courses included "God and the World" (autumn 1923), "Fundamental Questions of a Living Ethic" (spring 1924), "Augustine's Religious View of the World and Its Significance for Today" (autumn 1924), and "Christianity and Culture in View of Søren Kierkegaard's Posing of the Issues" (spring 1925). Moreover, he engaged in this dialogue as he lectured on the writings of Plato, Blaise Pascal, Michel Montaigne, Fyodor Dostoyevsky, Dante, Friedrich Nietzsche, Friedrich Hölderlin, Socrates, and the Buddha.[2] Further, he found occasions at the university, at Burg Rothenfels, and elsewhere to give addresses on the works of Sigmund Freud, Eduard Mörike, Wilhelm Raabe, and Rainer Maria Rilke.[3] Guardini's success with this dialogical approach in Berlin led him to continue it after the Second World War as he lectured in Tübingen and Munich. As a consequence, over four decades Guardini gained recognition as an interpreter of world literature and brought about the kind of encounter between Christian faith and culture that Scheler had proposed to him in 1923.[4]

As an interpreter of literature, Guardini made a significant contribution to German literary criticism. For this reason, his literary interpretations are discussed in such respected commentaries as Paul Fechter's *Geschichte der deutschen Literatur* (1956), Albert Soergel's and Curt Hohoff's *Dichtung und Dichter der Zeit* (1963), and Hermann Kunisch's *Handbuch der deutschen Gegenwartsliteratur* (1969).[5] Moreover, he influenced studies in religion and literature outside of Germany, as evident in the references to his work in the writings of Nathan A. Scott.[6] Finally, his literary interpretation was so original that even recent works on theology and literature, for example, those of Walter Jens, Hans Küng, and Theodore Ziolkowski, cite his texts.[7]

This fifth chapter examines how Guardini established a dialogue between Christian faith and world literature. In the quotation above, Guardini recalls Scheler's dialectical statement that the young scholar should both analyze specific texts and also explain how the ideas in these texts appear from a Catholic point of view. As we will see, he pursued this approach of both/and, and he rejected conservative Catholics' approach of either/or, that is, either Catholic literature or world literature. Because of his inclusive orientation, Guardini generated an encounter between the existential insights of the West's great writers and the wisdom of the Judeo-Christian tradition. In this endeavor he went beyond historical and textual analysis as he explained the view of personal existence expressed in a literary work and then compared and contrasted the work's existential outlook with his Christian understanding of God and human life.[8]

In order to glimpse Guardini as a literary interpreter, I will first review Germany's Catholic revival in literature, within which he emerged as a "foremost representative of cultural Catholicism."[9] Against this background, I will recollect Guardini's love of literature from childhood into his last years. The chapter's second section examines his masterful study of Rainer Maria Rilke's *Duino Elegies* (1923). This book of 1953 is entitled *Rainer Marie Rilkes Deutung des Daseins* (Rainer Maria Rilke's meaning of personal existence), and in 1961 it appeared in English as *Rainer Maria Rilke's Duino Elegies: An Interpretation.*[10] The chapter's third section will summarize how three respected interpreters of literature—Hermann Kunisch, Martin B. Green, and Hans Georg Gadamer— have assessed Guardini's literary studies. Finally, I will consider how Guardini's dialogue between faith and culture anticipated the Second Vatican Council's constructive stance toward the contemporary world.

Into the Cultural Mainstream

THE CATHOLIC LITERARY MOVEMENT IN GERMANY, 1890–1933

Romano Guardini found himself standing between two schools of thought as he lectured in Berlin on Christian faith and world literature. On the one hand, most of his academic colleagues judged that his approach was out-of-date, and, on the other hand, some Catholic intellectuals held that his approach was too liberal. Why did Guardini's literary studies satisfy neither group? In each of his studies Guardini analyzed and evaluated a literary classic not only in terms of its aesthetic quality but also in regard to its existential truth in light of Catholic belief. Guardini's academic colleagues held that it was incorrect for him to claim that an objective norm of truth should function in literary criticism. They could not agree with his approach, for they had adopted the relativistic view of the history of religions school, whose leader, Ernst Troeltsch, taught at the University of Berlin from 1915 until his death in 1923. At times, for example, Guardini found himself at odds with the Protestant theologian Walter F. Otto.[11] However, some Catholic intellectuals were suspicious of the theologian because he acknowledged the excellent aesthetic quality and existential truth of literature that was not written by Catholics.[12] This Catholic context and Guardini's place in it requires elaboration.[13]

After the *Kulturkampf,* progressive Catholics sought ways to enhance Catholics' participation in Germany's cultural and intellectual life. Toward this goal the Görres-Gesellschaft was founded in 1876, dedicated to strengthening Catholic scholarship. This effort gained momentum during the pontificate of Leo XIII (1878–1903) who was committed to the church's scholarly renewal. In his encyclical *Aeterni Patris* (1879), Leo called for the advancement of Catholic philosophy and theology by means of the teachings of St. Thomas Aquinas. This momentum increased during the reign of Kaiser Wilhelm II (1888–1918), in part because of the rise of the Catholic Center party and in part because of intellectual forces within German Catholicism. At the Katholikentag (Catholic Conference) of 1894 in Cologne, speakers addressed ways in which Catholics could overcome their "inferiority" in science, culture, and scholarship.[14] Two years later at a conference in Constance, Georg Freiherr von Hertling, who twenty years earlier was the founding president of the Görres-Gesellschaft, argued that Catholics' work in the natural sciences did not measure up to the research of their non-Catholic peers. Soon afterwards, this same assessment was also voiced by the *Historische-politische Blätter* which, founded by Joseph and Guido Görres in 1837, was the foremost Catholic intellectual journal of the nineteenth century.[15] In 1898 the Catholic writer Heinrich Federer observed that while a renewal of Catholic literature was underway in France, little was taking place in Germany.[16] Finally, throughout the 1890s, German Catholic theologians such as Albert Ehrhard, Franz Xavier Kraus, and Hermann Schell—who were identified with reform Catholicism—urged that the church's teachings be restated so as to become more intelligible to Germans whose thinking operated within the horizon of the *Aufklärung* (Enlightenment) and modern science.[17]

One preeminent representative of this intellectual awakening was Carl Muth (1867–1944). Muth grew up in Worms and then studied in Strasbourg where he participated in the revival of French Catholic literature which Louis Veuillot, Ernst Hello, and Léon Bloy had initiated. Influenced, too, by Hermann Schell's writings, Muth was convinced that Catholicism could contribute to contemporary thought and culture if it would express its deepest beliefs and values in the categories of the day.[18] In 1898, writing under the pseudonym "Veremundus," he published his pamphlet *Steht die katholische Belletristik auf der Höhe der Zeit?* (Does Catholic literature stand among the best of the time?). In response to his own question, the thirty-one-year-old layman answered that German Catholic literature fell short of the quality of contemporary writing for various reasons: the prudery and pedagogical narrowness of Catholic authors, Catholics' disinterest in world literature and the arts, and the scarcity of good Catholic literary journals. One year later, Muth issued his second pamphlet *Die literarische Aufgaben der deutschen Katholiken* (The literary challenges facing German Catholics) in which he exhorted Catholic writers to adopt the classic literary form as spelled out by Goethe. Further, in Muth's judgment these writers should treat not primarily Catholic topics but the urgent, existential issues of all Germans.[19]

Not satisfied solely with describing the situation, Muth also took steps to remedy it. He attracted to his cause other intellectuals such as the Catholic convert Julius Langbehn and the Protestant Friedrich Leinhard as well as Ehrhard, Freiherr von Hertling, and Schell. With their encouragement, in 1903 he founded the journal *Hochland* ("high ground") in Munich. Its aim, as Muth stated at the outset, was to become a "journal of high quality, [based] on a Catholic-Christian foundation," which would "influence the whole, contemporary life of culture in all of its expressions and emanations [which are] essential to its recognition and effective for its progress."[20] In concrete terms, *Hochland* would present Catholic views on world literature, the arts, and religious thought. Towards this goal, Muth published essays of literary criticism on "non-Catholic" literature and also Catholic authors' literary writings which ranked in his judgment with world literature. For example, in 1904 *Jesse und Maria* by Enrica von Handel-Mazzetti appeared in serial form in *Hochland*. German literary critics praised this novel, which concerns the Catholic Church's suppression of Protestants in Austria during the Counter-Reformation, but conservative Catholics sharply criticized it.

Not surprisingly, Muth's pamphlets and issues of *Hochland* disturbed conservative Catholics in Germany and Austria who judged that there was little to respect in current literature and art. Indeed, they saw Muth's agenda as going contrary to the Vatican's cautions against modernity, as spelled out in Pius IX's "Syllabus of Errors" and encyclical *Quanta cura* of 1864. These intellectuals were heartened, therefore, when Pope Pius X (1903–14) made known his opposition to contemporary thought. Among the opponents of Muth's program were the Jesuit literary critics Wilhelm Kreiten (d. 1902) and Alexander Baumgartner (d. 1910), who in the Jesuit journal *Stimmen aus Maria Laach* criticized Muth's work.[21]

One of the most outspoken critics of Muth's undertaking was the Austrian Catholic Richard von Kralik (1852–1934). An admirer of the operas of Richard Wagner, Kralik was convinced, first, that the German-speaking world should undergo a cultural rebirth by retrieving its ancient Teutonic culture and, second, that a revival of medieval Catholicism and nineteenth-century romanticism would bolster this German renaissance. He vigorously expounded his "cultural program" in his book *Deutsche Götter-und Heldbuch* (The book of German gods and heroes [1903]), and he also promoted it in his pamphlets *Kulturstudien* (1900), *Neue Kulturstudien* (1903), *Kulturarbeiten* (1904), and *Kulturfragen* (1907).[22] In 1905 Kralik founded in Vienna the Catholic association called "Gralbund" ("association of the Grail") along with the journal *Der Gral, Monatschrift für Schöne Literatur.*[23] In the first issue of *Der Gral* Kralik explained that this journal would provide a forum for those writers whose works conveyed what the journal's editors judged to be a true "artistic worldview."[24] In pursuing his "literary program," Kralik agreed with Pius X's stance against modernity and advocated "integralism."[25] In 1907, Kralik and his circle rejoiced when the Vatican condemned modernism in Pius X's encyclical *Pascendi Domini gregis* and the Holy Office's decree *Lamentabili sane exitu.*

What became known as the *Literaturstreit* ("literature controversy") started in 1906 when *Der Gral* published articles which criticized Muth and the progressive editors of *Hochland* for printing Handel-Mazzetti's *Jesse und Maria*. Kralik and his associates charged that Handel-Mazzetti's work was tainted by anti-Catholic ideas and that Muth's real agenda was to promote secular ideas at the expense of Catholicism. Shortly afterwards, *Hochland* published a review of Johannes Mumbauer's essay "Ein literarisches Ghetto für die Katholiken?" (A literary ghetto for Catholics?). The review praises Mumbauer for arguing that Catholics should enter into the literary mainstream of the German-speaking world and resist conservatives' efforts to promote a Catholic subculture. Then, it points out that circles of Catholic intellectuals in Austria and southern Germany saw little of value in the twentieth century and were trying to lead Catholics into a cultural ghetto. Angered by this review in *Hochland*, Kralik and his editors published another issue of *Der Gral* criticizing the modernist ideas of *Hochland*. In 1908, in a short statement in *Hochland*, Muth expressed his concerns about Kralik's reactionary stance.[26] Kralik immediately responded in *Der Gral* by charging that Muth lacked the skills to discern great literature.[27] Then, in their respective journals, Muth defended himself and *Hochland*, and Kralik responded by maintaining that it was wrong to speak about the inferiority of Catholic literature, for the problem lay with the inadequacy of contemporary standards. In 1909 Muth published his book *Wiedergeburt der Dichtung aus dem religiösen Erlebnis* (The rebirth of poetry out of religious experience) in which he presents anew his understanding of the classic form in literature and, reiterating the concerns of reform Catholicism, argues that Catholics must present their beliefs within contemporary categories of thought and style. Soon afterwards, Kralik completed his book *Die katholische Literaturbewegung der Gegenwart* (The Catholic literary movement of the day). Voicing his agreement with Pius X's opposition to modernity, he contends that Catholicism must sustain its own literary tradition amid the decay of twentieth-century culture.

The *Literaturstreit* ended in 1910. On the occasion of the death of Baumgartner, Muth wrote in *Hochland* that Baumgartner and he had expressed their opposing views in a high manner and, as a result, had contributed to a strengthening of Catholic literature.[28] After this article, Muth decided that he would no longer engage in a debate with *Der Gral* and its supporters. For their part, the conservatives claimed victory when *Der Gral* published a letter written by Pius X in the autumn of 1910 to a professor at the University of Freiburg in which the pope praised those who resisted the infiltration of contemporary ideas into Catholic literature. Implicit in the letter is the papacy's criticism of *Hochland*. Interpreting the pope's letter as a victory, Kralik and his associates continued to snipe at Muth and the progressive Catholics. In June 1911 Rome's Holy Office placed *Hochland* on the Index of Forbidden Books, but this action had little effect, for as a result of the intervention of the Vatican's nuncio to Munich, Andreas Frühwirth, and the Bavarian royal family, the Wittelsbachs, the Holy Office's decision was not made public.[29]

From our post–Vatican II perspective, we can see that while *Der Gral* coincided with Pius X's defensive stance toward modernity, *Hochland* anticipated John XXIII's dialogical posture toward the world. In other words, while Kralik and his circle took their bearings from the past, in particular from Pius IX and the First Vatican Council, Muth and his friends helped to prepare the way into the future, especially to the Second Vatican Council. Perhaps these divergent attitudes determined the prospects for their respective journals. *Der Gral* ceased publication in 1936, but *Hochland* thrived until 1972, when it was renamed *Neues Hochland* in order to reflect its editors' shift to issues in the Christian-Marxist dialogue.[30] Further, during its sixty-nine years *Hochland* published the literary works of some of Germany's foremost Catholic authors and also scholarly essays by its most influential Catholic theologians.[31] These works include writings by Heinrich Böll, Gertrud von le Fort, Elisabeth Langgässer, and Ernst Toller and theological texts by Hans Urs von Balthasar, Walter Kasper, Hans Küng, Erich Przywara, Karl Rahner, and Joseph Ratzinger.

Where did Romano Guardini stand in the conflict between *Hochland* and *Der Gral?* Statistics provide the answer. On the one hand, Guardini published seventeen articles or selections from his books in *Hochland,* and his writings were reviewed in thirty articles in *Hochland.* On the other hand, he contributed no articles to *Der Gral,* which reviewed only four of his books.[32] Undoubtedly, Guardini worked within the theological orientation of Carl Muth and *Hochland.* In fact, diocesan officials in Mainz viewed Guardini as a liberal theologian and hence with suspicion simply because he subscribed to *Hochland.*[33]

A LIFELONG LOVE OF LITERATURE

Romano Guardini's support for Muth's view of Catholicism and literature is evident in many ways. After the Great War, he became friends with Muth and, in the early 1920s, was invited by him to join the editorial board of *Hochland.* Guardini declined the invitation, however, in order to remain engaged with Quickborn as well as to maintain his teaching at the University of Berlin. At the same time, he was also friends with Richard Knies, who in Mainz founded Matthias Grünewald Verlag in 1918 with a vision in book publishing similar to Muth's in journalism. Guardini supported the new company by having it publish some of his most successful books and also by serving as one of its editors.[34] Guardini's backing for the orientation of Muth and Knies is also evident in the fact that when he became an editor of Quickborn's *Die Schildgenossen* in 1924, he immediately took steps to shape it into a journal similar to *Hochland* and published his own essays in *Die Schildgenossen* which previously would have appeared in *Hochland.*

Along with these indications of Guardini's literary kinship with Muth, there is a more internal clue, namely, his abiding interest in world literature. As a boy, he was a voracious reader; among his favorite books were Karl May's stories of the American west. As a youth, he immersed himself in Dante's *Divine Comedy* and made it the cornerstone of his own collection of literary classics. He also gathered prints of major works of art, including paintings by Raphael and Michelangelo.[35]

Philipp Harth, an artist and theologian, has written that during his youth in Mainz he was struck by Guardini's love of literature and art:

> When I visited [his room] for the first time, I was surprised to see the prints of works of art which hung on the wall, since I would have selected them myself. Romano owned a bookcase with many books. . . . Full of awe, I would listen when Guardini described the content of a book which he had read. Also poetry interested him, and he himself wrote poetry. . . . For school he translated *Oliver Twist* into German. . . . The greatest and most beautiful book which Guardini possessed was Dante's *Divine Comedy* with the illustrations by Doré. We often took note of these illustrations, and Romano explained them to me since he had read the [entire] book.[36]

Karl Berger, who studied with Guardini in Munich, has corroborated Harth's recollection. On Guardini's eightieth birthday, Berger recalled that in 1905 when their circle of friends met at Munich's cafés, "[y]ou occasionally had the *Divine Comedy* with you and offered to read to us some passages, which you selected, and to comment on them. I have never forgotten your soft, meditative voice and its effect on the small circle of hearers."[37]

In fact, literature sustained Guardini through his student years. During the unhappy year (1903–4) in which he studied chemistry at the University of Tübingen, he survived in part by reading Fritz Reuter's novels in the evenings.[38] When he visited Mainz, he enjoyed the discussions on Léon Bloy, Joris Karl Huysmans, and Cardinal Newman at the home of Wilhelm and Josephine Schleussner.[39] From 1906 into 1908, Guardini delighted in the literary circle at Tübingen's Wilhelmsstift, and, as the chaplain for Mainz's Iuventus beginning in 1915, he frequently discussed with the young people literature such as that by Joseph von Eichendorff (d. 1857).[40]

This review of Guardini's early literary interests sheds light on the reason for the success of his writings in literary interpretation. In 1923 when Scheler advised Guardini what he should teach in Berlin, he made this recommendation because he had already noted the young theologian's genius for analyzing literature in light of his Catholic faith. When Guardini eventually lectured on the writings of Dante, Dostoyevsky, Kierkegaard, and Pascal, he was not doing something new; he was doing in public what he had done in private since his youth.

Finally, what kind of literature did Guardini treat in his lectures? Unlike Richard von Kralik and the friends of *Der Gral,* he read non-Catholics as well as Catholics and selected literature primarily on the basis of two criteria: content and form. He studied a text when it conveyed an author's insight into the fundamental issues of personal existence and simultaneously possessed a high literary style.[41] (Guardini's standards of literary form were shaped in part by Stendahl's reflections on style.[42]) By holding these two norms, Guardini clearly agreed with the progressives in the *Literaturstreit.* Like Muth, he wanted to understand all respected literary works, especially those being read by students.[43] Given these criteria, it is not surprising that he took seriously the writings of Rainer Maria Rilke.

A "Dialogue" with Rainer Maria Rilke

RAINER MARIA RILKES DEUTUNG DES DASEINS (1953)

Over a span of approximately sixty years, Romano Guardini published numerous literary studies. Among the earliest of these texts were his reflections on the poetry of Michelangelo, which appeared in 1907, and his translation, with an introduction, of the spiritual journal of the Franciscan mystic Lucie Christine (d. 1908), which was published in 1912. However, most of his literary interpretations grew out of his lectures in Berlin, Tübingen, and Munich as well as from discussions at Burg Rothenfels. He studied Dostoyevsky's novels in *Der Mensch und der Glaube* (The human being and faith [1933]) and again in *Religiöse Gestalten in Dostojewskijs Werk* (Religious figures in Dostoyevsky's work [1939]). In *Christliches Bewusstsein* (1935) he analyzed Pascal's writings in order to understand a modern Christian's reconciliation of faith and reason. Guardini's two major works on Dante are *Der Engel in Dantes Göttlicher Komödie* (The angel in Dante's *Divine Comedy* [1937]) and *Landschaft der Ewigkeit* (Landscape of the eternal [1957]). One of the books which most pleased him is his study of the thought of the poet-philosopher Friedrich

Hölderlin, entitled *Hölderlin: Weltbild und Frömmigkeit* (Hölderlin: Image of the world and spirituality [1939]). Guardini's interest in comparing Jesus of Nazareth and the world's great philosophers and religious leaders resulted in his work *Der Tod der Sokrates* (1947). After publishing essays on a few of Rainer Maria Rilke's *Duino Elegies,* he examined all ten poems in *Rainer Maria Rilkes Deutung des Daseins* (1953). Guardini's last literary studies are *Gegenwart und Geheimnis* (Presence and mystery [1957]), which treats the poetry of Eduard Mörike, and *Sprache, Dichtung, Deutung* (Language, poetry, meaning [1962]), a collection of essays on the works of Rilke, Shakespeare, and Wilhelm Raabe.

Since synopses of Guardini's literary studies are already available, I will discuss *Rainer Maria Rilkes Deutung des Daseins* as one instance of his literary hermeneutics.[44] I begin with a review of the origins, aims, and method of the book and then examine Guardini's commentary on the *First Elegy.*

Rainer Maria Rilkes Deutung des Daseins was the fruit of approximately fifty years of reading, reflection, and discussion.[45] Many young Germans read the poetry and stories of Rainer Maria Rilke (1875–1926) during the early 1900s, and it is likely that Guardini discussed these works at Burg Rothenfels.[46] In the 1930s, he discussed the *Duino Elegies* (1923) at the University of Berlin and in 1938 wrote an essay on the first of the ten poems.[47] Subsequently, he treated Rilke's writings in his lectures at the universities of Tübingen and Munich and published essays on the second, eighth, and ninth poems.[48] He held off giving his manuscript on all ten elegies to a publisher until he was satisfied that he was being fair to the poems. Even then he admitted that there is more to Rilke's work than he had grasped, for "[n]o interpretation of these prophetic utterances can claim to be final and authoritative."[49] Finally, Guardini displayed his high regard for Rilke's writing by dedicating *Rainer Maria Rilkes Deutung des Daseins* to his mother on her ninety-first birthday.[50]

Guardini's personal investment in this work is revealed in his diary entry for August 20, 1953:

> I have just packed up the galley proofs of the book on Rilke. I am happy. The work on the *Elegies* began in Berlin in the middle of the 1930s, initially as an exercise in the seminar. Then [my work continued] in the first year of the war, I believe, as lectures within a private circle to which at that time Countess Hatzfeld belonged, in whom I subsequently confided and who had such a tragic destiny. . . . Through Grassi my interpretations of three *Elegies* (numbers 2, 8 and 9) appeared in the *Schriften zur geistigen Überlieferung.* Now the whole [text] is done. I wonder whether the result deserved the great amount of work that I have given it. However it is, as far as I see, the first critical philo-

sophical engagement with Rilke, and this engagement must be undertaken since its aim is to understand [the poem]—and [this understanding] is important for guiding our age.[51]

While waiting for the book to appear, Guardini read more of Rilke's poetry.[52] Then, when he received the new book, he did something characteristic of him: he questioned whether he had done justice to the *Duino Elegies*. His diary entry for November 27, 1953, reads: "The first copies of the book on Rilke arrived today. I have thought about and written the sentences so many times that they appear flat to me. I invested so much work [in this book]—and now I do not know whether all the effort has any significance."[53]

What were Guardini's aims and method in *Rainer Maria Rilkes Deutung des Daseins?* He pursued the two goals that Scheler had recommended to him in 1923: a literary analysis of the *Duino Elegies,* on the one hand, and, on the other, an assessment of the poems' truth, as determined in the light of Christian faith. Going beyond a clarification of the meaning of these elegies to an appraisal of their validity is required by Rilke himself who at times stated that these poems were religiously inspired. In Guardini's words: "Rilke thus demands more from his reader than an appreciation of the beauty of his verses or comprehension of great thoughts."[54] In writing the *Duino Elegies* (1923), as in writing his *Sonnets to Orpheus* (1922), Rilke saw himself as the "bearer" or "prophet" of a message which was dictated to him by something or someone apart from himself. As a result, he made implicit claims not only about his own experience of reality, his "subjective truth," but also about reality itself, "objective truth." For this reason, one must assess the validity of these poems as well as their meaning and truthfulness. In other words: "The question to be answered here is not whether Rilke's message commands respect, but whether his impressive account of life and death, of humanity and personal relations really corresponds to the truth."[55]

Guardini was aware that his evaluation of the *Duino Elegies* would be controversial. In his book he notes that some scholars had criticized his earlier studies because he weighed the truth of literary works. Referring to himself, he states: "The author has already provoked a certain amount of criticism whenever he left the path of historical or aesthetic appreciation in order to make a philosophical assessment of poetic works—in other words, whenever he was concerned with the question of their objective truth."[56] Such criticism did not stop Guardini, however, for he was convinced that, "despite the relativistic spirit of our age," responsible literary criticism must include a concern for the truth of a literary work, especially a work such as the *Duino Elegies* which makes an overt claim about the nature of reality.

How did Guardini examine the *Duino Elegies?* In a manner not unlike the "new criticism" of René Wellek (d. 1995), he focused primarily on the meaning of the poems as conveyed by their verbal sense. That is, he examined Rilke's use of words, phrases, patterns of expression, and images within the *Elegies* themselves. He also compared the usage of words and images in the *Duino Elegies* with Rilke's use of language and images in his other writings. Along with this study of factors internal to the poems, Guardini brought in some external factors. He noted what Rilke said in his letters about the genesis of the *Duino Elegies* and his intentions. At the same time, without delving into the poet's psyche, he considered the ways in which the poems were influenced by experiences in Rilke's life such as the loneliness of his childhood. Further, he made associations to literary works by other authors which treat issues, themes, and motifs similar to Rilke's. For example, since these elegies speak of angels, Guardini reviewed the character of angels in the writings of Dante and Hölderlin. In sum, in order to illumine the meaning of the *Duino Elegies,* he looked primarily at the text itself and secondarily discussed the text's background.

Guardini undertook his appraisal of the truth of the *Duino Elegies* on the basis of his understanding of Catholicism. In particular, he worked on the basis of three assumptions. First, he held that Christian belief witnesses to the truth about God and human life. As explained in his writings on revelation, he held that belief in Jesus Christ provides the point of view from which one can see reality as God sees it. Second, he assumed that there exists an opposition, though not a contradiction, between natural revelation and historical revelation.[57] Someone like Rilke or Hölderlin who does not stand within the church may have a religious experience, but this person has probably not attained the right perspective on our lives in relation to God. Third, in Guardini's judgment there is a limited spectrum of acceptable interpretations of the major tenets of Christian faith. For example, some statements about God and angels may be truthful in that they communicate someone's experience, but they would be objectively wrong if they did not conform to the church's teachings.

AN INTERPRETATION OF THE *FIRST ELEGY*

Rainer Maria Rilke began the *Duino Elegies* in 1912 while he was residing at the castle of Duino near Trieste. When he left Duino in mid-1912, he had in hand drafts of the entire first and second poems and also fragments of the third and tenth poems. For the next few years, he occasionally worked on the elegies, but from 1915 until early 1922 he found little time for them. In February 1922 at the Chateau Muzot in the Swiss Valais, he gave his undivided attention to this project and, during a period of a few weeks, felt driven to complete the eight remaining poems. Since each of the ten poems is highly complex, it must suffice to paraphrase Rilke's *First Elegy* and then to summarize Guardini's interpretation of it.[58]

The *First Elegy* speaks of loneliness and the pain of recognizing life's fleeting character. It opens with the question: "And if I cried, who'd listen to me in those angelic orders?" (v. 1).[59] And, the answer unfolds that we should not seek communion with an angel, for we cannot bear its powerful presence. Indeed: "Every angel's terrifying" (v. 7). Yet, if we cannot commune with angels, to whom can we turn? How should we live, especially since we also find ourselves disconnected from other human beings? We must live as "the hero who lives on: even his fall was only an excuse for another life, a final birth" (vv. 41–42). Our situation is similar to that of a "deserted" lover. Consider the young Milanese woman Gaspara Stampa of the sixteenth century who, after she was abandoned by Count Collaltino di Collalto, sought consolation in religion, poetry, and new lovers. Aren't we like her? "Isn't it time our loving freed us from the one we love and we, trembling, endured: as the arrow endures the string, and in that gathering momentum" (vv. 50–52).

In this situation we must "listen as only saints have listened: until some colossal sound lifted them right off the ground" (vv. 54–55). Listen, in particular, to "those who died young" (v. 61). Of course, death itself is not the answer, for in death we will find it "strange not living on earth anymore" (vv. 69–70). Yet, we can learn from the dead that we must mature to the point where "we're weaned from the things of this earth as gently as we outgrow our mother's breast" (vv. 87–88). According to legend, the spring god Linos relinquished his expectation of fulfillment in love, was overwhelmed with sadness, and eventually found consolation in music. "Is this story meaningless?" (v. 91) No, for it is possible that, in "the Void," we will feel "that vibration which charms and comforts and helps us now" (vv. 94–95).

THE THEMES OF THE *FIRST ELEGY*

As Guardini notes, the *First Elegy* comprises seven units. In the first unit (vv. 1–7), Rilke expresses his desire to communicate with the angels, but, in the second unit (vv. 8–25), he reasons that he must relinquish this desire for intimacy and live an asceticism which will bring his "inner" life into union with the "outer" world. In the third part (vv. 26–35), the poet avers that the outer world, the cosmos, wants to come to realization in some manner through each person's "inner world." The fourth unit (vv. 36–53) presents the poet's pessimistic view of love: a person cannot truly give to and receive from another person but, in the name of love, must renounce the yearning for reciprocity in love. The fifth segment (vv. 54–68) describes the "saints" as those who "have listened" to the call of the cosmos and allowed their inner selves to become one with it. In the sixth unit (vv. 69–85), Rilke declares that the living must follow the example of the dead by letting go of every attachment to other persons and even to their individual identity—"throwing out even your own name like a broken toy" (v. 75). In the seventh and final unit (vv. 86–95), the poet concludes that we attain true personal existence when we renounce our desire for meaning and love.

In his literary analysis, Guardini highlights the key themes of the *First Elegy* as he discusses the meaning of individual phrases and verses within the poem's seven units. On occasion, he offers his assessment of Rilke's ideas in the light of Christian belief. According to Guardini, three themes stand out in Rilke's first poem: the impossibility of love, the loss of belief in God, and renunciation as the fundamental act of personal existence. I will review Guardini's analysis of these three themes and then consider his evaluation of them.

First, the *First Elegy* declares that mutual love is not possible in human life; "I-you" ("I-Thou") relationships are ultimately not successful. As Guardini states, for Rilke "there is no such thing as love which enables one human being to find a spiritual home with another—any more than one can make one's home in a given country."[60] One expression of this conviction occurs in the poem's second unit: "Ah, who [sic] can we turn to, then? . . . Maybe what's left for us is some tree on a hillside we can look at day after day" (vv. 9, 13–15). Since we cannot find intimacy with one another, perhaps we feel closest to the tree which we see each morning through our kitchen window. Another expression of this negative view of love arises in the poem's fourth part: when we long for communion with others, we should "sing about great lovers" who were abandoned. We will find that "the deserted . . . could love you so much more than those you loved" (v. 38). People who have known failure in love know the truth about life. "For Rilke the true lover is not," Guardini says, "the one who finds fulfillment; he is the one who remains unfulfilled but none the less continues to love" (p. 31). A case in point is Gaspara Stampa, who handled her sorrow by writing poetry.

At this point, Guardini recalls that in his *Notebooks of Malte Laurids Brigge* (1910) Rilke discusses the parable of the Prodigal Son (Lk 15:11–32). In Rilke's judgment, this parable is "the legend of a man who didn't want to be loved."[61] The younger son renounced the kind of love that seeks to control the lover and fled home in order to love in a way that lives "in unspeakable fear for the freedom of the other person." The son remained disconnected from the ones whom he loved. Rilke states: "Slowly [the son] learned to let the rays of his emotion shine through into the beloved object, instead of consuming the emotion in her." As a result, the son moved toward "that profound indifference of heart" which directed him to transcend the object of his love and embrace the entire universe. Guardini writes that for Rilke "true lovers do not face one another as 'objects' of love. [Rather] each is the occasion for the other's free act of love which leads into 'Openness'" (p. 34).

Rilke's skepticism concerning love leads to a second theme: the loss of belief in God. Since we are unable to fulfill our desire to care for one another, we remain isolated. How then are we to cope with this isolation? Can we find solace in God or angels? The *Duino Elegies* makes no mention of God as known within the Judeo-Christian tradition but speaks of angels. However, according to the first poem, an angel is not a truly transcendent being. It possesses the fullness of finite existence and, for this reason, is too "terrifying" for us (v. 7). It frightens us because it is so much more alive than we are. Or, in Guardini's words, according to Rilke, "[t]he Angel thus stands for man at the furthermost limit of experience, illustrating what an earthly creature is *not*" (p. 21). In any case, since we can receive no comfort from an angel, we feel even more isolated. Hence, the first poem says: "So I control myself and choke back the lure of my dark cry" (v. 8). This verse, Guardini observes, refers to the primal longing that in previous ages brought about "the religious act of prayer." But this is not the case today. "Instead, the language of devotions is replaced," the theologian notes, "by words which belong to life on this earth, describing the cry of one creature to another." For twentieth-century people, God is dead, and, therefore, we could address our religious invocations to powerful, though finite beings, the "angels," who however cannot assist us. According to Guardini, our awareness of God's absence means that "the loneliness becomes still deeper."

Rilke's loss of a sense of divine transcendence surfaces in his view of the saints. According to the poet, "the saints have listened: until some colossal sound lifted them right off the ground" (vv. 55–56). Guardini points out that Rilke emphasizes the act of listening in the *Sonnets to Orpheus* as well as in the *Duino Elegies*. For instance, in the *First Elegy* Rilke praises the holy women and men for listening to "the voice of God" (v. 59). But he does not mean "God" and "saints" in the traditional sense. For the poet, "God" is a force within the cosmos which is capable of literally lifting people off the ground, and the "saints" are those people who are so attentive to this cosmic force that they lose themselves in it (v. 68).

At this point, a third theme emerges. If "I-you" relationships are impossible and if God does not exist, then we are alone in the cosmos. But how are we to live? We must accept that life has no meaning and that love cannot be fulfilled. According to Rilke, we must live "not giving the meaning of a human future to roses and other things that promise so much" (vv. 71–72). Or, in Guardini's restatement: "Admit that your arms remain empty. Accept their emptiness and fit it into the cosmic space." If we admit our loneliness and accept it, we may paradoxically give meaning to our lives and the world. To quote Guardini again: "In other words, by letting your heart receive the emptiness you will endow the space outside with 'fervor' or spiritual depth" (p. 25). As we forego our desire for intimacy, we can attain a spiritual depth that gives meaning both to our lives and also to the world. By our new asceticism, we reconcile our inner world and the outer world, and, in effect, impart into the universe what Guardini, paraphrasing Rilke, calls a "divine essence."

According to the *First Elegy,* life asks for our self-emptying, and love invites our union with the cosmos. When we realize what life requires, we face the poet's question: "Isn't it time our loving freed us from the one we love and we, trembling, endured: as the arrow endures the string, and in that gathering momentum becomes more than itself" (vv. 50–53). As analyzed by Guardini, Rilke's first poem exhorts us to detach ourselves from both our loved ones and ourselves so that, like an arrow, we can be sent into the unknown.

THE TRUTH OF THE *FIRST ELEGY*

According to Guardini, once we understand the *First Elegy's* themes, we must decide whether they are true in themselves. To be sure, the poem accurately expresses painful experiences in Rilke's own life, especially his difficult childhood, and it also puts into words what many people undergo today. However, we must not confuse the issue of the elegy's truthfulness with the question of its truth. Guardini makes it clear that while he values Rilke's ten poems as a faithful expression of our twentieth-century dilemma, he cannot agree with the work's implicit ontological claims.

In Guardini's judgment, the views on love, religious belief, and self-denial in the *Duino Elegies* sprang from two sources in Rilke's life: his impoverished childhood and his lack of Christian faith. Throughout his early years, Rilke was neglected by his parents and separated from his father. Then, as an adult, the poet himself failed in his interpersonal relationships. In April 1901, he married Clara Westhoff but in 1902 bid farewell to Clara and their newborn daughter. In light of this family history, Guardini concluded that Rilke's negative comments regarding love stem from his own inability "to establish firm personal relations" (p. 36). Further, a second source of the poem's view of life's emptiness was the poet's strong urge to believe in God and yet his inability to do so. Given the questions which Rilke asked and his attentiveness to life's deeper dimensions, one must recognize, Guardini says, that Rilke's life remained "rooted in a fundamentally religious impulse" (p. 33). Nevertheless, for reasons beyond human apprehension, Rilke could not make an act of Christian faith. The poet rightly sensed that human life is meant to bring one into communion with a truly transcendent reality, and yet he could not get beyond his conviction that talk about God is nothing more than a human projection into the unknown.

In Guardini's judgment, while Rilke's experience of "I-you" relationships manifests a subjective truth, it is objectively wrong. The theologian states: "Rilke's view [of love] is fundamentally false. To love means to love *someone*" (p. 33). The Judeo-Christian tradition attests that a human being matures into full personal existence as he or she enters into relationships marked by mutual, committed love. Not only are such human ties possible, they are necessary in our lives. As Guardini declares: "For a life which lacks the 'I-Thou' relationship . . . is no longer true to itself. An inner vacuity is created which manifests itself in relation to everything else: to things, to destiny, and . . . to God" (p. 37).

Guardini also insists that Rilke's view of God and the saints is wrong. Rilke has deliberately cast aside the rich language of the Judeo-Christian tradition and replaced it with "secular terms" which cannot express the meaning and truth of Christian faith. Rilke's nonreligious discourse is not capable of communicating God's absolute transcendence and the reality of revelation. In the theologian's words:

> There is no need of special proof to show that the God spoken of by Rilke is not the God to whom the "saints" listened. They were addressed by the Living God of Revelation. They stood in a direct relationship of prayer to Him, and in His service they were consumed by the fire of love and sacrifice. They would have rejected Rilke's God with their whole being. (p. 42)

After disagreeing with Rilke's theological ideas, Guardini takes issue with the poet's assertion that we must renounce our search for meaning. The *First Elegy* declares that "we're weaned from the things of this earth as gently as we outgrow our mother's breast" (vv. 87–88). Paraphrasing these words, Guardini writes: "And so the wheel comes full turn. The repeated negative—in *not*-possessing, *not* being able to use people or things—which runs through the *Elegy* is really [for Rilke] part of the mystery of becoming" (p. 50). But in the Judeo-Christian view, healthy acts of self-emptying lead not to a kind of symbiosis with the cosmos but to union in Jesus Christ with the living God.

Guardini's assessment of Rilke's *First Elegy* is nuanced. On the one hand, Guardini is empathetic with Rilke's loneliness and conveys respect for the poet's truthfulness. He states: "These poems express the experiences and ideas of perhaps the most sensitive and subtle German poet of modern times" (p. 9). On the other hand, Guardini also asserts that these beautiful, profound verses fail to articulate what Christians know about God and human life on the basis of their faith in Jesus Christ and participation in the church.

The Reception of Guardini's Literary Interpretations

When Romano Guardini was a university student, his interest in world literature placed him among progressive Catholics. In the *Literaturstreit*, he agreed with Carl Muth in acknowledging the wisdom and beauty of writings like those of Dostoyevsky, Hölderlin, and Rilke. However, among literary critics, Guardini was seen as a conservative, for he brought his Christian belief into dialogue with a literary work's implicit religious claims.[62] In order to glimpse the theologian within the literary world, I will briefly review statements on his work by Albert Soergel and Curt Hohoff, Hans Georg Gadamer, Martin B. Green, and Hermann Kunisch.[63]

Observing that the meaning and truth of personal existence is better expressed in literature than in philosophy and theology, Soergel and Hohoff point to Romano Guardini as a scholar who perceived the religious aspects of literary works and labored to illumine them. Indeed, they praise him for having thought through the interrelationship between existential truth and aesthetics. They state: "Mind and heart, thought and love, become one in literature. This 'existential' contact point between the spheres, which are inseparable in life, was worked out by Guardini." In their judgment, he saw that a person's "persistent engagement with literature is important," for the works of great writers like Dante, Dostoyevsky, Hölderlin, Kierkegaard, and Rilke are "testimonies about perceived (envisioned) reality." According to Soergel and Hohoff, Guardini benefited by possessing a "liturgical mentality" which enabled him to discern that, in literature as well as in ritual, meaning is a function of form.[64]

The philosopher of hermeneutics Hans Georg Gadamer has referred to Guardini's literary interpretations on numerous occasions.[65] In his *Truth and Method* (1960) Gadamer criticizes his literary studies, for in his view Guardini violated the hermeneutical principle that we must interpret a literary text on its own terms and not according to our religious and philosophical convictions. In Gadamer's judgment, an interpreter's values, while perhaps valid in themselves, do not apply to literary interpretation. Referring explicitly to Guardini's work, Gadamer writes: "Whoever would put Hölderlin or Rilke to the proof to see if they really believe in their gods or angels is missing the point."[66]

This criticism in *Truth and Method* derives from Gadamer's essay "Rainer Maria Rilkes Deutung des Daseins: Zu dem Buch von Romano Guardini" (1955). Here, Gadamer argues that while Guardini has provided fine insights into the meaning of the *Duino Elegies*, he has overstepped the boundaries of literary criticism by trying to judge the truth of these poems. Gadamer voices his objection to Guardini's kind of hermeneutics by rhetorically asking: "What is criticism of a poet which concerns not poetic success but truth?"[67] With regard to the issue of meaning, there is no doubt, Gadamer says, that Guardini has helped us to understand Rilke's poems, for he has provided "sensitive explanations" of "many individual passages" of the *Elegies*. Of course, as is the case in all literary criticism, some of his comments fall short of the mark. This inadequacy is especially evident with regard to the fourth, fifth, and tenth poems, where Guardini has not perceived "the unity of the poetic intentions" in each elegy (pp. 272, 280).

Guardini's work is problematic in principle, however, with regard to the issue of truth. In Gadamer's judgment, the theologian is correct in asking about the truthfulness of Rilke's poems but has erred in attempting to evaluate whether their view of personal existence is right or wrong—an evaluation which he must undertake according to criteria which are external to the *Elegies* themselves. Gadamer gives three reasons for his negative assessment. First, since the genre of these poems is that of a lamentation, an elegy, it is inappropriate to expect them to treat aspects of personal existence (e.g., life's blessings) which would not fit within this genre. Second, Rilke did not experience God within his life and, therefore, should not be faulted for his silence about something with which he was not familiar. Third, the validity of a literary work is always "the truth of aesthetic relativism," not the correctness that is established on the basis of a comprehensive philosophical or religious system. Thus, to criticize the *Duino Elegies* because of its "aesthetic relativism" is to misunderstand the kind of truth which poetry expresses. "The task of the interpreter

. . . is to find out the status of the truth expressed and simultaneously to set out its limits by means of opposing instances." In Gadamer's view, the "truth of art" displays the interpreter's limitations, for "[a]ll criticism of poetry . . . is always self-criticism of the interpretation" (p. 277).

In conclusion, Gadamer thanks Guardini for raising the question of truth in literature and proposes that the theologian should have pursued his concern for truth by relying upon criteria within the *Duino Elegies* themselves. Gadamer concedes that Guardini is correct when he says that Rilke's existential claims are not Christian. In fact, Rilke's thought has similarities to Hegel's, for Rilke like Hegel urges us to say yes to life even in the face of death but this yes has no basis in Christian belief in the resurrection (pp. 280–81). According to Gadamer, a philosophical or theological assessment of this sort must, however, always remain marginal to the literary interpreter's primary task of aesthetic analysis.

By contrast to Gadamer, the British literary critic Martin B. Green has offered a positive evaluation of Guardini's literary studies.[68] Specifically referring to *Rainer Maria Rilkes Deutung des Daseins,* Green judges that "Guardini is unanswerable" when he observes that in the *Duino Elegies* Rilke is asking the reader to make a religious as well as an aesthetic assent (p. 186). For this reason, he is correct when he questions the validity of the existential claims of the *Duino Elegies.* Nor does he stand alone in assessing the truth of these poems, for the British scholar E. M. Butler has done the same in her *Rainer Maria Rilke* (1941). Indeed, she "is even sharper in her tone about [Rilke]." As Green notes, Guardini's and Butler's disagreement with Rilke's existential claims does not lessen their respect for the literary accomplishment of the *Duino Elegies.* Indeed, "[i]t is clear that both Guardini and Butler enthusiastically appreciate the poetry, completely acknowledging the poet's powers, but find full consenting response impossible" (p. 187).

Further, Green calls attention to Guardini's insight that the *Duino Elegies* communicates a "weak sense of human personality." According to Green, the same observation applies to the writings of Yeats, Pasternak, and "all our representatives of modern art" who stress "extreme individualism" (p. 188). It is noteworthy, Green claims, that Guardini highlighted the impoverished view of personal existence in Rilke's writings, and, in hindsight, we can see that Guardini was correct. Rilke's emphasis upon the autonomous, isolated person contributed to the milieu in which Adolf Hitler accomplished the complete denigration of personal existence. In Green's words: "Guardini is saying that the humanism which should be our instinctive defence against all totalitarian temptations is betrayed where it should be strongest by Rilke's kind of individualism."

In conclusion, Green acknowledges that he has studied Guardini's literary interpretation of Rilke's work because it is an excellent example of how today's readers can bring their Christian belief into discourse with the fine arts. Green writes: "Guardini's book is of particular interest to me because it is a Catholic humanist's approach to a representative modern poet." In relating his faith to his literary interpretation of the *Duino Elegies*, Guardini was similar to Baron Friedrich von Hügel (d. 1925) who brought his Christian convictions into a "confrontation" with the writings of William Butler Yeats (d. 1935). Both Guardini and von Hügel judged that they must incorporate their religious belief into their literary studies, and they accomplished this synthesis in a judicious manner. In contrast to many Christian conservatives, they refused to engage in an "ideological broadside" against modern letters. Rather, in their respective ways, Guardini and von Hügel focused on specific works and highlighted the merits and shortcomings of each. By maintaining this focus, "Guardini can concentrate his fire on the aesthetic problem proper, and above all he can give that problem its deepest range of meaning." In Green's judgment, therefore, Guardini engaged in true "humanistic literary criticism" as he clarified where Rilke's "style opened up new possibilities of expression but also has had a destructive effect" (p. 188).

The German literary critic Hermann Kunisch has expressed in two ways his appreciation of Guardini's interpretations of world literature. First, Kunisch has commented on Guardini's type of literary criticism. In his essay of 1985, entitled "Interpretatio Christiana" (Christian interpretation), Kunisch observes that Guardini's work has points of similarity and difference with Goethe's. Both scholars were committed to a form of literary realism. That is, they were intent upon describing everyday reality in such a way as to shed light on its depths. However, Guardini deliberately differed from Goethe and was critical of him on the question of bringing the Christian faith to one's perceptions of the world. Kunisch writes:

Along with purely glimpsing, taking [something] seriously is connected for Guardini with the capability of differentiation, the *discretio: sapientis est ordinare* (Thomas Aquinas). That is, [it entails] drawing the boundaries by means of Christian belief that rests upon the acceptance of revelation: *interpretatio christiana.* Liberal critics view [this approach] with suspicion as necessarily "narrowness."[69]

Kunisch adds, however, that Guardini did not automatically dismiss literary masters like Goethe and Rilke because they did not explicitly bring Christian belief into their writings. On the contrary, as in the case of Rilke's *Duino Elegies,* he spoke of his numerous "attempts" to understand a great literary work on its own terms and left open the possibility that he misunderstood the work of a person whom he regarded as an extraordinarily gifted writer. In Kunisch's judgment, Guardini rightly insisted upon "caution" whenever one engages in "*interpretatio christiana.*"[70]

A second way in which Kunisch has shown his esteem for the theologian's work is by drawing on Guardini's writings and adopting his method. In *Rainer Maria Rilke: Dasein und Dichtung* (1975), Kunisch lays out his understanding of Rilke's texts and assesses their truth in light of his understanding of Catholic belief.[71] Along with Guardini, he judges that Rilke's god is not the God of the Judeo-Christian tradition. He notes, too, that he must give this evaluation because a Christian literary critic has the responsibility to highlight the points of agreement and disagreement between the views of a writer like Rilke and Christian belief.[72]

It is not my task here to adjudicate among these differing appraisals of Guardini's literary interpretations. It suffices that we have seen that literary critics took seriously Guardini's work. Even when scholars like Gadamer have disagreed with aspects of Guardini's analysis and approach, they have had such respect for his studies that they have explained where they differed from him and why.

Toward Vatican II's *Gaudium et Spes (1965)*

At the start of his career, Guardini felt virtually no encouragement from the official church for his dialogical approach to Christian faith and culture. However, during the last years of his life, he found that the Second Vatican Council had affirmed and even amplified his orientation to the fine arts. In the Pastoral Constitution on the Church in the Modern World, *Gaudium et Spes,* Vatican II embraced the coincidence of polarities as Guardini had. *Gaudium et Spes* acknowledges the appropriate independence or "autonomy" of all intellectual and artistic endeavors. It states: "Culture, since it flows from humanity's rational and social nature, has continual need of proper freedom of development

and a legitimate possibility of autonomy according to its own principles."[73]
Then, quoting from Vatican I's *Dei Filius,* the pastoral constitution declares
that "the church does not forbid 'that human arts and sciences have recourse
to their own principles and methods in their respective fields'; therefore, 'it acknowledges this lawful freedom' and affirms the legitimate autonomy of culture and especially of the sciences" (n. 59). Yet, while upholding the proper
autonomy of learning and culture, *Gaudium et Spes* also holds that the church
has a responsibility to engage in a "dialogue" with every culture. In fact, the
church "is to be a leaven and, as it were, the soul of human society in its renewal
by Christ and transformation into the family of God" (n. 40). The church "can,
then, enter into communion with different forms of culture, thereby enriching
both itself and the cultures themselves" (n. 58).

Along with speaking in general about the independence and dialogue which
should exist between church and culture, the pastoral constitution speaks specifically about Christian faith and the arts. It recognizes the legitimate autonomy of writers and artists when it holds that "[i]n their own way literature and
art are very important in the life of the church" (n. 62). *Gaudium et Spes* reiterates this point when it states: "Every effort should be made, therefore, to
make artists feel that they are understood by the church in their artistic work
and to encourage them, while enjoying a reasonable standard of freedom, to
enter into happier relations with the christian community." The statement's
mention of "happier relations with the christian community" implies the importance of an exchange of views between the members of literary and artistic
circles and the members of the church. This emphasis upon a dialogue as well
as independence is specifically conveyed when the pastoral constitution adds
that Christians must understand the literature and sciences of their day and
simultaneously seek a new synthesis between the Christian faith and contemporary ideas. In a dialectical statement the document states:

> Therefore, the faithful ought to work closely with their contemporaries and
> ought to try to understand their ways of thinking and feeling, as these find
> expression in current culture. . . . [I]n this way they will succeed in evaluating
> and interpreting everything with an authentically christian sense of values.
> (n. 62)

These statements in *Gaudium et Spes* on faith and culture evince the orientation of both/and that Guardini pursued for six decades prior to Vatican II.
Contrary to the attitudes of many pre–Vatican II church officials, this theologian appreciated modernity's ideas and artistic expressions. At the same time,

he did not relinquish his Christian perspective but sustained a constructive conversation between Catholicism's *Weltanschauung* and society's worldview. Thus, long before the council advocated it, Guardini actually did what Vatican II called for when it said that "the faithful ought to work closely with their contemporaries"; in anticipation of the council's view, he succeeded "in evaluating and interpreting everything with an authentically christian sense of values." In short, *Gaudium et Spes* advocates a view similar to the one that Scheler proposed to Guardini: "Investigate, for example, the novels of Dostoyevsky and study their outlook [on life] from your Christian standpoint, in order to illuminate, on the one hand, the works under consideration and, on the other hand, [your] standpoint itself."[74] In following Scheler's counsel so fruitfully, Guardini helped to pioneer the way which ultimately led to Vatican II's view that literature and the arts should enjoy "a reasonable standard of freedom" and, without relinquishing this independence, "enter into happier relations with the christian community."

❖ 6 ❖

NAZISM
A Negation of the Person

ON THE EVENING of May 10, 1933, Nazi youth with torches paraded down Berlin's Unter den Linden and reached the University of Berlin at midnight. At Franz-Josephs-Platz, near the Staatsoper, with the SA and SS bands playing "patriotic melodies," the marchers tossed their flaming timbers onto already prepared pyres, after which they threw armfuls of "un-German" literature into the conflagration. Among these texts were writings by German authors such as Albert Einstein, Thomas and Heinrich Mann, Hugo Preuss, Walter Rathenau, Erich Maria Remarque, and Arnold and Stefan Zweig. There were also texts by foreign writers, including Sigmund Freud, André Gide, Helen Keller, Jack London, Marcel Proust, Upton Sinclair, H. G. Wells, and Emile Zola. At the height of the event, Dr. Joseph Goebbels, the Reich's propaganda minister, gave a "fire-side sermon" in which he declared: "The soul of the German people can again express itself. These flames not only illuminate the final end of an old era; they also light up the new."[1] By dawn, Berlin's so-called students had destroyed approximately twenty thousand books, and their peers in other German cities had done the same.

Today we see the book burning as a harbinger of the Shoah. However, at the time most Germans—and most of the world, for that matter—failed to discern the significance of this debacle. Some ignored it as the impetuous action of fanatical students, and others perceived it as the action of extremists within the "Nationalsozialische Deutsche Arbeiter Partei," the NSDAP or Nazi party—extremists who, it was said, would fall by the wayside as the National Socialist German Workers' party matured. One hundred years earlier, Heinrich Heine (d. 1856) had said that those who burn books would eventually burn people.[2] Nevertheless, in May 1933, hardly anyone perceived that the Nazi book burning was a foreshadowing of the destruction of printing presses, the torching of synagogues, the bombing of cities, the extermination of six million Jews, and Hitler's decree for a "scorched earth" in Germany.[3]

We do not know Romano Guardini's opinion in January 1933 of the new chancellor, Adolf Hitler, nor his perception of the book burning on May 10. But we can surmise that this lover of world literature must have been horrified by the conflagration. He most likely thought of the destruction of literature as barbarian, for he eventually disclosed that he saw Nazism as an attack upon Western civilization and, more precisely, upon the idea of personal existence, which the West holds as sacred.

Although Guardini deliberately refrained from politics and political theories, he eventually offered a theological critique of the Third Reich. In his essay of 1935, "Der Heiland" (The savior), Guardini rejected the religious ideology of National Socialism by distinguishing between pagan savior-figures and the true savior, Jesus Christ. Two years later, he tried to identify the true savior in his verbal portrait of Jesus Christ in *Der Herr* (1937), and subsequently in *Welt und Person* (1939) he laid out a theological anthropology to support his claim that authentic personal existence comes about as we commit ourselves to the living God. When a person is faithful to God as known within the Judeo-Christian tradition, he or she "cannot ultimately be possessed by any other authority."[4] In 1946, Guardini made explicit what had remained implicit in his earlier writings. In *Der Heilbringer in Mythos, Offenbarung und Politik* (The savior in myth, divine revelation and politics) he declared that the Nazis had replaced Jesus Christ with their idol, Hitler, thereby turning away from the absolute point of reference which is necessary for the preservation of human dignity.

In this chapter, as we review Guardini's analysis of Nazism, we will see that, in his judgment, Hitler gained control over peoples' lives because he succeeded in substituting a pagan mythos for the symbolic structure of the Christian faith. Lacking the language by which to live in relationship to the true God, the German people lost their inner bearings and hence their freedom. In this vacuum they became subservient to the *Führer* who deprived them of their rights and dignity as persons. Writing in 1946, Guardini observed:

> In order to give their power a definitive religious basis, those who possessed power in the recent past awoke that "kernel of meaning" which is found in the fundamental structure of the soul but had lost its proper place and referent. They gave this kernel of meaning a form of expression which could only extinguish Christ, his victory, and his simultaneous fulfillment of our desire for the savior—a form of expression which put in the place of Christ an earthly savior. . . . The new myth of the earthly savior was intended to eliminate Christ and his salvation and bind human beings to this world. Whoever believed in this earthly savior [Hitler] no longer had the possibility of resisting the grip which seized them. They were given over—with body and soul, with spirit and will, with everything which they were and did—to the power which controlled Germany.[5]

Guardini's analysis of the twelve years of Nazi rule is insightful, and yet it is limited in at least two ways.[6] First, Guardini neglected to consider the Third Reich's political origins. That is, lacking an appreciation for democracy, he did not see that Germany's Catholic bishops and theologians, including Guardini himself, had indirectly helped to usher in Hitler's Reich by their lack of support for democratic rule in general and the Weimar Republic in particular.[7] Second, he did not struggle sufficiently with the question which urgently faces us today: ought Christian faith be the religious basis of a society, especially since it has a history of tolerating and even nurturing anti-Semitism?[8]

This sixth chapter describes and assesses Guardini's analysis of Nazism in three steps.[9] First, it reviews both the political stance of Germany's Catholic bishops and theologians in early 1930s and also the emergence of Nazism's German Faith Movement.[10] Second, turning to Guardini's writings on Nazism, it summarizes "Der Heiland" and *Der Heilbringer in Mythos, Offenbarung und Politik* in relation to events in Guardini's life, for example, his dismissal by the Reich in 1939 from the University of Berlin. Although Guardini's *Der Herr* was situated within this context, it will be treated in chapter 7. However, we will consider here Guardini's postwar view of Germans' moral responsibility to the Jewish people, as expressed in his essay "Verantwortung: Gedanken zur jüdischen Frage" (Responsibility: Thoughts on the Jewish question [1952]). Third and finally, the chapter evaluates Guardini's analysis of Nazism by asking, what more could one theologian have done?

Religion and Politics in the Early 1930s

THE CHURCH'S POLITICAL CONSERVATISM

During the Weimar Republic, Germany's Catholic bishops and theologians held a politically conservative vision for Germany. Along with the German people, they had no previous experience of democracy. Bishops Michael Faulhaber of Munich, Clemens August Graf von Galen of Münster, and Conrad Gröber of Freiburg represented many in the episcopacy in preferring that Germany still have a constitutional monarchy which would respect both the Protestant and Catholic churches and rely on the churches to provide the religious and moral underpinnings for Germany's political and social life. Adhering to Vatican I, the bishops and theologians regarded the church as an institution, a "true society," that should serve as the spiritual foundation of the nation's political institutions. In the public arena they conveyed this view in the rituals they performed on market squares throughout Germany on the feasts of Christ the King and Corpus Christi.[11]

Among the Catholic bishops, only Konrad Graf von Preysing, bishop of Eichstätt (1932–35) and then bishop of Berlin (1935–50), had received a formal education in jurisprudence. A large majority of the church leaders had been trained within the seminary with its hierarchical authority and monarchical view of the church. Further, having firsthand knowledge of the *Kulturkampf,* many bishops and theologians were concerned to avoid any overt confrontations with civil authorities and also to provide legal protection for the church. Therefore, some of them looked for ways to attest to their nationalism. In March 1932, Bishop Nikolaus Bares of Hildesheim claimed to speak for Germany's Catholics when he said, "We are patriotic to the core, German through and through, prepared to make every sacrifice for *Volk* and Fatherland."[12] It is not surprising therefore that in 1932, from their politically conservative vantage point, most bishops and theologians saw dangers primarily to their left and to a lesser extent to their right on the political spectrum.

To their political left church leaders placed both Bolshevism and democracy. To be sure, they perceived the greatest threat from the communist or socialist movement with its avowed atheism. They knew how Joseph Stalin had brutally suppressed the churches in the Soviet Union, and they feared that German Bolshevists would try to bring about a socialist republic of the sort that was established in Bavaria by Kurt Eisner in February 1919 and then exploded into the communist revolution of April 1919, which the German army violently crushed. However, most bishops and theologians were also uncomfortable with the Weimar Republic. Along with the Vatican, they were not enthusiastic about the Enlightenment's espousal of "liberalism," including democracy, and disapproved of the French Revolution.[13] They readily acknowledged that the Catholic Center party, which was officially constituted on December 13, 1870, had increasingly succeeded in representing well the interests of the Catholic Church in Germany. Nonetheless, most bishops and theologians had misgivings in principle about a parliamentary democracy. As a result, they did little to support Germany's first attempt at democracy and by their silence tolerated talk by Catholic publicists like Fritz Büchner and Albert Mirgeler concerning the possibility of Germany's new Holy Roman Empire.[14]

To their right on the political spectrum, the bishops and theologians placed Adolf Hitler's National Socialism. After the elections of 1930, they became increasingly concerned about the Nazi party. Also, they were aware that the majority of German Catholics did not accept Hitler's ideology of racial anti-

Semitism and neopaganism. (At the time, there were two conferences of Catholic bishops in Germany: the Fulda Bishops' Conference and the Bavarian Bishops' Conference.) In fact, in Germany's last free election (March 5, 1933), in which the Nazi party came out ahead with 44 percent of the vote, Catholics still did not support National Socialism.[15]

By the early 1930s, the German bishops had publicly banned Catholics from joining Hitler's National Socialist party. On October 30, 1930, Bishop Ludwig Maria Hugo of Mainz backed one his pastors who had condemned National Socialism from the pulpit. On February 12, 1931, the Bavarian bishops, led by Archbishop Michael Faulhaber, condemned five teachings of National Socialism and in doing so received public support from Cardinal Adolf Bertram of Breslau, Archbishop Carl Joseph Schulte of Cologne and the bishops of the Upper Rhine. A few months later, in August 1931, Cardinal Bertram as the chairman of the Fulda Bishops' Conference wrote a pastoral letter to German Catholics in which he stated that Nazism "actually stands in the most pointed contradiction with the fundamental truths of Christianity and with the organization of the Catholic Church created by Christ." During this same period, many pastors throughout Germany refused to give communion to those who wore Nazi insignia to Mass, and some pastors even denied a Christian burial for known members of the Nazi party.[16]

However, in an effort to adjust to political realities, some bishops and theologians held that National Socialism possessed positive qualities which could work for the good, especially if church leaders would communicate with the Nazi officials so as to influence their decisions. Shortly after being named archbishop on June 20, 1932, Conrad Gröber of Freiburg im Breisgau urged his priests to take a more conciliatory approach to Nazism and gave funds to the Nazi party.[17] Also, Osnabrück's Bishop Wilhelm Berning supported Hitler and eventually served as a Prussian *Staatsrat* (councilor) in the Third Reich.[18]

The German bishops' official stance against the Nazi party changed in the spring of 1933. On January 30, 1933, President Paul von Hindenburg appointed Adolf Hitler as Germany's chancellor; then on March 23, 1933, the Reichstag passed the Enabling Act which suspended the Weimar Constitution and gave Hitler dictatorial powers. (Under the leadership of Monsignor Ludwig Kaas, the Center party with its affiliated Bavarian Peoples party voted in favor of the Enabling Act, thereby putting itself out of existence.) On March 28, as Hitler promised to support the Protestant and Catholic churches, the Catholic bishops, intent upon avoiding a new *Kulturkampf,* dropped their prohibition against Catholics' membership in the Nazi party. Then, having sought a concordat with the German government since 1920, the Vatican and the German bishops worked with Hitler's regime throughout the spring on this legal agreement and concluded the concordat on July 20, 1933. (Key figures in these negotiations were Monsignor Kaas and Vatican's secretary of state Eugenio Cardinal Pacelli, who became Pope Pius XII in 1939.) In the late summer, many Catholic leaders were pleased that the Catholic Church had a legal boundary to protect its institutions, especially its schools, from the government's interference.[19]

After the bishops lifted their prohibition against membership in the Nazi party on March 28, 1933, some Catholic theologians publicly endorsed the bishops' support for Germany's new chancellor, while others protested this shift in policy. Positive statements came from theologians like Karl Adam, Karl Eschweiler, Joseph Lortz, and Michael Schmaus, most of whom gave the theological argument that, since grace builds on nature, it was important to cooperate with a chancellor who had pledged himself to restoring Germany's traditional values.[20] However, disapproval of the bishops' decision of March 28 was voiced by Catholic thinkers such as Konrad Algermissen, Fritz Gerlich, Waldemar Gurian, Dietrich von Hildebrand, Georg Moenius, Ingbart Nabb, O.F.M., Hermann Platz, and Franziskus Stratmann, O.P.[21] (Both Gurian and Platz were Romano Guardini's friends.[22]) These critics were joined by Fritz Tillmann, Guardini's professor at Bonn, who declared that Jesus Christ, not the *Führer*, stands at the center of the moral life, and also by Theodore Brauer and Gustav Gundlach who in 1935 observed that Nazism eroded the dignity of personal existence.[23]

While the period from 1930 into 1933 was marked by the German bishops' opposition to National Socialism, after March 1933 the relationship of the Catholic Church to Hitler's government unfolded in two phases over the next six years.[24] In the first phase, from the spring of 1933 until the end of 1934, the bishops sought to accommodate Germany's legitimate chancellor and his new government. However, because of the regime's efforts to achieve the "synchronization" (*Gleichschaltung*) of all aspects of German life, the bishops time and again protested Nazi actions. For instance, the bishops condemned the "Night of the Long Knives" (June 30, 1934), when Nazis executed over one hundred "dissidents," including the Catholic leaders Erich Klausner and Adalbert Probst. In the second phase, from 1935 into 1939, the Catholic bishops and the Third Reich stood at odds. This "church conflict" included the government's banning of Catholic associations, destruction of Catholic printing presses, "currency law trials" against religious congregations for "illegally" sending funds to their houses in the foreign missions, and show-trials against priests and members of religious orders on allegations of pedophilia.[25] At the height of this persecution, Pope Pius XI denounced racism and the tenets of Nazism in his encyclical *Mit brennender Sorge* (March 14, 1937).[26] Beginning in 1939, though, the Reich took a less confrontational stance against ecclesiastical institutions as it turned its attention to the invasion of Poland on September 1, 1939.

In 1935, as the struggle between the churches and the Reich grew, Catholic writers increasingly took issue with Nazism by challenging its religious claims.[27] Since this ideology was embodied in the Nazis' German Faith Movement, Romano Guardini publicly criticized this neopagan organization.

THE GERMAN FAITH MOVEMENT

On April 26, 1935, the German Faith Movement held a national rally in Berlin's Sportspalast. Over 10,000 supporters gathered to hear speeches on the necessity of the nation's recovery of ancient Teutonic symbols, myths, and rituals. This event manifested National Socialism's religious views, especially as found in the writings of Alfred Rosenberg (d. 1946) and Jakob Wilhelm Hauer (d. 1962). A review of this offshoot of the *Volk* movement will set the stage for Guardini's writing on Nazism.

In the late 1800s, some Germans took steps to heighten their sense of themselves as a *Volk,* as a people shaped by their race, history, and culture. Amid their nation's rapid industrialization and urbanization, these people found stability and promise by reasserting those things that to their minds were essential elements of their German heritage. They cherished the neoromantic revival in the operas of Richard Wagner (d. 1883) and in the writings of Friedrich Nietzsche (d. 1900). The extremists went so far as to insist that Germans must reclaim their race, their "blood." Representative of this racism were Paul de Lagarde's *Über das Verhältnis des deutschen Staates zu Theologie, Kirche und Religion* (1873), Julius Langbehn's *Rembrandt als Erzieher* (1890), and Houston Stewart Chamberlain's *Grundlagen des Neunzehnten Jahrhunderts* (1899).[28] After Germany's surrender in 1918, the *Volk* movement gained both in numbers and in radicalism as voiced by Theodor Fritsch, Dietrich Eckart, and Artur Dinter.[29]

The growing interest in the *Volk* possessed a strong religious stream which eventually broke into two distinct currents: the German Christian Movement (Deutsch-christliche Bewegung) and the German Faith Movement (Deutsch-gläubige Bewegung). The German Christian Movement espoused the incorporation of German myths and symbols into the Christian churches and produced studies in the history of religions that argued for affinities between Christianity and Teutonic beliefs.[30] Writings appeared on the similarities between Wotan and Jesus, and in 1920 Friedrich Andersen argued in *Der deutsche Heiland* that Jesus, the *Heiland*, was not a Jew but an Indo-European who possessed Nordic traits. By contrast, the radical proponents of *Volk* religion, who eventually formed the German Faith Movement, were anti-Christian. They held that Germans must extirpate Christianity from their land so that they could recover the mythos that had inspired the Teutonic tribes prior to the "negative" influence of Christian missionaries such as St. Remigius in the fifth century and St. Boniface in the eighth century. These neopagans initially formed small associations: the Schäfferbund und Deutsche Erneuerungsgemeinde (1904), the Germanische Glaubensgemeinschaft (1911), the Volkschaft der Nordungen (1917), the Tannenbergbund (1925) founded by General Erich Ludendorff, and the Nordische Glaubensgemeinschaft (1928).[31]

These groups within what eventually became the German Faith Movement promoted pagan symbols and reconstructed Germanic rituals. Instead of Christmas, they celebrated the Birth of the Holy Light or winter solstice observance. Good Friday became Silent Friday in honor of the 4,500 pagan Saxons slain by Charlemagne at Verdun. Easter was replaced by the feast of Ostara, the goddess of spring; Ascension Thursday by the Return of the Holy Hammer of Donar; and Pentecost by the High May Festival. Along with these feasts, the neopagans rejected the Christian sacraments and held pagan ceremonies to mark the crucial junctures in a person's life: birth, adulthood, marriage, and death.[32]

Alfred Rosenberg was a leading proponent of German neopaganism. In *Der Mythus des 20. Jahrhunderts* (1930) he contended that the German people would regain their self-esteem and fulfill their destiny within world history if they would embrace their *Volk* heritage. In his view, this affirmation entailed the purification not only of Germany's culture and religion but also of its race, its "blood." Indeed, the ideology of National Socialism rests upon a belief in biological dualism. According to this "theory," there exist men and women who because they are genetically healthy possess physical strength, high intelligence, upright moral character, and true religious inspiration.[33] Yet, there also exist men and women who because of their inferior biological makeup are plagued with physical deformities, inferior intellectual abilities, immoral conduct, and warped religious values. Whether a person possesses the right or wrong constitution ("blood") is determined by whether or not the individual belongs to the Aryan race.[34]

Rosenberg described the racial *Mythus* or mythology of the *Volk* as follows:

But the values contained in the racial soul which are the driving forces behind the new world conception have not yet become a living consciousness. Soul means race seen from within and vice versa; race is the outer form of the soul. To bring to life the soul of the race means to recognize its supreme value and under its rule to assign to the other values their proper organic place in the State, in art and religion. This is the task of our century: to create a new human type out of a new life-myth.[35]

According to Rosenberg, "a new human type" would spring from a "purified" German race. In his words:

It has been a truism for a long while that all the Western states and their creative values have been produced by the Germans. Houston Stewart Chamberlain, however, was the first who drew the necessary conclusions from this fact: if German blood were to disappear from Europe. . . . the entire culture of the West would go with it. . . . Today we are conscious that we stand before a final decision of terrible significance. Either we rise to an ennobled achievement by a revival and purification of the ancient blood, thus renewing our will to fight, or the very last Germanic-Western values of civilization and State discipline will be submerged in the polluted human masses of the cities of the world.[36]

In July 1933 the various neopagan groups formed a single organization, called the Working Association of the German Faith Movement. The leaders of this organization were Count Ernst zu Reventlow and Jakob Wilhelm Hauer, Professor of Indology and the History of Religion at the University of Tübingen. One year later, the Working Association of the German Faith Movement shortened its name to the German Faith Movement and simultaneously named Hauer as the organization's *Führer* and Reventlow as its deputy *Führer*. With backing from Rosenberg, Hauer immediately took steps to raise the movement's public profile throughout Germany. Among them, Hauer and Reventlow undertook a campaign in early 1935 to introduce the German people to the movement's teachings and to recruit more members into their organization. Within this campaign, they held a rally in Berlin's Sportspalast on April 26, 1935.[37]

Guardini's View of Nazism

A CRITIQUE OF THE GERMAN FAITH MOVEMENT IN 1935

After the burning of world literature outside the university on May 10, 1933, Guardini remained silent. In normal circumstances, silence usually means consent or at least toleration. But, after only a few months of the Third Reich, life in Germany was no longer normal. Hitler's government was already incarcerating "political dissidents" in concentration camps at Dachau and Oranienburg. Silence could indicate prudence. Moreover, while Karl Adam, Karl Eschweiler, Joseph Lortz, and Michael Schmaus published essays in support of Hitler's government in the summer of 1933, Guardini said nothing. In light of these theologians' positive statements, Guardini's silence clearly had a negative connotation.[38]

In 1935, in response to the propaganda of the German Faith Movement, Guardini formulated his critique of Nazism's religious ideology in "Der Heiland." In order to understand this text, we need to note the ambiguous meanings of *Heil*. As is well known, *Heil* was used in the Nazi salutation "*Heil Hitler*," that is, "Hail [in the name of] Hitler." In general, the word *Heil* means "Hail!," "Greetings!," "Good luck!" For instance, the expression *Heil dem König!* conveys the sense of "Long live the king!" To wish someone "Good skiing!" one would say, *Ski Heil!* As Hitler took Germany into war, he exclaimed *Sieg Heil!*, meaning "To victory!" As a noun *das Heil* means "prosperity," "happiness," and "salvation." Hence, *das ewige Heil* means "the eternal salvation." "Es war mir zum Heil" states, "It was fortunate for me." Finally, *der Heiland* or *der Heilbringer* means "the bringer of blessings," hence "the savior."[39] Two distinct meanings of *Heil* are evident in Richard Wagner's "Die Meistersinger von Nürnburg" (1862–67). The opera opens with the church chorus singing: "Da zu dir der Heiland [Jesus Christ] kam, . . . gab er uns des Heils Gebot." That is: "When the savior came to you, . . . he gave us the message of our salvation." However, the opera ends with the townsfolk applying *Heil* not to Jesus Christ but to the opera's hero; they sing: "Heil Hans Sachs!" It was because the Nazis took advantage of the ambiguities of *Heil* that Guardini wrote "Der Heiland."

His thesis in "Der Heiland" is that while there have been many figures— some mythical and others actual—who have been regarded as bearers of blessing (*Heil*), there is in fact only one true savior: Jesus of Nazareth, whom Christians call the Christ. Guardini's implicit message is that while Adolf Hitler may be *a* bearer of blessings, he is not *the* savior.[40.]

At the outset, Guardini notes that according to the phenomenology of religion, especially Gerardus van der Leeuw's *Phänomenologie der Religion* (1933), many religious beliefs rest upon myths that are somewhat similar to biblical narratives regarding Jesus of Nazareth. In light of this phenomenon, one may ask: what are we to make the affinities among the various religions' stories about a savior, *ein Heiland?*

There is, Guardini says, a form of religious experience that is common to men and women regardless of their specific religion. All people can have moments in which they sense a "numinous" or transcendent power within such ordinary occurrences as the rising of the sun and its setting, and in the change of seasons throughout the year. At times, people feel this power to be healing and health-giving, hence it is viewed as *Heil*. At other times, they experience this power as destructive, as *Unheil*. As the phenomenology of religion has highlighted, ancient peoples expressed their experience of *Heil* and *Unheil* in images, myths, and other imaginative forms. *Unheil* became associated with darkness, winter, snakes, dragons, and witches. *Heil* was spoken of in terms of light, spring, and savior-figures. Further, the *Heil*-bearers engaged in struggles with the *Unheil* and overcame it, though usually by first having to undergo death themselves after which they gained new life for themselves and others. This pattern appears, for example, in the myths concerning Dionysius, Baldur, Osiris, and Mithras.

Societies have also applied the imagery of a *Heiland* to their rulers. Guardini notes that for many peoples, "[t]he king is the bearer of sacred [*heiliger*] power" (p. 369). For instance, at one time the Chinese held that when a new ruler assumed the throne, he or she brought *Heil* to everyone in the kingdom. Further, some societies have formed their calendar according to the start of a ruler's reign. They have used expressions such as, "In such and such year of the rule of Emperor X...." At times, people have attributed their well-being to the ruler's relationship to a numinous power. When the harvest was poor, they judged that the emperor had become a bearer of *Unheil*, and, as a result, they put him or her to death, either in fact or in a ceremonial drama.

In light of this history, what are we to make of Jesus? Is he merely one *Heiland* among others like Dionysius, Baldur, Osiris, and Mithras? Jesus was not a mythic figure but a historical individual. He lived, suffered, died, rose from the dead, and appeared to his followers who then bore witness to him. In Guardini's words: "Jesus Christ is historical. To be sure, he exists in relation to eternity: by means of his preexistent origin, his departure from eternity and the singular return to it. However, he exists at the same time in history and, indeed, in an essential manner" (p. 374).

The myths about Dionysius, Baldur, Osiris, and Mithras, on the one hand, and the narratives about Jesus, on the other, rely on different notions of time. In the mythic world, time is cyclical. What is important happens time and time again in the cycle of coming to life, maturing, dying, and then coming to life again. By contrast, the gospels portray Jesus in a linear drama in which events occur only once. They present Jesus as the one who breaks the cycle of the natural order. Hence, he is not just one more *Heiland* among many others, but the Christ.

Implicitly condemning Hitler and the German Faith Movement, Guardini maintains that those who regard the gospels as merely a set of myths revert to a mythical view of the world. They dismiss God's singular revelation in Jesus Christ and also what this divine disclosure has inspired in Western civilization about the sanctity of personal existence. Under the influence of neopagan symbols and legends, advocates of the German Faith Movement are disposed to treat men and women as nonpersons, as pawns in the Nazi dream. Guardini adds an observation that in light of the Shoah appears prophetic. The return to a mythic consciousness, he states, not only destroys respect for human beings as persons but also puts people at the beck and call of "demonic" forces within the human psyche (pp. 382–84).

This observation about forces of evil leads to the question, "How does the Christ save us?" According to Guardini, since Jesus Christ enters this world from outside it, he is able to free us from the powers of this world, from "Satan." Also, the true *Heiland* reveals the identity of God and our identity. Guardini states: "When human beings accept what comes to them in Christ, their eyes open to who God is and who they are" (p. 385). He adds that the relationship between the myths of a *Heiland* and the Bible is one of opposition (*Gegensatz*). The gospels affirm, overturn, and fill out the ancient legends of a *Heiland*. That is, first, Christian belief recognizes the value of images, symbols, and myths of savior-figures, for it regards these as anticipations of the genuine savior. Second, it rejects these imaginative constructs, for it shows that they are the product of human projection. Third, Christian faith fulfills these myths because it presents Jesus Christ as the one person who was free to act responsibly and uniquely in history, and, therefore, it presents the relationship with Christ as the one within which all men and women can become genuine persons (pp. 386–88).

In Guardini's judgment, the confrontation between Jesus and Pilate in John's Gospel (18:33–19:11) reveals the heart of the matter. Jesus, the bearer of the truth, is brought before Pilate, the legitimate civil authority, who condemns Jesus to death. This decision displays the world's preference for Satan's power. The world has rejected the *Heil* that is borne to us in Jesus Christ (p. 388).

Guardini's "Der Heiland" is an implicit condemnation of National Socialism. It opposes Rosenberg's and Hauer's contention that the Teutonic mythos should displace Christian faith on German soil. Further, it implicitly undercuts the view of Hitler as the *Heiland* and, therefore, indirectly denounces the salutation, "*Heil* Hitler." Implying that something demonic is at work in Germany, Guardini conveys a point that Nazism is an attack upon the dignity of personal existence.[41]

DISMISSAL FROM THE UNIVERSITY IN 1939

Romano Guardini paid a personal price for the publication of "Der Heiland" in 1935. Soon after its appearance, Nazi spies attended his lectures in order to record any comments that might be construed as an attack upon the *Führer* and the Third Reich.[42] Although he did not speak about political matters, his silence was taken as a criticism. In 1939 the Reich dismissed Guardini from his professorship at the University of Berlin, seized Burg Rothenfels, and banned the publication of *Die Schildgenossen*.[43] Finally, in 1941 it prohibited the theologian from giving public addresses.[44]

In his autobiographical reflections of 1944, Guardini has recalled what transpired in January 1939 when he met with the Reich's minister of cult:

The official representing the government opened the meeting with the words regarding its purpose, which I remember well. When the state itself has a worldview, there can be no room for a chair of Catholic *Weltanschauung* at the University. No discussion concerning this axiom was of course possible, and I could do nothing other than indicate a nod of acceptance. Apart from this foundational principle, the conversation developed in a cordial manner.[45]

The minister of cult next discussed with Guardini ways for the theologian to keep his professorship. He suggested academic chairs in dogmatic theology at the universities of Bonn, Freiburg, and Tübingen. But Guardini explained that he was no longer prepared to teach dogmatic theology in the strict sense. The official then proposed that Guardini take a year's leave of absence during which time he could consider his future. When Guardini mentioned that he was currently doing research on the cultural ties between Germany and Italy, especially with regard to Dante's *Divine Comedy,* the official responded favorably to this project since it might strengthen the political ties between Hitler's government and Benito Mussolini's. The minister ended the meeting by promising to look into the prospects for the theologian's future. A few days later the minister of cult called Guardini and stated that, if he wished, he could choose early retirement but he would not receive the status of professor emeritus nor would he receive a pension. Guardini accepted the offer. When the spring semester began at the University of Berlin in March 1939, Guardini's courses were canceled. His students, saddened by his dismissal, were not permitted to hold a ceremony in his honor. Hence, they quietly sent him a "book of flowers," that is, a thick folder filled with letters of gratitude, poems in Guardini's honor, and assurances that they would keep him in their prayers.[46]

Guardini has also described the impact on him of the SS's seizure of Burg Rothenfels:

> The life and work which now [in February] unfolded were truly different from previously, and even more so when six months later even Burg Rothenfels was seized, and I lost both of the great points of reference to which, until that time, my concern and work were related and which had fulfilled my life with a consciousness of fruitful activity and of profound human connectedness.[47]

Deprived of his public roles, Guardini had become a nonperson in the country in which, at the age of twenty-six, he had received citizenship. Nevertheless, he continued to reside in his home in Berlin's suburb of Zehlendorf until 1943 when he moved to Josef Weiger's rectory in the Allgäu.[48]

A CRITIQUE OF NAZISM IN 1946

In early 1946, while teaching in Tübingen, Guardini expanded "Der Heiland" into *Der Heilbringer in Mythos, Offenbarung und Politik*. Much of this book repeats the earlier work, but there are three new ideas.[49]

First, according to Guardini, the human subconscious reasons by means of images, symbols, and myths. Even when we are not aware of it, our psyche applies imaginative constructs to the everyday world, so that we perceive meaning in people, things, and situations. As a result, this perception influences how we relate to life. Appealing to the work of C. G. Jung, Guardini claims that our psyche's "kernel of meaning"—conveyed in imaginative motifs—functions in us even after we have moved into the critical awareness of the Enlightenment.[50] Even though we may have adopted a critical consciousness that distances us from the natural world, we may invest political figures with meanings determined by our unconscious, collective images of a savior-figure. As these motifs influence our thought and actions, we may permit the human psyche's demonic forces to take control of our lives and motivate us to harm our neighbor.

Second, Hitler's tyranny provides a case study of a political leader's seizure of a people's subconscious. Hitler attained absolute authority over German society, in part by engaging people's imaginations in his ideology of "blood and race" (p. 62). Central to this doctrine was the myth of Hitler as Germany's *Heilbringer*. Hitler claimed to embody the *Heil* for the *Volk*. He gave himself the title *Führer* and claimed to possess the ability to judge all aspects of life—politics, military strategy, science, economics, and even art. Presenting himself as the mediator between God and the German people, he assumed the role of "the messenger of God." New buildings included the inscription, "For everything, we thank our *Führer*," and Germans spoke of sunny days as "Hitler weather." In fact, the *Führer* transferred to himself the images that Christians usually apply to Jesus Christ. For instance, the Nazi party distributed pictures of Hitler standing among children and looking benignly at them. Also, it encouraged people to hang a photograph of Hitler in their homes in the place usually reserved for a cross or a portrait of Christ. Many parks included altar-like tables on which were placed flowers surrounding a picture of the *Führer*. In at least one church, German Christians placed a photograph of Hitler on the altar. In the schools, the government required that children pray: "Small hands folded, small heads bowed, thinking within on the *Führer*, who gives us work and bread, who delivers us from all need." In other words, many Germans directed their religious sentiments away from Christ and to the *Führer* (pp. 68–71).

According to Guardini, the salutation "*Heil* Hitler" manifested this idolatry. People spoke this greeting countless times each day, allowing it to replace their use of the Christian salutation, "Gelobt sei Jesus Christus" ("Praised be Jesus Christ"). To greet someone with "*Heil* Hitler" was to pray that blessings would continue to come down upon Hitler and through him to all who wished him well (pp. 71–73). In short, Hitler had replaced Jesus Christ as the object of people's reverence. In Guardini's words: "The new myth of the earthly savior was intended to eliminate Christ and his salvation and to bind human beings to this world. Whoever believed in this earthly savior [Hitler] no longer had the possibility of resisting the grip which seized them" (p. 74).

Guardini's third and last major point—one which is seemingly undermined by the fact that Europe's Christian faith has at the very least tolerated anti-Semitism—is that the future of Europe depends upon its affirmation of its Christian tradition: "Either Europe becomes Christian, or Europe will no longer exist."[51] That which gives Europe its identity and direction is its belief in Jesus Christ. "Christ's essence freed the heart of the European. His personality has given to the European the extraordinary ability to live in history and experience his destiny." Over the centuries, Christ empowered Europeans to live in relation to the "personal, holy God" and therefore to attain "the freedom of the redeemed." It was this freedom, this character of personal existence, that Nazism hated and attacked with the aim of taking "a formless mass into its hands." Therefore, if Europe is to flourish, it must remain committed to its primary "kernel" of meaning and truth, Jesus Christ.[52]

Guardini's *Der Heilbringer in Mythos, Offenbarung und Politik* offers accurate insights into the ways in which Hitler manipulated the German people by his use of rhetoric, symbols, and public ceremonies. However, it unfortunately neglects to consider how Germany's Christian ethos of anti-Judaism fueled Nazi anti-Semitism. Also, it does not treat such issues as the status of religious pluralism and ethnic and racial pluralism within German society. Given Guardini's silence on these crucial matters, it is surprising to find that four years after writing *Der Heilbringer in Mythos, Offenbarung und Politik* he urged Germans to admit their moral responsibility to the Jewish people.

ON GERMANY'S MORAL RESPONSIBILITY TO THE JEWS

In the postwar years, as Germans were rebuilding their society and government, the question arose concerning their "collective guilt."[53] Asked to speak to this issue, Romano Guardini gave an address on May 23, 1952, at the University of Tübingen. In "Verantwortung: Gedanken zur Jüdischen Frage" he argued that Germans needed to seek reconciliation with Jews. Why? Such an action was necessary not only to make amends to the Jewish people but also so that the German people could overcome the evil that had infected their lives. Guardini reasoned as follows.[54]

In his judgment, since the university is the place in which the truth must be pursued—even when this truth may not be welcome—it is appropriate that a university reflect upon anti-Semitism within society. The fact of the matter is that the Third Reich systematically put to death six million Jews. Although some Germans deny this reality, no one with a sense of integrity can turn away from this horror. "These things have occurred, and today anyone with intellectual honesty must acknowledge them" (p. 13). Prior to 1945, many Germans were not aware of the Nazis' extermination of the Jews, but by 1952 everyone should know about it and face the question of what this demonic occurrence means.

Guardini notes that, by raising this question within a university, we can perceive the Shoah in relation to the West's tradition of learning. Consider some of the outstanding figures in the human search for truth: "Planck and Helmholtz; Mommsen and the brothers Grimm; Goethe and Hölderlin; Mozart and J. S. Bach; Leibnitz and Pascal; Raphael and Erwin von Steinbach; Gottfried von Strassburg and Dante; Augustine and Plato, Aeschylus, Heraclitus, and

Homer." These individuals stand out for their originality in human knowledge and the arts. Remembering them, we should ask: "What would these people say if we showed them what occurred [at Auschwitz]? How would we ourselves perceive it through their eyes?" (p. 15).

The West's great minds have generated centuries of knowledge and creativity, norms of right and wrong, and standards of what is noble and what is debasing. In light of these principles, they would be shocked by the Holocaust and ask: "Where at the time was conscience? Where was honor? Indeed, where was—if we may understand the word to mean more than mere conceptual work—reason?" They would likely go on to inquire: "How could it have happened? What kind of human beings were they who brought this about?" In response, Guardini answers: "Here something has come out of the dark underpinnings of human beings: the *barbarian* [my emphasis], the animal in the human being. Here it has become clear how little has been realized of that upon which we worked; how fruitful the powers of chaos and destruction still are" (p. 16).

But something becomes more evident upon inspection. What occurred in the Shoah is new insofar as it resulted from the combining of "the instincts of the animal directly with human calculations and technology." As a result, "something has come about which until then had not yet occurred: the unity of the subhuman and the machine" (p. 17). A government decided that one group of human beings had no right to exist and implemented this decision at its concentration camps. This regime saw itself standing above all human norms of right and wrong and also above all divine laws. It arrogantly declared that it possessed the authority to exterminate Jews simply because of their race. Moreover, these officials had at their disposal the technology by which to implement their decision, and in a cold, systematic, and efficient manner killed millions of Jews as well as other human beings.

This action attacked, Guardini observes, personal existence itself. With the assistance of technology, some human beings treated other human beings solely as objects, as things to be destroyed at will. In other words, a program such as that undertaken by the Nazis "eradicates the personal character of the human being. It steps apart from good and evil and thus reaches something which is more terrifying than evil, something which fits no categories because it fundamentally obliterates the basis of every ethical judgment, namely the person" (p. 21).

How did we get to this frightening state of affairs? The process began,

Guardini avers, with modernity's stress upon autonomy, technology, and free-dom. Out of this convergence of ideas and abilities came the twentieth-century state with its vast power, lack of moral norms, and claim that it "must have a free hand for its endeavor of comprehending and forming all of life" (p. 24).

The extermination of millions of Jews is a manifestation of what a govern-ment can now do. It demonstrates the state's assertion that it "has fundamen-tally transcended every [human] right." But herein is darkness. When the rights of some human beings as persons are violated, then the rights of all human beings are denied. "For [human] rights exist absolutely, for every per-son as such, or they do not exist at all" (p. 27). Representative of the modern state gone awry, the Third Reich attacked the very heart of the human com-munity; in seeking to eliminate the Jewish people, it sought to destroy the prin-ciple of the dignity of personal existence.

Now that the Third Reich no longer exists, what can the German people do? "How can we work out what took place so that it does not have a further effect as a poison and become a blueprint for what is to come?" (p. 32).

Germans must not hide from what happened but must publicly admit it, understand it, and act responsibly toward the Jewish people. When a moral fail-ing occurs in human life, it must be recognized and remedied, for otherwise it erodes the character of the whole life. So too the German people must speak about what seems unspeakable and does not fit within rational categories. Also, they must resist talk about the ways in which they were wronged, for example, in the bombing of Dresden. Further, instead of speaking about their collec-tive guilt, they must affirm their solidarity with and moral responsibility to the Jews. Finally, it must be seen that in following this course of action, Germans will act as persons. The German people must reclaim and strengthen the reality of personal existence that they relinquished to Hitler.

Concluding the address, Guardini returned to his initial thought that the university is the context in which people can pursue the truth and safeguard it. This recognition concretely means that "[t]he university is the place where the growing responsibility for the common good must live."[55]

With this address, Guardini assumed a public role in leading Germans in an effort to become reconciled with the Jewish people. Along with Konrad Ade-nauer, he promoted the conviction that the German government should pay reparations to the Shoah's survivors, and the Federal Republic of Germany translated this conviction into a national policy.[56] However, it remains unclear how Guardini linked this call to moral responsibility with his belief that Ger-man society needed to remain anchored in Christian faith.

What More Could One Theologian Have Done?

As we have seen, a recurring theme in Romano Guardini's writings on the Third Reich was that Nazism sought to destroy the character of personal existence. National Socialist leaders regarded millions of people as racially flawed human beings whose extermination would benefit humankind by eliminating their blood from the human family. At the same time, they judged that the German people were not capable of living as responsible citizens and, therefore, should be deprived of their civil rights, civic responsibility, and religious liberty. In the early 1930s, Germans permitted Hitler to take over the state. Why? What was the underlying cause of Nazism's success? The deep ailment was, Guardini judged, Germany's loss of the sense of objective, transcendent reality, namely the God of Jesus Christ. Lacking an orientation toward the true God, Germans turned to an idol, Adolf Hitler, and, as a result, they became depersonalized.

Guardini's reflections on the religious character of Nazism raise, of course, large issues concerning secularization—issues with which we struggle today. For example, to what extent and in what ways are Western society and culture dependent upon the Judeo-Christian tradition? Can a society rest on Christianity without excluding non-Christians and becoming anti-Semitic? Also, is there such a thing as a nonreligious or secular society, or is it the case—as Guardini holds—that, in the absence of an explicit religious tradition, a society will unwittingly draw on subconscious mythologies which then generate unconscious religious beliefs and practices? What is the interconnection between a society's regard for the dignity of human life and its adherence to religious beliefs, for example, to Christian faith?[57]

Guardini pursued some of these questions in his writings during the Third Reich, and, as we will see in chapter 8, he worked further on them after the Second World War. At this point, we will limit ourselves to answering two questions. First, what did this theologian do to resist Nazism? And second, what more could he have done?[58]

Guardini's opposition to Nazism showed itself in a few concrete ways. In some of his writings, he took issue with Nazism's religious tenets. He did so most notably in "Der Heiland" (1935). Moreover, he challenged Nazism, as we will see in chapter 7, by identifying the true savior, Jesus Christ, in *Der Herr* (1937). Printed four times by 1942, *Der Herr* was read in many German Catholic households throughout the war.[59] Further, in *Welt und Person* (1939) Guardini presented a clear account of personal existence which stood in opposition to

Nazi ideology.[60] Also, Guardini helped sustain *Die Schildgenossen* with its articles against National Socialism.[61] In sum, during the Third Reich, Guardini's writings gave many people the faith and courage to resist Nazism in quiet, daily ways, and they also nourished more overt opponents, including the members of the White Rose resistance group.[62]

Along with his writings, Guardini resisted Nazism by his pastoral leadership. Until 1939 he remained an inspirational, national leader of the Catholic youth movement, especially of Quickborn, and thus helped the movement to maintain its independence, thereby obstructing Hitler's efforts to bring all young men and women into the "Hitler Youth."[63] Further, as a leader of the liturgical renewal, Guardini gave direction to a movement that offered a covert means by which Catholics were able to express their opposition to Nazi idolatry and also able to strengthen their hope for a new society.[64]

In effect, Guardini put sand in the Reich's *Gleichschaltung* of German society, and, for this reason, the Reich stripped the fifty-four-year-old theologian of the public roles that had defined him: university professor, leader of Quickborn, editor of *Die Schildgenossen,* and public speaker. However, while recognizing the significant ways in which Guardini resisted National Socialism, we must ask too: could he have done something more? There is a twofold answer.

First, Guardini could have taken concrete steps to help the victims of Nazi oppression. For instance, he could have assisted Bishop Konrad von Preysing, Canon Bernhard Lichtenberg, and other Catholics in Berlin as they tried to assist Berlin's Jews, especially after *Kristallnacht* (November 8, 1938).[65] It is not evident today that Guardini offered extensive help to the Reich's victims. One must add, however, that such action would have likely led to Guardini's arrest, incarceration, and death. Such was the fate of Lichtenberg who, arrested by the Gestapo, died in 1943 en route by truck to Auschwitz.

Second, during the 1920s and into the 1930s, Guardini could have voiced public support for democracy in general and the Weimar Republic in particular. Granted, he admitted his ignorance of politics and deferred to others' judgment in practical areas.[66] Yet, he did think about political matters and expressed his thoughts in writings, most of which were not made public until after his death.[67] It is now clear that, as a political conservative, Guardini described himself as an advocate of democracy who acknowledged "absolute values and objective authorities" and judged that for a democracy to succeed it must maintain a "balance between individual selfhood and the objective order."[68] Guardini's postwar clarifications shed light on his stance toward the Weimar Republic. One can surmise that in his judgment the republic was inadequate because of its emphasis on self-autonomy and pluralism. His lack of public support for the republic fits into the pattern of disinterest among Germany's intellectuals and religious leaders who by their neglect permitted the collapse of Germany's first attempt at parliamentary democracy.[69]

Two postwar comments by Guardini are pertinent. First, in his diary for January 12, 1964, he criticizes the "blindness of liberalism" and laments the loss of "absolute norms" within democracy. Then he adds: "German liberalism was the father of Nazism—and will be again in some kind of form."[70] This comment by the seventy-nine-year-old theologian reveals his distrust of democracy. It is also the kind of assessment that has been challenged by those who argue that the seedbed of Nazism was German neoromanticism with its strong conservative backlash against Germany's modernization. In this regard, the Protestant theologian Wolfhart Pannenberg has observed that the attraction of Germans to Hitler's National Socialism was not "the logical outcome of the history of modern [liberal] Protestantism." On the contrary, Germans joined the German Christian Movement because it was "another form of revolt against modernity." Indeed, it was "a romantic reaction to modernity, and that was also its affinity with the Nazis."[71] Assessments such as Pannenberg's clearly oppose Guardini's linking of liberal thought and Nazism.

Second, after the war, Guardini also observed that his best experience of democracy occurred with the Catholic youth movement, for at Burg Rothenfels he discovered "what democracy is," namely, "a fortunate unity of order and freedom."[72] This statement is noteworthy, for Guardini seemingly did not see that, despite its many positive qualities, Quickborn—along with other groups in the *Volk* movement—inadvertently played into fascism.[73] Life at Burg Rothenfels depended upon a charismatic leader (namely, Guardini) and the desire of the young people to belong to an "organic" community. Such a form of life did not teach young people the skills to assert their political views according to an agreed upon set of rights and clearly defined process of decision-making. Also, the emphasis upon community (*Gemeinschaft*) often resulted in the disengagement of Catholic youth from the political affairs of the larger society (*Gesellschaft*).[74] Hence, in pointing to the community at Burg Rothenfels as an instance of democracy, Guardini conveyed his limited understanding of the Nazism's political origins.

Finally, I should conclude by recalling that, despite his uneasiness with democracy, Romano Guardini contributed in the 1950s to the intellectual and spiritual foundations of the Federal Republic of (West) Germany. In *Der Heilbringer in Mythos, Offenbarung und Politik* he helped Germans gain critical distance on the Nazi indoctrination that had determined their thoughts and actions for twelve years. In "Verantwortung" he assisted his nation's conscience in facing a harsh truth and supported the government's decision to make reparations to Jews. Also, he promoted a healthy society by describing the university as a locus for freedom of thought and speech and also by extolling the value of conscience as displayed in the martyrdoms of the White Rose group.[75] Further, soon after the war, he worked at reknitting Germany's ties with the other European nations. For instance, in 1948 he spoke in Paris on "the search for peace," thereby becoming one of the first German citizens to give a public lecture in postwar France, and in 1949 he contributed an article on Jean Pierre de Caussade to the prestigious French journal *Dieu Vivant*.[76]

Although it would be inaccurate to claim a direct tie between Guardini's writings and the Second Vatican Council's Declaration on the Relation of the Church to Non-Christian Religions, *Nostrae Aetate* (October 28, 1965), it is true that Guardini's considerations on the sanctity of the person anticipated Vatican II's recognition of the respect that is due to all women and men as human beings. Surely, Guardini's statements on the dignity of personal existence and Germans' moral responsibility to Jews helped to prepare the way for the council's condemnation of all forms of prejudice and racism. In *Nostrae Aetate* the council states that the church "deplores all hatreds, persecutions, displays of anti-semitism levelled at any time or from any source against the Jews."[77] It declares, further, that "the church reproves, as foreign to the mind of Christ, any discrimination against people or any harassment of them on the basis of their race, color, condition in life or religion."

On May 10, 1933, Romano Guardini must have been appalled by the Nazis' burning of books. Given his love of world literature, he must have seen that this horrendous act struck at the heart of Western civilization. In any case, as we have seen, he eventually characterized Nazism as a barbarism.[78] This tragic experience convinced Guardini that the surest safeguard against a demagogue is the development of personal existence in relation to the God of the Judeo-Christian tradition. In chapter 7 we will see that in his christological writings Guardini sought to identify the person who is "the way" to God: Jesus Christ.

$$\clubsuit \quad 7 \quad \clubsuit$$

JESUS CHRIST, MEDIATOR

In his diary for Easter Monday, April 26, 1943, Romano Guardini noted the way in which a small group of German soldiers perished in the battle of Stalingrad. The fighting had ended on February 2 with the surrender of Germany's Sixth Army, and, although this defeat was announced on the German radio on February 3, it took many weeks for the German people to piece together the reports. Amid national mourning, Guardini wrote:

> An acquaintance has told me of his friend who was ordered at the last moment out of Stalingrad and [earlier] experienced the following: On one occasion, as a group of soldiers were about to meet their end, a Protestant chaplain took his New Testament out of his satchel, tore off its binding, and gave a page of the sacred book to each soldier. No one has denied this report.[1]

This statement is Guardini's sole entry for Easter Monday 1943. It lacks an explanation of why Guardini thought about how a few men—out of approximately 300,000 German casualties—faced death because the *Führer* ordered General Friedrich von Paulus not to surrender. Yet, no additional words are needed when one knows Guardini's Christology. This seventh chapter examines his reflections on Jesus Christ and, as a result, sheds light on the theologian's interest in the poignant account of soldiers dying with pages of the New Testament in their hands or pockets.

Romano Guardini's theology is rightly called "christocentric," for its foundational ideas are linked to God's revelation in Jesus Christ.[2] Curiously, however, Guardini never formulated a Christology, in the strict sense of the term. That is, he did not give a systematic elucidation of the church's belief in Jesus Christ. Such an endeavor was not Guardini's primary concern. Rather, in numerous writings, the theologian aimed at depicting Jesus Christ as he is presented in scripture. He comments on this aim at the conclusion of his 500-page book *Der Herr:* "We attempted to prove nothing, only to clear the way for Revelation." Then, referring to Jesus Christ, he adds:

> Once we meet him the only way he can be met, in faith; once we renounce all personal judgment, letting Scripture speak with the full weight of its authority, every line of the New Testament comes alive. The Son of God and man . . .

steps out of eternity, the unknown, an immeasurable Being revealed to us bit by bit through the word of his messengers or through some personal trait.[3]

As these sentences convey, Guardini worked in Christology with the goal of a preacher, or, more precisely, a kerygmatic theologian: to identify the living Christ who is present to people of every age.[4] On the one hand, he had little interest in the so-called historical Jesus whom he judged to be a mental construct of modern historians, and, on the other hand, he did not want to investigate the Christ of dogma whom prior to Vatican II a Catholic theologian could safely discuss only within the categories of neoscholasticism. Rather, Guardini was intent upon giving an individuating account of Jesus Christ whom the believing community meets in the church, scripture, service to others, and liturgy, prayer, and the sacraments.[5]

Why did Guardini focus his theological attention on the living Christ? As we noted in chapter 1, Guardini held that knowledge begins with "living-concrete" persons. Hence, he wanted to single out the one whom church teachings presuppose. Beyond this epistemological rationale there was a theological reason: Guardini regarded Jesus Christ as the one "mediator" between God and humanity, the one in relation to whom all men and women can know God and simultaneously mature into full persons before God. Without a conscious relationship to Jesus Christ, people may find their way to God but with greater difficulty than if they believe in Christ. In 1935 Guardini expounded this point in *Christliches Bewusstsein:* "Christ is the foundation of creation: the Logos. He is the canon of true existence. He is the key to the questions which it poses. In him is the point of convergence of elements, which, taken alone, stand in insoluble contradictions."[6] In 1953 he reiterated this idea when he wrote in his diary that Jesus Christ "is the mediator. He tells us how God is to be thought of, and how we should speak to God."[7] Convinced that Christ is the full revelation of God, Guardini wanted to keep an image of him before his readers and listeners so that they could meet the one who is "the way, the truth, and the life" (Jn 14:6).[8]

How did Guardini specifically focus on Jesus Christ? He was guided by the question, Who is Jesus Christ?, or, in biblical terms, "'And, you, who do you say that I am?'" (Mk 8:29). His answer consisted of his retelling of scripture and reflecting on its meaning.[9] In a broad sense, he was a biblical theologian, not unlike Karl Barth (1886–1968), and his christological presentations were kerygmatic, that is, efforts to proclaim anew the living Christ and facilitate an encounter between Christ and modern readers.[10] Whereas Rudolf Bultmann (1884–1976) sought to "demythologize" the Bible, Guardini tried to revive biblical images and narratives of the anointed one, especially as they function in the liturgy.[11] To put this another way, he relied on a literary rendering of the Bible in order to provide identifying or individuating descriptions of Jesus Christ.[12] In his judgment, a theoretical or metaphysical account of the person and work of Jesus Christ—for example, as provided by the neoscholasticism of his day—has value, but it presupposes that one already possesses a knowledge, anchored in faith, of Christ not as an idea or as an exemplar of religious life, but as the absolutely unique, living person. For while systematic theology answers our conceptual or speculative questions, a biblical or kerygmatic theology addresses our existential questions, thereby speaking to our "hearts" as well as our minds.[13]

Our study of Guardini's Christology primarily treats the book for which Guardini is still remembered: *Der Herr.* He himself mentioned this book as a favorite among his writings.[14] During the five years after its publication in 1937, it went through four printings as tens of thousands of German Catholics turned to the book for spiritual sustenance. Some Germans even brought it with them to air-raid shelters.[15] Translated into English in 1950 as *The Lord,* it awakened in thousands of North American Catholics a new appreciation of the living Christ and also of the New Testament. (Many readers still remember the book's cover: Georges Rouault's "Christ Mocked by Soldiers.") Eventually available in at least four other languages, *Der Herr* became an international best-seller.[16]

Our consideration of *Der Herr* proceeds in four steps. First, it recalls the Catholic biblical movement and considers three ways in which Guardini could have engaged in Christology between the wars. Second, the chapter recounts the genesis of *Der Herr,* reviews the book itself, and examines the book's "introduction"—the monograph *Das Wesen des Christentums* (The essence of Christianity [1938]). Third, the chapter highlights the biblical hermeneutics of *Der Herr* by discussing Guardini's essay "Heilige Schrift und Glaubenswissenschaft" (Sacred scripture and critical study of the faith [1928]). Fourth, we note how Guardini's christological work nurtured ideas that came to expression in Vatican II's representation of Jesus Christ.

Interpreting the Bible

THE BIBLICAL MOVEMENT AND CHRISTOLOGY

On November 18, 1893, a momentous event occurred within the Catholic Church: Pope Leo XIII issued his encyclical *Providentissimus Deus.* Prior to this papal instruction, the Vatican had refused to recognize the validity of "critical" interpretation, also called "higher criticism," in the study of the Bible. But in this official statement, Leo XIII encourages Catholic biblical scholars to learn how to use critical methods and thus to know firsthand both their promise and their limits. In particular, he acknowledges the importance of historical study of "the origin and handing down of writings" (n. 17) and also the necessity of knowing that, unlike modern scientists, the Bible's writers "did not seek to penetrate the secrets of nature, but rather described and dealt with things in more or less figurative language, or in terms which were commonly used at the time" (n. 18). For this reason, the sacred writers "have sometimes expressed the ideas of their own times, and thus made statements which in these days have been abandoned as incorrect" (n. 19). To be sure, Catholics cannot accept all of the results of higher criticism, since it is an "inept method" for understanding the Bible (n. 17). Nevertheless, they must keep in mind that "truth cannot contradict truth" and, therefore, in light of the scientific findings it may be necessary at times to rethink some conventional interpretations of biblical passages (n. 23). Given these thoughts, Leo XIII calls for an increase both in the number of biblical scholars and also in these scholars' "diligence and industry in reading, meditating, and explaining Scripture" (n. 2).[17] Nine years after this momentous encyclical, the pope established the Pontifical Biblical Commission, giving it the task of comprehending and assessing the results and methods of modern biblical studies.[18]

Encouraged by *Providentissimus Dei,* Catholic scholars began to produce new translations of and commentaries on the Bible. However, after Pius X's condemnation of modernism in 1907, they proceeded cautiously. The French Dominican Marie Joseph Lagrange (d. 1938), who was a preeminent Catholic exegete, used source criticism and form criticism in his books *Historical Criticism and the Old Testament* (1905) and *Mark* (1911), *Luke* (1920), *Matthew* (1923), and *John* (1925). Exegetical works by German Catholics included Heinrich J. Vogels' *Textkritik des Neuen Testament* (1923) and *Einleitung in das Neuen Testament* (1925) and J. B. Goettsberger's *Einleitung in das Alten Testament* (1928). There appeared, too, new translations of the New Testament by Fritz Tillmann in 1912 and also by Konstantin Rösch in 1921. Building on these works, the Katholisches Bibelwerk, an institute founded in Stuttgart in 1933, made available to dioceses and parishes new editions of the Bible and also accessible commentaries on the Bible.[19]

During the first half of the twentieth century, Catholic biblical scholars depended on the research of their Protestant colleagues. They took careful note of the studies of Julius Wellhausen, H. J. Holtzmann, and B. H. Streeter in source criticism and also of Hermann Gunkel, K. L. Schmidt, Martin Dibelius, and Rudolf Bultmann in form criticism.[20] In 1928 Augustin Bea, S.J., then professor at Rome's Pontifical Biblical Institute, wrote a balanced, insightful review of recent studies on the history and archaeology of the Holy Land and Near East, which discusses the work of Wellhausen, Gunkel, and their students. In concluding this survey, he states: "There can be no doubt that a new era has begun for work on the sacred scriptures."[21]

Today, as a consequence of "critical" approaches to the Bible, mainstream Christians have increasingly called into question "precritical" interpretations of the Bible. A precritical view of the Bible takes little interest in the human origins of the Bible and is primarily interested in its "content," namely, revelation. Precritical interpretation frequently seeks to apprehend God's word by means of a conventional notion of scripture's four levels of meaning: its literal, allegorical, moral, and anagogical senses. By contrast, viewing the Bible within the horizon of human endeavors, critical interpretation applies to the Bible the same criteria and methods of interpretation that are employed in the interpretation of any text. In other words, critical methods seek to account for the oral and written origins of a text and also for its literary and structural aspects. It is not necessarily concerned to illumine the way in which a biblical text expresses God's word but neither is it opposed in principle to this aspect of a text's meaning. In light of this critical approach, the precritical one is inadequate because it does not take sufficient notice of the external and internal human factors that shape a text's meaning.[22]

As we will shortly see, this distinction between precritical and critical hermeneutics proves useful in clarifying Guardini's use of scripture in his christological writings. So too does a second distinction. This is the distinction between a text's "literal sense" and its "more-than-literal sense"—a distinction which the Pontifical Biblical Commission used in its *The Interpretation of the Bible in the Church* (1994).[23] A text's literal sense is its primary meaning at the time the text was produced. It is "[t]he sense which the human author directly intended and which the written words conveyed." It is distinct from the "simplistic literalism" of precritical interpretation which relies on "surface impressions" of a text.[24] The literal sense of a text is arrived at by means of historical-critical methods such as textual criticism, source criticism, form criticism, and redaction criticism—all of which seek to understand a text in relation to its origins and earliest contexts. It answers the question, what did this text originally mean?

This first consideration leads into a second which is guided by the question, what does this text mean today?, and this question is answered in terms of a text's more-than-literal sense, its *sensus plenior* or "fuller sense." The fuller sense of a text is "the deeper meaning, intended by God but not clearly intended by the human author, that is seen to exist in the words of scripture when they are studied in the light of further revelation or of development in the understanding of revelation."[25] To arrive at a text's more-than-literal meaning readers must rely on a "literary hermeneutics" which itself depends on "noncontextual" (or "postcritical") approaches to scripture. These include structuralism, deconstruction, rhetorical criticism, reader-response criticism, narrative criticism, sociological and psychological criticism, and phenomenological criticism.[26]

These conceptual distinctions and interpretative methods were not available to biblical scholars and theologians in the first half of this century. If they had been, they would have helped Guardini and other theologians clarify their biblical hermeneutics. Guardini brought to scripture an aim similar to the one which he brought to his reading of poetry and novels: he was intent upon understanding a text's verbal sense, its more-than-literal meaning. However, his interpretative approach to the Bible differed from his way of rendering world literature. In the case of the writings of Dante, Hölderlin, and Rilke, he considered (at least in a minimal way) the author's context, life, and intention in his analysis of the text, but, in the case of the church's sacred book, he judged—erroneously—that one could attain a fuller sense of scripture without first reaching an understanding of a text's origins and its author's or editor's intentions. In other words, Guardini was not consistent in his hermeneutics, for he included factors external to a text in his interpretation of world literature but refused to consider the results of historical critical inquiry in his interpretation of scripture. Given this refusal, Guardini's biblical hermeneutics was precritical. We will observe his approach to the Bible in *Der Herr,* but first we need to locate Guardini's work in relation to the Christologies of his day.

THREE KINDS OF CHRISTOLOGY

The nineteenth century's fermentation in biblical exegesis and hermeneutics had a direct impact upon theology. Theologians of the 1920s who worked in Christology had to choose one out of at least three ways of investigating the mystery of Jesus Christ. These three kinds of Christology—two of which cut across the denominational lines of Protestant and Catholic—were determined in large part by the way in which a scholar wanted to use scripture within theology. Each of these orientations possesses shortcomings as well as positive traits.[27]

One form of Christology was the neoscholastic type, which included such works as Christian Pesch's *Praelectiones Dogmaticae* (1894–99) and Adolphe Tanquerey's *Brevior Synopsis Theologiae Dogmaticae* (1911). Relying on the scholastic method, these Latin manuals took a precritical approach to scripture and church teachings, with the result that verses from the Bible and sentences from ecclesial doctrines were marshaled as "proof texts" in support of theological premises which functioned within the deductive reasoning of Aristotelian syllogisms. A literalist reading of the doctrine of Chalcedon provided the starting point and format for neoscholasticism's christological reflections and also functioned as the interpretative lens for understanding biblical testimony concerning Jesus Christ. According to its proponents, the merits of neoscholastic Christology included its safeguarding of centuries of teaching and also its emphasis upon the ontological uniqueness of Jesus Christ. Its critics have noted, however, that its abstract notions obscured the person of Jesus Christ, that its use of scripture and tradition was ahistorical and hence distorted the original meaning of texts, and that its discussion within distinct tracts of the incarnation, Christ's miracles and resurrection, and his death lost sight of the coherence of Christ's life and person.[28]

A second form of Christology was the *Leben-Jesu-Forschung* ("life of Jesus research"), which is also called the "liberal quest" and "old quest" for the historical Jesus. It originated with H. S. Reimarus's *Wolfenbüttel Fragments* (1774–78), gained strength in David Friedrich Strauss's *Leben Jesu, kritisch bearbeitet* (1835), and came to full expression in Adolf Harnack's *Das Wesen des Christentums* (*What Is Christianity?* [1900]). Among Catholics one of the most popular books in this vein was Ernest Renan's *Vie de Jésus* (1863). In light of their historical consciousness, the scholars within the *Leben-Jesu-Forschung* took for granted the distinction between the Bible's historical facts and its religious interpretations of events, which were often given the ambiguous label of "mythology." Assuming that twentieth-century historiography can determine "what actually happened" in the past, the old questers culled from the New Testament what they judged to be the facts about Jesus and used them within their so-called biographies of the Nazarean. They claimed that this reconstructed figure is the true object of Christian belief and thus should serve as the starting point for faith and Christology. In making this claim, they held that the gospels and also church dogmas (e.g., the doctrine of Chalcedon) are interpretations of the facts, interpretations which should play at best a secondary role in the faith of modern Christians. The proponents of the old quest claimed that their use of critical historiography provided an intellectually respectable view of Jesus, distinct from symbolic, metaphysical, and theological interpretations (with their possible distortions). According to Harnack, historical reconstruction frees Jesus and his message from its "Hellenization" by the early church.[29] The critics of the liberal quest have argued that a biography of Jesus Christ is not in fact possible and, even if it were, it would remain of limited theological worth since the object of Christian belief is the risen Christ.[30]

A third form of Christology entailed a kerygmatic approach to the mystery of Jesus Christ. That is, it reflected on God's word, as proclaimed in the church. The Protestant proponents of this view were Martin Kähler, Karl Barth, and Emil Brunner, among others. Among the Catholic representatives of kerygmatic theology were Karl Adam, Romano Guardini, Engelbert Krebs, Peter Lippert, and members of the theological faculty of Innsbruck such as Franz Lakner and Hugo Rahner. Kerygmatic Christology sought to identify the individual whom Christians confess to be "the Christ." In focusing on this living person, it tried to assist Christians in knowing Christ as well as in knowing about him. In this orientation the sources for knowledge of Jesus Christ include scripture, the sacraments, especially the Eucharist, religious devotions, and church teachings. According to its proponents, this kind of Christology rightly treated the Bible as the church's sacred book and remained true to Anselm's view that theology is faith seeking understanding. In doing so, it did not turn theology into a metaphysics or a theory, as occurred in neoscholasticism, nor did it reduce theology to history, as happened in the old quest. Its critics have charged, however, that it was fideistic, closed to modern thought (e.g., historiography), and precritical in its biblical hermeneutics.[31]

When Leo XIII issued *Providentissimus Deus* in 1893, he did so within his vision of renewing Catholic theology, especially by means of Thomistic philosophy and theology. At the time, it seemed possible to adopt a limited use of critical methods in the study of the Bible and simultaneously to recover the teachings and method of Thomas Aquinas and other scholastic theologians. However, it soon became clear to biblical exegetes and some theologians that a synthesis of the sort envisioned by Leo XIII was not possible.[32] Among these theologians was Romano Guardini, who in the tradition of Bonaventure and Pascal, was more interested in the human heart with its "reasons" than in "reason" as defined by the Enlightenment. Steering clear of neoscholastic Christology, on the one side, and the life-of-Jesus research, on the other, he opted for a kerygmatic Christology.[33]

The Living Christ

GUARDINI'S CHRISTOCENTRIC ORIENTATION

Near the end of his life, Romano Guardini commented on his conversion of 1905, perhaps addressing his remarks to the disaffected students of the 1960s. In *Die Kirche des Herrn* (*The Church of the Lord* [1965]) he observes that young Christians may come to a point at which they find themselves in a "crisis" of faith. Such a moment occurred in his own life, Guardini recalls, when he was twenty years of age. In Mainz he anguished over his faith and then considered, as though for the first time, Jesus' exhortation in Matthew 10:39: "Those who find their life will lose it, and those who lose their life for my sake will find it." At that moment, he saw that the living Christ is essential to Christianity, and he chose to dedicate his life to Christ. Remembering this moment at the age of eighty, he advises others that when they find themselves unsure of their religious belief, they must put their questions to God and await an answer. In Guardini's words:

> In answer there appears the figure of Christ. The more clearly our gaze is fixed upon Him, the more plainly we see that His claim to be the revealer of the living God is justified. He stands in a close proximity to the true God, and this enables Him to know more of the mind of God than anyone else. He lives in a relation of unity with God, and, for this reason, what He speaks is spoken by God Himself. So we understand the fundamental Christian truth of the Mediator and Redeemer.[34]

Guardini's religious experience in 1905 and his reflection upon it in 1965 pertain to *Der Herr*, which appeared in 1937. These three dates—1905, 1937, and 1965—stand as markers of the theological orientation that governed the theologian's adult years.[35]

For at least two reasons, Guardini's emphasis on the centrality of Jesus Christ for the Christian life came to an intense, clear expression in the 1930s. First, the financial collapse which took place in the United States in October 1929 brought about an economic crisis in Germany in July 1931, and by December 1932 unemployment in Germany rose from 3 million to 6.5 million. During these eighteen months, the number of Nazi Storm Troopers increased from 80,000 to 600,000.[36] Amid Germany's economic and political turmoil, Guardini perceived that Germans were desperately searching for someone in whom to place their trust. For many years at Burg Rothenfels, members of Quickborn had discussed Jesus Christ as the true *Führer*, and, by the early 1930s, Guardini saw that this understanding of Christ warranted elaboration so that people would better know the one absolute savior: Jesus Christ.[37] In 1935, as we saw in the previous chapter, he gave his analysis of the different kinds of savior figures in his essay "Der Heiland," and by 1937 he was ready to make public his verbal portrait of the true *Heilbringer*.

A second reason for Guardini's writing *Der Herr* was that throughout the early 1900s Berlin's museums had enhanced their exhibits of the ancient world, and in 1930 workers completed the construction of Berlin's Pergamon Museum. The general public now had access to such marvels as the Sphinx of Hatshepsut (1500 B.C.), the sculpture of Nefertiti (1200 B.C.), the Ishtar Gate and Processional Way from Babylon (580 B.C.), and Turkey's Pergamon Altar (180 B.C.).[38] As a result of these exhibits, people were becoming aware of the world's religions and asking about the uniqueness of Christian belief. If they read only the writings of Max Weber (d. 1920) or Ernst Troeltsch, they might conclude that Christian belief is merely one religion among others. As Guardini reflected on world religions, he found that this endeavor clarified and strengthened his faith in Jesus Christ. It is likely, too, that one stimulus for Guardini's reflections on this topic was Max Scheler's comparative study of the Buddha, Lao-Tzu, Socrates, Jesus, and Muhammad in his essay "Vorbilder und Führer" (Role models and leaders [1921]).[39] In any case, beginning in the early 1930s, Guardini envisioned writing on the "parallelism" that he perceived among the founders of major religious movements. In his words: "Thus, I had the intention to write a type of trilogy that would analyze the deaths of [the] Buddha, Socrates, and Jesus Christ in their similarities, however also and above all in their differences."[40] Guardini did not fully realize his aim of a trilogy, but he did complete two of the three works. In 1937 he finished *Der Herr*, which includes numerous comments concerning Jesus in relation to the Buddha and Socrates, and, six years later, he completed his reflections on Socrates' life and teachings in *Der Tod des Sokrates* (1943).

These two concerns—Germans' search for a *Heilbringer* or *Führer* and their growing consciousness of world religions—prompted Guardini to preach a series of "meditations" on Jesus Christ from 1932 through 1936 with students in Berlin's St. Benedict Chapel and also with farmers, laborers, and students at Burg Rothenfels. Prior to each mass, he wrote out his thoughts on some aspect of Christ's life or teachings, and, then at mass, he presented what he had written. Afterwards, he revised what he had written and then saved his text. When he had amassed texts on major aspects of the mystery of Christ, he reworked the entire collection of eighty-six meditations into a single, coherent work.[41] In

1937, as Berlin held a "Nazi festival" celebrating the seven-hundredth anniversary of the city's founding, *Der Herr* arrived in bookstores.

DER HERR (1937)

In *Der Herr* Guardini presents Jesus Christ as the "revealer" and "mediator" of God within history, and he develops these views not so much in conceptual and philosophical terms as in images, metaphors, and narratives, most of which are drawn from the Bible.[42] For Guardini, Jesus Christ is God's word who became a human being, disclosed God's love and truth, and then returned to God. More specifically, he revealed God in his teaching, wondrous works, and passion, death, and resurrection. In this supreme act of self-emptying love, Jesus Christ reconciled us with God and released the Holy Spirit into creation. Because of his extraordinary life, Jesus Christ is the "rescue pilot" who has boarded the ship of humanity, which was headed toward disaster, and charted the new, correct course that will lead the human family to its proper harbor.[43]

Guardini conveys his view of Christ in part by the *exitus-reditus* design according to which he orders his meditations. After a preface, the book consists of seven parts, each of which comprises approximately twelve meditations, and the book ends with a brief conclusion. "Part One: The Beginnings" reflects on Christ's "origins" in God's triune life, his incarnation and ministry among the people of Palestine, especially the sick, lost, and sinful. "Part Two: Message and Promise" considers Jesus' teachings about God's forgiveness, "the enemy" (Satan), and our conversion in the Holy Spirit. "Part Three: The Decision" explores Jesus' realization that since the world was rejecting his message, he faced the choice of abandoning the world or undertaking a journey of suffering and death by which he would bring about the new creation. "Part Four: On the Road to Jerusalem" probes the mystery of Jesus' transfiguration and the life of discipleship to Jesus Christ. "Part Five: The Last Days" meditates on Jesus' entry into Jerusalem, last supper, prayer in the Garden of Gethsemane, trial, crucifixion, and death. "Part Six: Resurrection and Transfiguration" considers the appearances of the risen Christ, the meaning of history, the role of the Holy Spirit in history, and Christ as the High Priest. "Part Seven: Time and Eternity" reflects on the images of Christ in the Book of Revelation. *Der Herr*'s design shows the divine word going out from God, becoming incarnate in Jesus Christ, and then returning to God, and this form is meant to convey the absolute uniqueness of Jesus Christ and the importance of our conversion to Christ.

Running through the eighty-six meditations of *Der Herr* are numerous themes concerning personal existence in relation to God. Of these recurring ideas, I will review five: the "fallen" world, Jesus Christ as revealer, the uniqueness of Jesus Christ, the humanity of Christ, and Christian conversion.

First, the world exists in a "fallen" state. To be sure, creation springs from grace and is sustained by it. But it has rebelled against God and is, therefore, marked by ambiguity. We discover particular truths about natural reality and human life, and yet we turn away from truth itself, from God. In the deepest recesses of our hearts we yearn for God but resist God's overtures of love. In all honesty it must be admitted that "human existence *in toto* has fallen away from God." It is like a ship that has gone off course, and now "the whole ship is headed for disaster" (pp. 293–94). Guardini states: "Existence itself is forsaken because it is as it is: estranged from God and sinking into nothingness. No human can rescue here, only Christ, the God-man, who has overcome the void" (p. 163).

What are the causes of our resistance to God? They are rooted in our minds and hearts. The human intellect can easily err and refuse to acknowledge its mistakes. Our very rationality can function as a "protective covering that man has constructed between himself and God" (p. 84). Through the Enlightenment the mind has come to see the world as "complete in itself and self-isolated from its Creator and Sustainer" (p. 321). Further, our alienation from God originates in our hearts. In Guardini's words: "At the bottom of the human heart, side by side with our longing for the eternal source and fulfillment of all things, lurks resistance to the source: elementary sin in its lair" (p. 45). The heart's movement to God is further complicated by the allure of Satan. The modern mind fails to admit the existence of evil in history. Nevertheless, the New Testament is clear that "Jesus recognizes a personal power that fundamentally wills evil: evil *per se*" (pp. 79–80). This malevolent force is not God's "dark side" or "antipode," as is proposed by some psychologists (e.g., C. G. Jung). On the contrary, the devil is an independent will intent upon spreading "murkiness and confusion" among us. As a result, the world remains estranged from its source and goal: God.

Second, Jesus Christ is God's word who has come into the world to reveal God's love for all people and to turn all minds and hearts to God. He is the Son of God who, out of faithfulness, entered into history in order to disclose the true *telos* of human life and to provide the means by which people can attain this goal. In his teaching and actions, he undertook the "Great Revaluation" of human values, the disclosure of the true values in human life. He accomplished this transformation of creation not solely by means of something he did (e.g., his teaching) but also in his very person. "What Jesus revealed there on the mountainside was no mere ethical code, but a whole new existence—admittedly, one in which an *ethos* is immediately evident" (p. 321). In his own existence, Jesus Christ brought about the "new beginning" within creation and history, and, after fulfilling his mission, returned to the divine circle of love.[44] The world's religions show reverence to God and are indeed inspired by God. Yet, they do not express the entirety of God's word and hence full union with God. Guardini declares: "Certainly God speaks through everything and to everything, also to me. . . . But all this remains vague. . . . It is ambiguous and needs the ultimate clarification that can come only through the word of God, and this he does not speak to everyone" (p. 295). Jesus Christ is, therefore, "the envoy," "the heavenly messenger," and "the eternal Logos" who has become a human being. Although Jesus Christ was born into the world, he does not fit within it. As a result, he is "the Stranger." But this is not all. Since the world can be likened to a ship that has veered off course and is headed "straight for destruction," Jesus Christ is "the Rescue-pilot" who comes aboard the ship and "puts us back on the right course."[45]

Third, Jesus Christ is absolutely unique. He was not one exceptional prophet or teacher among others. It is inappropriate to describe Jesus Christ as one insightful "guide" along with the Buddha, Lao-Tzu, Socrates, Muhammad, and Goethe. Jesus Christ is more than a teacher of the truth, he is truth itself embodied in a human being. "For he is the *Logos,* the source of Living Truth" (p. 294).

The distinctiveness of Jesus Christ is evident, Guardini insists, when Jesus' approach to death is compared with the approaches of the Buddha and Socrates. At first glance, it seems that each is an instance of "the leave-taking of a departing master." Nearing death, with his disciples close by, the Buddha proceeds up the steps of meditation and dies as he reaches the top. Socrates welcomes his disciples to his side when he drinks the cup of hemlock. Jesus bids farewell to his disciples as they are gathered around him at the last supper. Seemingly, the Buddha, Socrates, and Jesus are instances of the same pattern (p. 357). But closer inspection uncovers an essential difference. The Buddha "is convinced that he has discovered the law of illusion that reigns everywhere, but which only the extremely rare individual is privileged to perceive." In making this law known to everyone, he has accomplished his life's work, thereby attaining perfection. In dying as in living, Socrates "refuses to claim any authority." He is searching for the truth, and he urges others to do the same in their own ways. By contrast, Jesus does not belong in the company of the Buddha, Socrates, and others who are searching for the truth. He does not look for the truth, because he already possesses it. "Jesus, who was Truth, never sought it." He goes to his death as one who throughout his life had already reached perfection. "Humanly speaking, his life was not perfected, but destroyed in the plumbless mystery of his sacrificial destiny" (pp. 357–58).

Fourth, Jesus Christ is a full human being. He possesses a complete human nature and, therefore, participated in all aspects of human life, except sin. "Jesus was no cold Superman—he was more human than any of us" (p. 225). He did not lead by asserting himself but by living with weakness and humility. Jesus radiated human warmth and vitality. He exhibited a profound respect and love for creation, as is evident in his parables. Also, he experienced the pain of human limits and suffering, especially in the face of persecution and death. "Jesus really lived our life and died our death, real death (its terrors were only the more terrible for the divine strength and sensitivity of his life) yet everything was different both in his living and in his dying" (p. 234). In his suffering and death, he surrendered himself to the movement toward "negative nothingness" that began when human beings rebelled against God. In disobeying the source of life, human beings have chosen death, thereby initiating a human tendency toward the point of annihilation. This point of nothingness could not, however, be reached by human beings since they lack the ability to create themselves and hence to eradicate themselves. In order to undo the movement toward destruction, God sent his Son into the world so that, as a human being, he could succumb to the destructive tendency. In Guardini's words: "Thus in the midst of human history stood one who was both human and God. Pure as God; but bowed with responsibility as man. He drank the dregs of that responsibility—down to the bottom of the chalice. Mere man cannot do this" (p. 398).

Fifth, conversion is the appropriate response to Jesus Christ. But this act is demanding, for it requires overcoming one's innate resistance to God. Therefore, it can only be initiated by and sustained in the Holy Spirit. Simultaneously, it requires faith, which is a form of knowledge. In John's Gospel, Nicodemus is drawn by the Holy Spirit to Jesus, and yet he must choose to follow him (Jn 5). We, like Nicodemus, yearn for God, the living truth, but we are unsure whether to surrender to God. We are also similar to the Samaritan woman at Jacob's well (Jn 4) who initially resists the encounter with Christ but then finds that he is the source of living water, God's word.[46] As believers, we perceive the world in a new way because of our change of heart and mind. We can identify with the man born blind (Jn 9) who now realizes that those who claim to have sight are in fact blind. God's word guides believers to the truth. We look through the "fog" that has obscured the depths of reality. There is a sense in which we ultimately apprehend reality with our hearts. The Christian sees the world as Christ sees it, and, as a result, there occurs the overturning of the world's values (p. 153).

These five themes stand out in *Der Herr*. But, they do not exhaust Guardini's ideas in this work. The book also describes the triune God as a circle of love in which the Father, Son, and Spirit relate to one another in unity and differentiation.[47] Further, it contains an implicit critique of Nazism, for it repeatedly condemns those who are closed to truth and insists that there is only one savior: Jesus Christ. For the book's readers in the Third Reich, the message is clear: Jesus Christ, not Adolf Hitler, is the one, true *Heiland*.[48]

DAS WESEN DES CHRISTENTUMS (1938)

The Christology of *Der Herr* is not similar to most of today's books on Jesus Christ. For instance, it does not rely on an approach "from below" that theologians like Karl Rahner (d. 1984) and Edward Schillebeeckx employ. Also, it does not accentuate Jesus' resurrection as occurs in the christological writings of Walter Kasper and Gerald O'Collins. How then should we classify *Der Herr*?

Guardini himself answered this question in *Der Herr*'s "introduction," *Das Wesen des Christentums*, which is an elaboration of his essay by the same title that appeared in 1929.[49] Guardini gives his rationale for *Der Herr* when he explains that the "essence" of Christian faith is something more than the "fatherhood" of God and universal love. Its center is Jesus Christ. In Guardini's words: "That which is Christian is ultimately no theory of truth or meaning of life. It is also these things. But its essential kernel does not exist in them. Rather its kernel is Jesus of Nazareth, his concrete existence, work, and destiny—in other words, a historical person" (p. 7). This individual is, however, not simply a human being, but God's word within history. Such a revelation is necessary because, as a result of sin, the world has alienated itself from God. We need to be "saved" by the truth which comes from outside of ourselves in the *Heilbringer* (pp. 33–38). In relation to Jesus Christ, all human beings can experience the truest "I-you" relationship and move toward the proper way of relating to God, themselves, and others. In other words, Jesus Christ is the mediator for all of creation (pp. 25–29). The aim of *Der Herr* is, therefore, to identify Christian faith's "essence," namely, the living Christ. By means of biblical images and narratives, this book is meant to provide an individuating account of the Lord who is contemporaneous with the people of every age.[50]

Expanding upon Guardini's introduction, we can observe that *Der Herr* is basically a form of Christology "from above," for it assumes from the outset that Jesus Christ is God's word who has become "flesh" (Jn 1:14).[51] Moreover, it stands in the christological trajectory that runs from John's Gospel, through Cyril of Alexandria and Augustine, to Bonaventure.[52] A neo-Platonic influence is clearly at work here. The book presents the motif of *exitus,* going out, and *reditus,* going back, both in what Guardini says about Jesus Christ and also in the way in which he has arranged the meditations. Further, *Der Herr* is directed to the "heart," to the whole person. It aims at a knowledge that is self-involving: as readers commit themselves more completely to Christ, they know the Lord more fully, and, as they grow in the knowledge of Christ, they respond with greater faithfulness to the Lord. In short, *Der Herr* is intended to facilitate encounters between Jesus Christ and all those who are searching for the truth.[53] For this reason, the book is best classified as a form of kerygmatic Christology.[54]

Finally, *Der Herr* is a clear alternative to two other kinds of Christology. On the one hand, it challenges the *Leben-Jesu-Forschung,* which asserts that Christology's starting point must be historical reconstruction. *Der Herr* provides no biography of Jesus; it does not distinguish between the Jesus of history and the Christ of faith.[55] Also, Guardini deliberately gave his explanation of *Der Herr* the same title that Harnack used for his introduction to Christology: *Das Wesen des Christentums.* On the other hand, *Der Herr* differs from the Christology that dominated Catholic thought at the time. It makes no use of neoscholastic Christology, which in Guardini's judgment obscures the individuality of Jesus Christ.[56] *Der Herr* does not provide a theory or a metaphysics concerning the person of Christ. It does not even include an adequate discussion of the doctrine of the Council of Chalcedon.[57] As a kerygmatic Christology, *Der Herr* is designed to communicate not an idea but an account of a person.

Literary Interpretation and Christology

IN SEARCH OF THE BIBLE'S FULLER SENSE

Romano Guardini deliberately fashioned his Christology in *Der Herr* without reference to the results of historical studies about Jesus' life and times. It is true, of course, that if he had made explicit use of such findings when he wrote *Der Herr* in 1937, he would likely have come into conflict with the Vatican's Holy Office. But, even within the narrow limits set by Pius X's condemnation of modernism in 1907, he could have shaped his use of scripture to recognize some of the conclusions of historical studies concerning the formation of the Bible and the symbolism of some biblical accounts. For example, in light of the insights of source criticism and form criticism, he could have remained silent concerning the details of Jesus' infancy and childhood. But in fact Guardini treated the infancy narratives as though they were newspaper reports. Moreover, in his later writings he made little use of the methods and findings of source criticism and form criticism even after Pius XII's encyclical *Divino af-flante Spiritu* (1943). Therefore, the question arises, how are we to make sense of the rejection of higher criticism by a theologian who in so many other ways was open-minded?

The answer lies in Guardini's conviction that since the Bible conveys God's word, it must be approached in a singular manner—a manner which appreciates scripture's divine message and is not concerned about a biblical text's human origins.[58] Using the categories reviewed earlier in the chapter, we can say that Guardini wanted to uncover scripture's more-than-literal sense, its *sensus plenior*, but he did not execute his intention in a way that respected scripture's literal sense, that is, what it meant in its earliest settings. As a result, Guardini employed a precritical approach to the Bible.[59] In order to see what he wanted and what he in fact attained, I will review his essay on biblical hermeneutics and then one of his meditations in *Der Herr.*

In his essay "Heilige Schrift und Glaubenswissenschaft" (1928), Guardini argues for an appreciation of the Bible's *sensus plenior.* To make his case, he initially observes that the process of human knowledge is not uniform, mechanical, and rigid, but diverse, complex, and flexible. Without usually adverting to it, we adjust our way of knowing something to the specific reality that we are trying to apprehend. We rely on one form of knowledge when we understand the chemistry of some entity, and we employ a different mode of apprehension when attempting to know a person as a person. In the former case, we remain detached from the object and follow a method that focuses our attention on one aspect of the object. By contrast, in the latter case, we establish a relationship of "faithfulness" with the person and we seek to know the individual as a whole reality.[60]

Similarly, in our study of the Bible what we find when we read the church's book is in part a function of what we are looking for. In Guardini's judgment, if we regard the Bible as primarily a source of historical information, then we can appropriately apply historical-critical methods to these texts. We can treat the gospels as we might study Thucydides' *History of the Peloponnesian War*, or we can analyze the letters of St. Paul as we would examine Seneca's *Epistolae morales ad Lucilium.* But if we regard the Bible as the written witness to what God has said and done in history, then we cannot settle for the results of critical methods but must adopt an approach which directs our attention to the Bible's primary referent, God's word.[61]

According to Guardini, Christians should allow three factors to shape their reading of the Bible. First, they must attend to the literal sense of the text.[62] However, what Guardini means by "literal sense" is not what we mean today, but what we would call its "literalist" sense, that is, a rendering of a text which does not consider its author's intention, its genre, and its early uses and settings. Second, Christians must approach the text with the eyes and ears of faith. In order to apprehend the Bible's subject matter, i.e., God's word, believers must be disposed to hear it.[63] Third, they must interpret the Bible within the church's living tradition. Although God's self-communication is addressed to us as individuals, it comes to us within the believing community. Hence, we should permit the church's interpretation of a text to guide our understanding of it.[64]

"Heilige Schrift und Glaubenswissenschaft" contains a significant flaw: it presents the relationship between critical interpretation and more-than-literal interpretation as a relationship of either/or, rather than both/and. It reaches for a text's fuller sense, its witness to revelation, without first having a clear understanding of its literal sense as determined by critical methods.[65] In other words, Guardini perceived a contradiction (*Widerspruch*) where there exists an opposition, a creative tension (*Gegenstand*). In order to accomplish his goal of discerning God's word in scripture, he should have held that the biblical hermeneutics includes *both* critical methods *and also* literary (noncontextual) methods.[66]

Two further observations are pertinent. First, by omitting critical inquiry from his biblical hermeneutics, Guardini broke with the way in which he interpreted world literature. As we saw in chapter 5, in order to make sense of Rilke's *Duino Elegies,* he studied its origins in Rilke's life. Unfortunately, he did not follow this same procedure in his interpretation of biblical texts.[67] Second, by disregarding the findings of higher criticism, Guardini's approach to the Bible includes no critical checks upon his (and our) tendency to impose preconceptions and assumptions on scripture.[68] As we will now see, this consequence is evident in his scriptural interpretations in *Der Herr.*

A MEDITATION ON THE INCARNATION

Guardini's precritical hermeneutics in *Der Herr* shows itself in his reflection on the birth of Jesus Christ, entitled "Incarnation."[69] The meditation begins by recalling that the Christmas mass (in the pre–Vatican II liturgy) includes a reading from the Book of the Wisdom of Solomon: "For while gentle silence enveloped all things . . . your all-powerful word leaped from heaven, from the royal throne, into the midst of the land that was doomed" (Wis 18:14–15). This description of what Guardini calls "the infinite stillness" is the meditation's dominant motif. Building on it, he recalls that according to Luke, Mary quietly consents to God's will; according to Matthew, Joseph agrees to what takes him by surprise; and according to John, God's word became flesh without any fanfare. These passages attest, Guardini says, to the fact that God intervened in the lives of Mary, Joseph, and Jesus as God acts in our lives, that is, in "stillness." But God's ways should not upset us since "the greatest things are accomplished in silence . . . in the almost imperceptible start of decision, in quiet overcoming and hidden sacrifice."

How are we to understand God's action in Jesus Christ? Although transcending creation, God freely chose to enter into it. Why? There is no reason, except the reasoning of love. "None of the great things in human life springs from the intellect; every one of them issues from the heart and its love."

Mary eventually gives birth to an infant who is utterly unique: "this child *is* God in essence and in being." This claim to absolute singularity may offend us. If so, we should admit it, for "[i]t is not good to suppress anything; if we try to, it only goes underground, becomes toxic, and reappears later in far more obnoxious form." It is better that we try once again to fathom the scandal of the incarnation. However, according to Guardini, we cannot receive clues from psychology since Jesus fits no psychological categories. Nor can we find help in neoscholastic theology, since it is "necessarily abstract." Rather, motivated by faith and following a phenomenological approach, we must stay focused on the specific person who is involved in this birth.

The child born in Bethlehem was called "to proclaim the sacred tidings, to stir mankind with the power of God, to establish the Covenant, and shoulder the sin of the world, expiating it with love and leading mankind through the destruction of sacrifice and the victory of the Resurrection into the new existence of grace." Here is the one human being who embodied and lived out God's saving will for us. In other words: "Jesus' self-realization meant that his human being 'took possession' of the divine being he had always intrinsically been." In his life, Jesus was able "to place divine reality and power squarely in the realm of his human consciousness and will."

It is important to note, Guardini says, that the process begun at the incarnation unfolds in hiddenness for most of Jesus' life. Prior to Jesus' brief public ministry, the mystery of his being breaks into view when the youth Jesus teaches in the Temple. On this occasion, Mary questions her son about his be-havior, and he rhetorically asks, "Did you not know that I must be in my Fa-ther's house?" (Lk 2:49). In this exchange it becomes evident what had taken place: when Jesus enters the Temple, "something in him seems to rise and grip him," and, as a result, he spontaneously begins his divinely appointed task of proclaiming the good news. "His reply to Mary's shaken question best reveals how remote from theirs is the world in which he stands even then. Nevertheless, he obediently returns to Nazareth with his parents to grow with the years in wisdom and grace before God and men."[70] At this juncture, the Christmas meditation ends.

This meditation is both profound and problematic. It is insightful in its ob-servations on the way in which God's activity remains hidden among us and how, by analogy, a divine initiative also occurred in Jesus. Much more is hap-pening in our lives than we usually know. Grace operates through "secondary causes" (our family, a physician, an accidental meeting) and only occasionally do we glimpse that God has acted in our daily lives. What at the time seemed ordinary may afterwards show its extraordinary or supernatural elements, and then we marvel at all that God has done in "stillness." Guardini reasons that if God acts in concealment in our lives, God must have also done the same in Jesus' life. In short, the incarnation is the perfect instance of God's presence in hiddenness.

At the same time that Guardini's meditation on the incarnation is insightful, it is also problematic in its use of scripture. It exhibits no attempt to recognize the historical, literary, and theological differences among the various texts from which it draws: the Wisdom of Solomon and the Gospels according to Mat-thew, Luke, and John. There is no mention of the discrepancies between Mat-thew's view that Joseph and Mary originally resided in Bethlehem and Luke's statement that the couple resided in Nazareth and traveled to Bethlehem for a census, or between Matthew's report that the holy family fled to Egypt and Luke's account that the family immediately returned to Nazareth. Moreover, Luke's story of the child in the Temple (Lk 2:41–51) is handled as though it were a scene in a biography. There is no acknowledgement that this pericope con-tains symbolism.[71] The findings of the source criticism and form criticism of Guardini's day would have raised these issues. Not adverting to them, Guardini approaches the Bible in a precritical manner. That is, he assumes that the in-fancy narratives describe what factually happened at Jesus' birth and in his twelfth year. Also, without noting the distinct theologies of the biblical texts which he cites, he inserts these texts into his preconceived idea of the hiddenness of grace. As a result, when Guardini quotes biblical verses, he does so with little regard for the entire passage in which the verse occurs.

What are we to make of Guardini's use of the Bible? We should appreciate that he was intent upon going beyond the texts' historical, literary, and even theological differences to what he perceived to be their fuller sense. Today, in light of advances in biblical hermeneutics since the 1930s, we recognize that, in order to reach a text's *sensus plenior,* we must first secure its literal sense. From our vantage point, we see that Guardini short-circuited the process of biblical interpretation and, thus, had few checks upon his tendency to inject his preconceived ideas into his reading of scripture.

Six years after the publication of *Der Herr,* Pope Pius XII issued his encyclical *Divino afflante Spiritu* (September 30, 1943) concerning the study of the Bible. In promoting biblical studies, this letter affirms Guardini's persistent emphasis upon the centrality of the Bible in Christian life and theology. However, Pius XII's statement also challenges Guardini's theology, because it acknowledges the validity of the use of critical methods in the interpretation of scripture. In contrast to the theologian's precritical biblical hermeneutics, *Divino afflante Spiritu* declares that, as part of our efforts to understand a biblical text, we must "endeavor to determine the peculiar character and circumstances of the sacred writer, the age in which he lived, the sources written and oral to which he had recourse and the forms of expression he employed" (n. 33).[72] Unfortunately, this principle of interpretation is not followed in Guardini's work, even after this encyclical.

Toward Vatican II's View of Jesus Christ

During the thirty years after the appearance of *Der Herr,* Catholic Christology underwent major changes. Breaking out of neoscholasticism, it recovered a sense of the humanity of Jesus Christ by linking Christology and theological anthropology (e.g., Karl Rahner's transcendental Christology), and, using critical methods in biblical exegesis, it turned anew to the New Testament (e.g., Rudolf Schnackenburg's and Raymond Brown's writings on Jesus Christ).[73] These two developments came to expression in the Vatican II's Pastoral Constitution on the Church in the Modern World, which envisions the human family moving through history toward full realization in union with Jesus Christ.[74] *Gaudium et Spes* states: "The Lord is the goal of human history, the focal point of the desires of history and civilization, the center of humanity, the joy of all hearts, and the fulfillment of all aspirations."[75] This statement expresses relatively recent insights in Christology, for it views Jesus Christ within a theological anthropology (e.g., "the center of humanity") and implicitly draws on a biblical view of Jesus Christ within world history (e.g., Eph 1).

At this point, we can ask two questions: first, how did Guardini view the christological changes that came about in the 1950s and 1960s and are contained in *Gaudium et Spes?* And, second, to what extent did Guardini's writings foster these new ideas?

First, Guardini was uneasy with the christological trends that emerged after he wrote *Der Herr.* Concerned in 1958 that a Christology which is fashioned in relation to a theological anthropology risks losing sight of the uniqueness of Jesus Christ, Guardini wrote *Die menschliche Wirklichkeit des Herrn (The Humanity of Christ)* in which he argues for the absolute singularity of Jesus Christ.[76] In doing so, he implicitly challenged the thought of Catholic theologians such as Karl Rahner who wished to overcome the latent monophysitism in Catholic Christology.[77] At the same time, seeking to illumine the *sensus plenior* of the New Testament, he wrote biblical meditations on the mystery of Jesus Christ. These works include *Jesus Christus: Geistliches Wort (Jesus Christ: Meditations* [1959]), *Nähe des Herrn* (The nearness of the Lord [1960]), *Das Christusbild der paulinischen und johanneischen Schriften* (The image of Christ in the Pauline and Johannine Writings [1961]), and *Johanneische Botschaft* (The Johannine Message [1962]). Although Guardini's postwar christological writings were engaging and edifying, they ignored the findings of Catholic biblical scholars, findings that were available after 1957 in the *Biblische Zeitschrift* and also in the second edition of the *Lexicon für Theologie und Kirche* (1957–67).[78] In his later christological texts, Guardini also disregarded Pius XII's *Divino afflante Spiritu* (1943). In 1965 Guardini must have been unsettled, therefore, when he read *Gaudium et Spes.* He would have seen that Vatican II took a more positive stance than he judged appropriate toward the changes in Christology and biblical studies.

Since Guardini did not work with the results of historical-critical studies of the Bible, he allowed his Christology to become out of date. Although Joseph Ratzinger would seemingly not agree with this assessment, most biblical scholars and theologians would accept Herbert Vorgrimler's evaluation: "[I]t is no longer possible to concur with Guardini's reflections on Jesus Christ. Our understanding, our efforts to understand, and our questions have changed. It would be unfair to bring our questions now to Guardini's works."[79]

Second, we must acknowledge that *Der Herr* tilled the soil for the growth that eventually troubled Guardini. In fact, by this book and his other christological writings he had promoted theological changes in at least three ways. First, he pioneered a path away from neoscholastic Christology by formulating a kerygmatic Christology. Second, he reached many of his insights concerning Jesus Christ by correlating Christology and theological anthropology. We have seen that, in his meditation "Incarnation," he illumines the hiddenness of grace in Christ's life by discussing grace in human life in general. Third, because his writings drew so heavily on scripture, he awakened in Catholics a desire to study the Bible, even by means of critical methods.

Today, scholars recognize Guardini's contributions to the renewal of Catholic Christology. Thomas Ruster has observed that Guardini heightened among Catholics the recognition that theology must be grounded in scripture.[80] According to Arno Schilson, Guardini was "the pioneer of the new Christology" who opened the way for theologians such as Walter Kasper and Hans Küng.[81] In this same vein, Monika Hellwig has pointed to Guardini's *Der Herr* as one of the earliest texts that led Catholic Christology into contemporary thought.[82] Similarly, Horst Georg Pöhlmann has observed that "[t]he 'christological turn' in Catholic theology proceeds not only from Karl Adam, Erich Przywara, and others, but above all from Guardini. . . . His book of 1937 *Der Herr,* which shaped the postwar generation of Catholic priests more than almost any other theological work, is the manifestation of this christological turn."[83] The journalist Walter Dirks has expressed well the importance of *Der Herr* in the church's life:

> Guardini's book *Der Herr* made many Catholics into Christian Catholics and [also made] countless Catholics into ecumenical, Catholic Christians. It relativized "Catholicism" in the direction that could lead not to its weakening but only to its self-realization: in the direction of Jesus Christ, the Lord. During the Nazi time, we lived spiritually out of this book. It was no less an impetus toward Vatican II. It was the necessary fulfillment and completion of the liturgical and ecclesiological themes [of the previous decades].[84]

Finally, although *Der Herr* is now out of date, it can still alert us to topics that need new consideration. One of these issues is the necessity of a hermeneutics that delves into the *sensus plenior* of the Bible.[85] A second topic is that of the uniqueness of Jesus Christ in relation to other religious leaders such as the Buddha, Lao-Tzu, Moses, and Muhammad. In other words, there is a growing interest in finding new ways to speak about the divinity of Jesus Christ.[86] A third topic springs from the awareness—found among liberation theologians—that Christology is self-involving. Critical reflection on the person and work of Christ presupposes one's commitment to the living Christ and seeks an understanding which entails Christian witness.[87] Today's emphasis is on a discipleship of justice, but Guardini saw Christology's participatory aspect in relation to prayer and the formation of personal character.[88]

In *Der Herr* Romano Guardini fashioned a Christology for Germans living in the Third Reich, most of whom judged that they had little choice but to endure Hitler's tyranny. With them in mind, he crafted a book which strengthened their integrity and spiritual life. This accomplishment is linked to Guardini's entry in his diary on Easter Monday in 1943 concerning the soldiers at Stalingrad who went to their deaths holding a page of the New Testament. It is likely that Guardini's interest in this tragic incident sprang from his christological orientation. Convinced that Christian faith rests primarily upon a relationship with Jesus Christ, Guardini intuited that at Stalingrad these soldiers did what all Christians must do throughout their lives, especially before death: with the help of the New Testament, they must strengthen their union with Christ.

❖ 8 ❖

A CHRISTIAN VIEW
OF THE MODERN WORLD

"*Stunde Null.*" "Zero hour." This is the name for the months in 1945 when time stopped in Germany. It was the moment with no past since armies had destroyed it and with no future since there was little with which to work. There was only the present. Residing in basements and ruined buildings, many Germans lived from one day to the next worried about food.[1] They often had to be satisfied with merely three slices of bread per person each day, which initially was their ration from the Allied forces.[2] They feared that they and their children would suffer the fate of those, twenty-five years earlier, who had died of hunger after the First World War. Throughout the day, they looked for loved ones returning from refugee and prisoner-of-war camps.[3]

In this apocalyptic moment, Germany's new leaders struggled with fundamental questions regarding their new society and government. Among these issues were those related to the role of Christian faith in the new social and political order.[4] In the last years of his life, Dietrich Bonhoeffer (d. April 9, 1945) had foreseen these challenges and advocated that since the world had "come of age," Christians should promote a "religionless Christianity," a society which embraces the gospels but avoids explicitly Christian language.[5] In many ways, this pastor and martyr anticipated the agenda of postwar Germany. For, as the people of West Germany rebuilt their lives, they saw the further secularization of the public realm and sought the appropriate relationship between their religious beliefs and their new government.

Romano Guardini contributed to this discussion of religion and secularity in Germany. While remaining silent on the relationship between the Christian churches and the state, he commented on the interdependence between the Christian faith and Germany's social and cultural life. In this regard, on the one hand, he recognized an appropriate autonomy of human affairs. In *Das Ende der Neuzeit* (*The End of the Modern World* [1950]) he acknowledged the limited role of the church within the contemporary age. On the other hand, he also stressed the important contribution of Christian faith to human beings' self-realization. In *Freiheit, Gnade, Schicksal* (*Freedom, Grace and Destiny*

[1948]) as well as in *Das End der Neuzeit,* he presented the view that belief in Jesus Christ guides and strengthens us so that we mature into full persons. This eighth chapter reviews the creative tension (*Gegensatz*) in Guardini's thought concerning Christian faith and modernity and concludes by showing how his views anticipated the Second Vatican Council's vision of the church's role in society. At the outset, the chapter recalls Germany's secularization in the nineteenth century and highlights Guardini's attempt to understand society in the twentieth century. This effort is evinced in *Briefe vom Comersee* (*Letters from Lake Como* [1927]). After laying out this background, I will consider Guardini's discussion of personal freedom in *Freiheit, Gnade, Schicksal* and then his reflections in *Das Ende der Neuzeit* on Christian existence in postwar Germany.[6] Finally, the chapter will highlight the line of continuity between Guardini's thought and Vatican II's Pastoral Constitution on the Church in the Modern World, *Gaudium et Spes* (1965).[7]

The Secularization of Germany

The *Aufklärung* or Enlightenment promoted belief in the self-sufficiency of human reason, the goodness of human nature, and the possibility of improving the quality of human life by means of human ingenuity and effort. At the same time, it criticized Christian faith as superstition and Christian dogma as an antiquated metaphysics. Appealing to principles of reason, the *Aufklärung's* influential representatives, among whom were H. S. Reimarus, G. E. Lessing, and J. G. Herder, questioned the authority of the church and the Bible. In this vein, they also called for the separation of church and state and for a society freed from the imposition of Christianity. These ideas and the political and social changes which they initiated in nineteenth-century Germany met resistance from Catholic officials and eventually from some German intellectuals, especially in the early twentieth century.[8]

On March 24, 1803, the diet of the expiring Holy Roman Empire, which had gathered in Regensburg, resolved some of the issues created by Napoleon's victories within Germany-speaking lands. In particular, the diet formally adopted the recommendations of the representatives from the major German states concerning the compensations for losses of estates and property west of the Rhine and also concerning the reorganization of the three hundred German states into new governmental units. These recommendations, called the "Final Recess of the Imperial Delegates," had a lasting impact upon Christianity in German lands. It was agreed that the churches would relinquish their civil powers and their properties to the state and would henceforth confine their mission to people's moral and spiritual well-being. As a result of the Final Recess, government officials redrew diocesan boundaries and demanded that some bishops vacate their sees. Moreover, the government closed or took control of Protestant and Catholic institutions such as schools, universities, seminaries, and monasteries as well as church-owned farms and vineyards.[9] This process of alienation between church and state was called "secularization" or, in German, *Säkularisation.*[10]

It gradually became evident that *Säkularisation* was changing the relationship between Christian faith and German society. Not only had the churches relinquished their formal authority over civil matters and property, but they were also losing their control over values, attitudes, and the arts. Explicitly Christian language was waning in Germans' social and cultural lives and being replaced by "this-worldly" or secular language, determined by what was deemed beneficial for human life in itself and not in relation to God and the Judeo-Christian tradition. In this situation, Germans employed the term *Säkularisation* to designate the suppression of the ecclesiastically governed states and the term *Säkularisierung* to refer to the differentiation between Christian faith and society.[11]

Throughout the nineteenth century, German philosophers and Protestant theologians gave theories in support of *Säkularisation* and *Säkularisierung.* According to G. W. F. Hegel, the political and social changes throughout German-speaking lands had come about as the human spirit or consciousness had rightly moved to a new, inner appropriation of the Christian faith. Religion and theology were being surpassed by reason and philosophy. Ludwig Feuerbach supported all efforts to remove Christianity from people's lives, since he judged that religious belief is the projection of one's deepest wishes onto the unknown. Further, recasting Hegel's thought into "dialectical materialism," Karl Marx saw secularization as a phase within the liberation of the working class from the "opium" of religion. Finally, Friedrich Nietzsche heralded the "death of God" and the emergence of the *Übermenschen* ("superior human beings") who would step into the place once reserved for God and assert their vision upon history by means of their will-to-power.[12]

The views of Germany's nineteenth-century philosophers and the processes of *Säkularisation* and *Säkularisierung* did not go unchallenged. The exclusion of the church from civil matters went contrary to the Catholic Church's long-standing views of the interconnection between church and state and between Christian faith and society. These views had become institutionalized in the

Holy Roman Empire which King Otto I had founded in 962. But this incarnation of the "Christendom" ideal of society officially ended in 1806 when the Austrian Hapsburg emperor, Francis I, dissolved the Holy Roman Empire. Throughout the 1800s and into the 1900s, conservative German Catholics held that the Holy Roman Empire was the perfect political order, and they pointed to the Middle Ages as the paradigm of the interrelationship between state and church and also between society and Christian belief. During the Weimar Republic, influential Catholics such as Franz von Papen and Carl Schmitt envisioned, in distinct ways, the day when Germany would rid itself of the social, political, and religious effects of the *Aufklärung* and establish a society and government with similarities to the Holy Roman Empire.[13]

The Catholic Church's response to political and cultural secularization, to *Säkularisation* and *Säkularisierung*, assumed at least three forms. First, there arose ultramontanism as a way to safeguard the Christian faith by means of ecclesiastical centralization in Rome. One of ultramontanism's high points was the First Vatican Council's declaration in 1870 on papal infallibility in its Dogmatic Constitution on the Church of Christ, *Pastor Aeternus,* which in effect asserts the pope's authority against the absolutist claims of political figures like Otto von Bismarck. Second, beginning with Pope Pius IX and Pope Leo XIII, the Vatican promoted neoscholasticism as the intellectual bulwark against the Enlightenment. As a result, Catholic philosophers and theologians studied the "perennial" thought of medieval scholasticism and rejected the conceptual categories of the *Aufklärung* and secularization. While thinkers such as Hegel and Marx were struggling with issues related to the meaning of history, neoscholastic scholars held that the topics of history and eschatology had already been treated by medieval theologians in their tracts on "the four last things," namely, death, judgment, heaven, and hell. A third expression of the Catholic Church's response to secularization came in the form of its social teachings. Guided by a belief in natural law, episcopal leaders tried to uphold fundamental human values. Leo XIII defended the rights of workers in his encyclical *Rerum Novarum* (1891). In this constructive approach to urgent social issues, he built on the work of Bishop Wilhelm Ketteler of Mainz.[14]

By the early 1900s other voices were also questioning the new political and social order. Some German intellectuals, influenced by neoromanticism, noted the effects of their nation's industrialization upon society and doubted whether the changes brought about by modernization had been for the best. They observed that whereas in 1871 36 percent of the German people lived in cities, in 1910 60 percent resided in urban areas where they often endured inadequate housing, air pollution, poor health, and unemployment. Also, over these forty years, the German population had jumped from 40 million to 65 million, thereby causing anxiety about sufficient living-space and the quality of life in the future.[15] Criticism sharpened during World War I as its violence cast a dark shadow across the *Aufklärung*'s beliefs in the sufficiency of human reason, the goodness of human nature, and the idea of progress. During the postwar years, conservative views came to expression in Oswald Spengler's two-volume *Decline of the West* (1918, 1922), Karl Jasper's *Psychologie der Weltanschauungen* (1919) and *Man in the Modern Age* (1932), Max Scheler's *On the Eternal in Man* (1921), and Martin Heidegger's *Being and Time* (1927). At the same time, many Protestants felt betrayed by the "cultural Protestantism" of Adolf Harnack and Ernst Troeltsch and discovered the "neo-orthodox" theologies of Karl Barth, Rudolf Bultmann, and Friedrich Gogarten. Amid this social criticism by Catholic officials, conservative intellectuals, and dialectical theologians, Romano Guardini worked to resolve his outlook on contemporary German society.

Coming to Terms with Modernity

THREE SOURCES OF RESISTANCE

Romano Guardini brought his theory of opposition to his view of the *Aufklärung* and the social tendencies within Germany. On the one hand, he disapproved of some aspects of the Enlightenment, for example, its emphasis upon self-autonomy and the separation of social and cultural life from the church.[16] On the other hand, he also perceived the merits of the Enlightenment, for instance, the breakthroughs in the natural sciences and engineering. Further, he realized that the West could not return to the medieval world. As Guardini explains in his *Briefe vom Comersee* and also in *Das Ende der Neuzeit,* the dream of restoring the Middle Ages' political, social, and cultural order is a flawed, neoromantic idea. A realistic assessment recognizes that we cannot go back to an earlier era and that we are, in fact, living through the end of the modern era. At this time, Christians must reject the lure of the past and shape the present and future in the light of Judeo-Christian wisdom.

Guardini did not hold this view at the start of his career but worked toward it during the 1920s. In particular, he overcame three sources which militated against his acceptance of modernity: his lack of roots in Germany, his intellectual attraction to the Middle Ages, and his melancholy.

First, Guardini was never fully rooted in Germany. Throughout his life, he sensed to varying degrees his distance from German life. During his childhood, his family lived on Gonsenheimer Strasse as though on an island. Speaking Italian, they were not connected to Mainz.[17] Although the young Romano fared well at school, he found that "school was an isolated realm to which I went and from which I departed. . . . When I ask myself to which feeling was school linked for me, it was above all estrangement which often increased to fear."[18] According to one of his childhood friends, "Romano Guardini did not act like a foreigner, but we knew that his family had come from distant Italy."[19] In light of this early alienation, it is noteworthy that, during his adult years, the theologian never secured a permanent residence in Germany. As a priest in Mainz, a young professor in Berlin, and a mature professor in Munich, he changed his dwelling every few years. For seven years, he cherished his house in Berlin, which the architect Rudolf Schwarz designed for him, but he had to abandon it. Finally, not only did Guardini never feel settled in Germany, he also eventually realized that he felt most at home on his mother's estate, Isola Vicentina, near his birthplace of Verona.[20]

A second element which inclined Guardini to resist the *Aufklärung* and contemporary life was his intellectual attraction to the medieval world and his discomfort with empirical investigation. As noted in earlier chapters, he grew up with Dante's *Divine Comedy;* in the Schleussner circle, he delighted in the writings of the medieval mystics; and his first publication treated Michelangelo's poetry and letters. By contrast, his lack of success in chemistry and economics was evidence of his inability to grasp twentieth-century empirical methods. At the seminary in Mainz, Guardini was immersed in the church's effort to revive the Middle Ages by means of neoscholastic philosophy and theology—an effort that he found unsatisfactory. Further, in his graduate studies in Freiburg and Bonn, he engaged in his own retrieval of medieval thought as he studied Bonaventure's writings. By 1923, as Guardini assumed his professorship in Berlin, he was very familiar with medieval ideas and less at ease with Enlightenment thought. It is not surprising, therefore, that he initially saw the Middle Ages as embodying the ideal relationship between Christian faith and society.[21]

A third factor which colored Guardini's perceptions of his times was his melancholy. Throughout his life, Guardini struggled with bouts of depression.[22] As a child, he was so strongly afflicted by this mental state that, in his adult years, he spoke of seeing his youth as though situated "under water."[23] Also, as already noted, in 1906 Guardini became so despondent over his studies that he entertained suicidal thoughts.[24] Once he was settled in his vocation as a priest and professor, he coped with his depression and wrote about it in "Vom

Sinn der Schwermut" ("The Meaning of Melancholy" [1928]).[25] Nevertheless, he continued to suffer from it.[26] This melancholic disposition surely influenced his perceptions of life, so that he readily saw the world's inadequacies.[27]

Given these three factors, Guardini was not spontaneously inclined to see the good in modernization. Yet, he came to a point in the mid-1920s when he accepted the current state of affairs and resolved to improve it through Christian humanism. In 1926 he expressed his point of view in "Gedanken über das Verhältnis von Christentum und Kultur" (Thoughts on the relationship between Christianity and culture).[28] One year later, he shared his struggle to reach this outlook in *Briefe vom Comersee.*

BRIEFE VOM COMERSEE (1927)

Throughout the 1920s Guardini's mother resided at Lake Como, and Romano visited her there in the summers. In this majestic natural setting the young scholar reflected on the differences between life at Lake Como and life in Berlin. Desiring to put his impressions on paper, Guardini wrote nine letters to his friend Pastor Josef Weiger from 1923 through 1925. Then, with encouragement from Weiger, he published these letters in *Die Schildgenossen* over a period of two years, and in 1927 he collected them in *Briefe vom Comersee.*[29] Since these letters convey Guardini's steps toward his point of view on modernity, I will review three of them: the first, second, and ninth letters.

In the first letter (summer 1923), written from Lake Como, Guardini describes his trip through the valleys of Brianza from Milan to Como. As he tells it, after the train left the urban area, there appeared vistas of green fields and wooded hills with clusters of houses and gardens. At one point, however, they passed a factory where wood crates and waste littered the surrounding area. Struck by the contrast between the refuse and the landscape, he saw that the negative effects of industrialization had spread into Italy, and he felt sadness "for a life which is doomed to perish" (p. 8).

In the second letter (summer 1923), also written from Lake Como, Guardini describes in romantic imagery the old culture. In his judgment, this way of life rests on the harmony of human beings, nature, and human artifacts. It is an "organic" world, a world in which people use their technology to bring human life and nature into closer cooperation. This harmonious arrangement is evident in the sailboat, which permits people to harness the wind but does not distance them from the wind and water. Similar manifestations of the coherent character of the old order include the plough, the candle, and the traditional Italian homes with their open hearths. This culture is also embodied in rural family physicians who, because they know their patients from birth into adult-hood and are familiar with their extended families, view a particular illness within the bigger picture of a person's life. But this interconnected way of life is dying, even in Italy, and "[t]he sphere in which we live is becoming more and more . . . *barbarian* [my emphasis]. The profound sadness of this whole pro-cess [of decline] lies over Italy" (p. 17).

Before proceeding to the ninth letter, two observations are appropriate. First, in his initial letters Guardini, like a romantic artist, painted bright, naturalis-tic scenes in the foreground of his canvas and dark, urban scenes in the back-ground. The young scholar surely viewed the world through the neoromanti-cism that predominated in postwar Germany. Second, these two letters exude a melancholy that suggests a desire to withdraw from the twentieth century. If we read no further, we would expect that he eventually retreated from Berlin to a secluded haven in Italy. However, the later letters tell a different tale.

In the ninth and last letter (autumn 1925), written from Berlin, Guardini states that he has made a "decision." He now sees that he cannot flee to the past, to the old order. Such a flight is easy to entertain, for people do not feel linked to the new order; indeed, "we are homeless in the midst of *barbarism* [my em-phasis]" (p. 79). Yet, he has come to see that to flee to the past would be to succumb to romanticism. Instead of fleeing, one must accept modernity with the aim of changing it from within itself. According to Guardini, the present era (beginning prior to the Enlightenment) came about in part because Chris-tianity set people free from their deification of natural powers. There is reason to believe, therefore, that Christian faith can continue to influence Western thought and culture. Christians must strive to understand this new era—its presuppositions, methods, and goals—so that they can shape it for the better-ment of all peoples and nature. In sum: "We must first say yes to our age" (p. 84).

There are grounds for hope, Guardini states. Perhaps with the Bauhaus school in mind, he asserts that imaginative people are fashioning forms of art and architecture that display a harmony of human life, nature, and culture. Moreover, since people possess an inner "dynamic core" that God has planted in them and still nourishes, they have the potential of rediscovering their inner selves and creating a new, humane world. Indeed, in Guardini's judgment, a fresh impulse from God is at work in human minds and hearts. We can be confident, therefore, that the human community will take new steps to renew God's creation. He concludes: "History is going forward in the depths, and we must be ready to play our part, trusting in what God is doing and in the forces that he has made to stir within us" (p. 96).

As this last letter shows, Guardini's outlook changed from 1923 to 1925. He removed his image of the old order from the pedestal and began to measure the new order on its own terms. At the same time, he stopped sketching sentimental scenes of Italy and pursued a more analytic approach to the situation. As a result, his mood became more positive. Having resolved some of his ambiguity toward the present day, he made acceptance the starting point for his reflections on contemporary culture.[30] As though signaling this shift in perspective, he wrote the ninth letter from Berlin, not from Lake Como. Guardini maintained this hopeful attitude, even during the Third Reich, and eventually conveyed it in *Freiheit, Gnade, Schicksal* and *Das Ende der Neuzeit.*

Personal Existence in the Modern World

FREIHEIT, GNADE, SCHICKSAL (1948)

During Hitler's tyranny, Romano Guardini reflected on personal freedom and expressed some of his thoughts in a talk entitled "Freiheit, Schicksal, Gnade," which he gave at Greifswald outside of Berlin in 1943.[31] Four years later, he expanded on this paper as he lectured at the University of Tübingen (1947–48) on Pascal's understanding of personal existence. These lectures produced *Freiheit, Gnade, Schicksal* (*Freedom, Grace and Destiny*), in which Guardini observes that, for twelve years, the German people had relinquished their personal independence to the state, and, in the postwar years, they would need to learn once again how to exercise it.[32] Towards this goal, he proposes a Christian understanding of personal freedom that he anchors in the thought of Augustine and Pascal.[33]

According to Guardini, personal freedom possesses three major aspects. First, the form or mode of freedom consists of personal initiative. A free action is one which ultimately originates out of a person's self-agency. A person comes to see that he or she is "the effective starting point of the process, which must now be more precisely termed the action" (p. 15). Contrary to philosophies of determinism, human beings possess the ability to shape their thoughts, actions, and relationships on the basis of their independent choice. Second, the goal or object of personal freedom is fullness of life, our "right relation to being" (p. 70). Contrary to the skepticism of Kant and Nietzsche, we can apprehend objective reality with its inherent values. In fact, our freedom is directed toward reality, for we seek to participate in being itself (p. 51). Third, personal freedom arises from self-relating and reflection, and is constitutive of personal existence. For this reason, we must protect and nurture our self-knowledge and ability to think critically (pp. 62–63).

From a solely humanistic point of view, Guardini could end his pheno-menological analysis at this point. However, from a Christian point of view he needs to shed light on our relationship to the one who is the wellspring of per-sonal freedom: the God of Jesus Christ. Christian faith perceives that our independence increases as we become united with God. Such a thought is, of course, judged to be wrong by many contemporary minds—Feuerbach, Marx, Nietzsche, and Freud—who insist that human beings reach full maturity only by outgrowing their religious beliefs and disavowing God, in other words, by a secularization that results in atheism (p. 87). But this narrow view of self-autonomy misconceives the relationship between human initiative and divine initiative, for it holds that for the one to increase the other must decrease. But such is not the case. On the contrary, a human being's self-agency does not compete with God's self-agency, rather grace ignites and strengthens the hu-man will. What the Christian discovers is that "because Christ lives in me, I am finally able to be *myself*—that *self* which God had in mind when He created me and there awoke in me my power of initiative, decision and self-develop-ment." In faith, we see that "God's initiative is everything and yet, because of it, [a person] becomes free and endowed with vigor" (p. 75).

According to Guardini, the paradigm of true independence is St. Paul. As a Pharisee, Saul of Tarsus relied on his own strength. He displayed his form of personal freedom as he asserted himself in pursuit of faithfulness to the Jewish Law. Paul "had a passionate longing for justice; he desired earnestly and sin-cerely to be free and struggled for this freedom against very difficult obstacles." But this self-will eventually broke down. "He failed to understand that evil must not only be combatted but also overcome through wisdom and patience." Then, at the trial of Stephen, Saul sensed "a mysterious spiritual power" among Jesus' followers—a power which contains "nothing of that weariness of for-mal fulfillment of the law, that tortuous struggle to achieve good by one's own strength, that futility and frustration he had been experiencing." This in-cident led to Saul's encounter with Christ on the road to Damascus, a meeting in which he arrived at a radically new experience and understanding of free-dom. With his fall, he discovered a strength—namely, grace—which was not his own. Then, in surrendering himself to Christ, he found himself liberated to live at once in closer union with God and also in greater personal wholeness.

In Guardini's words: "Paul stands now in a totally new attitude of life which subsequently he will express in the often recurring words: 'I in Christ and Christ in me.'" In light of Paul's conversion and profound witness to it, he "appears expressly as the prophet of the new freedom" (pp. 66–68).

Guardini's analysis of personal freedom may seem at first glance to be solely a scholarly exercise within the church's ongoing discussion of grace and free will. To be sure, it provides a Christian response to Enlightenment views of self-autonomy, and it also contributes to a theological topic that, emerging in St. Paul's letters, runs through the writings of Augustine, Martin Luther and John Calvin, Thomas Aquinas and Louis de Molina, and Pascal. But *Freiheit, Gnade, Schicksal* also establishes the foundation for Guardini's view of the way in which the German people should rebuild their lives and society after the Third Reich. This view came to expression in *Das Ende der Neuzeit.*

DAS ENDE DER NEUZEIT (1950)

The lectures which Guardini gave at the University of Tübingen in 1947 led not only to *Freiheit, Gnade, Schicksal* but to another book as well. During his stay at Mooshausen from 1943 into 1945, Guardini returned to the topic that he had treated twenty years earlier in *Briefe vom Comersee:* a Christian view of the twentieth century. Then, as he endured *Stunde Null,* his thoughts crystallized.[34] He brought these reflections to his lectures at Tübingen and subsequently to his lectures at the University of Munich. In 1950 he published them in *Das Ende der Neuzeit.*

In order to glimpse some of the many ideas in this short, complex text, I will address three questions. First, according to Guardini, what is the character of the modern age? Second, what are the properties that distinguish Western society in the postwar years? Third, what is the status of Christian faith at mid-century?

The Modern Era

In Guardini's judgment, Western civilization is nearing the end of its third epoch. The first age, antiquity, began in the fifth century B.C., especially in Greece, and ran until the eighth century A.D. It rested on the assumption that "the universe itself was the whole of reality." For example, when Parmenides spoke about a "pure being," he had in mind "a principle [within the universe] to which the multiplicity of experience turned as to its ultimate source." The second era, the Middle Ages, commenced in the ninth century and proceeded into the fourteenth century. It was founded on an understanding of divine transcendence. The medieval mind acknowledged the disclosure "of a God who holds his Being separate and beyond the world." It appropriated Ptolemy's insight that God dwells outside creation in the "empyrean" and yet is active within the world. The third epoch, modernity, emerged in the fifteenth century, reached its zenith in the nineteenth century, and during the twentieth century is moving toward its conclusion when a new, as yet unknown epoch will emerge.[35]

As in previous eras, the modern age has its own sense of the universe. It assumes that the universe is constituted by "an unending space-time relationship" (p. 17). The universe itself is seen to be an infinite or endless reality, open to determination by the human intellect and will. As understood by Giordano Bruno (d. 1600), the cosmos consists of an endless number of possible universes. Today, the notion of infinity does not concern a transcendent reality, rather it expresses the limitless reality of time and space. One manifestation of this outlook is our persistent explorations both outward, beyond geographical boundaries, and simultaneously inward, into the subatomic elements of matter. Inherent in this mentality is an optimism about the natural order, human beings, and the relationship between the two. There persists a "faith in progress" (p. 50). This positive attitude is exhibited in the three major aspects of modern consciousness: its view of the natural order, its understanding of human beings, and its sense of culture (p. 94). I will consider here only what Guardini says about our age's understanding of personal existence.

An identifying element of our consciousness is the notion of human subjectivity. Modernity is marked by the turn to the knowing subject, the "I." As perceived by Kant, a human being is an autonomous, rational being whose capabilities and processes of inquiry and self-reflection shape what is known and what comes about. The "I" then possesses ultimate value. In relation to the material world, human beings recognize their subjectivity, that is, their awareness of themselves as knowers who can comprehend the principles of the natural order and also the laws of their own knowing. The ideal for human life is to develop one's full potential, to become a full "personality." To a large extent, human subjects are the makers of their world. Hence, the human subject stands as a value in himself or herself. Or, according to Guardini, in our epoch "[t]he 'I'—particularly the 'I' of the extraordinary genius—became the measure by which all human life was judged" (p. 56).

Given its self-understanding, modernity leaves no conceptual space for revelation. When it considers the autonomy of the human intellect, it sees little point in talking about God's involvement in human affairs. The contemporary mind asks: "If God is truly God, what does this mean for the autonomy of human life? Does God really act [in history] if human beings have initiative and creativity, as claimed by modernity?"[36] Further, the independent use of the human mind demands that we set aside tradition and authority, which are essential properties of religious belief. Although avoiding explicitly Christian language, the twentieth century has nevertheless adopted some Christian ideas and values, as in the notion of person, the dignity of the human being, and the demythologizing of human activity. All the same, it has tried to establish its own "rational" basis for these notions and convictions apart from their true foundation in revelation. For instance, it has preserved Christian ethics while discarding Christian doctrine. It is fair to say, therefore, that contemporary thinkers have displayed a "dishonesty" regarding modernity's origins and sources (p. 65).

The End of the Modern Age

Guardini perceives that since the early 1900s the West has entered into the "dissolution" (*Auflösung*) of modernity. More and more voices have questioned belief in progress, and by mid-century there emerged a fresh awareness of the presence of evil in the human heart and history. As a consequence, people now take issue with the Enlightenment's assumptions concerning the self-sufficiency of reason, the goodness of human nature, and the notion of progress. Given our doubts, we are living in the last phase of the modern epoch (pp. 68–69).

One manifestation of our late modernity is our revised understanding of personal existence. At its height in the 1700s and 1800s, the modern mind stressed the importance of a few people becoming "personalities," that is, becoming unusually creative individuals (e.g., Goethe). Now, however, we recognize that every human being is a person, an inviolable reality who possesses a dignity in himself or herself regardless of his or her explicit originality. Guardini points out that "the idea of the creative personality formed out of its own inner resources, that is, the [fully] autonomous subject, is apparently now no longer the ideal."[37] We currently acknowledge that each human being is a knowing subject with a dignity that stems not from what he or she accomplishes but simply from his or her being.

Concurrent with this awareness of each human being as a personal subject, there has surfaced the view that a human being is an object which we can study in empirical ways, for example, by means of statistical studies. We now perceive someone as one among the "masses." This perception of human existence has resulted in an ambiguity. On the one hand, there are occasions when a man or woman receives unparalleled respect simply for being a human being and, on the other hand, there are situations in which we completely lose sight of someone's dignity as a person (pp. 80–81). Although Guardini does not give these examples, we need think only of the conflicting ways in which we treat the unborn and the elderly. In some cases, we go to great lengths to preserve life, and, in other cases, we choose death.

One thing that is refreshing about late modernity, Guardini points out, is that there is a new consistency and honesty in the rejection of the Judeo-Christian tradition. Contemporary society not only disavows Christian doctrines, it has also rid itself of its implicit espousal of Christian ethics. People are no longer required by law to protect human life in its first months or in its last years. The culture is now so thoroughly secular that it no longer takes for granted the values generated by Christian faith. In short, we live in a post-Christian world. One merit of this order, Guardini notes, is that people are now able to choose their values and live them out (pp. 90–92).

Finally, as modernity approaches its end, we live in a situation with much potential for good and also for evil.[38] We face opportunities to discover anew the wonders of creation, human life, and personal relationships. Yet, simultaneously, we have at our disposal the means to deprive people of their dignity. Without an agreed upon system of values and beliefs, society is vulnerable to the control of one group with great power. It is imperative, therefore, that people reflect on the uses and abuses of power (pp. 108–12). As we will see, Guardini himself undertook such a reflection in *Die Macht* (*Power and Responsibility* [1951]).

Being Christian Today

How then does Christian faith relate to society in this last phase of the modern era? Or, to be more specific, where is there a point of difference and also a point of convergence between Christian life and modern society? According to Guardini, a source of misunderstanding between Christians and their nonreligious contemporaries will increasingly be the reality of the holy. Guardini predicted that, in a secular, technological culture, few people will have a "natural religious experience" (p. 116, n. 4). They will not have a sense of a being greater than themselves and thus will find the Christian faith incomprehensible and consider it an irrational attitude left over from an earlier age. Talk about God and prayer will highlight the gap between Christians and their nonreligious neighbors.

Yet, according to Guardini, the Christian faith may be able to engage in a dialogue with society concerning the inherent value of personal existence. As already noted, there is a consensus that all human beings are persons and, therefore, possess dignity regardless of their accomplishments. One expression of this secular value is the recognition of the importance of a collegiality in which all participants contribute to an endeavor according to their respective talents. Less and less will a single person stand out for his or her creativity. Rather, teams of people will jointly accomplish something which, because of its complexity, could not be attained by one researcher working alone (e.g., breakthroughs in medicine). Another indication of the value of personal existence will be the acknowledgment that the social sciences do not give a complete view of human existence (p. 98). They do not possess categories by which to glimpse the human spirit and its potential for independence.

In Guardini's judgment, the new awareness of the dignity of human beings as persons can serve as a point at which Christian faith can contribute to late modernity. The Judeo-Christian tradition possesses a wealth of wisdom about personal existence. This treasure includes the insight that a person is an "incommunicable being," "that uniqueness who comes to life not because of special talent and advantage of social circumstance but because she or he has been called forth by God."[39] Contained in these comments are three distinct points. First, a person is a mystery, an irreducible reality, who is constituted by more than other human beings can know. Second, a person's dignity rests not in an activity or accomplishment but in his or her very being. These two ideas are ones with which our secular society would agree. There is, however, a third point that is more troublesome.

According to the Christian faith, human dignity is anchored in its transcendent source, God. The only sure safeguard of the value of a person is the acknowledgment of the person's calling by God. This claim is, of course, unacceptable to the secular mind. Yet Guardini insists that there is only one guarantee against the pressure in a totalitarian state or a utilitarian society to treat human beings as objects. This one assurance is the recognition that personal existence is grounded in the God of Jesus Christ. Pressing his point, Guardini asks, "what is the decisive element of a human being?" and answers that it is

[t]o be a person. Called forth by God. Thus capable of being responsible for oneself and of entering into the real world by means of one's inner powers of initiative. This element makes every person unique. Not because the person

would have singular talents, but because in the clear and absolute sense every person is indispensable, irreplaceable, and inviolate. . . . [A] person is one who exists in relation to God, one who is inviolate in dignity, one who is irreplaceable in the responsibility, which is called forth with a spiritual decisiveness, that was previously not possible.[40]

The Christian faith speaks also to the value of solidarity, for it highlights the fact that relating to God is essential if one is to relate well to oneself and others. To be sure, the secular mind can apprehend the importance of interpersonal relationships for human life. But what it fails to see is that all of our "I-you" relationships with other human beings rest upon our "I-you" relationship with God. In standing before God who is the perfect "you," each of us discovers himself or herself as an "I" who also depends on other human beings. Guardini writes:

> Being a person is essential to being human. A person comes clearly into view and is affirmable by ethical choice when a relationship to the living-personal God comes about by means of the revelation of God's communal life and providence. . . . Thus knowledge of what it means to be a person is bound up with Christian faith.[41]

In noting points of convergence and difference between Christian faith and society at mid-century, Guardini brought to *Das Ende der Neuzeit* topics that he previously treated in *Briefe vom Comersee* and *Freiheit, Gnade, Schicksal*. Reaffirming his decision of the mid-1920s, he has conveyed the view that the starting point of a cultural analysis must be an acceptance of the current state of affairs. A Christian view of the modern world must first of all understand a culture on its own terms. Then, one must proceed by recognizing that there exists an opposition or creative tension but not a contradiction between Christian faith and secular society. It is essential to acknowledge what is held in common and what is an area of disagreement. In this regard, the notion of personal existence is a fruitful point for dialogue with modernity.

In *Freiheit, Gnade, Schicksal* and *Das Ende der Neuzeit* Guardini discusses what is distinctive to the Christian understanding of personal existence but he does so from two different points of view. In *Freiheit, Gnade, Schicksal*, he explains that personal existence requires a freedom which is a function of one's relationship with God. Contrary to modern views on the matter, the greater a person's trust in God, the greater the person's independence in relation to God. Christian faith should not, therefore, stifle freedom but should ignite it. In *Das Ende der Neuzeit*, Guardini observes that personal existence is characterized by interpersonal relationships, whose wellspring is one's intimacy with God. Although the secular mind ignores it, at the heart of all "I-you" relationships among people is each person's intimacy with God. Christian belief should not, therefore, erode our interdependence but provide the foundation for faithfulness and forgiveness. In effect, Guardini has shown that Christianity need not withdraw from contemporary life but should take the initiative to make its wisdom available to all people.

Toward Vatican II on the Church in the Modern World

THE NEED FOR A THEOLOGY OF THE WORLD

At mid-century Romano Guardini was not the only German scholar who was reflecting upon freedom, history, and Christian faith. From the mid-1940s into the 1950s, in response to the terror of Hitler's Reich and the rebuilding of German society, numerous German philosophers and theologians wrote on these topics. Among the books that appeared were Friedrich Meinecke's *Die deutsche Katastrophe* (1946), Alfred Weber's *Abschied von der bisherigen Geschichte* (1946), Karl Jasper's *Vom Ursprung und Ziel der Geschichte* (1949), Karl Löwith's *Meaning in History* (1949), Ernst Jünger's *Über die Linie* (1950), Josef Pieper's *Über das Ende der Zeit* (1950), Friedrich Gogarten's *Verhängnis und Hoffnung: Die Säkularisierung als theologisches Problem* (1953). Also, Walter Benjamin, Theodor Adorno, and Jürgen Habermas collaborated through Frankfurt's Institute for Social Research.[42] Whereas after the First World War German scholars such as Karl Barth, Romano Guardini, Rudolf Otto, and Max Scheler wrote on the transcendent, objective reality of God, after the Second World War German philosophers and theologians took up the issue of meaning and history, and Guardini was again among them.[43]

Guardini's work stands out among these diverse postwar writings for a number of reasons. First, his *Das Ende der Neuzeit* (1950) and Pieper's *Über das Ende der Zeit* (1950) are two of the earliest writings by German Catholics on the issue of faith and history. Second, since his text was accessible to general readers, it influenced the thinking of many German Catholics. Third, Guardini followed this book with further analyses of modernity. And fourth, *Das Ende der Neuzeit* contributed to a discussion that fifteen years later influenced Vatican II's Pastoral Constitution on the Church in the Modern World.[44] The third and fourth points warrant elaboration.

In 1951, one year after the publication of *Das Ende der Neuzeit*, Guardini completed *Die Macht*, in which he develops the insight that, since the Enlightenment, the Western mind has gained greater and greater access to forces within nature, the human psyche, and society, and it has simultaneously shown that it is capable of using these energies for both good and ill. With the totalitarian regimes of Stalin, Mussolini, and Hitler in mind as well as the bombing of Dresden, Hiroshima, and Nagasaki, he writes: "In the coming epoch, the issue will ultimately concern not how to increase power . . . but how to limit it. This challenge will form the epoch's central concern, to direct power so that human beings can remain human beings in their use of it."[45] One of the indications that we are living at the end of the modern age, Guardini points out, is that we now question the Enlightenment's assumptions about the sufficiency of reason, the goodness of human nature, and the inevitability of progress. As Nietzsche argued in the late 1800s, we stand, like Prometheus, in the place that we once reserved for God. But, contrary to Nietzsche's vision, we have employed our power in "demonic" ways. As a result of these abuses, we suffer from a high degree of anxiety. At mid-century many people have asked, can we direct the energies that we have released solely to constructive uses?[46] In Guardini's judgment, we can give an affirmative answer if our age can see the world as God's creation in which God calls the human family to care for the earth and make it fruitful (Gen 1:28).

After the publication of *Das Ende der Neuzeit* and *Die Macht* Guardini intended to write a third book on the thought of Nietzsche, entitled "Die Macht und der Nihilismus," and hence have a trilogy on modernity. Unfortunately, he did not finish this manuscript.[47] Nevertheless, in the 1950s he proposed the fashioning of a "theology of the world"—a topic which has received much attention in the post–Vatican II church, for example, in the writings of Johannes Metz.[48] In his essay "Zur Theologie der Welt" (Toward a theology of the world [1959]) Guardini observes that, while in the Enlightenment's view the world is "nature," in the biblical view the world is God's "creation." In this perspective, Christians have a responsibility to witness to God's intention for the earth by acting for its well-being. It no longer suffices for Christians to examine their consciences solely in reference to their personal sins. For the Christian "a new task has become clear: to preserve God's work." To bring creation to the fulfillment which God intends, each follower of Jesus Christ "must comprehend the ethical obligation in which he or she not only says 'I should guard myself against sin' but also 'I should be concerned that all becomes right in the world.' "[49]

In an effort to promote the proper use of power, Guardini described those human qualities or traits which are good in themselves and also result in action on behalf of creation.[50] In 1963 he provided a phenomenological analysis of sixteen "virtues" in his *Tugenden: Meditationen über Gestalten Sittlichen Leben* (*The Virtues: On Forms of the Moral Life*). This insightful book, inspired in part by Max Scheler's writings on moral values, was not an afterthought in the theologian's literary corpus but the fruit of forty years of lecturing and writing on Christian values.[51] In 1921 Guardini published a collection of essays on the moral life, entitled *Gottes Werkleute: Briefe über Selbstbildung* (God's laborers: Letters on the formation of the self), which went through four revised editions, the last of which appeared in 1930 entitled *Briefe über Selbstbildung.*[52] Moreover, in Berlin and Munich Guardini regularly lectured on Christian ethics.[53] Further, in both *Das Ende der Neuzeit* and *Die Macht* he discusses the virtues needed in our age: honesty, courage, and asceticism.[54] In order to glimpse Guardini's thought on the moral life we will look at his "meditation" in *Tugenden* on the virtue of reverence (*Ehrfurcht*).[55]

According to Guardini, reverence or respect is the personal trait or virtue which "creates a spiritual space in which that which deserves reverence can stand erect, detached and free, in all its splendor" (p. 46). Having originated in the primal sense of honor and fear in the presence of "the holy," reverence shows itself today as respect for another person. It recognizes that a human being is a person, an "I." "Respect desires privacy for the other person, in the sphere of his own being and in connection with those with whom he lives and to whom he is related, his family and friends." For example, I would show respect if I did not photograph someone who is weeping at the funeral of a loved one. Further, our respect becomes reverence when we figuratively "stand back" in the presence of a great person or work of art. In religious belief, reverence is our "adoration of God" which we manifest in such gestures as kneeling, bowing, and not speaking. This reverence is our acknowledgment of God's otherness. What we fail to realize, Guardini notes, is that as we may show reverence to God, God conveys reverence to us, for God has created us with personal freedom so that we can choose or reject God. Concluding this meditation, he observes that God's "creative reverence is the 'space' in which we exist. In our day, when that terrible mixture of arrogance and folly which is called atheism is flooding the world, it is good to think of that truth" (p. 54).

After the publication of *Tugenden,* Guardini intended to publish his complete theological ethics but did not realize this intention.[56] However, Hans Mercker and the Katholische Akademie in Bayern have edited and recently published the manuscript, entitled *Ethik.* This two-volume work contains the theologian's reflections on the pursuit of "the good" in the twentieth century.[57]

TOWARD *GAUDIUM ET SPES* (1965)

Vatican II's Pastoral Constitution on the Church in the Modern World is "a document unprecedented in conciliar history."[58] Breaking with the heritage in which councils have focused their attention on the church's inner life and teachings, this council spoke not only *ad intra* but also *ad extra*, not only to issues primarily within the Christian community but also to the challenges facing the human family. Further, overcoming the negative posture toward the world conveyed by Pope Pius IX in his Syllabus of Errors (1864) and by Pope Pius X in *Pascendi Dominici gregis* and *Lamentabili* (1907), Vatican II adopted a positive, though not uncritical, stance toward modernity. These two shifts came about not as the result of thunderbolts from the sky but because of the labor and hardship of Catholic leaders over many decades. Romano Guardini was one of these forerunners of the pastoral constitution.[59] *Gaudium et Spes* embraces his cultural analysis and simultaneously goes beyond it.

Gaudium et Spes possesses the polarities or opposition that Guardini had earlier described: on the one hand, human autonomy, and, on the other hand, our relationship with God in Jesus Christ. It recognizes the value of appropriate independence, which it understands not as rebellion against God but as the rightful dignity of human beings before God and in relation to the church. The document states: "Women and men as individuals and as members of society crave a life that is full, autonomous, and worthy of their nature as human beings"[60] (n. 9). Admittedly, there is "apprehension today that a close association between human activity and religion will endanger the autonomy of humanity, of organizations and of science." This wariness has, of course, come about because of unfortunate incidents when the Vatican interfered in human learning, for example, in its censoring of Galileo (d. 1642). Renouncing this kind of interference, the pastoral constitution recognizes the "rightful autonomy of earthly affairs" (n. 36). Also, it declares that "we cannot but deplore certain attitudes (not unknown among Christians) deriving from a shortsighted view of the rightful autonomy of science." The guiding principle is this: "By the very nature of creation, material being is endowed with its own stability, truth and excellence, its own order and laws" (n. 36).

While affirming the proper autonomy of human life, *Gaudium et Spes* upholds the importance of our relationship to God in Jesus Christ. It observes that life's central issues, such as suffering and evil, have their ultimate solution in relation to Jesus Christ (n. 10). Further, it observes that women and men realize their personal freedom only as they cooperate with God's grace (n. 17).

Speaking of Jesus Christ as the "new Adam," the pastoral constitution states that personal autonomy is attainable as the human community enters into union with Jesus Christ. "For since Christ died for everyone, and since all are in fact called to one and the same destiny, which is divine, we must hold that the Holy Spirit offers to all people the possibility of being made partners, in a way known to God, in the paschal mystery" (n. 22). It reiterates this idea when it declares that "the Spirit makes all of them free . . . stretching out to that future day when humanity itself will become an offering acceptable by God" (n. 38).

These ideas bear a resemblance to Guardini's thoughts on freedom, history, and Christian faith. In acknowledging the proper autonomy of human life, on the one hand, and, on the other, the necessity of union with God in Jesus Christ, *Gaudium et Spes* embraces the creative tension or opposition (*Gegensatz*) that Guardini recognized in *Das Ende der Neuzeit, Die Macht,* and "Zur Theologie der Welt." However, the council also went beyond Guardini's work in at least two ways.

First, the council assumed a more positive stance toward the contemporary age than Guardini had.[61] Whereas he stressed that the church's message about revelation necessarily "offends" those who do not possess Christian faith, Vatican II emphasized that the church must acknowledge the truths which are already held by those outside the church. The pastoral constitution points out that there is much of value in modernity and that the church has learned from those who stand outside the church. One manifestation of this positive regard is the pastoral constitution's affirmation of democracy (n. 75). By contrast, as we noted in chapter 6, Guardini remained skeptical about democracy.[62] A second expression of Vatican II's positive stance is its affirmation of religious liberty in *Gaudium et Spes* (n. 17) and also in its Declaration on Religious Freedom, *Dignitatis Humanae* (December 7, 1965). For the first time, the Catholic Church officially acknowledged that the church itself as well as governments must respect people's dignity in choosing and exercising their religious beliefs. In this regard, contrary to Guardini's prediction, people have continued to have religious experiences in the second half of the twentieth century.[63] With these specific views, Vatican II communicated a stronger positive regard for modern life than is evident in Guardini's writings.[64]

Second, Vatican II went beyond Guardini's work in its acknowledgment that history and society are more complex than his cultural analysis considered.[65] This outlook is evident in the council's attentiveness to sociopolitical issues and its formulation of principles within social ethics. It deliberately adopted the trajectory of social teachings that includes Bishop Ketteler's work in Germany, Leo XIII's *Rerum Novarum* (1891), Carl Sonnenschein's programs in Berlin, and John XXIII's *Mater et Magister* (1961) and *Pacem in Terris* (1963). Whereas Guardini focused solely on personal morality in his *Tugenden* and *Ethik,* the council widened its scope to include the ethical responsibilities of institutions, organizations, and governments. Moreover, *Gaudium et Spes* sees that sociopolitical issues and culture are intertwined. It implicitly calls into question, therefore, Guardini's tendency to discuss cultural topics without also considering the social and political factors surrounding this topic.[66] Finally, the council also surpassed the work of Guardini by presenting the church as the advocate for human dignity and values within society. As we saw in chapter 3, he highlighted four aspects of church: its communal, sacramental, institutional, and prophetic dimensions. While the council surely upheld these essential elements of the church, it also described the church as the servant for the coming of God's kingdom.[67]

Gaudium et Spes is an extraordinary document, whose vision of the church's mission in society continues to challenge Catholicism. It is a statement that few, if any, episcopal leaders foresaw when John XXIII convoked the Second Vatican Council on December 25, 1961. Nevertheless, in hindsight we know that, in the decades prior to the council, Catholic minds were formulating ideas about Christian faith and modernity that prepared the way for *Gaudium et Spes.* To be sure, a number of scholars (e.g., Jacques Maritain) directly contributed to the council's emphasis on the dignity of the person. All the same, Guardini's recurring thoughts on the character of personal existence and on the possibilities for fruitful dialogue between Christian faith and modernity prepared the way for some of Vatican II's most visionary statements.

AN INTERPRETER OF TRUTH

The previous chapters have highlighted three ways in which Romano Guardini helped to prepare the way for the Second Vatican Council. Chapter 1 has shown that Guardini was a forerunner of the council by means of his life itself. Long before it was acceptable in ecclesiastical circles, he broke out of a self-enclosed church and entered into a dialogue with current ideas and culture. The first chapter has also explained how he set aside the deductive logic of neoscholasticism and adopted an inductive approach to theology. In his readiness to learn from his pastoral activities, he aided in the formation of a theological method anchored in experience which Vatican II followed in its attempt to read "the signs of the times." Guardini's third contribution to the renewal of Catholicism consisted of the themes that he developed in his many writings. Chapters 2 through 8 have clarified his understanding of revelation, the church, the liturgy, world literature, Nazism, Jesus Christ, and Christian faith in a modern world, and they have also elucidated how the ideas that Guardini promoted came to maturity in *Dei Verbum, Lumen Gentium, Sacrosanctum concilium, Nostra Aetate,* and *Gaudium et Spes.*

One major question remains: what was the unifying dynamism of Guardini's thought? What held together this scholar's wide-ranging interests?

The answer is that Guardini integrated his thought in relation to his twofold commitment to mine the wisdom of the Judeo-Christian tradition and to bring this truth into dialogue with twentieth-century thought. He pinpointed this dynamism when, in 1944, he observed that "[w]hat I wanted from the beginning—initially by instinct, then always more deliberately—was to bring the truth to light."[1] Ten years later, he made the same point: "The truth has a bright and calm power. In my pastoral work I have one aim: to help by means of the truth."[2] (Today this statement is cast in a bronze plaque in memory of Guardini that hangs in Munich's St. Ludwig Church.) About the same time, he also wrote: "I have the feeling that I have presented not something specialized, a specific thought or a specific form, but a consistent interpretation of the Christian-Catholic reality."[3] In other words, Romano Guardini saw himself as an interpreter of the truth about God and our personal existence.[4]

In order to glimpse this unifying drive in Guardini's life and thought I will review his late autobiographical writings and then recall the impression that he made upon his readers. Thus, this chapter has two parts. First, it shows that as Guardini neared the end of his life, he anguished anew over questions about God and human life. Second, it describes how his pursuit of wisdom influenced Catholics in North America and Germany.

Waiting on God

GUARDINI'S LAST YEARS

On Romano Guardini's eightieth birthday (February 17, 1965) the University of Munich held an *akademische Feier*, an "academic celebration," in honor of its professor emeritus. Karl Rahner, Guardini's successor at the university, gave the main address, and afterwards Guardini himself made a short statement.[5] (Both talks are reviewed below.) Also, the celebration's hosts presented the octogenarian with a *Festschrift* entitled *Interpretation der Welt* (Interpretation of the world). This 750-page book contains forty-four essays, written by preeminent scholars such as Hans Urs von Balthasar, Jean Daniélou, Friedrich Heiler, Gabriel Marcel, Josef Pieper, Karl Rahner, Paul Ricoeur, and Michael Schmaus. The letter of dedication at the start of the *Festschrift* explains the book's title. Addressed to Guardini, it states in part:

> You have spoken to us as *an interpreter* [my emphasis]—not only of the divine word but also of the world, which discloses itself in the word. Thus, you have sought us out where we, as this world's children and sons and daughters of this age, already stand with our opinions and thoughts. However, this interpretation has not allowed us to remain where we stood: it possesses an anagogical sense. For, it has uncovered the indications of our kinship with God in our participation in the world, the eternal element in our participation in our age.[6]

This *akademische Feier* was a fitting tribute to an "interpreter" of God's word and world. Amazingly, throughout his last years, Guardini continued to work on his books *Die Existenz des Christen* (1976) and *Ethik* (1993). Further, Munich's academic celebration culminated many celebrations which, beginning in the early 1950s, had honored Romano Guardini. These honors included the Peace Prize of the German Book Association in 1952, the Federal Republic of Germany's Great Medal of Merit in 1959, and the European community's Erasmus Prize in 1962. It was on the occasion of his eightieth birthday, too, that Paul VI invited the theologian to join the college of cardinals.[7] The scholar, who felt little respect in academic and ecclesiastical circles during his years in Berlin, was time and again lauded during his tenure in Munich.

Guardini cherished these honors. On February 22, 1954, he wrote in his diary: "[Professor Hermann] Kunisch has written that the University of Berlin's faculty of philosophy has decided to give me an honorary doctorate! The honors are coming, and life goes on."[8] But, while enjoying the acclaim of professors and church leaders, Guardini was simultaneously undergoing some difficult moments, for he was afflicted with physical ailments, depression, and an intense religious questioning.

Among Guardini's infirmities was trigeminal neuralgia which caused sudden, sharp seizures of pain in his face and head. Also, the asthma from which he had suffered since youth worsened. He frequently found it difficult to breath and, on occasion, was stricken by violent asthma attacks during which he feared that he would die of suffocation. During these same years, he had a loss of hearing and became almost blind in his left eye. Further, a few months after Munich's *akademische Feier*, he suffered a heart attack which hospitalized him from late July to early December 1965.[9]

As evident in his diary, these ailments distressed Guardini. On December 4, 1953, he worried that he would soon need a hearing aid. Three weeks later, on Christmas day, he wrote that "the depression, which always comes during Christmas season, has also occurred again this time." In January 1954, he mentioned that "as a result of the weather, the asthma has come again and, as it seems, also some form of influenza." His frustration comes through a fragmentary entry on January 6, 1960: "Large gaps [in the diary] . . . Neuralgia, hospital, surgery,. . . . " Four years later, he wrote: "From May 1, 1961 until today January 11, 1965, [is a] great gap [in the diary]. Many health-related obstacles. Now I stand at the start of my seventy-ninth year and again begin [to write in the diary]."[10] A few months later, the diary ends.

While enduring his physical ailments and bouts of depression, Guardini pondered immediate existential issues. In his diary he made notes on suffering and death as he read Goethe, Nietzsche, and Sartre, and jotted down his anxieties about Germany's increasingly technological society. Also, he thought anew about God. On September 16, 1959, he wrote: "What determines everything in the Christian faith—however also simply everything in thinking, acting, and being—is whether the reality of God will be experienced, whether God exists as the real one, as the ultimate, singular reality in existence." In 1961 he reflected on "faith being put to the test."[11] Then, on May 3, 1964, he observed: "'What God is, no one is able to know.' [This is] a basic axiom of theology.

Everything in theology and its formulations goes into this statement. God is the individual in relation to whom we should know about our existence."[12]

Guardini never tired of thinking about personal existence in relation to God. Even during the last months of his life, he asked about suffering and evil. In the summer of 1968 the journalist Walter Dirks visited his former teacher and friend who, now bedridden, was nearing death. Dirks subsequently described what took place during his farewell visit:

> To hear what the elderly man confided on his sick bed was an unforgettable experience. [He said that] at the Last Judgment he would not only be questioned, but would also in his turn ask questions [of God]. He firmly hoped that the angel would not deny him the true answer to the question which no book, not even the Bible, no dogma and no teaching authority, no "theodicy" or theology, not even his own theology, had been able to answer for him: why, God, these fearful detours on the way to salvation? [why] the suffering of the innocent? why sin?[13]

Dirk's recollection shows that Guardini sought the meaning of life even as he faced death. His suffering as well as his knowledge of others' hardships, for example, during the Third Reich, had generated questions to which he had found no adequate answers. He longed for the moment when he could ask God about "these fearful detours on the way to salvation," "the suffering of the innocent," and "sin."

The last months of his life were not, of course, the first time that Romano Guardini had asked about suffering. Beginning in the mid-1950s, he had raised these issues in some his published works. In 1963 in *Tugenden* he observed that some questions can receive answers only in "a living encounter" with God after death.[14] In three other texts as well, he spoke of the prospect of a face-to-face dialogue with God. Each of these texts warrants a brief review.

THE QUESTION OF GOD

On Turning Seventy, 1955

In the 1960s the topic of the "death of God" was widely discussed among scholars. Previously, it had appeared in the 1800s in the writings of Hegel, Feuerbach, and Nietzsche, and again in the early 1900s in the works of Sigmund Freud and Albert Camus. Then, at mid-century it again surfaced in the aftermath of World War II, the Shoah, and Hiroshima and also with Western society's secularization. Literature on this topic included Martin Stallmann's *Was ist Säkularisierung?* (1960), Gabriel Vahanian's *The Death of God* (1961),

Harvey Cox's *The Secular City* (1965), Thomas Altizer's and William Hamilton's *Radical Theology and the Death of God* (1966), and Johannes Metz's *Zur Theologie der Welt* (1968). These writings discuss the experience of people who speak of God's absence in their lives.[15] Amid this discussion, Guardini struggled with his own questions about God.

On his seventieth birthday, Guardini took up the issue of God's absence in an essay on the role of philosophy within the stages of life. In implicitly autobiographical statements, the theologian describes an elderly man sitting in his apartment and looking around as though he were visiting a stranger's room. He writes:

> There are times in the evening when he is in his study, his books all about him, read and reread a hundred times. There is the furniture, the pictures on the wall, the statues on the table. Of a sudden, all these lose their familiarity, seem odd, far away, and oppressive. It is then that the thought comes: How strange that you are seated in this room this evening, that you are you and that you continue doing what each day asks of you. That you are simply there! What is behind it all?[16]

Guardini compares this situation to a painting which awakens a sense of life's ambiguities. In such a moment "[e]verything takes on the air of an enigma." As the aged scholar puts it:

> Existence now takes on the character, we might say, of the still-life in Cézanne. There is a table. Upon the table, a plate. Upon the plate, some apples. Nothing else. Everything is there, clear and evident. Nothing left to ask nor to answer. And yet, mystery is everywhere. There is more in these things than meets the eye: more than the simple individuality of each thing. (p. 78)

The two statements above provide a poignant glimpse of the elderly scholar's solitary thoughts. They indicate that, in his last years, Guardini felt God's absence and ultimately trusted in the unknown. In his words: "Here is a moment when you are called upon to cling to this sense of the absolute, when the very meaning of things seems to give way" (p. 78).

Guardini was aware that the backdrop to his malaise was the imminence of his death. How someone finds meaning in life is ultimately tested, he notes, as one nears death: "[i]t makes a lot of difference whether you face up to death or try to wave it aside or talk it away." In his judgment, Christians ought not to turn away from death but integrate it into their sense of life. Indeed, they may even reach a spiritual maturity in which they can accept their death "as atonement for the sins of life." In any case, "our attitude toward death influences our understanding of existence. As a matter of fact, it is altogether decisive" (p. 79).

At seventy years of age, Guardini asked about life's meaning. Despite his accomplishments, honors, and Christian faith, he still searched for God. This theme appeared again in his letters to Josef Weiger and also in his lecture at his *akademische Feier*.

The Theologische Briefe, 1963–66

When Guardini was seventy-eight, he began writing to Josef Weiger in Mooshausen on the relationship between God and creation. (It was to Weiger from 1923 to 1925 that Guardini wrote *Briefe vom Comersee* [1927].) These "theological letters" gave him an opportunity to sort out his impressions as he struggled with failing health. After three years, he and Weiger agreed that the ten letters he had sent to Weiger should eventually appear as a book, to which Guardini would add a foreword, postscript, and a prayer, entitled "Prayer in the Hour of Enduring." In 1976 they were published as *Theologische Briefe an einen Freund*.

Although Guardini proposes no wholly new ideas in *Theologische Briefe*, he does communicate three noteworthy things.[17] First, he admits in his eighth letter (September 1964) that he does not understand Germany's new culture, for instance, the cartoon character of Mickey Mouse, which he finds grotesque.[18] Not surprisingly, therefore, in the ninth and tenth letters he voices pessimism about trends in society and an uneasiness about the post–Vatican II church. In other words, these letters exhibit an absence of the creative tension, the coincidence of opposites (*Gegensatz*), that had shaped Guardini's thought throughout his adult years. (Since it was during this period that he wrote his controversial letter to the Third Liturgical Conference, one cannot help but suspect that his pessimism influenced this letter, too.)

Second, in his ninth letter (1965), Guardini indicates that he was shifting away from his Christ-centered theology to a God-centered theology. He writes: "a new character is being given to theology—a character which does not change anything substantially but could place everything in a different light" (p. 59). This statement is amazing, for it suggests that, after sixty years of thinking in one way, the theologian was exploring an alternative theological framework.

Third, throughout the letters, Guardini poses questions about God. His references to Nietzsche and Freud indicate that he undertook his inquiry partially in response to the death-of-God debate.[19] But he was also motivated by something more. As he tells Weiger, his deteriorating health was directing his thoughts to God's relation to the world. He states: "In God's self, God is complete and perfect. What can it mean, therefore, for God to create finite reality which, as far as we can tell, reaches its zenith in human beings?" (p. 8). In response, he considers that "the absolute" has freely chosen to establish and sustain a living bond with contingent reality because God is love. This answer, he admits, is what one might expect from a Christian. But, going beyond the conventional view, he explores the idea that God has taken finite reality into God's infinite life. God has created the world and has remained active in it, not in some detached manner but by drawing creation into the absolute. Guardini writes:

> God became a human being. God was not only concerned about human existence but also "became" a human being. This means that, in Jesus, God "becomes" finite. After Jesus' death God did not shed . . . the human element but remained a human being. That is, after Jesus' death the humanity of Jesus "was seated at the right hand of the Father." (p. 12)

This insight, Guardini adds, means that the church needs a new theology of history. Neoscholasticism does not take history seriously enough, for it holds that history is accidental to the drama of salvation, as though God's activity on behalf of the human family occurs apart from time and space. But such a view devalues the incarnation. Crediting the Jesuit anthropologist Pierre Teilhard de Chardin (d. 1955) for his fresh ideas about history, Guardini observes that "the incarnation should not be understood as an isolated event, but must be understood as the ultimate expression of something which was already given from the first suggestion of creation and is effective in the whole relationship of God to creation" (p. 22).

These reflections lead to the issue of evil, on which Guardini offers three thoughts. First, God does not intend evil, rather he wills the freedom of creation so that it can choose to enter into a relationship of love with God. The creator allows for the possibility that some created beings will wrongly claim absolute status for themselves. Second, God foresaw this possibility and nevertheless chose to endure evil. God has affirmed creation and struggles with evil even in the face of creation's rebellion against its maker and sustainer (pp. 11–12). Third, in speaking about God and evil, we must recognize the difference between the Christian view and the "romantic," somewhat "gnostic," view of writers such as Goethe and C. G. Jung who hold that good and evil are essential to life. This dualism stands at odds with the Judeo-Christian tradition which attests that evil is the absence of reality (pp. 50–52).

If God enters into the heart of finite existence, how is it that many people today speak about the absence of God in their lives? Why have they accepted the atheistic views of Nietzsche and Freud? According to Guardini, modernity's crisis of faith has resulted not from God's withdrawal from us but from our reliance on a constricted view of reason, as a result of which we live in a "world" of our making and have lost touch with the "natural" world. Indeed, we see ourselves as Promethean: "Human beings have undertaken to exist with an absolute disposition without being absolute" (p. 37). Insofar as God is absent from our modern age, God is not the source of the difficulty, we are.

These thoughts bring Guardini to consider life after death. He contends that we must discard the image of the Last Judgment as condemnation and adopt the image of the Last Judgment as fulfillment, as the moment when God brings to completion what the Holy Spirit began in our lives at conception. Moreover, fulfilling our I-you relationship, we will enter into a dialogue with God.[20] Mentioning to Weigert what he eventually said to Dirks, Guardini writes that in our encounter with God, "[i]t is not only the case that God asks and human beings answer out of the unevasiveness of their being, but also that human beings themselves may ask [questions]. . . . Indeed, God expects that human beings will question [God]" (p. 30).

How then can we experience God in our time? Christians should pursue three approaches. First, we must assume responsibility for the world so as to relate to it as God does, and, in doing so, we may become conscious of our proximity to God's intention and actions in history (pp. 32–34). Second, we must seek the truth, knowing that such an endeavor goes against today's "liberal skepticism." In this effort, we can gain inspiration from the passion narrative in John's Gospel in which Jesus Christ upholds the truth before Pilate's interrogation (p. 57). Third, we must abandon ourselves to God even when God seems absent. Not sensing God's presence (natural revelation), we must purify our faith by relying solely on historical revelation, especially God's disclosure in Jesus Christ (pp. 62–64).

Guardini concludes with the tenth letter, entitled "Trust" (*Vertrauen*), in which he reflects on blind faith. Even when we have no sense of God's presence in our lives, we must abandon ourselves to the darkness, where we may paradoxically meet God. Building on this thought, Guardini gives his "Prayer in the Hour of Enduring" (*Gebet in der währenden Stunde*), which concerns the trust we must have in a seemingly absent God (pp. 65–66). (For this prayer, see the appendix.) At one point, the prayer reads: "Living God, we believe in you. Give us the strength to persevere when everything becomes meaningless." Then it adds: "In your love alone must we trust [*vertrauen*]" (p. 65). These lines are striking in themselves, but they gain even more weight from the fact that Guardini alluded to them in the epitath that he asked to have inscribed on his grave's bronze memorial plaque: "Romano Guardini. Born in Verona, 17 February 1885. Died in Munich, 1 October 1968. Believing in Jesus Christ and his church. Trusting [*Vertrauen*] in his merciful judgment."[21]

On Turning Eighty, 1965

At the University of Munich's *akademische Feier* for his eightieth birthday, Romano Guardini gave a short address entitled "Wahrheit und Ironie" (Truth and irony). After thanking his colleagues, students, and friends, he stated that, as his birthday neared, he had asked himself: "What really emerges for you as the lasting fruit of this long life?"[22] In answer, he had decided that the ultimate benefit of his life had been his pursuit and partial attainment of truth. But he saw, too, that the quest which he had undertaken is characterized by irony, because those who undertake it become aware of their "insufficiency" for the task before them. They attain "a knowledge of the truth and at the same time a knowledge of the incommensurability of their capability in relation to it; a knowledge of the true insufficiency which arises not from skepticism but from the very highest confidence" (p. 41). In other words, truth-seekers insist that they have not reached their goal and must simply trust (*vertraut*) that truth exists.

Developing this theme, Guardini praised Plato for opposing the Sophists who—not unlike contemporary skeptics—argued diverse points of view on any topic while believing that there exists no objective reality to which their ideas should refer. Plato must have had an "overwhelming experience of truth," for his commitment to it is evident in the *Symposium,* the *Phaedo,* the sixth book of the *Republic,* and the seventh of his *Letters.* These writings also convey Plato's awareness of the irony of the quest. In the *Symposium* Socrates says that he does not see himself as a teacher of truth. In Book VI of the *Republic* Glaucon makes a fool of himself when, after Socrates' discourse, he "very ludicrously" tells his teacher that "hyperbole can no further go" (509c).[23] By contrast, Socrates knows that much more can be said. Commenting on this Socratic exchange, Guardini noted that Socrates and all truth-seekers are ironically consciousness of how far they remain from the truth, and, hence, may seemingly bear a resemblance to the Sophists. In Guardini's words:

> And the irony of knowledge exists in that inquirers recognize what goes beyond their capacity of apprehension. As an Augustinian of the High Middle Ages, such as Bonaventure, would say, "truth" is no rationalistic simplification but an *excessivum,* and for this reason the situation of inquirers is that they experience that there is indeed absolute truth, however they cannot adequately attain it by means of their finite intellectual powers since they themselves are not absolute. (pp. 40–41)

In concluding, Guardini encouraged his listeners to search for the truth, for God, knowing that they may increasingly realize their "insufficiency" before the truth, before "that which is above them." The octogenarian ended by stating:

> In the spirit of Plato it would be good, I believe, to say that human beings abandon their nobility when they understand themselves by that which is beneath them. They live much more properly when they live by that which is above them—also when they are not able to grasp it and hence when they come before themselves "very ludicrously" as occurs to the young Glaucon in the *Republic.* (p. 41)

"Wahrheit und Ironie" was Romano Guardini's last public lecture. It was appropriate that he should depart from the public arena by exhorting everyone to pursue the truth. Given his persistent questioning, it was also proper that he should implicitly admit that he felt far from the truth and had chosen simply to "trust" in God.

The Reception of Romano Guardini's Writings

A WORLDWIDE INFLUENCE

A person's identity is more than his or her self-perceptions, words, actions, and interpersonal relationships. Personal identity also includes the influence that someone has had upon others, many of whom the person may never have known. Speaking to this point, Edward Schillebeeckx has noted: "No individual can be understood . . . independently of the effect he has had on subsequent history. . . . In other words, an individual human being is the personal focal point of a series of interactive relations to the past, the future and his own present."[24] Although this observation is valid for all human beings, it is especially pertinent to authors whose works have touched many lives. For this reason, if we are to reach an adequate view of Guardini's life and work, we must attain a sense of his impact on others.

Not surprisingly, recent popes have read Guardini's books and articles. Eugenio Pacelli, who in 1939 became Pius XII, likely read Guardini's work during his years as the Vatican's nuncio to Germany (1917–30), for as pope he made Guardini a papal prelate in 1952. In 1953 Monsignor Giovanni Battista Montini, who at the time was the Vatican's pro-secretary of state and became Paul VI (1963–78), encouraged Guardini to visit the Vatican, but the theologian could not fit the trip into his schedule.[25] Montini valued Guardini's books and articles, and in 1965 he invited the eighty-year-old scholar to join the college of cardinals.[26] John Paul II (1978–) knows Guardini's works, for he like Guardini has drawn extensively on phenomenology, including the work of Max Scheler, in his scholarly reflections on the character of personal existence.[27] Moreover, during his visit to Germany in November 1980, he conveyed his high regard for Guardini by listing him among the most significant German-speaking theologians in the church's history. Addressing an assembly of professors of theology at Altötting, the pontiff stated:

> I warmly greet you and through you all theological scholars. You stand in a great tradition. I need think only of Albert the Great, Nicholas of Cusa, Möhler and Scheeben, Guardini and Przywara. I name these prominent theologians as representatives of the many others who in the past, as also in the present, have enriched and still enrich not only the church in the German-speaking world but also the theology and life of the entire church.[28]

Along with earning the respect of at least three popes, Guardini's writings, especially *Der Herr* touched tens of thousands of Catholics in many lands. This global impact is evident in the fact that numerous scholars outside of Germany have analyzed Guardini's work.[29] Since I cannot survey Guardini's worldwide influence, I will review of the reception of his texts in North America and in the work of three German-speaking scholars.

PREPARING NORTH AMERICAN CATHOLICS FOR VATICAN II

Although a few of Guardini's books, most notably *The Spirit of the Liturgy* of 1935, were read in North America prior to 1950, it was from 1950 until the late 1960s that many of his texts circulated in Canada and the United States. During this period there appeared in English at least thirty-four of his books, along with ten excerpts from his books and at least nine articles by him in *Cross Currents* and *Philosophy Today*. Further, after the Second World War and prior to the Second Vatican Council *America, Catholic World, Commonweal,* and *Jubilee* carried articles on him. After Vatican II, North American interest in Guardini's thought waned, and his books went out of print. Only a few English-speaking periodicals mentioned Guardini's death on October 1, 1965.[30] However, North Americans have recently taken a new interest in his work. Some of his books have been reissued, and in 1994 there appeared *Letters from Lake Como.*[31] In 1995 the first book in English on Guardini was published, and in 1997 an anthology of his writings in English became available.[32]

It is too soon to explain the current interest in Guardini's writings among North Americans. Some readers are seemingly returning to his texts because they judge that something is missing from today's spiritual writings.[33] However, insofar as some people are using Guardini's books to promote a pre–Vatican II view of the church, this aim goes contrary to Guardini's intention and also to the role that these texts played prior to the Second Vatican Council.[34]

A select list of North American Catholics who were influenced by Guardini's writings reads like a "who's who in Catholicism." In the early 1920s, the Benedictine monk Virgil Michel (1888–1938) at St. John's Abbey, Collegeville, read *Vom Geist der Liturgie* and dedicated the rest of his creative, though unfortunately short life, to the renewal of worship in North America.[35] Further, George Shuster (1894–1977), the educator, writer, and statesman, mentioned Guardini in *Commonweal* in 1930 and described his *Der Gegensatz* as "one of the really important Catholic books."[36] Beginning in the early 1950s, Dorothy Day (1897–1980), the journalist and social activist, frequently referred to Guardini's writings in her columns in the newspaper *The Catholic Worker* and cited them too in her autobiography, *The Long Loneliness* (1952).[37] In 1958 Joseph B. Gremillion (1919–94), the Southern pastor and Catholic leader in social justice, published his engaging interview with Guardini in Munich, thereby giving English-speaking Catholics one of their first glimpses of Guardini.[38] The poet Anne Sexton (1928–74), on the recommendation of a Catholic monk, read a couple of Guardini's books and brought some of his ideas to her *The Awful Rowing Toward God* (1975).[39] The theologian Monika Hellwig has noted that she and her contemporaries in the Netherlands were influenced by Guardini's writings beginning in the 1930s and also that at the Catholic University of America in the mid-1950s students were forbidden to read Guardini's *The Lord* "because the translator or publisher had chosen an unauthorized translation for the biblical quotations."[40] In recent years, the theologian Avery Dulles has continued to draw on Guardini's writings in his own theological inquiries, for instance, in *The Assurance of Things Hoped For.*[41]

Along with having an impact on these people, Guardini touched two others: Thomas Merton and Flannery O'Connor.

Thomas Merton (1915–68) apparently began reading Guardini's works in the mid-1950s (interestingly, Guardini had already discovered the Trappist's writings).[42] In his journal and also in letters, Merton wrote in glowing terms about such books as *The Lord's Prayer* (1958) and *Prayer in Practice* (1963), calling attention in particular to Guardini's thought on divine providence.[43] In 1959 he mentioned in a letter to the poet Czeslaw Milosz that "[a]mong the Catholics Bouyer is writing some good things, also of course De Lubac, Daniélou, etc. And then there is Guardini, who is splendid."[44] In his *Conjectures of a Guilty Bystander* (1966) Merton attributed to Guardini—seemingly referring to *The End of the Modern World* (1956)—the idea that Christians should work as leaven in secular society, transforming it from within. In Merton's words: "Guardini is speaking of the true situation of the Christian in the world today: called by what does not yet exist, called to help it come into existence *through and by a present dislocation of Christian life.*"[45] Finally, a year prior to his untimely death, the monk delighted in Guardini's *Pascal for Our Time* (1966). In January 1967, he became so excited by this book that, as he read it, he had to walk back and forth in his hermitage.[46] A couple of months later, in his "circular letter" to friends, he said:

> I have in fact just been reading Romano Guardini's excellent little book on Pascal. He analyzes the "demon of combativeness" in Pascal—a demon which is no prerogative of Jansenists. At times one wonders if a certain combativeness is not endemic in Catholicism: a "compulsion to be always right" and to prove the adversary wrong.[47]

A year later, Merton attended an interreligious monastic conference in Bangkok and tragically died there. Since he participated in the conference in order to learn from non-Christian religions regarding prayer and meditation, one may wonder whether *Pascal for Our Time* was one source of the monk's inspiration to move beyond Catholicism's "combativeness."

The writer Flannery O'Connor (1925–64), though younger than Thomas Merton, seemingly read Guardini's writings ahead of the Trappist and also with a more critical eye.[48] She came upon *The Lord* soon after it appeared in 1954 and afterwards resolved to read "everything I can of Romano Guardini."[49] In her letters and book reviews in *The Georgian Catholic* she praised *The Lord, The Rosary of Our Lady* (1955), *Meditations Before Mass* (1955), *Jesus Christus* (1959), *The Conversion of Augustine* (1960), *Freedom, Grace and Destiny* (1961), and *Prayer in Practice*. She valued not only Guardini's ideas but also his lack of "smugness"—"the Great Catholic Sin"—which she perceived in writings by most clergy.[50] Also, she appreciated his clear prose, especially "the total absence of pious cliché."[51] She even credited Guardini's reflections on Prince Myshkin in Dostoyevsky's *The Idiot* with shaping her depiction of the schoolteacher's boy in *The Violent Bear It Away* (1960).[52] Not surprisingly, in her letters she mentioned most frequently *The Lord*, of which she said: "In my opinion there is nothing like it anywhere, certainly not in this country."[53] However, O'Connor did not hesitate to point out shortcomings in the German theologian's texts. In 1958 she commented that in his ecclesiology Guardini needed to move beyond his idealized view of the church and "take in the corrupt organization."[54] Further, she noted that in his Christology he neglected to draw on the results of historical-critical study of the Bible and, as a consequence, relied too exclusively on his own "spiritual intuition."[55] Nevertheless, she listed Guardini among the contemporary thinkers whose work shaped her thought. In 1957, when asked for advice on how to develop one's understanding of Catholicism, she wrote:

> Anyway, to discover the Church you have to set out by yourself. The French Catholic novelists were a help to me in this—Bloy, Bernanos, Mauriac. In philosophy, Gilson, Maritain and Gabriel Marcel, an Existentialist. They all seemed to be French for a while and then I discovered the Germans—Max Picard, Romano Guardini and Karl Adam.[56]

Statements like those by Merton and O'Connor show that Guardini's writings brought to many in the New World both fresh religious insights and also an enthusiasm for rethinking the basic tenets of Christian belief. As Flannery O'Connor pointed out in 1956, while North American Catholics were learning from Fulton J. Sheen (d. 1979), European Catholics were studying Guardini's works, and the difference between their theologies displayed "how far Europe is ahead of us on that score."[57] For this reason, to the extent that Catholics in Canada and the United States were theologically prepared for the Second Vatican Council, some credit for this initial renewal must go to Romano Guardini and his North American publishers and translators.

SHAPING THE THOUGHT OF GERMAN-SPEAKING CATHOLICS

In early October 1968 *Der Spiegel* printed this obituary:

> Romano Guardini. The German-Italian theologian, priest, and author on the philosophy of religion succeeded in his gentle revolution in Catholicism in the

1920s. As the mentor of a Catholic version of the youth movement, "Quickborn," this spiritual innovator challenged the official church—which had hardened itself against modernism—not only with his articulation of new ideas (e.g., *Vom Geist der Liturgie,* 1918) but also with his implementation of these new ideas within the tradition-laden forms of the liturgy, an implementation which occurred chiefly at Burg Rothenfels am Main. In hundreds of writings Guardini, as professor in Berlin, Tübingen, and Munich, persisted with a strength in humility which wanted the things of the earth to become as they should be. Consistently a political conservative, the papal prelate with a lively spirit saw the challenge of Europe in the "critique of power," so that this power will not bring a [demonic] metaphysical reality to expression. The spectacular reforming zeal of the Second Vatican Council, which (according to Karl Rahner) would be hardly thinkable without Guardini's life and work, made Guardini himself uneasy. He had always lived according to the maxim: "A gentleman is one who causes no public disturbance." On last Tuesday evening, Guardini died of a cerebral hemorrhage in Munich.[58]

This statement expresses well the complexity of Romano Guardini's personality and thought—a complexity or breadth of polarities which means that he does not fit into the categories by which we tend to classify religious thinkers. He was in one sense a liberal in that he brought about radical changes in the liturgy, and yet he was also a conservative in that he wanted to retrieve the ancient forms and was fearful when, after Vatican II, he perceived that ecclesial and liturgical innovations were being made without guidance from the past. Moreover, he was a "political conservative," for he distrusted democracy, and yet he criticized authoritarianism, whether in the state or the church. For his balanced views, Guardini won the respect of conservatives and liberals alike. Perhaps, too, he gained their admiration because they recognized his commitment "in humility" to the truth. In any case, he is misrepresented if he is depicted as standing in an ecclesiastical camp.[59]

Using this obituary as our point of reference, we can turn to the portraits of Romano Guardini by Karl Rahner, Hans Urs von Balthasar, and Joseph Ratzinger. Each of these theologians has painted a different picture of Guardini.

In his main address at the *akademische Feier* for Romano Guardini, Karl Rahner (1904–84) described the octogenarian as a Christian humanist who led Catholics "out of an intellectual and cultural ghetto [and] into the contemporary age." According to the Jesuit theologian, Guardini's foremost concern was not to engage in ecclesiastical politics but to understand "that unspeakable mystery which we call God" and also the reality of being human "in its ultimately unspeakable qualities." In his effort to shed light on "the eternal in human beings," Guardini assumed at least five roles in the church's life. First, he was a leader in the liturgical movement who renewed worship in relation to the living Christ. Second, he was a theologian who began his inquiries not with the conventional scholastic questions but "from the point of view of human beings and the urgent questions of their personal existence." Third, he was a biblical exegete, in a broad sense of the term. Although Guardini did not use the critical tools of scholarly interpretation, he delved into the Bible "in service of the [divine] word." Fourth, he was a phenomenologist of religion who pursued fundamental issues concerning personal existence, freedom, and community, and thus "opened us to the eternal questions of [philosophical] anthropology." Fifth, Guardini was an interpreter of writers and poets who were "masters of life" as well as "masters of texts." By means of these involvements, he taught Catholics both how "to live in a pluralistic world without becoming relativistic" and also how "to speak the message of the gospels so that it is not a priori incomprehensible to those who stand outside the church."[60]

A year after Guardini's death, Hans Urs von Balthasar (1905–88) spoke at Munich's Katholische Akademie in Bayern on the life and work of the professor whose lectures had captivated the young Balthasar in the 1920s at the University of Berlin.[61] According to Balthasar, Guardini was a "reformer" of Catholicism who sought to renew the church by returning to its "source" or "wellspring": God's self-disclosure in Jesus Christ. After his conversion of 1905, Guardini saw that, out of faithfulness to revelation, the church must stand "in" the world without being "of" the world. He realized that in every era the church is "unmodern," a source of "offense" to the spirit of the age.[62] In particular, he believed that his "commission" was to focus his attention on the world, as seen in the light of God's word. Thus, he wrote not only about revelation itself but also about the thought of Bonaventure, Dostoyevsky, Augustine, Pascal, Dante, Hölderlin, Socrates, and Rilke. Further, he tried to mirror the "pure light" of Jesus Christ in texts such as *Der Herr, Die menschliche Wirklichkeit des Herrn,* and *Die Kirche des Herrn.* Guardini saw, too, that he must be a steadfast witness to God's word amid modernity's enthrallment by the power of technology, totalitarianism, and atheism.[63] Playing upon the Italian meaning of Guardini's last name, Balthasar compares the theologian to a watchman who, commissioned to defend the truth, found himself faced with one question: " 'Guardian, how far along is the night?' He always heard this question addressed to him. . . . It was his responsibility not to abandon what is normative [for faith] in its form as well as in its content."[64]

Joseph Cardinal Ratzinger (1927–) has also written on the life and work of

Romano Guardini. In 1985, at the Katholische Akademie in Bayern's celebration of the anniversary of Guardini's one hundredth birthday, the prefect of the Vatican's Congregation for the Doctrine of the Faith portrayed Guardini as a theologian who discerned that we are living at the end of the modern era. Beginning with his conversion of 1905, Guardini set his heart and mind on the truth of Jesus Christ which is proclaimed in the church. At the same time, on a philosophical level, he perceived the inadequacy of Kantianism. Making use of Max Scheler's phenomenology, he sought to hear God's self-communication, especially as known in the church's worship and prayer. It was not accidental, therefore, that his first major work was *Vom Geist der Liturgie*. In the 1920s he was optimistic that a new way of thinking would soon predominate among the German people. However, his positive outlook gradually changed. By the 1950s he saw—as evident in *Das Ende der Neuzeit*—that skepticism still prevailed in society. Troubled by the influence of contemporary ideas within the church's life, Guardini wrote his sobering letter to the German Liturgical Conference of 1964 on the difficulty of the liturgical act for twentieth-century men and women. Thus, sixty years after his conversion, he was still intent upon upholding the truth and safeguarding one of its loci, the church's worship.[65]

This brief review of the representations of Guardini by Rahner, Balthasar, and Ratzinger brings to light both the agreement and also the dissimilarity among their respective views of the theologian. All three highlight Guardini's commitment to the truth about God and personal existence. Rahner reiterates his attentiveness to "the eternal within human life." Balthasar emphasizes his deliberate, clear focus on revelation. And, Ratzinger accentuates his orientation to the wisdom that he finds in Catholicism. The three scholars differ among themselves, however, concerning Guardini's relationship to the church and society. Rahner emphasizes his critical role within the pre–Vatican II church. By contrast, Balthasar and Ratzinger stress that Guardini played a prophetic role within society. According to Balthasar, he stressed that true personal existence is realized only in relation to the God of Jesus Christ, and, according to Ratzinger, he recognized that the church is the protector of the truth about God and human life.[66]

What are we to make of the disparity among these three portraits? The differences in their depictions are explained in part by the fact that Guardini's life and thought were themselves an interplay of opposites and, for this reason, are not adequately described in any one portrait. As *Der Spiegel* observed, Guardini was a complex individual. He was a loyal critic both of the church and also of today's culture. The disparity in presentations also stems from the fact that each theologian has illuminated in Guardini's rich thought a theme that is central to his own theology: Rahner has accentuated the universality of grace; Balthasar, the uniqueness of God's word in Jesus Christ; and Ratzinger, the importance of doing theology in faithfulness to the church's teachings.

In this writer's judgment, Rahner's presentation of Guardini's life and thought is more faithful to the theologian and his historical context than Balthasar's and Ratzinger's. In Rahner's view, Guardini generated his most creative work during his years in Berlin. From 1923 through 1943, Guardini studied the work of Augustine and Rilke, reflected on the person of Jesus Christ, and explored the topics of personal existence, freedom, and grace. Also, during this time he led the liturgical movement out of the monasteries and into the parishes by means of his writings and his leadership of Quickborn. Finally, as Rahner points out, Guardini's work in Berlin and at Burg Rothenfels was not only worthwhile in itself but it also guided the Catholic Church into a constructive exchange with current ideas. By contrast, Balthasar and Ratzinger distance Guardini's works from the political, social, and ecclesial context in which he struggled for respect prior to 1950. As a result, they make too little of his points of friction with ecclesiastical authorities.[67]

The accounts by Rahner, Balthasar, and Ratzinger share, however, a similar oversight. Although they note that Guardini chose not to use historical-critical methods in his interpretation of scripture, they neglect to point out that this omission weakened Guardini's theology and his commitment to the truth. Heinrich Kahlefeld (d. 1980) took issue with Guardini on this point and rightly so.[68] Guardini's failure is especially glaring after Pius XII issued *Divino Afflante Spiritu* (1943) in which he confirmed the role of critical investigation in determining the literal meaning of a biblical text. Rahner, Balthasar, and Ratzinger are, of course, correct in saying that Guardini wanted to uncover scripture's fuller sense. But in light of *Divino Afflante Spiritu*, Vatican II's Dogmatic Constitution on Divine Revelation, and the Pontifical Biblical Commission's recent instructions, these theologians should have also clarified that, after 1943, Guardini erred by neglecting church teachings in his interpretation of scripture. As noted above, Flannery O'Connor, who had no formal education in theology, noted this inadequacy in the theologian's christological writings, without lessening her praise of his work. Following her example, we must acknowledge the flaw in Guardini's biblical interpretation while simultaneously respecting him for his accomplishments.

In concluding, we should note that Guardini influenced not only Rahner,

Balthasar, and Ratzinger, but also many German-speaking scholars.[69] After studying during the same years at Freiburg, Martin Heidegger and Guardini exchanged letters and read each other's writings. During the postwar years they visited together in Munich.[70] Also, Martin Buber and Guardini collaborated beginning in the 1920s.[71] In 1952 Guardini sent Buber his address "Verantwortung," concerning Germans' moral responsibility to Jews. In response, Buber, who had fled to Palestine in 1938, wrote to Guardini that: "While reading [your address], I noticed that something had changed for me. It was again possible for me to speak publicly in Germany."[72] Subsequently, Buber gave public lectures and visited with Guardini in Munich. Further, the Jewish philosopher Hannah Arendt was deeply affected by Guardini's courses in Berlin in the 1920s and, moved by his work on Augustine, subsequently wrote her doctoral dissertation on the bishop of Hippo, under the direction of Karl Jaspers.[73] Also, Otto von Simson (d. 1993), the art historian and civic leader, studied with Guardini in Berlin, taught at the University of Chicago during the Third Reich, and returned to Berlin in 1957, becoming a leader at Berlin's Free University and the Guardini Stiftung.[74] During the three semesters that Guardini taught at the University of Tübingen, he made a lasting impression on the thinking of the young Redemptorist Bernard Häring, who went on to fashion a theological ethics of virtue not unlike Guardini's.[75] At the University of Munich the theologian Michael Schmaus (d. 1995) was the first Catholic scholar to cite Guardini's work within a theological manual and delighted Guardini when he dedicated the first volume of his *Katholische Dogmatik* to him.[76] It is noteworthy, too, that Guardini's work is still cited by Walter Kasper, previously professor at the University of Tübingen and now the bishop of the diocese of Rottenburg-Stuttgart.[77] This list could go on.[78] In conclusion, I should mention, too, that Guardini's ideas were well received by Protestant scholars such as Paul Fechter, Gerhard von Rad, and Helmut Thielicke.[79]

This review of Guardini's impact upon German-speaking scholars has shown that this theologian has made a significant difference in German Catholic thought.[80] Although not fully appreciated as a theologian because of his refusal to engage in neoscholasticism, Guardini taught theologians and nontheologians alike how to understand anew Christian belief and bring it into dialogue with contemporary thought. In this regard, Walter Dirks has written: "The academic specialists had and have . . . their doubts about him, and they even do not grant him their deep respect. Nevertheless, the Catholic consciousness in Germany would appear quite different had this man remained in the land of his birth."[81]

Romano Guardini's Legacy Today

As we have seen, a passion for the truth about God and personal existence and its relevance unified Guardini's life and thought. That is, it propelled him out of Catholicism's intellectual and cultural ghetto and into an exchange with some of the twentieth century's best minds. Further, it motivated him to break away from neoscholasticism and employ an inductive theological method that rested on his theory of opposites. Also, this thirst for knowledge directed Guardini to restate Christian teachings concerning revelation, the church, the liturgy, and Jesus Christ. By means of his dialogue with the world, experiential method, and seminal ideas, Guardini contributed to the spiritual and intellectual fermentation that occurred within Catholicism in the decades prior to Vatican II. That he himself was surprised by the council's spirit of renewal and unsure of its results attests to the fact that he did not set out to spark a reform council. Rather, he resolved to uncover the riches of the Judeo-Christian tradition, share them with his contemporaries, and allow his work to bear fruit as God willed.

What is Guardini's legacy to the post–Vatican II church? In the last analysis, it is his dedication to knowing the truth about God and human life and to communicating it effectively to others. In relation to this commitment, there are some specific things that his writings can still teach us. One of these values is the commitment to learn from the Judeo-Christian tradition. Another is the use of opposites in theological reasoning. A third value concerns the character of worship; surely, *Vom Geist der Liturgie* is a minor classic in theology. Finally, Guardini's writings can still inspire us with their inclusive or catholic vision. As Guardini put it in 1944, throughout his life he wanted "to bring into relationship the unconditionality of Christian faith and an unbiased view of everyday reality and culture."[82]

One of the primary challenges facing the post–Vatican II church is that the Christian community must hold together its twofold responsibility both to draw on the wealth of the Judeo-Christian tradition and at the same time to learn from today's world. There currently exists the tendency to reduce this both/and involvement—both the past and the present—to an either/or stance which, in effect, divides the church. There is no doubt that it is difficult to reconcile continuity with past teachings and dialogue with the present age. Not long ago, Walter Kasper called attention to this challenge when he asked: "how can theology escape from the identity-relevance dilemma in which it finds itself? How can it escape the deadly logic of either preserving its relevance at the cost of its identity, or of keeping its identity at the cost of its relevance—and at the price of a retreat into the ghetto?"[83] In response, Kasper gave an answer that Guardini could have written: the church must sustain a "polarity" (*Gegensatz*) without allowing this creative tension to degenerate into a "'contradiction' [*Widerspruch*] that can no longer be integrated" into the church's life.[84]

Romano Guardini's primary legacy to the post–Vatican II church is, therefore, the spirit to discern and direct the tension between identity and relevance, between faith and culture, into a creative dynamism for the well-being of the church and society. During his life, Guardini retrieved the past's wisdom for the sake of the present and learned from present experience in order to draw out the insights of the Bible and church teachings. On his seventieth birthday, he observed that Christian belief should bring about "a methodical encounter between faith and the world," in which "faith should speak and give answers" and "the world should pose questions to the faith and be illuminated by that faith."[85] Ten years later, on his eightieth birthday, Guardini reiterated this idea when he said that "on the basis of Christian faith, there should open a view of the world, a glimpse of its essence, an assessment of its values, that is otherwise not possible." At the same time, the culture of the day should enrich our understanding of the Christian faith, for "from the world and its problems questions are posed to revelation which bring this otherwise silent content to speech. In this ever new, changing encounter, there is attained a fruitful illumination of Christian existence."[86]

Guardini described, too, what a fruitful dialogue between faith and culture requires in our time. As early as 1935 in *Vom Leben des Glaubens,* he observed that "[a]fter the luxurious use of symbols, images, and forms of past ages, there is emerging a form of faith which longs for simplification, for a return to the sources, for conciseness."[87] Consistent with this insight, he wrote with a bold simplicity and encouraged lean forms of expression in the liturgy and church leadership. He held that, remaining rooted in the church and everyday life, theology must be intelligible to its day. In 1960, at the age of seventy-five, Guardini observed: "One must create a theology which flows out of the basic realities of scripture, the fundamental content of the church, and the essence of human life, within a language that contemporary theologians and believers hold in common."[88] Here again is Guardini's commitment to the wisdom of the Judeo-Christian tradition and its relevance to modern life.

In conclusion, we can take heart from Guardini's insight concerning the power of truth. Noting that we live in a creative tension between faith and culture, Guardini pointed out that God's word possesses the strength to make itself known. This conviction sustained Guardini during many difficult years, especially during the Third Reich. Following Guardini's example, we need not lose heart when wisdom is seemingly rejected either by society or the church. As Guardini says in his "Prayer in the Hour of Enduring," we must ultimately make an act of trust that God's light will eventually shine in the apparent darkness. In early 1945, as he was entering his twelfth year under Nazi tyranny, Guardini stated this conviction:

> Truth is a power, however, only when one requires of it no immediate effect, but has patience and figures on a long wait. Still better, when one does not in general think about its effects but wants to present truth for its own sake, for its holy, divine greatness. . . . As already said, one must have patience. Here months may mean nothing and also years. And one must have no specific aims. Somehow, lack of an agenda is the greatest power. Sometimes, especially in recent years, I had the sense that truth was standing as a reality in the room.[89]

A case in point of this statement is Guardini's own pastoral leadership and writings. Guardini did not intend what *Der Spiegel* aptly called a "gentle revolution" in the church. Rather, he wanted to retrieve the church's wisdom and bring it into the light of his day. As he pursued this goal, he taught thousands of young Catholics to learn both from their Christian faith and also from current ideas. Without realizing it, he led Catholics to an ecumenical council whose results simultaneously pleased and troubled him. Guardini's legacy to us is the inspiration to discover and communicate—in word and deed—the truth about God and human life and, then, to trust that this truth will bear fruit as God wills.

APPENDIX 1

Romano Guardini
"Prayer in the Hour of Enduring"

Living God,
    we believe in you.
Teach us to understand the hour
    in which it is
    as though you have abandoned us,
        you whose faithfulness is eternity,
    [in which it is]
    as though you are not the one who told us your name:
        the one who is present.
Living God, we believe in you.
Give us the strength to persevere,
    when everything becomes meaningless.

Almighty Father,
    you who live, Lord, in yourself, needing no thing,
Eternally free you have created the world,
    although you do not need it.
The world exists because you desire that
    it exists, filled with your thought.
No earthly sense knows the intention
    from which the world originated.
However the revealer, the Son,
    has given us the word which means love.
Your love, O Father, springs from no earthly heart.
We believe in you,
    for what the world means to us are your divine works.
You have conceived them,
You have willed that they should exist, and that
    they should continue and shine through you alone.
You direct everything, even our small lives.
You direct our lives
    through the soundless guidance of your mystery.

We trust in your love alone.
Nevertheless your magnanimity requires ours.
You have given the world into our hands,
You desire that we should think your thoughts and
    work for your ordering of things.

Christ Jesus,
Redeemer of the world,
    who returned to the Father
        once everything was accomplished.
You are seated at God's right hand on the throne of glory,
    awaiting the hour
        in which you will come again in power,
        to judge the living and the dead.
We believe in you.
Teach us to live out the solitary faith which
    this hour demands of us,
        this hour when your light appears not to shine, and yet
            sheds light even more powerfully
                in the darkness than ever before.
In your mystery of love, in your obedience, in greatness
    you were obedient to the Father,
        saving everything and everybody.
Let your love for us not be in vain.

Most holy Spirit,
    sent to us,
        staying with us even when our space sounds empty
            as though you were far away.
The ages are given into your hands.
In the mystery of silence you guide
    and bring everything to fulfillment.
Therefore we believe and await the coming world.
Teach us to wait in hope.
Allow us to participate in the coming world,
    so that the promise of glory will be fulfilled in us.

Romano Guardini wrote this prayer shortly before he was hospitalized in July 1965. The prayer, entitled "Gebet in der währenden Stunde," first appeared in *Hochland* 61 (1969): 195–96.

APPENDIX 2

A Chronology of Romano Guardini's Life

The Youth, 1885–1905

1885 February 17: born in Verona.

1886 Moves with parents to Mainz. Three brothers: Gino, Mario, and Aleardo.

1903 August: graduates from Mainz's Gymnasium in Humanities.

1903–5 Studies chemistry and then economics in Tübingen, Munich, and Berlin.

1905 August: undergoes a religious conversion. November: decides to study for the priesthood.

The Student-Priest, 1906–22

1906–10 Studies theology in Freiburg, Tübingen, and Mainz.

1910 On May 28: ordained a priest.

1910–12 Serves as a curate in the diocese of Mainz.

1911 Becomes a German citizen.

1912 Begins doctoral studies at Freiburg in October.

1915 May: awarded Ph.D. Dissertation: *Die Lehre des heiligen Bonaventura von der Erlösung* (published in 1922).

1915–20 Serves as a curate in the diocese of Mainz and as the chaplain to "Iuventus."

1918 Publication of *Vom Geist der Liturgie*.

1919 Publication of *Der Kreuzweg unseres Herrn und Heilandes*. September: Guardini's father (b. 1857) dies in Mainz. His mother and brothers move to Lake Como and eventually to Isola Vicentina.

1920 Studies for his Habilitation in Bonn. At Easter, attends a gathering of "Quickborn" at Burg Rothenfels.

1922 Completes "Die Lehre vom lumen mentis" (published in 1964). Publication of *Vom Sinn der Kirche*.

The Young Professor, 1923–44

1923 Begins professorship for "Religionsphilosophie und Katholische Weltanschauung" at the University of Berlin. Participates in Quickborn at Burg Rothenfels.

1924 Becomes co-editor with Josef Aussem of *Die Schildgenossen*.

1925 Publication of *Der Gegensatz*. Karl Neundörfer dies in a hiking accident.

1927 Becomes Quickborn's national leader and the spiritual leader at Burg Rothenfels. Publication of *Briefe vom Comersee*.

1928–42 Preaches at St. Benedict Chapel in Berlin.

1929 Publication of *Von heiligen Zeichen*.

1930 Publication of *Vom lebendigen Gott*.

1935 Publication of *Christliches Bewusstsein; Die Bekehrung des Aurelius Augustinus; Vom Leben des Glaubens;* and "Der Heiland."

1937 Publication of *Der Herr* and *Der Engel in Dantes Göttlicher Komödie*.

1939 February: dismissed by the Reich from his professorship. August: the SS seizes Burg Rothenfels and the Reich disbands Quickborn. Publication of *Besinnung vor der Feier der heiligen Messe; Welt und Person;* and *Hölderlin: Weltbild und Frömmigkeit*.

1939–43 Remains in Berlin, continues to write, and lectures at St. Canisius Church.

1940 Writes "Ein Wort zur liturgischen Frage" to the bishops.

1941 The Reich stops *Die Schildgenossen* and prohibits Guardini from giving public addresses.

1943 Publication of *Vorschule des Beten* and *Der Tod von Sokrates*.

1943–45 Resides with Pastor Josef Weiger at Mooshausen.

The Mature Professor, 1945–68

1945 March: completes *Berichte über mein Leben* (published in 1984).

1945–47 Professor for "Religionsphilosophie und Christliche Weltanschauung" at the University of Tübingen. Publication of *Der Heilbringer in Mythos, Offenbarung und Politik.*

1948–63 Professor for "Religionsphilosophie und Christliche Weltanschauung" at the University of Munich. Preaches every Sunday at St. Ludwig's Church.

1950 Publication of *Das Ende der Neuzeit* and *Deutscher Psalter.*

1951 Publication of *Die Macht.*

1952 Pope Pius XII names Guardini a papal monsignor. Awarded the Peace Prize of the German Book Association.

1953 Publication of *Rainer Maria Rilkes Deutung des Daseins.*

1954 Awarded an honorary doctorate in philosophy by the University of Freiburg.

1957 Guardini's mother (b. 1862) dies at Isola Vicentina. The founding of the Katholische Akademie in Bayern (Munich).

1958 Received into the Peace Society of the Order "Pour le Mérite."

1959 Awarded the Medal of Distinguished Service by the West German government.

1962 Awarded the Erasmus Prize. In the autumn: withdraws from teaching at the University of Munich, due to illness.

1963 Retires from the University of Munich. Publication of *Tugenden* and *Weisheit der Psalmen.*

1964 Writes "Der Kultakt und die gegenwärtige Aufgabe der liturgischen Bildung" for the Third Liturgical Conference.

1965 Publication of *Die Kirche des Herrn.* Honored at an *akademische Feier.* Awarded an honorary doctorate by the University of Padua. Declines Pope Paul VI's invitation to become a cardinal. Writes "Prayer in the Hour of Enduring."

1965–68 Periods of hospitalization.

1968 Dies on October 1 and on October 4 is buried in the cemetery of the Oratorians at St. Laurence Church in Munich.

Posthumous Awards and Publications

1969 Awarded an honorary doctorate in philosophy by the University of Bologna.

1970 The Katholische Akademie in Bayern establishes the Guardini Prize, whose early recipients are Karl Rahner (1970), Hans Urs von Balthasar (1971), Oswald Nell-Breuning (1972), and Werner Heisenberg (1973).

1976 Publication of *Die Existenz des Christen* and *Theologische Brief an einen Freund.*

1993 Publication of *Ethik,* 2 volumes.

ABBREVIATIONS

1. Works by Romano Guardini

The date after each title indicates the work's appearance in German. See the bibliography for further information.

"Bäume"	"Die Bäume von Isola Vicentina" (1963)
Berichte	Berichte über mein Leben (1984)
Briefe	Theologische Briefe an einen Freund (1976)
Church	The Church and the Catholic (1922)
Conversion	The Conversion of St. Augustine (1935)
End	The End of the Modern World (1954)
"'Europa'"	"'Europa' und 'Christliche Weltanschauung'" (1953)
"Ironie"	"Wahrheit und Ironie" (1965)
Letters	Letters from Lake Como (1927)
Liturgy	The Spirit of the Liturgy (1918)
Lord	The Lord (1937)
Offenbarung	Die Offenbarung (1940)
Pascal	Pascal for Our Time (1935)
Power	Power and Responsibility (1951)
Rilke	Rilke's Duino Elegies (1953)
Verantwortung	"Verantwortung: Gedanken zur jüdischen Frage" (1952)
Wahrheit	Wahrheit des Denkens und Wahrheit des Tuns (1980)
"Warum?"	"Warum so viele Bücher?" (1955)
World	The World and the Person (1939)

2. Secondary Sources

Biblio	Bibliographie Romano Guardini (1885–1968). Edited by Hans Mercker and the Katholische Akademie in Bayern. Paderborn: Ferdinand Schöningh, 1978.
ChrPhil	Christliche Philosophie im katholischen Denken des 19. und 20. Jahrhunderts. Edited by Emerich Coreth et al. 3 volumes. Graz: Styria, 1987, 1988, 1990.

DicFTh	*Dictionary of Fundamental Theology.* Edited by René La-tourelle and Rino Fisichella. New York: Crossroad, 1995.
EnCa	*The HarperCollins Encyclopedia of Catholicism.* Edited by Richard P. McBrien. San Francisco: HarperCollins, 1995.
EnPhil	*The Encyclopedia of Philosophy.* Edited by Paul Edwards. 8 volumes. New York: Macmillan and The Free Press, 1967.
H	*Hochland*
HanCaTh	*Handbook of Catholic Theology.* Edited by Wolfgang Beinert and Francis Schüssler Fiorenza. New York: Crossroad, 1995.
HanFTh	*Handbuch der Fundamentaltheologie.* Edited by Walter Kern, Hermann J. Pottmeyer, and Max Seckler. 4 volumes. Freiberg: Herder, 1985–88.
HisCh	*History of the Church.* Edited by Hubert Jedin, Konrad Rep-gen, and John Dolan. Translated by Margit Resch and An-selm Biggs. 10 volumes. New York: Crossroad, 1981.
ITQ	*The Irish Theological Quarterly*
LitJb	*Liturgisches Jahrbuch*
LThK2	*Lexikon für Theologie und Kirche.* Second edition. 10 vol-umes. Freiburg: Herder, 1957–67.
LThK3	*Lexikon für Theologie und Kirche.* Third edition. 10 volumes. Freiburg: Herder, 1993–.
MoCa	*Modern Catholicism: Vatican II and After.* Edited by Adrian Hastings. New York: Oxford University Press, 1991.
NCaEn	*New Catholic Encyclopedia.* 15 volumes. Edited by the edito-rial staff of the Catholic University of America. New York: McGraw-Hill, 1967. Supplementary: volume 16 (1975); vol-ume 17 (1979); volume 18 (1988); volume 19 (1996).
NDicSWor	*The New Dictionary of Sacramental Worship.* Edited by Pe-ter Fink. Collegeville: The Liturgical Press, 1990.
NJBC	*New Jerome Biblical Commentary.* Edited by Raymond Brown et. al. Revised edition. Englewood Cliffs: Prentice-Hall, 1990).
RGG3	*Die Religion in Geschichte und Gegenwart.* Third edition. 6 volumes. Tübingen: J.C.B. Mohr (Paul Siebeck), 1957–65.
RGL	*Angefochtene Zuversicht. Romano Guardini Lesebuch.* Edited by Ingeborg Klimmer. Mainz: Matthias Grünewald, 1985.
RoGu	*Romano Guardini: Proclaiming the Sacred in a Modern*

	World. Edited by Robert A. Krieg. Chicago: Liturgy Training Publications, 1995.
Sch	*Die Schildgenossen.*
SysTh	*Systematic Theology: Roman Catholic Perspective.* Edited by Francis Schüssler Fiorenza and John P. Galvin. 2 volumes. Minneapolis: Fortress Press, 1991.
TuG	*Theologie und Glaube.*
TS	*Theological Studies.*
TRE	*Theologische Realenzyklopädie.* 24 volumes. Berlin: Walter de Gruyter, 1976–94.
VC2	*Vatican Council II.* Edited by Austin Flannery. Northport, N.Y.: Costello Publications, 1995.

NOTES

Chapter One: From Vatican I to Vatican II

1. See John Jay Hughes, *Pontiffs: Popes Who Shaped History* (Huntington, Ind.: Our Sunday Visitor, 1994), 192, 232, 262; Joseph Schmidlin, *Papstgeschichte der neuesten Zeit*, 2 (Munich: Kösel-Pustet, 1934), 93–101; idem, *Papstgeschichte der neuesten Zeit*, 3 (Munich: Kösel-Pustet, 1939), 18–27.

2. See Hermann J. Pottmeyer, "Vatican Council I," in EnCa, 1296–98; Marcel Chappin, "Vatican I," in DicFTh, 1147–51.

3. On the recent history of Catholic theology, see Thomas F. O'Meara, *Church and Culture: German Catholic Theology, 1860–1914* (Notre Dame: University of Notre Dame Press, 1991); Giacomo Martina, "The Historical Context in Which the Idea of a New Ecumenical Council Was Born," trans. Leslie Wearne, in René Latourelle, ed., *Vatican II: Assessment and Perspectives*, 1 (New York: Paulist Press, 1988), 3–73; Raymond Winling, *La théologie contemporaine (1945–1980)* (Paris: Le Centurion, 1983); T. Mark Schoof, *A Survey of Catholic Theology, 1880–1970*, trans. N. D. Smith (New York: Paulist Press, 1970); Roger Aubert, "Die Theologie während der ersten Hälfte des 20. Jahrhunderts," in Herbert Vorgrimler and Robert Vander Gucht, eds., *Bilanz der Theologie im 20. Jahrhundert*, 2 (Freiburg: Herder, 1964), 7–70; TS 50 (1989).

4. On Guardini's twofold commitment, see Arno Schilson, ed., *Konservativ mit Blick nach vorn* (Würzburg: Echter, 1994); Thomas Ruster, *Die verlorene Nützlichkeit der Religion* (Paderborn: Ferdinand Schöningh, 1994); Alfons Knoll, *Glaube und Kultur bei Romano Guardini* (Paderborn: Ferdinand Schöningh, 1993); Hans Mercker, *Christliche Weltanschauung als Problem* (Paderborn: Ferdinand Schöningh, 1988); Fridolin Wechsler, *Romano Guardini als Kerygmatiker* (Paderborn: Ferdinand Schöningh, 1973); Jakob Laubach, "Romano Guardini" (1960), in Leonhard Reinisch, ed., *Theologians of Our Time*, trans. Charles H. Henkey (Notre Dame: University of Notre Dame Press, 1964), 109–26; Paul Fechter, *An der Wende der Zeit* (Gütersloh: E. Bertelsmann, 1949), 159–67; Heinrich Getzeny, "Auf dem Wege Romano Guardini," H 21 (1924): 637–47.

5. See *Wahrheit*, 87.

6. Horst Georg Pöhlmann, *Gottes Denker* (Reinbek bei Hamburg: Rowohlt, 1984), 172.

7. Paul Misner, "Guardini, Romano," in NCaEn, 16, p. 198; see Heinz Robert Schlette, "Guardini, Romano (1885–1968)," in TRE 14, pp. 294–97, 296; Arno Schilson, *Perspektiven theologischer Erneuerung* (Düsseldorf: Patmos, 1986), 14; Walter Dirks, "Ro-

mano Guardini," in Heinz Jürgen Schultz, ed., *Tendenzen der Theologie* (Stuttgart: Kreuz, 1966), 248–52, 249.

8. This expression, found in Mt 16:3, was used by John XXIII in *Pacem in Terris* (1963), nn. 126–29, and then by Vatican II in *Gaudium et Spes* (1965), n. 4.

9. See Hans Mercker, "Vorlesungen und Schriften Guardinis in seiner Berliner Zeit," in Hermann Josef Schuster, ed., *Guardini Weiterdenken* (Berlin: Guardini Stiftung, 1993), 78–106; Hanna Barbara Gerl, *Romano Guardini 1885–1968* (Mainz: Matthias Grünewald, 1985); G. Maron, "Guardini, Romano," in RGG3 2: 1900; Karl Rahner, "Thinker and Christian: Obituary of Romano Guardini," in idem, *Opportunities for Faith*, trans. Edward Quinn (New York: Seabury, 1975), 127–31; Laubach, "Romano Guardini," 111.

10. See Hanna Barbara Gerl, *Anfechtung und Treue* (Donauwörth: Ludwig Auer, 1989), 23–29; idem, "Durchblick aufs Ganze," in Joseph Ratzinger, ed., *Wege zur Wahrheit* (Düsseldorf: Patmos, 1985), 32–69; RGL, 10; Hans Urs von Balthasar, *Romano Guardini: Reform aus dem Ursprung* (Munich: Kösel, 1970), 11–32.

11. See Gerl, *Romano Guardini;* idem, "Romano Guardini (1885–1968)," in Walter Seidel, ed., *"Christliche Weltanschauung"* (Würzburg: Echter, 1985), 11–36.

12. See Gerl, *Romano Guardini*, 20.

13. See Anton Wächter [Romano Guardini], "Thule oder Hellas? Klassiche oder deutsche Bildung?" *Der Wächter* 3 (1920): 2–16, 66–79; see RGL, 206–11. From 1916 through 1920, Guardini occasionally used the pseudonyms "Anton Wächter" and "Dr. A. Wacht" because he feared that diocesan officials would restrict his writing. He chose these names which are variations in German on the Italian "guardiniano" (Engl., "guardian"). See Biblio, 1–7; "'Europa,'" 9; Gerl, *Romano Guardini*, 17.

14. "Bäume," 37.

15. Gerl, *Romano Guardini*, 21.

16. See *Berichte*, 74–76.

17. See ibid., 77.

18. See ibid., 86–87.

19. Ibid., 81.

20. Romano Guardini, *Michelangelo* (Berlin: Pan, 1907). Hereafter, for Guardini's publications, his name will be omitted in the notes.

21. *Berichte*, 79–86; see Helmut Kuhn, *Romano Guardini* (Munich: Kösel, 1961), 20. Guardini dedicated *Christliches Bewusstsein* to Koch.

22. *Berichte*, 83. In 1913 the rector made a formal list of Koch's errors. Taking a leave of absence from the faculty in 1916, Koch served as a military chaplain on Germany's western front. Returning to Tübingen in 1918, he was told by the seminary's rector that he no longer had a teaching position at the seminary. For the remainder of his life, Koch served as a pastor in the diocese of Rottenburg-Stuttgart. See Max Seckler, *Theologie vor Gericht* (Tübingen: J.C.B. Mohr [Paul Siebeck], 1972).

23. *Berichte*, 92.

24. "'Europa,'" 13; see *Berichte*, p. 134. Throughout this book, translations from German texts are mine, unless otherwise noted.

25. It was published as *Systembildende Elemente in der Theologie Bonaventuras,* ed. Werner Dettloff (Leiden: Brill, 1964).

26. Nevertheless, Guardini felt deep affection for Mainz; see *Berichte,* 15; *Wahrheit,* 114. Today, Mainz has a small park named "Romano Guardini Platz."

27. Dr. Maria Schlüter-Hermkes, a leader within Berlin's Catholic organizations, promoted Guardini's appointment to the university. Her husband, Johannes Schlüter, worked in the Prussian Ministry of Cult (religious affairs). Subsequently, she wrote an essay on Guardini's theory of opposition: "Die Gegensatzlehre R. Guardinis," H 26 (1928–29): 529–39. See *Berichte,* 37–41; Gerl, *Romano Guardini,* 40–42.

28. Josef Pieper, *No One Could Have Known,* trans. Graham Harrison (San Francisco: Ignatius Press, 1987 [1979]), 34.

29. See Gerl, *Romano Guardini,* 279.

30. On February 12, 1945, Guardini asked his friend Johannes Spörl (d. 1977) to do what he judged best with Guardini's autobiography after his death; see *Berichte,* 15–17.

31. See *Wahrheit,* 70.

32. These sermons appeared in *Wahrheit und Ordnung: Universitätspredigten* (Würzburg: Werkbund, 1956–59).

33. See Kurt Hoffman, "Portrait of Father Guardini," *Commonweal* 60 (September 17, 1954): 575–77.

34. See William Dych, *Karl Rahner* (Collegeville: The Liturgical Press, 1992), 13.

35. "Ordinariats-Korrespondenz: Dokumentation," diocese of Munich-Freising (1968).

36. See Gerl, *Romano Guardini,* 352–56; Biblio, 466.

37. See Knoll, *Glaube und Kultur,* 496–99; Arno Schilson, "Romano Guardini und die Theologie der Gegenwart: Aspekte einer vergessenen Wirkungsgeschichte," TuG 80 (1990): 152–64; idem, *Perspektiven theologischer Erneuerung,* 14–16.

38. Even though Guardini wanted to work further on the book, the text of 1925 was reprinted in 1955 without revisions; see *Berichte,* 27; Knoll, *Glaube und Kultur,* 70; Gerl, *Romano Guardini,* 68, 250–53.

39. On Guardini's theological method, see Knoll, *Glaube und Kultur,* 74–99; Thomas Schreijäck, "Romano Guardini (1885–1968)—Sein philosophisches Werk," in ChrPhil 3, pp. 201–15; Gerl, *Romano Guardini,* 250–77; Schilson, *Perspektiven theologischer Erneueruung,* 19–20; Wechsler, *Romano Guardini als Kerygmatiker,* 15–29; Laubach, "Romano Guardini."

40. See Knoll, *Glaube und Kultur,* 46; Schilson, *Perspektiven theologischer Erneuerung,* 19; Gerl, *Romano Guardini,* 43; Balthasar, *Romano Guardini,* 23–53.

41. On the *Lebensphilosophie* and Catholic theology in the 1920s, see Richard Schaeffler, "Philosophie und katholische Theologie im 20. Jahrhundert," in ChrPhil 3, pp. 49–79; Leo Scheffczyk, "Main Lines of the Development of Theology between the First World War and the Second Vatican Council," in HisCh 10, pp. 260–72; H. O. Pappé, "Philosophical Anthropology," EnPhil, 6, pp. 159–66; Adolf Kolping, *Katholische Theologie* (Bremen: Carl Schüneman, 1965), 68–70.

42. See Hanna Barbara Gerl, "Unterscheidung aus Verstehen: Romano Guardini

und Nietzsche," in Schuster, ed., *Guardini Weiterdenken,* 61–77; idem, *Romano Guardini,* 185; Mercker, *Christliche Weltanschauung,* 106–7.

43. See Mercker, *Christliche Weltanschauung,* 140; Gerl, *Romano Guardini,* 28; Robert A. Krieg, *Karl Adam* (Notre Dame: University of Notre Dame Press, 1993), pp. 159–78.

44. "'Europa,'"20.

45. "Ironie," 50.

46. Gerl, *Anfechtung,* 20–23; Eugen Biser, *Interpretation und Veränderung* (Paderborn: Ferdinand Schöningh, 1979), 34; Heinz Robert Schlette, "Romano Guardini—Versuch einer Würdigung" (1969), in idem, *Aporie und Glaube* (Munich: Kösel, 1970), 247–87, 259. Adam Heinrich Müller's *Die Lehre vom Gegensatz* (1804) contributed to this discussion in Germany; see Gerl, *Romano Guardini,* 253.

47. Other phenomenologists of this period are Konrad Martius, Edith Stein, and Peter Wust. On German Catholics' adoption of phenomenology, see Mariasusai Dhavamony, "Religion II: Phenomenology," in DicFTh, 827–36; Bernhard Braun, "Der allgemein-philosophische Hintergrund: Der deutschsprachige Raum im 20. Jahrhundert," in ChrPhil 3, pp. 80–88; Kolping, *Katholische Theologie,* 62–70; Heinrich Fries, *Die katholische Religionsphilosophie der Gegenwart* (Heidelberg: F. H. Kerle, 1949).

48. "Warum?" 33.

49. See Herbert Spiegelberg, *The Phenomenological Movement,* 3d rev. ed. (The Hague: Martinus Nijhoff, 1982); Richard Schmitt, "Phenomenology," in EnPhil 6, pp. 135–51.

50. See *Wahrheit,* 71, 77, 112; Gerl, *Romano Guardini,* 87, 110, 263.

51. See Edward T. Oakes, *Pattern of Redemption: The Theology of Hans Urs von Balthasar* (New York: Continuum, 1994); Peter Hebblethwaite, "Husserl, Scheler and Wojtyla: A Tale of Three Philosophers," *The Heythrop Journal* 27 (1986): 441–45; Robert A. Krieg, "Cardinal Ratzinger, Max Scheler and Christology," ITQ 47 (1981): 205–19; George Huntston Williams, *The Mind of John Paul II* (New York: Seabury, 1981), 115–40.

52. See *Der Gegensatz,* 3d ed. (Mainz: Matthias Grünewald, 1985). Guardini dedicated this book to K. Neundörfer, who died in 1925 as the book was being published; see "Karl Neundörfer zum Gedächtnis," Sch 6 (1926): 387.

53. *Der Gegensatz,* 9.

54. See Hanna Barbara Gerl, "Leben in Ausgehaltener Spannung: Romano Guardinis Lehre vom Gegensatz," in *Der Gegensatz,* 217–35; idem, *Romano Guardini,* 250–66; E. Fastenrath, *"In vitam aeternam"* (St. Ottilien: EOS, 1982), 727–802; Biser, *Interpretation,* 52; Balthasar, *Romano Guardini,* 23–26; Laubach, "Romano Guardini," 114–15; Karl Wucherer-Huldenfeld, *Die Gegensatzphilosophie Romano Guardinis in ihren Grundlagen und Folgerungen* (Vienna: Verlag Notring, 1968); Fries, *Die katholische Religionsphilosophie,* 272–74; Erich Przywara, "Tragische Welt," *Stimmen der Zeit* 111 (1926): 183–98.

55. On the notion of the living-concrete, see Werner Löser, "Universale Concretum," in DicFTh, 1145–46; idem, "Universale concretum als Grundgesetz der oeconomia revelationis," in HanFTh 2, pp. 108–21.

56. *Der Gegensatz,* 16.

57. Ibid., 29.

58. Ibid., 30.

59. See *Wahrheit*, 131, 133; *Briefe*, p. 51. On the view that life must include evil as well as good, see Gordon A. Craig, *Germany, 1866–1945* (New York: Oxford University Press, 1978), 218; Ronald Gray, *The German Tradition in Literature, 1871–1945* (Cambridge: Cambridge University Press, 1965), 1–15.

60. *Der Gegensatz*, 19.

61. Ibid., 25.

62. See Ernst Tewes, "Romano Guardini," LitJb 19 (1969): 129–41, 130.

63. See "Warum?" 30; Mercker, *Christliche Weltanschauung*, 11; Wechsler, *Romano Guardini als Kerygmatiker*, 54.

64. See Knoll, *Glaube und Kultur*, 131, 343; Gerl, *Anfechtung*, 25.

65. See "Ein Gespräch vom Reichtum Christi" (1923), in *Auf dem Wege* (Mainz: Matthias Grünewald, 1923), 151–65; Joseph Ratzinger, "Vom Liturgie zur Christologie," in idem, *Wege zur Wahrheit*, 137–42.

66. See *Berichte*, 26–27.

67. See Mathia Köck, "Quarrachi—Der franziskanische Beitrag zur Erforschung des Mittelalters," in ChrPhil 2, pp. 390–97.

68. See Gerald McCool, *From Unity to Pluralism* (New York: Fordham University Press, 1989), 5–38; idem, *Catholic Theology in the Nineteenth Century* (New York: Seabury, 1977), 241–67.

69. As noted by Schoof (*A Survey*, 83), prior to Vatican II Catholic theologians turned to Bonaventure's writings as a source for theological renewal. Mainz's Bishop Albert Stohr (1890–1961) studied Bonaventure, as did Joseph Ratzinger (b. 1927): see J. Ratzinger, *The Theology of History in St. Bonaventure*, trans. Zachary Hayes (Chicago: Franciscan Herald Press, 1971 [1959]).

70. See *Berichte*, 27.

71. See Francis Schüssler Fiorenza, "Systematic Theology: Task and Methods," in SysTh 1, pp. 1–88, 28–30. On neoscholasticism, see Benedict Ashley, "neo-Scholasticism," EnCa, 911; Heinrich M. Schmidinger, "'Scholastik' und 'Neuscholastik,'" in ChrPhil 2, pp. 23–53; James A. Weisheipl, "Neoscholasticism and Neothomism," NCaEn 10, p. 337; idem, "Scholastic Method," NCaEn 12, pp. 1145–46; idem, "Scholasticism, Contemporary," NCaEn 12, pp. 1165–70.

72. Yves Congar, *A History of Theology*, trans. Hunter Guthrie (Garden City: Doubleday, 1968), 179.

73. See Walter Kasper, *The Methods of Dogmatic Theology*, trans. John Drury (Glen Rock, N.J.: Paulist Press, 1969 [1967]), pp. 11–21.

74. On Bonaventure's thought, see Zachary Hayes, *The Hidden Center* (New York: Paulist, 1981); idem, "Christology and Metaphysics in the Thought of Bonaventure," *The Journal of Religion* 58: *Supplement* (1978): S82-S96; Ewert Cousins, *Bonaventure and the Coincidence of Opposites* (Chicago: Franciscan Herald Press, 1978).

75. See "St. Francis and Self-Achievement" (1927), in *The Focus of Freedom*, trans. Gregory Roettger (Baltimore: Helicon, 1966), 7–32.

76. See Gerl, *Romano Guardini*, 85–86; Balthasar, *Romano Guardini*, 61–65; Klaus

Hemmerle, *Theologie als Nachfolge* (Freiburg: Herder, 1975); Laubach, "Romano Guardini," 111.

77. Guardini, *Systembildende Elemente*, 148.

78. Ibid., 212.

79. "Anselm von Canterbury und das Wesen der Theologie" (1921), in *Auf dem Wege*, 33–65, 61; see Knoll, *Glaube und Kulture*, 141.

80. See Joseph A. Komonchak, "Theology and Culture at Mid-Century: The Example of Henri de Lubac," TS 51 (1990): 579–602; Martina, "The Historical Context in Which the Idea of a New Ecumenical Council was Born."

81. See Herbert Vorgrimler, *Understanding Karl Rahner*, trans. John Bowden (New York: Crossroad, 1986), 55–56; Schoof, *A Survey*, 73; Tewes, "Romano Guardini," 139.

82. On Vatican II's theological approaches, see Giuseppe Alberigo and Joseph A. Komonchak, eds., *The History of Vatican II*, 1 (Maryknoll, New York: Orbis, 1996); Richard P. McBrien, "Vatican Council II," in EnCa, 1299–1306; René Latourelle, "Vatican II," in DicFTh, 1151–62; Otto Pesch, *Das Zweite Vatikanische Konzil* (Würzburg: Echter, 1993), 21–104; Hermann J. Pottmeyer, "The Traditionalist Temptation of the Contemporary Church," *America* 168 (September 5, 1992): 100–104; idem, "Die zwiespältige Ekklesiologie des Zweiten Vaticanums—Ursache nachkonziliarer Konflikte," *Trierer Theologische Zeitschrift* 92 (1983): 272–83; Michael A. Fahey, "Church," in SysTh 2, pp. 4–74; Alexandre Ganoczy, "Kirche im Prozess der pneumatischen Erneuerung," in Elmar Klinger and Klauz Wittstadt, eds., *Glaube im Prozess* (Freiburg: Herder, 1984), 196–206.

83. Guardini admitted that he did not have a mind for historical research; see *Berichte*, 27, 32–34.

84. Early in Guardini's career this shortcoming was noted by Ernst Michel, "Toter und lebendiger 'Liberalismus,'" in Karlheinz Schmidthüs, ed., *Christliche Verwirklichung* (Rothenfels am Main: Burgverlag, 1935), 284–91. Also see Otto Weiss, *Der Modernismus in Deutschland* (Regensburg: Friedrich Pustet, 1995), 535–40.

85. See Ruster, *Die verlorene Nützlichkeit*, 191.

86. According to Karl Rahner, Guardini never forgot the trauma of seeing how Rome's condemnation of modernism brought hardship to his professors, especially W. Koch; see K. Rahner, *I Remember*, trans. by Harvey D. Egan (New York: Crossroad, 1985), 73–75; *Berichte*, 27. Bishop Karl Lehmann of Mainz has observed that Rahner's work had a greater impact upon the church's official theology than Guardini's because Rahner spoke explicitly about the church's teachings and, as a result, engaged neoscholastic theologians and church authorities; see K. Lehmann, "Karl Rahner: A Portrait," in K. Lehmann, Albert Raffelt, and Harvey Egan, eds., *The Content of Faith*, trans. Robert J. Braunreuther (New York: Crossroad, 1992), 1–43, 11–12.

87. See Knoll, *Glaube und Kultur*, 131, 540.

88. "Warum?" 30.

89. Ibid., 31.

90. Guardini did not significantly change the content of his themes during his life; however, his emphases changed, depending upon the situation; see Mercker, *Christliche Weltanschauung*, 41; Balthasar, *Romano Guardini*, 30–32. This view is challenged by Biser, *Interpretation und Veränderung*, 94–100.

91. See Gerl, *Anfechtung*, 9, 29.

92. See the articles by P. Beer, J. Meyer zu Schlochtern, H.J. Pottmeyer, and H. Waldenfels in TuG 86 #2 (1996); Ruster, *Die verlorene Nützlichkeit*, 33–34; Marcel Chappin, "Theologies VI: Contextual Theology," in DicFTh, 1097–1102.

93. Erich Przywara and Adolf Kolping have characterized the period after World War I as German Catholicism's "decade of movements"; see E. Przywara, "Le Mouvement théologique et religieux en Allemagne," *Nouvelle Revue Théologique* 56 (1929): 565–75; Kolping, *Katholische Theologie*, 71; Schlette, "Romano Guardini—Versuch," 250–60.

94. See Schlette, "Romano Guardini—Versuch," 285; Gerl, *Romano Guardini*, 15–16. According to Schlette (p. 285 n. 106), in *Romano Guardini* Balthasar has not adequately described the historical context of Guardini's thought, and, as a result, has simplified his complexity. This same observation applies to Joseph Ratzinger's discussions of Guardini's theology; see, for example, J. Ratzinger, "Guardini on Christ in Our Century," *Crisis* 14 (June 1996): 14–15. To be sure, both Balthasar and Ratzinger illumine Guardini's thought. However, by not saying enough about the circumstances in which Guardini worked, they have softened the coincidence of opposites in Guardini's writings and actions. I return to this observation in chapter 9.

Chapter Two. The Self-Disclosure of God

1. Vatican I, Dogmatic Constitution on the Catholic Faith, in Norman P. Tanner, ed., *Decrees of the Ecumenical Councils, 2: Trent—Vatican II* (Washington, D.C.: Georgetown University Press, 1990), 806.

2. Vatican II, Dogmatic Constitution on Divine Revelation, n. 2, in VC2, 97–98.

3. Gotthold Lessing, "On the Proof of the Spirit and of Power" (1777), in *Lessing's Theological Writings*, ed. Henry Chadwick (Stanford: Stanford University Press, 1956), 53.

4. See Avery Dulles, *Models of Revelation* (Garden City: Doubleday, 1983), 21–23.

5. Adolf Harnack, *What Is Christianity?* trans. by Thomas Bailey Saunders (New York: Harper and Row, 1957), 125–26.

6. See O'Meara, *Church and Culture*; McCool, *Catholic Theology in the Nineteenth Century*; Avery Dulles, *Revelation Theology* (New York: Herder and Herder, 1969).

7. Adolphe Tanquerey, *A Manual of Dogmatic Theology*, 1, trans. John J. Byrnes (New York: Desclée Company, 1959), 22–23.

8. Wolfgang Beinert, "Revelation," in HanCath, 598–604, 600. See René Latourelle, "Revelation," in DicFTh, 905–50; Josef Schmitz, "Das Christentum als Offenbarungsreligions im kirchlichen Bekenntnis," in HanFTh 2, pp. 15–28; Avery Dulles, "Faith and Revelation," in SysTh 1, pp. 89–128.

9. See Weiss, *Der Modernismus in Deutschland*; Daniel Donovan, "Church and Theology in the Modernist Crisis," *Proceedings of the Catholic Theological Society of America* 40 (1985): 145–59; Gabriel Daly, *Transcendence and Immanence* (Oxford: Clarendon, 1980); Thomas M. Loome, *Liberal Catholicism, Reform Catholicism, Mod-*

ernism (Mainz: Matthias Grünewald, 1979); Norbert Trippen, *Theologie und Lehramt im Konflikt* (Freiburg: Herder, 1977); Roger Aubert, "Reform Catholicism in Germany," in HisCh 9, pp. 422–30; Wilhelm Spael, *Das katholische Deutschland im 20. Jahrhundert* (Würzburg: Echter, 1964), 148–77.

10. See George Griener, "Herman Schell and the Reform of the Catholic Church in German," TS 54 (1993): 427–54; Werner Sosna, *Selbstmitteilung Gottes in Jesus Christus* (Paderborn: Ferdinand Schöningh, 1993). On Koch, see Seckler, *Theologie vor Gericht.*

11. See Bernhard Langemeyer, *Der dialogische Personalismus in der evangelischen und katholischen Theologie der Gegenwart* (Paderborn: Ferdinand Schöningh, 1963), 247–64.

12. *Berichte,* 68; see Gerl, *Romano Guardini,* 42–45. Unless otherwise noted, Guardini's statements in this chapter concerning his conversion are quoted from *Berichte.*

13. *Berichte,* 71–72. The biblical verses in this passage and throughout this book are quoted from the *Holy Bible: The New Revised Standard Version* (Nashville: Thomas Belson Publishers, 1990).

14. Mercker, *Christliche Weltanschauung,* 24–30.

15. *Conversion,* xvi-xvii. Guardini dedicated this book to Josef Weiger; Gerl, *Romano Guardini,* 42–45, 285.

16. Mercker, *Christliche Weltanschauung,* 28; Gerl, *Anfechtung,* 22.

17. Rudolf Otto, *The Idea of the Holy,* trans. John W. Harvey (New York: Oxford University Press, 1958), 6–7.

18. Ibid., 12–24.

19. See *Briefe,* 41.

20. "Religiöse Erfahrung und Glaube" (1934), in *Unterscheidung des Christlichen,* rev. ed., ed. by Hans Waldmann (Mainz: Matthias Grünewald, 1963), 307–39, 328.

21. See "The Meaning of Melancholy" (1928), in *The Focus of Freedom,* 55–92; *Die Existenz des Christen* (Paderborn: Ferdinand Schöningh, 1977), 6; *Briefe,* 41; Gerl, *Romano Guardini,* 62–63, passim.

22. See Knoll, *Glaube und Kultur,* 90–95, passim. Guardini lectured on Kierkegaard's thought in spring 1925, autumn 1925, and autumn 1927; see Biblio, 17–22; Hermann Josef Schuster, "Vorlesungen und Lehrveranstaltungen Romano Guardinis in Berlin, Tübingen, München," in idem, ed., *Guardini Weiterdenken,* 273–85.

23. "Der Ausgangpunkt der Denkbewegung Søren Kierkegaards" (1927), in *Unterscheidung des Christlichen,* 471–501, 478.

24. Ibid., 481.

25. "Religiöse Erfahrung und Glaube," 355.

26. See Ruster, *Die verlorene Nützlichkeit,* 117–21; Mercker, *Christliche Weltanschauung,* 56–65.

27. Wilhelm Dilthey, *Weltanschauungslehre,* in idem, *Gesammelte Schriften,* 8 (Leipzig: B.G. Teubner, 1931), 82.

28. See H. P. Rickman, "Dilthey, Wilhelm," in EnPhil 2, pp. 403–7; Herbert A.

Hodges, *The Philosophy of Wilhelm Dilthey* (London: Routledge & Kegan Paul, 1952), 72–95.

29. See G. Söhngen, "Weltanschauung," LThK2 10: 1027–29; J. Klein, "Weltanschauung," RGG3 6: 1603–6.

30. See *Berichte*, 45; Gerl, *Romano Guardini*, 142–44; idem, "'Durchblick aufs Ganze,'" 66.

31. "Vom Wesen katholischer Weltanschauung" (1923), in *Unterscheidung des Christlichen*, 1–22, 10.

32. Ibid., 11.

33. Ibid., 23.

34. A similar view is expressed in Karl Rahner, "Thoughts on the Possibility of Belief Today," in idem, *Theological Investigations*, 5, trans. Karl H. Kruger (New York: Crossroad, 1983), 3–22.

35. See Knoll, *Glaube und Kultur*, 545; Ludger Honnefelder, "Weltanschauung und Glaube," in L. Honnefelder and Matthias Lutz-Bachmann, eds., *Auslegungen des Glaubens* (Berlin: Morus, 1987), 107–24; Mercker, *Christliche Weltanschauung*, 12.

36. See Maurice Friedman, *Martin Buber's Life and Work: The Later Years, 1945–1965* (New York: E.P. Dutton, 1983), 111.

37. Buber's letter is quoted in Gerl, *Romano Guardini*, 133 n. 38; see Haim Gordon and Jochanan Bloch, *Martin Buber: A Centenary Volume* (New York: KTAV, 1984), 446. For the letter itself, see M. Buber, *Briefwechsel*, 2 (Heidelberg: L. Schneider, 1973), #114.

38. Guardini's statement is quoted in Gerl, *Romano Guardini*, 133–34.

39. Martin Buber, *I and Thou*, trans. Walter Kaufmann (New York: Charles Scribner's Sons, 1970), 78. Unless otherwise noted, Buber's statements are quoted from *I and Thou*.

40. An early expression of Guardini's theological anthropology is: "Über Sozialwissenschaft und Ordnung unter Personen" (1926), in *Unterscheidung des Christlichen*, 34–63. See Knoll, *Glaube und Kultur*, 338–73; Gunda Böning, "Strukturen der Freiheit," in Schilson, ed., *Konservativ mit Blick nach vorn*, 49–68; Schilson, *Perspektiven theologischer Erneuerung*, 158–96; Mario Farrugia, "Man's Quest for Truth" (Ph.D. Dissertation, Gregorianum University, 1986); Jörg Splett, "Zum Person-Begriff Romano Guardinis," in Seidel, ed., *"Christliche Weltanschauung,"* 80–109; Schlette, "Romano Guardini—Versuch einer Würdigung"; Ursula Berning-Baldeaux, *Person und Bildung im Denken Romano Guardini* (Würzburg: Echter, 1968); Helmut Kuhn, "Romano Guardini: Christian Existence," trans. William G. Kramer, *Philosophy Today* 4 (1960): 158–71.

41. *World*, viii. Unless otherwise noted, Guardini's statements on personal existence in this chapter are quoted from *World*.

42. See Wechsler, *Romano Guardini als Kerygmatiker;* Dulles, *Revelation Theology*, 145–46; Aubert, "Die Theologie während der ersten Hälfte des 20. Jahrhunderts," 24–27. Guardini's notion of revelation is similar to the later thought of F. W. J. Schelling (d. 1854). On Schelling's philosophy, see Thomas F. O'Meara, "Revelation and History: Schelling, Möhler and Congar," ITQ 53 (1987): 17–35; idem, "Christ in Schelling's Philosophy of Revelation," *The Heythrop Journal* 27 (1986): 275–89; idem, *Romantic Idealism*

and Roman Catholicism (Notre Dame: University of Notre Dame Press, 1982); Walter Kasper, "Krise und Neuanfang der Christologie im Denken Schellings," *Evangelische Theologie* 33 (1973): 366–84; idem, *Das Absolute in der Geschichte* (Mainz: Matthias Grünewald, 1965). Given that both Guardini and Kasper have drawn on Schelling's thought, their theologies are similar.

43. See *The Life of Faith*, trans. John Chapin (Westminster, Md.: Newman Press, 1961 [1935]); *The Word of God on Faith, Hope and Charity*, trans. Stella Lange (Chicago: Henry Regnery, 1963 [1949]).

44. *Offenbarung*, 118–19; see "Die Offenbarung," Sch 19 (1940): 22–31. Unless otherwise noted, Guardini's statements on revelation in this chapter are quoted from *Offenbarung*.

45. See Knoll, *Glaube und Kultur*, 477–98; Gerl, *Anfechtung*, 20–24; Mercker, *Christliche Weltanschauung*, 14–48; Peter Eicher, *Offenbarung* (Munich: Kösel, 1977), 261–92; René Latourelle, *Theology of Revelation* (New York: Society of St. Paul, 1966), 315–76; Werner Bulst, *Revelation*, trans. Bruce Vawter (New York: Sheed and Ward, 1965), 26–27.

46. See Roger Aubert, *Le Problème de l'Acte de Foi*, 3d ed., (Louvain: E. Warny, 1958), 626–30.

47. Beinert, "Revelation," in HanCaTh, 601.

48. See Arno Schilson, "The Major Theological Themes of Romano Guardini," in RoGu, 31–42; idem, "Romano Guardini und die Theologie der Gegenwart"; Hans Waldenfels, *Offenbarung* (Munich: Max Hueber, 1969), 282–93.

49. Mercker, *Christliche Weltanschauung*, 158. Avery Dulles has observed (*Revelation Theology*, 145) that kerygmatic theologies have leaned toward "an excessively objectivist notion of revelation and of science."

50. See Gerl, *Romano Guardini*, 61.

51. See "Heilige Schrift und Glaubenswissenschaft," Sch 8 (1928): 24–57.

52. See *Berichte*, 84–86; Mercker, *Christliche Weltanschauung*, 42–48.

53. *Religion und Offenbarung* (Mainz: Matthias Grünewald, 1990), 7; see "Nur Wer Gott kennt, kennt den Menschen" (1952), in *Religiöse Erfahrung und Glaube* (Mainz: Matthias Grünewald, 1974), 102–17.

54. See Laubach, "Romano Guardini," 121.

55. *Conversion*, xvii.

56. *Berichte*, 46.

57. "'Europa,'" 22.

58. Ibid., 20.

59. Vatican II, Pastoral Constitution on the Church in the Modern World, n. 2 and n. 3, in VC2, 163–64.

Chapter Three. The Church: A Light to the Nations

1. Vatican Council I, Dogmatic Constitution on the Church of Christ, in Tanner, ed., *Decrees of the Ecumenical Councils*, 2: *Trent–Vatican II*, 811–16.

2. Vatican Council I, The First Draft of the Dogmatic Constitution on the Church

of Christ, in John Clarkson et al., eds. and trans., *The Church Teaches* (St. Louis: B. Herder, 1955), 88.

3. See Walter Kasper, "The Church as Communion" (1986), in idem, *Theology and Church*, trans. Margaret Kohl (New York: Crossroad, 1989), 148–65.

4. On *Mystici Corporis*, see Leo Scheffczyk, "Main Lines of the Development of Theology between the First World War and the Second Vatican Council," in HisCh 10, pp. 260–77; Avery Dulles, *Models of the Church* (Garden City: Doubleday, 1978), pp. 51–66.

5. *Berichte*, 88.

6. On Guardini's ecclesiology, see Ruster, *Die verlorene Nützlichkeit der Religion*, 183–96, 357–67; idem, "Vom 'Sinn der Kirche,'" in Schilson, ed., *Konservativ mit Blick nach vorn*, 103–14; Eva-Maria Faber, "Das Kirchenbild Guardinis," in Schilson, ed., *Konservativ mit Blick nach vorn*, 68–80; idem, *Kirche zwischen Identität und Differenz* (Würzburg: Echter, 1993), 11–116; Knoll, *Glaube und Kultur*, 114–29; Matthias Lutz-Bachmann, "Der Begriff der Kirche bei Romano Guardini," in Honnefelder and Lutz-Bachmann, eds., *Auslegungen des Glaubens*, 62–84; Schilson, "The Major Theological Themes of Romano Guardini"; idem, *Perspektiven theologischer Erneuerung*, 199–256.

7. See Dulles, *Models of the Church*, 95–108; Faber, *Kirche zwischen Identität und Differenz*, 107–16.

8. Max Scheler, "Soziologische Neuorientierung und die Aufgaben der deutschen Katholiken nach dem Krieg" (1915/1916), in idem, *Gesammelte Werke*, 4, ed. Manfred Frings (Bern: Franck, 1982): 373–472, 440. See Alois Baumgartner, *Sehnsucht nach Gemeinschaft* (Munich: Ferdinand Schöningh, 1977), 156.

9. See Baumgartner, *Sehnsucht nach Gemeinschaft*; Peter Gay, *Weimar Culture* (New York: Harper, 1968), 70–101.

10. See René Wellek, "Romanticism Re-examined," in S. G. Nichols, ed., *Concepts of Criticism* (New Haven: Yale University Press, 1963), 199–21.

11. See Koppel S. Pinson, *Modern Germany*, 2d ed., (New York: Macmillan, 1966), 454–66, 461.

12. See Sefton Delmer, *Weimar Germany* (New York: American Heritage Press, 1972), 74.

13. See Gay, *Weimar Culture*, 17–27.

14. Friedrich Meinecke, *Die Idee der Staatsräson in der neueren Geschichte* (Munich: R. Oldenbourg, 1924), 490. See Gay, *Weimar Culture*, 81.

15. See Peter D. Stachura, *The German Youth Movement 1900–1945* (New York: St. Martin's Press, 1981); Hajo Holborn, *A History of Modern Germany*, 3 (New York: Alfred A. Knopf, 1969), 411–13; W. Uhsadel et al., "Jugendbewegung," in RGG3 3: 1013–24; Gay, *Weimar Culture*, 75–80; Otto Friedrich, *After the Deluge* (New York: Harper and Row, 1972), 243–45.

16. Franz Marc, "Die 'Wilden' Deutschlands," in F. Marc and Wassily Kandinsky, eds., *Der Blaue Reiter*, re-edited by Klaus Lankheit, *Dokumentarische Neuausgabe* (Munich: R. Piper, 1965), 30.

17. Gay, *Weimar Culture*, 101.

18. See Pinson, *Germany,* 177–78; Baumgartner, *Sehnsucht nach Gemeinschaft,* 19. On nineteenth-century German Catholicism, see Paul Misner, *Social Catholicism in Europe* (New York: Crossroad, 1991); O'Meara, *Romantic Idealism and Roman Catholicism.*

19. See Scheffczyk, "Main Lines of the Development of Theology"; Erwin Iserloh, "Movements within the Church and Their Spirituality," in HisCh 10, pp. 299–335.

20. See Iserloh, "Movements within the Church," 299–307; Heinz Hürten, *Kurze Geschichte des deutschen Katholizismus* (Mainz: Matthias Grünewald, 1986), 193; Johannes Binkowski, *Jugend als Wegbereiter* (Stuttgart: Konrad Theiss, 1981), 102–3; Franz Henrich, *Die Bünde der katholischen Jugendbewegung* (Munich: Kösel, 1968); Felix Messerschmid, "Katholische Jugendbewegung," in RGG3 3: 1020–22; Kolping, *Katholische Theologie,* 73–80; Spael, *Das katholische Deutschland,* 216–23.

21. See Guenther Lewy, *The Catholic Church and Nazi Germany* (New York: McGraw-Hill, 1964), 4.

22. See Gerl, *Romano Guardini,* 155–61, 193.

23. See Baumgartner, *Sechsucht nach Gemeinschaft,* 68–86, 121–23.

24. See *Berichte,* 88.

25. See Vatican II, The Dogmatic Constitution on the Church, in VC2; Dulles, *Models of the Church.*

26. Johann Adam Möhler, *Die Einheit in der Kirche,* ed. Josef Rupert Geiselmann (Cologne: Jakob Hegner, 1957), 5, 7. See idem, *Unity in the Church,* trans Peter C. Erb (Washington, D.C.: The Catholic University Press of America, 1996), 81, 82–83.

27. Johann Adam Möhler, *Symbolism,* trans. James Burton Robertson (London: Gibbings, 1906), 258–59; see idem, *Symbolism* (New York: Crossroad, 1997).

28. On Möhler's thought, see O'Meara, "Revelation and History: Schelling, Möhler and Congar"; idem, *Romantic Idealism and Roman Catholicism;* R. William Franklin, *Nineteenth Century Churches* (New York: Garland, 1989); James T. Burtchaell, "Drey, Möhler and the Catholic Tübingen School," in Ninian Smart et al., eds., *Nineteenth Century Religious Thought in the West,* 2 (Cambridge: Cambridge University Press, 1985), 111–39.

29. *Berichte,* 61; see Gerl, *Romano Guardini,* 25–28.

30. *Berichte,* 67–69.

31. Ibid., 68; Gerl, *Romano Guardini,* 49.

32. Quoted in Gerl, *Romano Guardini,* 48.

33. The first lecture, "Das Erwachen der Kirche," appeared in H 19/2 (1921–22). See *Berichte,* 36; Gerl, *Romano Guardini,* 137.

34. Guardini was included on a list of outstanding Catholic lecturers in *Das Jahrbuch der Deutschen Katholiken* (Augsburg: Haas & Grabherr, 1921); others on this list were N. Ehlen, H. Hoffmann, E. Krebs, M. Laros, H. Platz, and M. Scheler. See Guardini, *Berichte,* 34–36, 104–5, 112–13; Gerl, *Romano Guardini,* 122–48.

35. *Vom Sinn des Kirches* (Mainz: Matthias Grünewald, 1990), 19; *Church,* 11; Marc, "Die 'Wilden' Deutschlands," 30. Unless otherwise noted, Guardini's ecclesiological statements in this chapter are quoted from *Church.*

36. On Guardini's challenge to neoscholastic ecclesiology, see Lutz-Bachmann,

"Der Begriff der Kirche bei Romano Guardini," 73–79. On neoscholastic ecclesiology, see Richard P. McBrien, *Catholicism*, 3d ed. (New York: Harper Collins, 1994), 657–59; Avery Dulles, "A Half Century of Ecclesiology," TS 50 (1989): 419–42.

37. Tanquerey, *A Manual of Dogmatic Theology*, 1, p. 107.

38. "Universität und Synkretismus," in *Das Jahrbuch der Deutschen Katholiken*, 50. See Gerl, *Romano Guardini*, 58, 149.

39. See Knoll, *Glaube und Kultur*, 130.

40. See Faber, *Kirche zwischen Identität und Differenz*, 107–9.

41. Ketteler's tomb rests at a side altar in the Cathedral of Mainz. See Misner, *Social Catholicism in Europe*.

42. *Berichte*, 111–12, 128. Guardini likely knew, too, of the social outreach of Adolf Kolping (d. 1895).

43. Scheffczyk, "Main Lines of the Development of Theology," 261–62; see Iserloh, "Movements within the Church," 305–7.

44. Erich Przywara, "Corpus Christi Mysticum" (1940), in idem, *Katholische Krise*, ed. Bernhard Gertz (Düsseldorf: Patmos Verlag, 1967), 123–52, 133.

45. Roger Aubert, "Les grandes tendances théologiques entre les deux guerres," *Collectanea Mechliniensia* 31 (1946): 17–36, 27, 29.

46. See Josef Meyer zu Schlochtern, *Sakrament Kirche* (Freiburg: Herder, 1992), 43–44; Avery Dulles, "Theology and Philosophy" (1990), in idem, *The Craft of Theology*, expanded edition (New York: Crossroad, 1995), 119–34, 120; Walter Kasper, "The Church as the Place of Truth," in idem, *Theology and Church*, 129–147, 130–32; Heinrich Fries, "Der Sinn von Kirche im Verständnis des heutigen Christentums," in HanFTh 3, pp. 17–29, 18; Victor Conzemius, "Die Kritik der Kirche," in HanFTh 3, pp. 30–48, 47.

47. See Gerl, *Romano Guardini*, 212–24; Elisabeth Wilmes, *Jahre auf dem Burg Rothenfels. Chronik 1926–1937* (Burg Rothenfels: Theatinerkreis, 1983); Binkowski, *Jugend as Wegbereiter*, 51–84; Hermann Hoffmann, *Im Dienst des Friedens* (Stuttgart: Konrad Theiss, 1970), 160–68; W. Mogge, "Quickborn," in LThK2 8: 937; idem, "Rothenfels am Main, Burg," in LThK2 9: 67.

48. See Gerl, *Romano Guardini*, 94–100.

49. *Berichte*, 104.

50. See "Katholische Jugendgemeinschaft," *Quickborn* 8 (1920–21): 242–44; "Die Abende im Rittersaal," in Hermann Horrmann (ed.), *Wehender Geist* (Burg Rothenfels am Main: Deutsches Quickbornhaus, 1920), 86–89; "Quickborn," *Pharus* 12 (1921): 96–115; "Parzival," in Ludwig Neundörfer, ed., *Der neue Anfang* (Burg Rothenfels am Main: Deutsches Quickbornhaus, 1922), 17–18.

51. See *Berichte*, 36; Gerl, *Romano Guardini*, 158–80.

52. See Gerl, *Romano Guardini*, 100–103.

53. "Burg Rothenfels: Rückblick und Vorschau" (1949), in RGL, 229.

54. Quoted in Gerl, *Romano Guardini*, 178.

55. Pieper, *No One Could Have Known*, 39.

56. See Karl H. Neufeld, *Die Brüder Rahner* (Freiburg: Herder, 1994), 56–57.

57. Ibid., 252–53.

58. Rahner, *I Remember*, 28.

59. See *Berichte*, 106, 115; Gerl, *Romano Guardini*, 180–92.

60. See Gerl, *Romano Guardini*, 193–203.

61. See *Church*, 92–123; *The Church of the Lord*, 85–94.

62. This letter of March 29, 1952, is quoted in Gerl, *Romano Guardini*, 59.

63. *Lord*, 96. On the church's positive qualities, see pp. 238–42, 456–57.

64. See *Berichte*, 92–93; Gerl, *Romano Guardini*, 77–80.

65. According to Guardini, because of Bendix's interference, a conflict occurred in 1921 between Guardini and the religious superior of the convent where he resided as chaplain; see *Berichte*, 103.

66. See *Berichte*, 26–31; Gerl, *Romano Guardini*, 107–9.

67. See Gerl, *Romano Guardini*, 174; Binkowski, *Jugend als Wegbereiter*, 59, 168, 189.

68. See Binkowski, *Jugend als Wegbereiter*, 134–35.

69. *Berichte*, 116.

70. Ibid., 118–19.

71. Ibid., 44.

72. See ibid., 111–12; Henrich, *Die Bünde*, 54; Hans Gerhard Müller, "Carl Sonnenschein (1876–1929)," in Wolfgang Knauft, ed., *Miterbauer des Bistums Berlin* (Berlin: Morus, 1979), 9–22; Stanis Edmund Szydzik, "Romano Guardini (1885–1968)," in Knauft, ed., *Miterbauer des Bistums Berlin*, 77–92.

73. See Knoll, *Glaube und Kultur*, 148; Mercker, "Vorlesungen und Schriften Guardinis in seiner Berliner Zeit," 93 n. 2.

74. See Virgil C. Funk, "Liturgical Movement, The (1830–1969)," in NDicSWor, 695–715, 703; Iserloh, "Movements within the Church," 302–4; Albert Stohr, "Romano Guardini Fünfundsiebzig Jahre Alt," LitJb 10 (1960): 200–201.

75. *Berichte*, 117–18.

76. See Latourelle, "Vatican II"; Hastings, "Catholic History from Vatican I to John Paul II"; Giacomo Martina, "The Historical Context in Which the Idea of a New Ecumenical Council Was Born."

77. See Otto Dibelius, *Das Jahrhundert der Kirche*, 2d ed. (Berlin: Furche, 1927), 137–53.

78. See McBrien, "Vatican II"; Fahey, "Church," in SysTh 2, pp. 4–74, 30–43.

79. Pesch, *Das Zweite Vatikanische Konzil*, 136; cf. 168.

80. Schilson, "Romano Guardini und die Theologie der Gegenwart," 157.

81. See Kasper, "The Church as Communion"; Faber, *Kirche zwischen Identität und Differenz*, 359–69.

82. See *Berichte*, 99–100; Faber, "Das Kirchenbild Guardinis," 71–73; Schilson, "Romano Guardini und die Theologie der Gegenwart," 158; idem, *Perspecktiven theologischer Erneuerung*, 199–258; Mercker, *Christliche Weltanschauung*, 23–24.

83. See Meyer zu Schlochtern, *Kirche Sakrament*, 43–44; Walter Kasper, "The Church as a Universal Sacrament of Salvation" (1984), in idem, *Theology and Church*, 111–28. On the difference between Guardini's view of church as symbol and Vatican II's view of church as sacrament, see Lutz-Bachmann, "Der Begriff der Kirche bei Romano Guardini," 75.

84. On Vatican II's steps beyond the ecclesiology of the body of Christ, see Fahey, "Church," in SysTh 2, pp. 30–43; Dulles, *Models of the Church*, 56–59.

85. See Lutz-Bachmann, "Der Begriff der Kirche bei Romano Guardini," 75–77.

86. See Ruster, *Die verlorene Nützlichkeit*, 398.

87. See Faber, "Das Kirchenbild Guardinis," 75–80; idem, *Kirche zwischen Identität und Differenz*, 107–14.

88. On Guardini's view of Protestantism, see *Wahrheit*, 12–14, 133, 136; "Evangelisches Christentum in katholischer Sicht heute," *Una-Sancta-Rundbriefe* 13 (1958): 225–33; Mercker, *Christliche Weltanschauung*, pp. 15–18, 30–42; Gerl, *Romano Guardini*, 176–78. According to Peter Eicher, Guardini prepared the Catholic Church for ecumenism by stressing the centrality of Jesus Christ in Christian belief; see Eicher, *Offenbarung*, 261–92.

89. See Knoll, *Glaube und Kultur*, 497 n. 270; Mercker, *Christliche Weltanschauung*, 22–24.

90. See *The Church of the Lord*, trans. Stella Lange (Chicago: Henry Regnery, 1966), 111–14; Gerl, *Romano Guardini*, 350.

91. See Faber, *Kirche zwischen Identität und Differenz*, 8, 112.

92. *The Church of the Lord*, 113. See Balthasar, *Romano Guardini*, 104.

93. Romano Guardini, "Brief an Papst Paul VI" (1954), in Paul Schmidt, *Die pädagogische Relevanz einer anthropologischen Ethik* (Düsseldorf: Patmos, 1973), 9–10.

94. See Faber, "Die Kirchenbild Guardinis," 71–75; idem, *Kirche zwischen Identität und Relevanz*, 36–76.

95. *Berichte*, 88.

Chapter Four. Liturgy as Play before God

1. Regina Kuehn, "Romano Guardini in Berlin," in RoGu, 87–92, 88; cf. *Berichte*, 106–7.

2. Heinz R. Kuehn, "Fire in the Night: Germany 1920–1950," in RoGu, 1–14, 7–8.

3. On the liturgical movement, see Mark Searle, "liturgical movement," in EnCa, 783–84; Virgil C. Funk, "Liturgical Movement, The (1830–1969)," in NDicSWor, 695–715; Aidan Kavanagh, "Liturgical and Credal Studies," in Henry W. Bowden, ed., *A Century of Church History* (Carbondale: Southern Illinois University Press, 1988), 216–44; Alois Baumgartner, "Die Auswirkungen der liturgischen Bewegung auf die Kirche und Katholizismus," in Anton Rauscher, ed., *Religiös-kulturelle Bewegungen im deutschen Katholizismus seit 1800* (Paderborn: Ferdinand Schöningh, 1986), 121–36; Iserloh, "Movements within the Church"; idem, "Die Geschichte der liturgischen Bewegung" (1959), in idem, *Kirche—Ereignis und Institution*, 1 (Münster: Aschendorff, 1985), 436–51; R. William Franklin, "The Nineteenth-Century Liturgical Movement," *Worship* 53 (1979): 12–39; L. C. Shepperd, "Liturgical Movement, Catholic," in NCaEn 8, pp. 900–905; Ernest B. Koenker, *The Liturgical Renaissance in the Roman Catholic Church* (Chicago: University of Chicago Press, 1954).

4. On the movement's phases, see *Liturgie und liturgische Bildung* (Würzburg:

Werkbund, 1966), 15; *Wahrheit,* 31; Heinrich Kahlefeld, "Die Phasen der liturgischen Erneuerung" (1969), in idem, *Kleine Schriften* (Frankfurt am Main: Josef Knecht, 1984), 177–89.

5. In its choice of Guardini's texts, this chapter is similar to Theodor Maas-Ewert, "Anwalt des liturgischen Anliegens," in Siedel, ed., *"Christliche Weltanschauung",* 163–83.

6. See Bernard Botte, *From Silence to Participation,* trans. John Sullivan (Washington, D.C.: The Pastoral Press, 1988), 1–8.

7. See Funk, "Liturgical Movement, The," 695–700; Michael Kwatera, "Benedictines and Liturgical Renewal," in NDicSWor, 129–134.

8. See Shepperd, "Liturgical Movement, Catholic," 902–3.

9. Pius X, *Tra le sollecitudini,* in R. Kevin Seasoltz, ed., *The New Liturgy: A Documentation, 1903 to 1965* (New York: Herder and Herder, 1966), 3–10, 4.

10. See EnCa, 671; G. J. O'Brien, "Integralism," in NCaEn 7, pp. 552–53.

11. See Funk, "Liturgical Movement, The," 700.

12. This slogan has been mistakenly attributed to Pius X; see John H. McKenna, "Papacy, Modern, and Liturgical Renewal," in NDicSWor, 922–25, 923; Koenker, *The Liturgical Renaissance,* 12–13, 235 n. 10.

13. See Funk, "Liturgical Movement, The," 700; Sonya Quitsland, *Beauduin* (New York: Newman, 1973).

14. See Kwatera, "Benedictines and Liturgical Renewal," 131.

15. See Baumgartner, "Die Auswirkungen der liturgischen Bewegung," 124; Schilson, *Perspektiven theologischer Erneuerung,* 51–52; Holborn, *A History of Modern Germany, 1840–1945,* 3, p. 657; Pinson, *Modern Germany,* 462.

16. On Pius Parsch, see NCaEn 10, 1040; Koenker, *The Liturgical Renaissance,* 14–16.

17. *Berichte,* 60–61; Gerl, *Romano Guardini,* 22.

18. See Gerl, *Romano Guardini,* 35.

19. See ibid., 42.

20. See *Berichte,* 74; Gerl, *Romano Guardini,* 46.

21. See Gerl, *Romano Guardini,* 51–52.

22. *Berichte,* 87–88.

23. *Liturgie und liturgische Bildung,* 20–21; cf. *Berichte,* 88–89.

24. The monks with whom Guardini frequently spoke were Anselm Manser, who was acquainted with the thought of Max Scheler; Odilo Wolff, who spoke about Plato's philosophy; and Placidus Pflumm who was an advisor of Ildefons Herwegen at the Abbey of Maria Laach; see Gerl, *Romano Guardini,* 64.

25. *Berichte,* 96.

26. See Martin Marschall, *In Wahrheit beten* (St. Ottilien: EOS, 1986); Arno Schilson, "Romano Guardini: Wegbereiter und Wegbegleiter der liturgischen Erneuerung," LitJb 36 (1986): 3–27; Tewes, "Romano Guardini"; Walter Dirks, "Guardini als Führer zur Liturgie," LitJb 10 (1960): 202–10.

27. *Liturgy,* 122. Unless otherwise noted, Guardini's statements on the liturgy in this chapter are quoted from *Liturgy.*

28. Gerl, *Romano Guardini,* 109.

29. Henrich, *Die Bünde,* 40.

30. Hans Maier, "Nachwort," in *Vom Geist der Liturgie* (Mainz: Matthias Grüne-wald, 1983), 145–58, 152; cf. Schilson, *Perspektiven theologischer Erneuerung*, 37; John F. Baldovin, review of *Holy Things* by Gordon W. Lathrop, in TS 55 (1994): 569.

31. See Maas-Ewerd, "Anwalt der liturgischen Anliegens," 164.

32. On *Vom Geist der Liturgie*, see Marschall, *Im Wahrheit beten*, 51–111; Knoll, *Glaube und Kultur*, 100–14; Schilson, *Perspektiven theologischer Erneuerung*, 34–79; Gerl, *Romano Guardini*, 109–19.

33. See Henrich, *Die Bünde*, 78–79.

34. See Burkhard Neunheuser, "Romano Guardini and His Vision of the Liturgy" (1982), *Liturgy O.C.S.O.* 29 (1995): 73–81.

35. See Baumgartner, "Die Auswirkungen der liturgischen Bewegung," 132.

36. Ibid., 126.

37. On the impact of *Vom Geist der Liturgie*, see Franz Henrich, "Leben, Persön-lichkeit und Charisma Romano Guardinis," in Ratzinger, ed., *Wege zur Wahrheit*, 9–32; Tewes, "Romano Guardini"; Dirks, "Guardini als Führer zur Liturgie."

38. Kathleen Hughes, "Romano Guardini's View of Liturgy," in RoGu, 73–85, 83.

39. Henrich, *Die Bünde*, 96.

40. Maier, "Nachwort," 150.

41. See Henrich, *Die Bünde*, 30, 40, 76–82; Frederic Debuyst, "The Church: A Dwell-ing Place of Faith," *Studia Liturgica* 24 (1994), 30–31. On R. Schwartz, see Wolfgang Pehnt and Hilde Strohl, *Rudolf Schwartz, 1897–1961* (Stuttgart: Gerd Hatje, 1997).

42. Burkhard Neunheuser has recalled that "[t]owards four or five o'clock in the afternoon, [Guardini] used to excuse himself and break off his work in order to pray Vespers standing upright before a lectern on which a large breviary lay open"; see B. Neunheuser, "Romano Guardini and His Vision of the Liturgy," 74.

43. *Liturgy*, 123.

44. An instance is *Wille und Wahrheit* (Mainz: Matthias Grünewald, 1933). See He-inrich Dumovlin, *Zen Buddhism in the Twentieth Century*, trans. Joseph O'Leary (New York: Weatherhill, 1992), 107–10; Henrich, *Die Bünde*, 135.

45. See Henrich, *Die Bünde*, 93.

46. Dirks, "Guardini als Führer zur Liturgie," 203.

47. On Casel, see Theresa F. Koernke, "Mystery Theology," in NDicSWor, 883–91; Arno Schilson, *Theologie als Sakramententheologie* (Mainz: Matthias Grünewald, 1982).

48. See "Das Objektive im Gebetsleben," *Das Jahrbuch für Liturgie Wissenschaft* 1 (1921): 117–25.

49. See Gerl, *Romano Guardini*, 121–28; Neunheuser, "Romano Guardini and His Vision of the Liturgy," 78. Casel's lack of enthusiasm for liturgical renewal among the Catholic youth is evident in O. Casel, "Liturgische Bewegungen: 2. In der katholische Kirche," *Religion in Geschichte und Gegenwart*, 2d ed., 3 (1929): 1698–1701.

50. Funk, "Liturgical Movement," 702–4; Theodor Maas-Ewerd, *Die Krise der Litur-gischen Bewegung in Deutschland und Österreich* (Regensburg: Friedrich Pustet, 1981); Ferdinand Kolbe, *Die liturgische Bewegung* (Aschaffenburg: Paul Pattloch, 1964); Koenker, *The Liturgical Renaissance*, 18–20; Burkhard Neunheuser, "Report on Liturgi-cal Activities in Germany During the War," *Orate Fratres* 21 (1946–47): 114–22.

51. See Eugene O'Sullivan, *In His Presence* (Wilmington, Del.: Michael Glazier, 1980). On Guardini's influence, see Karl Fröhlich, "Das Volksliturgie Apostolat von St. Paul in München," in Georg Schwaiger, ed., *Das Erzbistum München und Freising in der Zeit der nationalsozialistischen Herrschaft*, 1 (Munich: Schell und Steiner, 1984), 122–30.

52. See "Ein Wort zur liturgischen Frage" (1940), in R. Guardini, *Liturgie und liturgische Bildung*, 193–213. An abbreviated text is: "Some Dangers of the Liturgical Renewal," in Alfons Kirchgässner, ed., *Unto the Altar*, trans. Rosaleen Brennan (New York: Herder and Herder, 1963), 13–22; Hughes, "Romano Guardini's View of Liturgy," 79–82; Maas-Ewerd, "Anwalt des liturgischen Anliegens," 167–69; Schilson, *Perspecktiven theologischer Erneuerung*, 43–47.

53. Albert Stohr, "Romano Guardini Fünfundsiebzig Jahre Alt," 200–201.

54. See Iserloh, "Movements within the Church," 302–5.

55. On Gröber's criticism of Guardini's view of the Eucharist, see *La Maison-Dieu* 7 (1946): 101.

56. See Karl Rahner, *Theologische und philosophische Zeitfragen im katholischen deutschen Raum (1943)*, ed. Hubert Wolf (Ostfildern: Schwabenverlag, 1994); J. Gülden, "Krise der Liturgischen Bewegung (1942–1944)," in Balthasar Fischer et al., eds., *Ein Leben für Liturgie und Kerygma* (Innsbruck: Tyrolia, 1975), 64–68; Vorgrimler, *Karl Rahner*, 32–42.

57. See Maas-Ewerd, *Die Krise der Liturgischen Bewegung*, 435–53; Iserloh, "Movements within the Church," 303–4.

58. See Maas-Ewerd, *Die Krise des Liturgischen Bewegung*, 453–76.

59. See Pius XII, *Mediator Dei* (November 22, 1947), in Claudia Carlen, ed., *The Papal Encyclicals, 1939–1958* (Raleigh: McGrath, 1981), 118–56; Funk, "Liturgical Movement," 705–6.

60. See Pius XII, *Mediator Dei*, n. 8; Shepperd, "Liturgical Movement," 903.

61. See Pius XII, *Mediator Dei*, n. 19.

62. See "Die liturgische Erfahrung und die Epiphanie," in *Die Sinne und die religiöse Erkenntnis* (Zurich: Verlag der Arche, 1950), 39–70.

63. See "A Letter from Romano Guardini," *Herder Correspondence* (Special Issue, 1964): 24–26; *Liturgie und liturgische Bildung*, 9–18.

64. Gerl, *Romano Guardini*, 356–57.

65. See Johannes Wagner, *Mein Weg zur Liturgiereform 1936–1986* (Freiburg: Herder, 1993), 42–43.

66. See Annibale Bugnini, *The Reform of the Liturgy, 1948–1975*, trans. Matthew J. O'Connell (Collegeville: The Liturgical Press, 1990), 938.

67. See Gerl, *Romano Guardini*, 360–64.

68. Vatican II, The Constitution on the Sacred Liturgy, in VC2, n. 7, p. 121.

69. Ibid., n. 14, p. 124.

70. See Aidan Kavanagh, "Liturgy," in MoCa, 68–74, 69; Baumgartner, "Die Auswirkungen der liturgischen Bewegung," 135.

71. See Pesch, *Das Zweite Vatikanische Konzil*, 115, 131.

72. See Bugnini, *The Reform of the Liturgy*, 544.

73. Schilson, "Romano Guardini und die Theologie der Gegenwart," 161; see idem,

"Die liturgische Bewegung," in Klemens Richter and A. Schilson, eds., *Den Glauben feiern* (Mainz: Matthias Grünewald, 1989), 11–48.

74. See Baumgartner, "Die Auswirkungen der liturgischen Bewegung," 131.

75. On liturgy and inculturation, see R. E. McCarron, "Inculturation, Liturgical," in NCaEn 19, pp. 179–86; David N. Power, *Worship: Culture and Theology* (Washington, D.C.: The Pastoral Press, 1990).

76. See Gerl, *Romano Guardini*, 210.

77. See Hughes, "Romano Guardini's View of Liturgy," 74–79; Knoll, *Glaube und Kultur*, 512–20; Albert Gerhards, "Romano Guardini als Prophet des Liturgischen," in Schuster, ed., *Guardini Weiterdenken*, 1, pp. 140–53; Klemens Richter, "Die Frage nach der Liturgiefähigkeit angesichts einer erneuerten Liturgie," in Honnefelder and Lutz-Bachmann, eds., *Auslegungen des Glaubens*, 85–106; Jennifer Glenn, "Twenty Years Later," *Assembly* 12 (April 1986): 325–28; Schilson, *Perspektiven theologischer Erneuerung*, 48–50; Walter Birnbaum, *Das Kultusproblem und die liturgischen Bewegungen des 20. Jahrhunderts* (Tübingen: Katzmann, 1966).

78. "A Letter from Romano Guardini," 25. Unless otherwise noted, Guardini's statements in this chapter on the situation in 1964 are quoted from "A Letter from Romano Guardini."

79. Tewes, "Romano Guardini," 136–37.

80. *Liturgische Bildung*, 22. Guardini's positive view also appears in his diary entry for June 19, 1953; see *Wahrheit*, 39.

81. See Knoll, *Glaube und Kultur*, 512; Richter, "Die Frage," 86.

82. *Spirit*, 139.

83. See Mercker, *Christliche Weltanschauung*, 135–37, 158.

84. See *Briefe*, 55.

85. See Gerl, *Anfechtung*, 25.

86. Neunheuser, "Romano Guardini and His Vision of the Liturgy," 81.

87. Regina Kuehn, *A Place for Baptism* (Chicago: Liturgy Training Publications, 1992), 13.

88. See Bugnini, *The Reform of the Liturgy 1948–1975*, 179; Regina Kuehn, "Romano Guardini: The Teacher of Teachers," in Robert L. Tuzik, ed., *How Firm A Foundation: Leaders of the Liturgical Movement* (Chicago: Liturgy Training Publications, 1990), 36–49, 36.

Chapter Five. Christian Faith and Literature

1. " 'Europa,' " 19–20; see *Berichte*, 45; Gerl, *Romano Guardini*, 142–44.

2. See Schuster, "Vorlesungen und Lehranstaltung Romano Guardinis."

3. See Biblio.

4. See Knoll, *Glaube und Kultur*, 261–77.

5. Paul Fechter, *Geschichte der deutschen Literatur* (Gütersloh: C. Bartelsmann, 1952), 190, 193; Albert Soergel and Curt Hohoff, *Dichtung und Dichter der Zeit*, rev. ed., 2 (Düsseldorf: August Bagel Verlag, 1963), 662–63; Hermann Kunisch, "Romano

Guardini," in idem ed., *Handbuch der deutschen Gegenwartsliteratur,* 2d ed., 1 (Munich: Nymphenburger Verlagshandlung, 1969), 244–48.

6. See Nathan A. Scott, *The Broken Center* (New Haven: Yale University Press, 1966), 23–24, 212–13; idem, "The Name and Nature of Our Period Style" (1959), in G. B. Tennyson and Edward E. Ericson, Jr., eds., *Religion and Modern Literature* (Grand Rapids: William B. Eerdmans, 1975), 121–37, 137.

7. Theodore Ziolkowski, "Theologie und Literatur," in Walter Jens, Hans Küng, and Karl Josef Kuschel, eds., *Theologie und Literatur* (Munich: Kindler, 1986), 113–28, 115–16; Walter Jens and Hans Küng, *Literature and Religion,* trans. Peter Heinegg (New York: Paragon House, 1991 [1985]), vii, 25, 118, 124, 297, 301, 306.

8. See Hermann Kunisch, "Interpretatio Christiana," in Ratzinger, ed., *Wege zur Wahrheit,* 96–120, 99.

9. G. Maron, "Guardini, Romano," RGG3 2: 1900; W. Sucker, "Der Katholizismus der Gegenwart," RGG3 3: 1219–26.

10. The English text lacks the foreword and postscript of the German text as well as a few paragraphs from the German introduction.

11. See Jens, *Literature and Religion,* vii; Gerl, *Romano Guardini,* 211; Schlette, "Romano Guardini—Versuch einer Würdigung."

12. See Spael, *Das katholische Deutschland,* 246–78.

13. On Catholic literary revival in Germany, see Weiss, *Der Modernismus in Deutschland,* 458–75; Jutta Osinski, *Katholizismus und deutsche Literatur im 19. Jahrhundert* (Paderborn: Ferdinand Schöningh, 1993); O'Meara, *Church and Culture,* 181–85; Manfred Weitlauff, " 'Modernismus litterarius,' " *Beiträge zur Altbayerischen Kirchengeschichte* 37 (1988): 97–175; Wolfgang Frühwald, "Katholische Literatur im 19. und 20. Jahrhundert in Deutschland," in Rauscher, ed., *Religiös-kulturelle Bewegungen,* 9–26; Vincent Berning, "Geistig-kulturelle Neubesinnung im deutschen Katholizismus vor und nach dem ersten Weltkrieg," in Rauscher, ed., *Religiös-kulturelle Bewegungen,* 47–98; T. A. Riley, "German Literature, 7: 1880 to the Present," in NCaEn 6, pp. 419–24; Mary Johannella Fiecke, *The Revival of Catholic Literature in Twentieth-Century Germany* (Milwaukee: School Sisters of Saint Francis, 1948).

14. The first *Katholikentag* was held in Mainz in 1848. On the "inferiority debate," see Frühwald, "Katholische Literatur," 12–17; Soergel and Hohoff, *Dichtung und Dichter,* 744.

15. See Schatz, *Zwischen Säkularisation und Zweitem Vatikanum,* 190–91.

16. See V. Conzemius, "Germany: Since 1789," in NCaEn 6, pp. 440–48; W. Grenzmann, "Literary Revival, Catholic," NCaEn 8, pp. 817–23.

17. In 1898 Joseph Müller, a priest and the editor of the journal *Renaissance,* coined the term *Reformkatholizismus,* and in that same year the Vatican censured Schell's writings. On "Reform Catholicism," see Weiss, *Der Modernismus in Deutschland;* Donovan, "Church and Theology in the Modernist Crisis"; Loome, *Liberal Catholicism, Reform Catholicism, Modernism;* Norbert Trippen, *Theologie und Lehramt im Konflikt;* Aubert, "Reform Catholicism"; Vincent Berning, "Modernismus und Reformkatholizismus in ihrer prospektiven Tendenz," in Franz Pöggeler, ed., *Die Zukunft der Glaubensunterweisung* (Freiburg: Seelsorge, 1971), 9–32, Schoof, *A Survey,* 72–93; John J. Heaney, *The*

Modernist Crisis (Washington, D.C.: Corpus Books, 1968), 422–30; Spael, *Das katholische Deutschland*, 148–75.

18. See Berning, "Geistig-kulturelle Neubesinnung im deutschen Katholizismus," 65–69; Spael, *Das katholische Deutschland*, 106–20.

19. Osinski, *Katholizismus und deutsche Literatur*, 343; Soergel and Hohoff, *Dichtung und Dichter*, 1, pp. 744–46.

20. Carl Muth, "Ein Vorwort," H 1 (1903–4): 1–4; reprinted in *Hochland (Neues)* 64 (1972): 1.

21. In 1914 *Stimmen aus Maria Laach*, which was founded in 1870, became *Stimmen der Zeit* and took a more positive stance toward modernity. On Kreiten and Baumgartner, see Osinski, *Katholizismus und deutsche Literatur*, 253–337; Frühwald, "Katholische Literatur im 19. und 20. Jahrhundert," 15–17, 24–26; Berning, "Geistig-kulturelle Neubesinnung im deutschen Katholizismus," 69–71; Fiecke, *The Revival of Catholic Literature*, 100–158.

22. Fiecke, *The Revival of Catholic Literature*, 105.

23. Soergel and Hohoff, *Dichtung und Dichter*, 1, p. 744.

24. Richard von Kralik, "Ein literarisches Programm," *Der Gral* 1 (1906–7): 50–51.

25. See Osinski, *Katholizismus und deutsche Literatur*, 381–88.

26. Carl Muth, "Vom *Gral* und der Gralbündlern," H 5 (1907–8): 603.

27. Richard von Kralik, "Literatur Umschau," *Der Gral* 2 (1907–8): 267.

28. Soergel and Hohoff, *Dichtung und Dichter*, 1, p. 746.

29. Weiss, *Der Modernismus in Deutschland*, 472.

30. Also in 1972 Hans Urs von Balthasar founded the *Internationale katholische Zeitschrift: "Communio"* as an alternative to *Concilium*, which Hans Küng, Johannes Metz, and Edward Schillebeeckx had begun in 1964; see *Internationale katholische Zeitschrift* 1 (1972): 1–17.

31. Muth (d. 1944) remained editor until 1941 when the Reich banned *Hochland*. After the war, Muth's associate Karl Schaezler assumed leadership of the journal; see NCaEn 10, pp. 144–45; Soergel and Hohoff, *Dichtung und Dichter*, 1, p. 746.

32. See Biblio.

33. *Berichte*, 103.

34. See Gerl, *Romano Guardini*, 103–5.

35. See ibid., 25, 20, 89–90.

36. Quoted in Gerl, *Romano Guardini*, 34.

37. Quoted in ibid., 40–41.

38. *Berichte*, 64.

39. See ibid., 67–68; Gerl, *Romano Guardini*, 47.

40. See Gerl, *Romano Guardini*, 53, 98.

41. See Hermann Kunisch, "Romano Guardini als Interpret," *Stimmen der Zeit* 195 (1977): 602–16; idem, *Handbuch der deutschen Gegenwartsliteratur*, 246.

42. See Gerl, *Romano Guardini*, 41.

43. See *Berichte*, 50.

44. See Knoll, *Glaube und Kultur*, 261–336; Gerl, *Romano Guardini*, passim; Balthasar, *Romano Guardini*, 53–89.

45. See Gerl, *Romano Guardini*, 349.

46. See Binkowski, *Jugend als Wegbereiter*, 184.

47. "Zu R. M. Rilkes Erster Elegie," Sch 17 (1938): 170.

48. See Schuster, "Vorlesungen und Lehranstaltungen Romano Guardinis," 273–85; Gerl, *Romano Guardini*, 332.

49. *Rilke*, 9.

50. Guardini dedicated two other books to his mother: *Über Wilhelm Raabes Stopfkuchen* (1932) and *Der Rosenkranz Unserer Lieben Frau* (1940). He dedicated his first book on Dante, *Der Engel in Dantes Göttlicher Komödie* (1937), to his father, with these words: "'To the memory of my father from whose lips I as a child plucked the first verses of Dante." He dedicated *Vom Geist der Liturgie* (1918) to both parents; see Gerl, *Romano Guardini*, 20, 23 n. 19.

51. *Wahrheit*, 52.

52. Ibid., 55.

53. Ibid., 72.

54. *Rilke*, 14.

55. Ibid., 14.

56. Ibid.

57. See "Religiöse Erfahrung und Glaube" (1934), 307–39.

58. On the *Duino Elegies*, see J. B. Leishman and Stephen Spender, Introduction, in Rainer Maria Rilke, *Duino Elegies*, trans. J. B. Leishman and S. Spender (New York: W. W. Norton, 1967), 9–18.

59. The verses of the *First Elegy* are quoted from Rainer Maria Rilke, *Duino Elegies and the Sonnets to Orpheus*, trans. A. Poulin, Jr. (Boston: Houghton Mifflin, 1977).

60. *Rilke*, 25. Unless otherwise noted, Guardini's statements on the *Duino Elegies* are quoted from *Rilke*.

61. Rainer Maria Rilke, *The Notebooks of Malte Laurids Brigge*, trans. Stephen Mitchell (London: Pan Books, 1988), 251–60.

62. See Knoll, *Glaube und Kultur*, 261–77; Mercker, *Christliche Weltanschauung*, 112–31. According to the philosopher Iring Fetscher, Guardini's essays on the *Duino Elegies* aided his religious conversion in 1946; see I. Fetscher, *Neugier und Furcht* (Hamburg: Hoffmann and Campe, 1995), 326–27.

63. Guardini's standing within literary circles is evident in that one of his essays on the *Duino Elegies* is included in Ulrich Fülleborn and Manfred Engel, eds., *Rilkes 'Duineser Elegien'*, 2: *Forschungsgeschichte* (Frankfurt am Main: Suhrkamp, 1982).

64. Soergel and Hohoff, *Dichtung und Dichter der Zeit*, 1, pp. 662–63.

65. See Hans Georg Gadamer, *Gesammelte Werke* (Tübingen: J.C.B. Mohr [Paul Siebeck], 1986–93): vol. 1, pp. 376, 492; vol. 4, p. 171; vol. 8, p. 113; vol. 9, pp. 11, 163, 271–81; 289, 291, 313.

66. Hans Georg Gadamer, *Truth and Method*, trans. Garrett Barden and John Cumming (New York: Crossroad, 1984), 444, 532 n. 123; also, 333, 527 n. 274.

67. Gadamer, *Gesammelte Werke*, 9, pp. 271–81, 272. Gadamer's statements on Guardini's approach are quoted from *Gesammelte Werke*, 9.

68. Martin B. Green, *Yeat's Blessings on von Hügel: Essays on Literature and Religion* (London: Longmanns, Green, 1967), 78, 94–96, 124, 186–88, 229, 247. Green's statements on Guardini's work are quoted from *Yeat's Blessings*.

69. Kunisch, "Interpretatio Christiana," 114.

70. Ibid., 117.

71. Hermann Kunisch, *Rainer Maria Rilke*, 2d ed. (Berlin: Duncker and Humblot, 1974), 227–37, 248–53, 391, 403, 443–49, 504.

72. See ibid., 227–37.

73. Vatican II, Pastoral Constitution on the Church in the Modern World, n. 59, in VC2, 235. The pastoral constitution is quoted from VC2.

74. "'Europa,'" 20.

Chapter Six. Nazism: A Negation of the Person

1. See Klaus P. Fischer, *Nazi Germany: A New History* (New York: Continuum, 1995), 366; Joachim C. Fest, *Hitler*, trans. Richard and Clara Winston (New York: Vintage Books, 1975), 424; Marshall Dill, Jr., *Germany* (Ann Arbor: University of Michigan Press, 1970), 363; William L. Shirer, *The Rise and Fall of the Third Reich* (New York: Simon and Schuster, 1960), 241.

2. See Fischer, *Nazi Germany*, 366.

3. See Pieper, *No One Could Have Known*, 89–100. Pieper recalls Germans' naive response to the events of 1933.

4. *World*, 114.

5. *Der Heilbringer in Mythos, Offenbarung und Politik* (Mainz: Matthias Grünewald, 1979), 74.

6. See Heinz Hürten, *Deutsche Katholiken 1918–1945* (Paderborn: Ferdinand Schöningh, 1992), 299–314; Fritz Stern, "National Socialism as Temptation" (1984), in idem, *Dreams and Delusions*, (New York: Alfred A. Knopf, 1987), 147–91, 148; F. Stern, "Germany 1933: Fifty Years Later" (1983), in idem, *Dreams and Delusions*, 119–46, 139; Fest, *Hitler*, 422–24.

7. See Ruster, *Die verlorene Nützlichkeit*, 183–96; Ulrich Bröckling, *Katholische Intellektuelle in der Weimarer Republik* (Munich: Wilhelm Fink, 1993); Knoll, *Glaube und Kultur*, 382–87; Hürten, *Deutsche Katholiken*, 112–15, 218, 228, 333–46; Donald J. Dietrich, *Catholic Citizens in the Third Reich* (New Brunswick, N.J.: Basic Books, 1988); idem, "Catholic Theologians in Hitler's Reich: Adaptation and Critique," *The Journal of Church and State*, 29 (Winter 1987): 19–45.

8. See Donald J. Dietrich, *God and Humanity in Auschwitz* (New Brunswick, N.J.: Transaction Books, 1995).

9. I am indebted to Donald J. Dietrich and J. Michael Phayer for their critiques of an earlier version of this chapter and to Kevin P. Spicer for his bibliographic advice.

10. See Fischer, *Nazi Germany*; Hürten, *Deutsche Katholiken*; Klaus Scholder, *Die Kirchen und das Dritte Reich*, 1: *Vorgeschichte und Zeit der Illusionen 1918–1934* (Frank-

furt am Main: Ulstein, 1986 [1977]); idem, *Die Kirchen und das Dritte Reich*, 2: *Das Jahr der Ernüchterung, Barmen und Rom* (Frankfurt am Main: Ulstein, 1988 [1985]).

11. See Georg Denzler, *Christen und Nationalsozialisten* (Frankfurt am Main: Fischer Taschenbuch, 1993); Klaus Breuning, *Die Vision des Reiches* (Munich: Max Hueber, 1969); Hermann Greive, *Theologie und Ideologie* (Heidelberg: Lambert Schneider, 1969); Guenter Lewy, *The Catholic Church and Nazi Germany* (New York: McGraw-Hill, 1964).

12. Quoted in Lewy, *The Catholic Church and Nazi Germany*, 16. See Rudolf Morsey, "Die katholische Volksminderheit und der Aufstieg des Nationalsozialismus 1930–1933," in Klaus Gotto and Konrad Repgen, eds., *Die Katholiken und das Dritte Reich*, 3d ed. (Mainz: Matthias Grünewald, 1990), 9–24, 10.

13. Pius IX condemned "liberalism" and implicitly democracy in his Syllabus of Errors (1864), but Leo XIII recognized the validity of democratic rule in *Immortale Dei* (1885). In his Christmas message of 1944 Pius XII spoke favorably of democracy, and John XXIII affirmed its value in *Pacem in Terris* (1963). Vatican II's *Gaudium et Spes* (1965), nn. 73–76, officially endorses democracy. See Paul E. Sigmund, "Democracy," in Judith A. Dwyer, ed., *The New Dictionary of Catholic Social Thought* (Collegeville: Liturgical Press, 1994), 269–75; idem, "Catholicism and Liberal Democracy," in R. Bruce Douglass and David Hollenbach, eds., *Catholicism and Liberalism* (Cambridge: Cambridge University Press, 1994), 217–41; Anthony Rhodes, *The Vatican in the Age of the Dictators (1922–1945)* (New York: Holt, Rinehart, and Winston, 1973).

14. See Ernst Wolfgang Böckenförde, *Der deutsche Katholizismus im Jahre 1933* (Freiburg: Herder, 1988). This book's second chapter appeared in *Hochland* (1961) and also in translation: Böckenförde, "German Catholicism in 1933," trans. Raymond Schmandt, *Cross Currents* 11 (Summer 1961): 283–304. See also Richard Fabers, "Politischer Katholizismus," in Hubert Cancik, ed., *Religions- und Geistesgeschichte der Weimarer Republik* (Düsseldorf: Patmos, 1982), 136–58; Breuning, *Die Vision des Reiches*; Heinrich Lutz, *Demokratie im Zwielicht* (Munich: Kösel, 1963); Kurt Stontheimer, *Antidemokratisches Denken in der Weimarer Republik* (Munich: Nymphenburger Verlagshandlung, 1962).

15. In the Reichstag elections on March 5, 1933, the Catholic vote was 5.5 million for the Center party and 7 million for the other parties; see Mary Alice Gallin, *German Resistance to Hitler* (Washington, D.C.: Catholic University of America Press, 1961); Holborn, *A History of Modern Germany*, 3, p. 664.

16. See Ernst Christian Helmreich, *The German Churches Under Hitler* (Detroit: Wayne State University Press, 1979), 117; Gallin, *German Resistance to Hitler*, 167, 204.

17. See Hugo Ott, "Conrad Gröber (1872–1948)," in Jürgen Aretz, Rudolf Morsey, Anton Rauscher, eds., *Zeitgeschichte in Lebensbildern*, 6 (Mainz: Matthias Grünewald, 1984), 64–75; Gordon C. Zahn, *German Catholics and Hitler's Wars* (Notre Dame: University of Notre Dame Press, 1992 [1962]), 119–42.

18. See Lewy, *The Catholic Church and Nazi Germany*, 17, 22; Zahn, *German Catholics and Hitler's Wars*, 72.

19. See Dietrich, "Catholic Theologians," 28; John Zeender, "The Genesis of the German Concordat," in Nelson Minnich et al., eds., *Studies in Catholic History* (Wilmington, Del.: Michael Glazier, 1985), 617–65.

20. See Hürten, *Deutsche Katholiken*, 214–30; Dietrich, "Catholic Theologians"; Krieg, *Karl Adam*, 107–36; Scholder, *Die Kirchen und das Dritte Reich*, 1, pp. 543–50; Lewy, *The Catholic Church and Nazi Germany*, 365. Also, Friedrich Muckermann, S.J., initially spoke in favor of Hitler but eventually changed his stance; see Franz Kroos, "Friedrich Muckermann (1883–1946)," in Rudolf Morsey, ed., *Zeitgeschichte in Lebensbildern*, 2 (Mainz: Matthias Grünewald, 1975), 48–63; also, the forthcoming essay on Muckermann by Donald J. Dietrich in *Church and State* (1997).

21. See Scholder, *Die Kirchen und das Dritte Reich*, 1, p. 320; Lewy, *The Catholic Church and Nazi Germany*, 17, 43–44, 171; Waldemar Gurian, *Hitler and the Christians*, trans. E. F. Peeler (London: Sheed and Ward, 1936).

22. See Gerl, *Romano Guardini*, 133. Carl Schmitt, who became a jurist for the Third Reich, did not remain a member of this circle; see Andreas Koenen, *Der Fall Carl Schmitt* (Darmstadt: Wissenschaftliche Buchgesellschaft, 1995), passim; Gerl, *Romano Guardini*, p. 201; Mark Lilla, "The Enemy of Liberalism," *New York Review of Books* 64/8 (May 15, 1997), 38–44.

23. See Dietrich, "Catholic Theologians," 35, 40.

24. See ibid., 28.

25. See Helmreich, *The German Churches Under Hitler*, 273; Richard Grunberger, *Social History of the Third Reich* (London: Weidenfeld and Nicolson, 1971), 449; John S. Conway, *The Nazi Persecution of the Churches, 1933–1945* (London: Weidenfeld and Nicolson, 1968); Gallin, *German Resistance to Hitler*, 173.

26. Subsequently, Gustav Gundlach and John LaFarge drafted an encyclical that would have condemned anti-Semitism, but did not complete their work prior to Pius XI's death in 1939; see Georges Passelecq and Bernard Suchecky, *L'encyclique cachée de Pie XI* (Paris: Éditions La Découverte, 1995); Robert Hecht, *An Unordinary Man: A Life of Father John LaFarge, S.J.* (Lanham, Md.: Scarecrow Press, 1996); Dietrich, "Catholic Theologians," 32–33.

27. See Dietrich, "Catholic Theologians," 34–39.

28. As already noted in chapter 2, Chamberlain's book helped to precipitate Romano Guardini's religious conversion in 1905; see *Berichte*, 70.

29. On the *Volk* movement, see Heinz Hürten, *Kurze Geschichte des deutschen Katholizismus* (Mainz: Matthias Grünewald, 1986), 209–43; Craig, *Germany 1866–1945*, 181–92, 486–95; Pinson, *Modern Germany*, 262–73, 454–66, 500–504.

30. See Doris L. Bergen, *The Twisted Cross* (Chapel Hill: University of North Carolina Press, 1996).

31. See Scholder, *Die Kirche und das Dritte Reich*, 1, pp. 100–105; Helmreich, *The German Churches Under Hitler*, 75–80; Grunberger, *Social History of the Third Reich*, 435–45.

32. See Helmreich, *The German Churches Under Hitler*, 180; Grunberger, *Social History of the Third Reich*, 440–45.

33. See Peter Haas, *Morality after Auschwitz* (Philadelphia: Fortress Press, 1992).

34. See Scholder, *Die Kirche und das Dritte Reich*, 2, pp. 119–58; Helmreich, *The German Churches Under Hitler*, 154–55.

35. Alfred Rosenberg, *"Mythus": I. The Worship of Race*, trans. Charles A. Beard

(London: Friends of Europe, 1936), 7; idem, *Der Mythus des 20. Jahrhunderts* (Munich: Hoheneichen-Verlag, 1935), 2.

36. Rosenberg, *"Mythus"*, 13; idem, *Der Mythus*, 81–2. See Helmreich, *The German Churches Under Hitler*, 264; Grunberger, *A Social History of the Third Reich*, 441.

37. See Helmreich, *The German Churches Under Hitler*, 178–80, 401–7.

38. See Anton Gill, *An Honorable Defeat* (New York: Henry Holt, 1994); Hürten, *Deutsche Katholiken*, 228, 523–40. According to Guardini, he was able to maintain silence because he did not serve on any of the University of Berlin's academic committees; see *Berichte*, 41.

39. See Fischer, *Nazism*, 130, 343; Harold T. Betteridge, ed., *The New Cassell's German Dictionary* (New York: Funk and Wagnalls, 1965), 223.

40. See "Der Heiland," in *Unterscheidung des Christlichen* (Mainz: Matthias Grünewald, 1935), 362–88. Hereafter, Guardini's statements in "Der Heiland" are quoted from *Unterscheidung* (1935).

41. See Johannes Schwarte, *Gustav Gundlach S.J. (1892–1963)* (Munich: Ferdinand Schöningh, 1975).

42. See Gerl, *Romano Guardini*, 317.

43. Beginning in 1933, the Reich denied Quickborn permission to hold large gatherings at Burg Rothenfels; see Knoll, *Glaube und Kultur*, 56.

44. In 1941 it was rumored that Guardini would be arrested; see Douglas Auchincloss, "Romano Guardini and the New Age," *Catholic Digest* 25 (November 1960): 35–40, 37.

45. *Berichte*, 52.

46. See ibid., 54.

47. Ibid.

48. See Hanna Barbara Gerl et al., eds., *Begegnungen in Mooshausen* (Weissenhorn: Anton H. Konrad, 1990). Today, the former rectory is a museum in honor of Josef Weiger, Romano Guardini, and their friends. On life in Berlin for Guardini and his students, see Heinz R. Kuehn, *Mixed Blessings. An Almost Ordinary Life in Hitler's Germany* (Athens, Ga.: University of Georgia Press, 1989).

49. Chapters 2, 3, and 4 of *Der Heilbringer* repeat portions of "Der Heiland," while chapters 1, 5, 6, and 7 make explicit what was implicit in "Der Heiland"; see Knoll, *Glaube und Kultur*, 382–87.

50. *Der Heilbringer*, 47. Unless otherwise noted, Guardini's statements of 1946 on Germany under Hitler are quoted from *Der Heilbringer*.

51. Ibid., 79. Guardini elaborated on this idea in his address upon receiving the Erasmus Award (April 28, 1962). See "Europe: Reality and Mission," in *Charactère et culture de l'Europe* (1962), 143–47.

52. *Der Heilbringer*, 79–81.

53. Manfred Malzahn, *Germany 1945–1949: A Source Book* (New York: Routledge, 1991), 90–92; Schatz, *Zwischen Säkularisation und Zweiten Vatikanum*, 287–88.

54. Unless otherwise noted, Guardini's statements concerning Germans' moral responsibility to the Jews are quoted from *Verantwortung*.

55. Ibid., 40. See "Wille zur Macht oder Wille zur Wahrheit? Zur Frage nach der Universität" (1965), in Felix Messerschmid, ed., *Geschichte in Wissenschaft und Unterricht* 21 (1970): 752–59; R. Guardini, W. Dirks, and M. Horkheimer, *Die Verantwortung der Universität* (Würzburg: Werkbund, 1954).

56. See Hoffman, "Portrait of Father Guardini"; Pinson, *Modern Germany*, 571.

57. See Dietrich, *God and Humanity in Auschwitz.*

58. On forms of Catholic resistance to Hitler, see Heinz Hürten, "Katholische Kirche und Widerstand," in Peter Steinbach and Johannes Tuchel, eds., *Widerstand gegen den Nationalsozialismus* (Berlin: Akademische Verlag, 1994), 182–92; idem "Die katholische Kirche zwischen Nationalsozialismus und Widerstand" (1989), in idem, ed., *Katholiken, Kirche und Staat als Problem der Historie* (Paderborn: Ferdinand Schöningh, 1994), 141–58; idem, *Verfolgung, Widerstand und Zeugnis* (Mainz: Matthias Grünewald, 1987); Georg Denzler, *Widerstand oder Anpassung?* (Munich: R. Piper, 1984).

59. See Hürten, *Deutsche Katholiken*, 455–56; Heinz Robert Schlette, "Romano Guardini—Versuch einer Würdigung," 263–66.

60. See Hürten, *Deutsche Katholiken*, 338.

61. See ibid., 218; Gerl, *Romano Guardini*, 199; Breuning, *Die Vision des Reiches*, 89–90.

62. Hans and Sophie Scholl of the student resistance group "White Rose" read Guardini's works and participated in Neudeutschland; see Hürten, *Deutsche Katholiken*, 533. The Scholls were put to death by the Reich on February 22, 1943, for "conspiracy to commit high treason" by writing and distributing literature in opposition to the Nazi state; see Hermann Vinke, *The Short Life of Sophie Scholl*, trans. Hedwig Pachter (New York: Harper and Row, 1984). On November 4, 1945, Guardini gave an address at the University of Tübingen in which he extolled the Scholls and the other martyrs of the White Rose for accepting the call or "weight" of full personal existence; see *Die Waage des Daseins* (Tübingen: Rainer Wunderlich, 1946); reprinted in Carl Georg Heise et al., eds., *Deutsche Stimmen 1945–1946* (1948). During the 1950s the University of Munich gave this text to all students when they matriculated.

63. See Grunberger, *Social History of the Third Reich*, 449.

64. See O'Sullivan, *In His Presence*; Fröhlich, "Das Volksliturgie Apostolat von St. Paul in München," in Schwaiger, ed., *Das Erzbistum München und Freising*, 1, pp. 122–30. An outspoken critic of Nazism, who was influenced by Guardini's writings, was Hans Anscar Reinhold (d. 1968); see Jay P. Corbin, "H.A. Reinhold: Liturgical Pioneer and Anti-Fascist," *The Catholic Historical Review* 82 (1996): 436–58.

65. See Frank M. Busch and Michael Phayer, "German Catholic Bishops and the Holocaust, 1940–1952," *German Studies Review* 11 (October 1988): 463–85.

66. See Ruster, *Die verlorene Nützlichkeit*, 360; Gerl, *Romano Guardini*, passim.

67. See "Gedanken über politische Bildung" (1926), Sch 13 (1933–34): 177–82; "Zum Problem des Demokratie" (1946), in *Geschichte in Wissenschaft und Unterricht* 21 (1970): 711–16. Other writings by Guardini on political matters are also published in *Geschichte in Wissenschaft und Unterricht* 21 (1970); these are listed in the bibliography under 1970.

68. "Zum Problem der Democratie," 712–13.

69. See Grunberger, *Social History of the Third Reich*, 304–10; Craig, *Germany*, 421; Gay, *Weimar Culture*, 23–25; Mary Alice Gallin, *Midwives to Nazism* (Macon, Ga.: Mercer University Press, 1968), 13.

70. *Wahrheit*, 132–33. In 1953 Guardini wrote in *Wahrheit* (p. 56): "Democracy is a utopia and at its depths unrealistic. . . . I believe that in twenty years we will again have authoritarian regimes. The difference [among them] will only be whether they respect the person or distrust the person." On Guardini's understanding of democracy's presuppositions, see Michele Nicoletti, "La democrazia e i suoi presuppositi in Romano Guardini," *"Communio"* (1993): 109–22.

71. Wolfhart Pannenberg, "The Christian West?" in *First Things*, 7 (November 1990): 24–31; see Craig, *The Germans*, 290; Gay, *Weimar Culture*, 96.

72. "Burg Rothenfels: Rückblick und Vorschau" (1949), in RGL, 224–30, 225; see Gerl, *Romano Guardini*, pp. 199–202.

73. See Bröckling, *Katholische Intellektuelle in der Weimarer Republik*, 38–55; Scholder, *Die Kirchen und das Dritte Reich*, 1, p. 93; Böckenförde, "German Catholicism in 1933," 293, 301.

74. See Ruster, *Die verlorene Nützlichkeit*, 185; Schlette, "Romano Guardini—Versuch einer Würdigung," 261–63.

75. See Michael C. Schneider and Winfried Süß, eds., *Keine Volksgenossen*, trans. George Low (Munich: Pressereferat der Ludwigs Maximilians Universität, 1993).

76. Guardini delivered *A la Recherche de la Paix* (Strasbourg: Éditions F.-X. Le Roux, 1948) in Paris on April 18, 1948, to the "Semaine des Intellectuels catholiques français." The article is "Introduction à Jean-Pierre de Caussade," trans. Claire C. Lossey *Dieu Vivant* 13 (1949): 83–96. The original German text is "Einführung," in Wolfgang Rüttenauer, ed., *Jean Pierre de Caussade* (Freiburg: Herder, 1940), 1–20.

77. Vatican II, Declaration on the Relation of the Church to Non-Christian Religions, n. 4, in VC2, p. 573.

78. See *Verantwortung*, 16.

Chapter Seven. Jesus Christ, Mediator

1. *Wahrheit*, 12.

2. See Schilson, *Perspektiven theologischer Erneuerung*, 82–155; Balthasar, *Romano Guardini*, 90–107; Gerhard Ludwig Müller, "Christocentrism," in HanCaTh, 71–74; Arno Schilson, "Christozentrik," LThK3 2: 1176–77.

3. *Lord*, 533. The German text's subtitle describes the book's content: "meditations on the person and life of Jesus Christ."

4. See ibid., 254–55.

5. See ibid., v–vi, 534–35.

6. *Pascal*, 78, cf. 80.

7. *Wahrheit*, 46.

8. See Herbert Vorgrimler, "Jesus Christus—Bemühungen um eine heute ange-

messene Deutung der Person Jesu Christi," in Honnefelder and Lutz-Bachmann, eds., *Auslegungen des Glaubens*, 46-61.

9. See Knoll, *Glaube und Kultur*, 462-77; Biser, *Interpretation und Veränderung*, 47; Leo Scheffczyk, "Das Christusgeheimnis in der Schau Romano Guardinis," in Seidel, ed., *"Christliche Weltanschauung"*, 110-40, esp. 110, 119.

10. See Schlette, "Guardini, Romano (1885-1968)," 294-97; Werner Dettloff, "Romano Guardini (1885-1968)," in Heinrich Fries and Georg Kretschmar, eds., *Klassiker der Theologie*, 2 (Munich: C. H. Beck, 1983), 318-30; Dirks, "Romano Guardini"; Laubach, "Romano Guardini."

11. See Ratzinger, "Von der Liturgie zur Christologie."

12. See Knoll, *Glaube und Kultur*, 466; Schilson, "Romano Guardini and die Theology der Gegenwart," 160.

13. Like Bonaventure and Pascal, Guardini emphasizes the centrality of the "heart" in our relationship to God; see *Lord*, 15, 25, 49, 70, 82, 87, 108-9, passim; *Pascal*, 113-37; Knoll, *Glaube und Kultur*, 70-73, 285-313, 457-77.

14. In a letter (1940) to Richard Knies, Guardini wrote: "That you are fond of *Der Herr* delights me a great deal. This is my favorite book, along with the one on Hölderlin" (quoted in Gerl, *Romano Guardini*, 306).

15. The Dominican scholar Ulrich Horst, director of the Grabmann Institute (Munich), made this comment on September 8, 1995, in a conversation with the author.

16. See Biblio; Schilson, "Romano Guardini and die Theologie der Gegenwart," 160-61.

17. Leo XIII, *Providentissimus Deus*, in Carlen, ed., *The Papal Encyclicals, 1878-1903*, 325-39.

18. See John R. Donahue, "A Journey Remembered: Catholic Biblical Scholarship 50 Years After *Divino Afflante Spiritu*," *America* 169 (September 18, 1993): 6-11; Raymond E. Brown and Thomas Aquinas Collins, "Church Pronouncements," in NJBC, 1166-74; Raymond F. Collins, *Introduction to the New Testament* (Garden City: Doubleday, 1983), 356-86.

19. See Kolping, *Katholische Theologie*, 82-86.

20. See Alexa Suelzer and John S. Kselman, "Modern Old Testament Criticism," and John S. Kselman, "Modern New Testament Criticism," in NJBC, 1113-29, 1130-45; Collins, *Introduction to the New Testament*, 41-195.

21. Augustin Bea, "Biblische Kritik und Neuere Forschung," *Stimmen der Zeit* 114 (1927-28): 401-12.

22. See Joseph A. Fitzmyer, *Scripture, The Soul of Theology* (New York: Paulist Press, 1994); John R. Donahue, "Things Old and New in Biblical Interpretation," *The Way. Supplement* 72 (Autumn 1991): 20-31; Raymond E. Brown and Sandra M. Schneiders, "Hermeneutics," in NJBC, 1146-65.

23. See Pontifical Biblical Commission, *The Interpretation of the Bible in the Church* (Boston: St. Paul Books and Media, 1993); Joseph A. Fitzmyer, "'Interpretation of the Bible in the Church,'" *America* 169 (November 27, 1993): 12-15; idem, *Scripture, The Soul of Theology*.

24. Brown and Schneider, "Hermeneutics," 1148-49.

25. Ibid., 1157.

26. See Donahue, "Things Old and Things New in Biblical Interpretation"; Edgar V. McKnight, *Post-Modern Use of the Bible* (Nashville: Abingdon, 1988); Collins, *Introduction to the New Testament*, 231–71; D. Robertson, "Literature, The Bible as," in Keith Crim et al., eds., *The Interpreter's Dictionary of the Bible. Supplementary Volume* (Nashville: Abingdon, 1976): 547–51).

27. See Jean Galot, "Christology IV: Various Approaches," in DicFTh, 126–31; Gerhard Ludwig Müller, "Christological Models" and "Christology," in HanCaTh, 77–81, 85–88; John F. O'Grady, *Models of Jesus Revisited* (New York: Paulist Press, 1994); John P. Galvin, "Jesus Christ," in SysTh, 1, pp. 249–324.

28. See Galvin, "Jesus Christ," 262–81; Gerald O'Collins, *What Are They Saying About Jesus?*, rev. ed. (New York: Paulist Press, 1983), 5–12.

29. See Harnack, *What Is Christianity?*; John Macquarrie, *Jesus Christ in Modern Thought* (Philadelphia: Trinity Press International, 1990), 260–64.

30. See Gerald O'Collins, *Interpreting Jesus* (New York: Paulist Press, 1983), 21–30; Walter Kasper, *Jesus the Christ*, trans. V. Green (New York: Paulist Press, 1976), 26–40; Norman Perrin, *Rediscovering the Teaching of Jesus* (New York: Harper and Row, 1976), 207–48.

31. See Galot, "Christology: Various Approaches," 128–29; Avery Dulles, "Contemporary Approaches to Christology," *The Living Light* 13 (1976): 119–44, especially 124–26, 136–38; idem, *Revelation Theology*, 144–46. On the use of scripture, see David H. Kelsey, *The Uses of Scripture in Recent Theology* (Philadelphia: Fortress Press, 1975), 32–55; Klaus Reinhardt, *Der dogmatische Schriftgebrauch in der katholischen und protestantischen Christologie von der Aufklärung bis zur Gegenwart* (Munich: Ferdinand Schöningh, 1970), 221–39, 331–48, 425–42.

32. See Gerald A. McCool, *From Unity to Pluralism* (New York: Fordham University Press, 1989); Oscar Köhler, "The Encyclical *Aeterni Patris*" and "Neo-Thomism, Neo-Scholasticism, and the 'New Philosophers,'" in HisCh 9, pp. 307–18.

33. See Scheffczyk, "Main Lines of the Development of Theology"; Aubert, "Die Theologie während der ersten Hälfte des 20. Jahrhunderts," 21–27.

34. *The Church of the Lord*, trans. Stella Lange (Chicago: Henry Regnery, 1966), 61.

35. For example, see "Der religiöse Gehorsam" (1916), in *Auf dem Wege*, 9–18.

36. See Delmer, *Weimar Germany*, 103.

37. Gerl, *Romano Guardini*, 166.

38. See Anthony Read and David Fisher, *Berlin Rising* (New York: W.W. Norton, 1994), 121–35; Laurenz Demps et al., *Geschichte Berlins von den Anfängen bis 1945* (Berlin: Dietz, 1987), 475–635.

39. See Max Scheler, "Vorbilder und Führer" (1921), *Schriften aus dem Nachlass*, Part 1, in idem, *Gesammelte Werke*, 10, ed. Maria Scheler (Bern: A. Francke, 1957), 257–88.

40. See Guardini's letter (1963) in Gerl, *Romano Guardini*, 305.

41. See ibid., 304–10.

42. On the role of narratives in theology, see Carlo Rocchetta, "Theologies III: Narrative Theology," in DicFTh, 1084–87; Robert A. Krieg, *Story-Shaped Christology* (New

York: Paulist Press, 1988); Gary L. Comstock, "Two Types of Narrative Theology," *Journal of the American Academy of Religion* 55 (1987): 687–71.

43. *Lord*, 295. Unless otherwise noted, Guardini's statements in this chapter on the living Christ are quoted from *Lord*.

44. Ibid., 306. Walter Kasper also emphasizes that Jesus Christ is the "new beginning" in history; see Kasper, *Jesus the Christ*, 52–58, 190–92. With this emphasis, Guardini and Kasper show their common philosophical roots in the later Schelling.

45. *Lord*, 141, 174, 213, 190, 272, 295.

46. Ibid., 438, 408, 145, 194–95, 489–90.

47. On the triune God, see *Lord*, 3–8, 26–30, 110–14, 139–44, 145–50, 219–23, 426, 431–38; "Zwei Kapitel zur Gotteslehre," in RGL, 63–75.

48. For Guardini's implicit criticism of Hitler's National Socialism, see *Lord*, 36–42, 79–85, 98–104, 115–21, 177–89, 240–41, 272, 290, 294, 318, 322, 330, 394–96, 471, 503, 513; Schlette, "Romano Guardini—Versuch einer Würdigung," 263–66.

49. *Das Wesen des Christentums* (1938) and *Die menschliche Wirklichkeit des Herrn* (1958), ed. Franz Henrich (Mainz: Matthias Grünewald, 1991), 9; see "Das 'Wesen des Christentums,'" Sch 9 (1929): 129–152. Unless otherwise noted, Guardini's statements in this chapter on Christian faith are quoted from *Das Wesen des Christentums*.

50. As Michael Theobald notes, Guardini developed a "narrative Christology"; see M. Theobald, "Die Autonomie der historischen Kritik," in Honnefelder and Lutz-Bachmann, eds., *Auslegungen des Glaubens*, 28, 33.

51. Leo Scheffczyk holds that Guardini used neither an approach "from above" nor one "from below"; see Scheffczyk, "Das Christusgeheimnis," 110–40, 119. However, according to Monika Hellwig, *The Lord* is an early expression of Christology "from below"; see M. Hellwig, "Re-Emergence of the Human, Critical, Public Jesus," TS 50 (1989): 466–80, 468.

52. See Theobald, "Die Autonomie der historischen Kritik," 23–24.

53. See Knoll, *Glaube und Kultur*, 262–77, 467–76; Schilson, *Perspektiven theologischer Erneuerung*, 120–37; Balthasar, *Romano Guardini*, 90–107.

54. See Schilson, *Perspektiven theologischer Erneuerung*, 82–119; Wechsler, *Guardini als Kerygmatiker*, 161–68.

55. See *Lord*, 534.

56. See *Wahrheit*, 21.

57. See *The Church of the Lord*, 76–78.

58. On Guardini's biblical hermeneutics, see Knoll, *Glaube und Kultur*, 457–76; Schilson, *Perspektiven theologischer Erneuerung*, 95–107; Alfred Mertens, "An den Grenzen der historisch-kritischen Methode" in Seidel, ed., *"Christliche Weltanschauung,"* 141–61; Theobald, "Die Autonomie der historischen Kritik"; Heinrich Kahlefeld, "Nachwort," in *Geistliche Schriftauslegung* (Mainz: Matthias Grünewald, 1980), 89–97.

59. See Scheffczyk, "The Main Lines of the Development of Theology," 295; Reinhardt, *Der dogmatische Schriftgebrauch*, 331–48.

60. See "Heilige Schrift und Glaubenswissenschaft," Sch 8 (1928): 24–57, 24–34.

61. See ibid., 35–42.

62. See ibid., 43–46.

63. See Kahlefeld, "Nachwort," 89.

64. "Heilige Schrift und Glaubenswissenschaft," 46–57.

65. See *Wahrheit*, 22.

66. See Fitzmyer, *Scripture, The Soul of Theology;* Donahue, "Things Old and New in Biblical Interpretation"; Brown and Schneiders, "Hermeneutics."

67. See Schilson, *Perspektiven theologischer Erneuerung*, 90–91; Kahlefeld, "Nachwort," 89. Guardini and his friend Kahlefeld disagreed with each other on the use of historical critical methods in biblical interpretation; see Gerl, *Romano Guardini*, 114, 194, 306, 335–36, 363–68.

68. See Biser, *Interpretation und Veränderung*, 66–70.

69. See *Lord*, 13–18. For similar analyses of Guardini's biblical hermeneutics, see Mertens, "An den Grenzen der historisch-kritischen Methode," 146–56; Kahlefeld, "Nachwort," 91–95.

70. Ibid., 18.

71. See Raymond E. Brown, *The Birth of the Messiah* (New York: Doubleday, 1993).

72. Pius XII, *Divino afflante Spiritu* (September 30, 1943), n. 33, in Carlen, ed., *The Papal Encyclicals 1939–1958*, 65–80, 73.

73. See Josef Pfammatter, "Katholische Jesusforschung im deutschen Sprachraum," in idem, ed., *Theologische Berichte VII* (Zurich: Benziger, 1978), 101–48; Kasper, *Jesus the Christ*, 17–19.

74. As Edward Schillebeeckx has noted, Vatican II did explicitly express a Christology; see E. Schillebeeckx, *Interim Report,* trans. John Bowden (New York: Crossroad, 1981), 103.

75. Vatican II, Pastoral Constitution on the Church in the Modern World, n. 45, in VC2, 216.

76. See *The Humanity of Christ,* trans. Ronald Walls (New York: Pantheon Books, 1964); Xavier Tilliette, *Le Christ de la Philosophie* (Paris: Les Éditions Du Cerf, 1990), 24, 84, 119–20.

77. See Robert A. Krieg, "A Fortieth-Anniversary Reappraisal of 'Chalcedon: End or Beginning?' " *Philosophy and Theology* 9 (1995): 77–116; Kasper, *Jesus the Christ*, 17–18, 48–52; Karl Rahner, "Current Problems in Christology" (1954), in idem, *Theological Investigations,* 1, trans. Cornelius Ernst (Baltimore: Helicon Press, 1964), 149–200; K. Rahner, "The Eternal Significance of the Humanity of Jesus for Our Relationship with God" (1956), in idem, *Theological Investigations,* 3, trans. Cornelius Ernst (Baltimore: Helicon Press, 1967), 35–46.

78. See Pfammatter, "Katholische Jesusforschung," 103; Franz Mussner, "Die katholische Leben-Jesu-Forschung und ihre heutigen Aufgaben," LThK2 7: 859–64; Kolping, *Katholische Theologie*, 265.

79. Vorgrimler, "Jesus Christus," 47–48; see Ratzinger, "Guardini on Christ in Our Century."

80. Ruster, *Die verlorene Nützlichkeit*, 194; see Theobald, "Die Autonomie der historischen Kritik," 23.

81. Schilson, "Romano Guardini und die Theology der Gegenwart," 159.
82. Hellwig, "Re-emergence of the Human, Critical, Public Jesus," 468.
83. Pöhlmann, *Gottes Denker,* 180.
84. Dirks, "Romano Guardini," 248–52, 250–51.
85. See Donahue, "Things Old and Things New in Biblical Interpretation"; Krieg, *Story-Shaped Christology;* Pontifical Biblical Commission, *Scripture and Christology,* trans. Joseph A. Fitzmyer with commentary (New York: Paulist Press, 1986).
86. See Hellwig, "Re-emergence of the Human, Critical, Public Jesus," 478–80.
87. See Vorgrimler, "Jesus Christus," 49.
88. See Markus Knapp, "Die Christologie Romano Guardinis im Kontext seiner These vom Ende der Neuzeit," TuG 83 (1993): 338–56.

Chapter Eight. A Christian View of the Modern World

1. See Golo Mann, *The History of Germany Since 1789,* trans. Marian Jackson (New York: Praeger, 1968), 495.
2. See Malzahn, *Germany 1945–1949,* 117.
3. See Marija Stankus-Saulaitis, "Forgotten Faces of War," *America* 173 (July 1, 1995): 6–7.
4. See Malzahn, *Germany 1945–1949,* 90–97; Hürten, *Deutsche Katholiken 1918–1945,* 552–53.
5. See Dietrich Bonhoeffer, *Letters and Papers from Prison,* enlarged edition, ed. Eberhard Bethge (New York: Macmillan, 1971), 271–407.
6. Guardini noted the continuity among these three texts; see Clemens Münster, Walter Dirks, Gerhard Krüger, and Romano Guardini, *Unsere geschichtliche Zukunft* (Würzburg: Werkbund, 1953), 28.
7. On Guardini's view of Christian faith and modernity, see Reinhard Haubenthaler, *Askese und Freiheit bei Romano Guardini* (Paderborn: Ferdinand Schöningh, 1995); Ruster, *Die verlorene Nützlichkeit;* Jan van der Vloet, "Romano Guardini und die (Nach-) Neuzeit," in Schilson, ed., *Konservativ mit Blick nach vorn,* 115–32; idem, "Romano Guardinis theologische Kritik des modernen Zeitalters," *Bijdragen, tijdschrift voor filosofie en theologie* 52 (1991): 159–84; Knoll, *Glaube und Kultur;* Heinz Robert Schlette, *Konkrete Humanität,* ed. J. Brosseder, N. Klein, and E. Weinzierl (Frankfurt am Main: Josef Knecht, 1991); Mercker, *Christliche Weltanschauung;* Wilhelm Schmidt-Biggemann, "Säkularisierung und Theodizee," in Honnefelder and Lutz-Bachmann, eds., *Auslegungen des Glaubens,* 125–43; Eugen Biser, "Romano Guardinis Rückwärtsgewandte Deutung des Epochenendes," in Rauscher, ed., *Religiös-kulturelle Bewegungen,* 99–120; Gerl, *Romano Guardini,* 180–90, 338–42; Hansruedi Kleiber, *Glaube und religiöse Erfahrung bei Romano Guardini* (Freiburg: Herder, 1985).
8. See Solange Lefebvre, "Secularity," in DicFTh, 976–86; Owen Chadwick, *The Secularization of the European Mind in the Nineteenth Century* (Cambridge: Cambridge

University Press, 1976); Albert Keller, "Secularization," in Karl Rahner et al., eds., *Sacramentum Mundi*, 6 (New York: Herder and Herder, 1970), 64–70.

9. See Schatz, *Zwischen Säkularisation und Zweitem Vatikanum*, 13–95; Victor Conzemius, "Die Kritik der Kirche," in HanFTh 3, pp. 30–48; idem, "Germany: Since 1789," in NCaEn 6, pp. 440–48; Hajo Holborn, *A History of Modern Germany 1648–1840*, 2 (New York: Alfred A. Knopf, 1964), 366–68; Mann, *The History of Germany since 1789*, 24–35.

10. See Lefebvre, "Secularity," 979; Keller, "Secularization," 64–70; Roger Aubert, "The Catholic Church after the Congress of Vienna," HisCh 7, pp. 85–104.

11. See Lefebvre, "Secularity," 979; E. Hegel, "Säkularisation," in LThK2 9: 248–53; A. Auer, "Säkularisierung," in LThK2 9: 253–54.

12. See Karl Löwith, *From Hegel to Nietzsche*, trans. David E. Green (Garden City: Doubleday, 1967). Originally published in German in 1941, Löwith's book argues that Christianity's influence on society and the state has come to an end; it fueled the discussion to which Guardini contributed *Das Ende der Neuzeit*.

13. See Ruster, *Die verlorene Nützlichkeit*, 35–112; Ludwig Volk, "The Church in the German-Speaking Countries," in HisCh 10, pp. 531–57.

14. See Misner, *Social Catholicism in Europe*, 30–31, 136–47; Wilhelm Weber, "Society and State as a Problem for the Church," in HisCh 10, pp. 229–59; Anton Rauscher, "Die katholische Sozialphilosophie im 20. Jahrhundert," ChrPhil 3, pp. 846–61.

15. Dill, *Germany*, 156.

16. See "Europe: Reality and Mission" (1962).

17. *Berichte*, 58–59. Nevertheless, Guardini felt strong ties to Mainz; see *Wahrheit*, 114.

18. *Berichte*, 58–59.

19. See Gerl, *Romano Guardini*, 36–38, 35.

20. See *Wahrheit*, 63, 92–93, 96; Gerl, *Romano Guardini*, 25–26.

21. See Knoll, *Glaube und Kultur*, 175–80, 235–60.

22. See *Berichte*, 76–77; Gerl, *Romano Guardini*, 21, 186.

23. *Berichte*, 60–61.

24. See ibid., 77; Gerl, *Romano Guardini*, 52.

25. See "The Meaning of Melancholy" (1928), in *The Focus of Freedom*, 55–90.

26. See *Wahrheit*, 40, 77, 96.

27. See "The Meaning of Melancholy," 69; *Prayer in Practice*, trans. Prince Leopold of Loewenstein-Wertheim (New York: Pantheon Books, 1957), 202–4.

28. See "Gedanken über das Verhältnis von Christentum und Kultur," Sch 6 (1926): 281–315.

29. Unless otherwise noted, Guardini's comments of the 1920s on culture in the chapter are quoted from *Letters*. See Lawrence S. Cunningham, "Romano Guardini as Sapiential Theologian," in RoGu, 61–72; Knoll, *Glaube und Kultur*, 183–96; Gerl, *Romano Guardini*, 38, 183, 338, 342. Cunningham has noted that *Letters* is "an innocently uncritical work," consisting of "romantic musings," and that when compared with Ignazio Silone's writings, it appears as "an exercise in sentimentalism, indeed in *Weltschmerz*" (p. 71).

30. According to Joseph Ratzinger, Guardini possessed a naive optimism in the 1920s but outgrew it; see Ratzinger, "Von der Liturgie zur Christologie," 125–26. Yet, Heinz Robert Schlette holds that Guardini became pessimistic in his last years as physical ailments led to melancholy; see Schlette, "Romano Guardini—Versuch einer Würdigung," 281–83.

31. Gerl, *Romano Guardini*, 319.

32. *Freedom, Grace and Destiny*, trans. John Murray (New York: Pantheon Books, 1961), 22–23; see Gerl, *Romano Guardini*, 338. Unless otherwise noted, Guardini's statements on personal freedom in this chapter are quoted from *Freedom, Grace and Destiny*.

33. See, *Freedom, Grace and Destiny*, 35, 43, 45, 46, 90; Knoll, *Glaube und Kultur*, 395–453. Walter Kasper, like Guardini, relies on Pascal's thought; see W. Kasper, *Jesus the Christ*, 61 n. 53.

34. See Gerl, *Romano Guardini*, 338–42; Schlette, "Romano Guardini—Versuch einer Würdigung," 265–67.

35. *End*, 18, 19, 45, 24, 28. Unless otherwise noted, Guardini's statements on modernity in this chapter are quoted from *End*. Guardini's thought anticipates some of the ideas associated with postmodernism; see Knoll, *Glaube und Kultur*, 542–46.

36. *Das Ende der Neuzeit* and *Die Macht* (Mainz: Matthias Grünewald, 1989), 45; *End*, 65.

37. *Das Ende der Neuzeit*, 52; *End*, 76.

38. Critics of today's culture misconstrue Guardini's thought when they neglect his recognition of its merits. For example, Walker Percy has quoted *End*, along with Søren Kierkegaard's *Either/Or*, on the title page of *The Last Gentleman* (New York: Farrar, Straus and Giroux, 1966).

39. *Das Ende der Neuzeit*, 55; *End*, 81.

40. *Das Ende der Neuzeit*, 56–57; *End*, 81–83.

41. *Das Ende der Neuzeit*, 86; *End*, 121.

42. See Rene Buchholz, *Zwischen Mythos und Bilderverbot* (Frankfurt am Main: Long, 1991), 234–39; Ludwig Watzal, *Das Politische bei Romano Guardini* (Percha am Starnberger See: R. S. Schulz, 1987), passim.

43. See Schmidt-Biggemann, "Säkularisierung und Theodizee."

44. See Münster, Dirks, Krüger, Guardini, *Unsere geschichtliche Zukunft*. Along with the texts already cited, critical discussions of Guardini's *Das Ende der Neuzeit* include: Alfons Auer, "Gestalt des christlichen Weltverständnis," in Herbert Vorgrimler et al., eds., *Gott in Welt*, 1 (Freiburg: Herder, 1964), 333–65; Heinz Robert Schlette, "Zur Kulturkritik im Spätwerk Romano Guardinis," *Zeitgeschichte* 12 (1984): 37–51.

45. *Das Ende der Neuzeit* and *Die Macht*, 98; *Power*, xiii. On the bombing of Dresden, Nagasaki, and Hiroshima, see *Power*, 84; *Briefe*, 38; Knoll, *Glaube und Kultur*, 398–428; Schlette, "Romano Guardini—Versuch einer Würdigung," 272–77.

46. *Die Macht*, 165; *Power*, 79–80. See "Das Phänomen der Macht" (1962), in *Sorge um den Menschen*, 2 (Mainz: Matthias Grünewald, 1989), 45–58.

47. See Knoll, *Glaube und Kultur*, 397; Gerl, "Unterscheidung aus Verstehen: Romano Guardini und Nietzsche."

48. See Johannes Metz, *Theology of the World,* trans. William Glen-Doepel (Freiburg: Herder and Herder, 1971 [1968]).

49. "Zur Theologie der Welt" (1959), in *Sorge um den Menschen,* 1, pp. 67–81, 81.

50. See Knoll, *Glaube und Kultur,* 428–30.

51. See Max Scheler, "Zur Rehabilitierung der Tugend" (1913), in idem, *Vom Umsturz der Werte: Gesammelte Werke,* 3, ed. Maria Scheler, 4th ed. (Bern: Francke, 1955), 13–31; Gerl, *Romano Guardini,* 143–44.

52. See Biblio, entries #63, #64, #330.

53. See Schuster, "Vorlesungen und Lehrveranstaltungen Romano Guardinis," idem, ed., *Guardini Weiterdenken,* 273–85; Knoll, *Glaube und Kultur,* 430 n. 250; Gerl, *Romano Guardini,* 344.

54. See *End,* 112–14; *Power,* 87, 98–104; *Briefe,* 32–34; Mercker, *Christliche Weltanschauung,* 168–70.

55. According to Gerl (*Romano Guardini,* 349), this meditation is a "masterpiece" which exhibits "the basic orientation of Guardini's view of reality." Unless otherwise noted, Guardini's statements on reverence are quoted from *The Virtues,* trans. Stella Lange (Chicago: Henry Regnery, 1967).

56. See *Wahrheit,* 34.

57. See *Ethik,* 2 vols., ed. Hans Mercker, Martin Marschall, and the Katholische Akademie in Bayern (Mainz: Matthias Grünewald, 1993); Arno Schilson, "Gottes Hoheit in die Welt hineintragen," *Herder Korrespondenz* 49 (February 1995): 94–99.

58. Enda McDonagh, "The Church in the Modern World," in MoCa, 96–112, 96. See Pesch, *Das Zweite Vatikanische Konzil,* 311–50.

59. See van der Vloet, "Romano Guardinis theologische Kritik des modernen Zeitalters," 160.

60. Vatican II, Pastoral Constitution on the Church in the Modern World, n. 9, in VC II, p. 170. See Anton Losinger, *"Iusta autonomia"* (Paderborn: Schöningh, 1989).

61. Although Guardini saw that we cannot return to the past, he implicitly measured modernity in relation to the Middle Ages; see Knoll, *Glaube und Kultur,* 338–40, 354, 512; Mercker, *Christliche Weltanschauung,* 78–87.

62. See *Wahrheit,* 56, 120; Ruster, *Die verlorene Nützlichkeit,* 146.

63. Guardini's prediction that people would not have religious experiences in a secular society has not proven accurate; see Schlette, "Romano Guardini—Versuch einer Würdigung," 267–72; William D'Antonio et al., *Laity: American and Catholic* (New York: Sheed and Ward, 1996).

64. Many of Guardini's fears about modern society have not proven true; see Lina Börsig-Horer, *Zeit der Entscheidung* (Fridingen: Börsig, 1990); Michael Theunissen, "Falscher Alarm Wiedergelesen: Romano Guardinis 'Das Ende der Neuzeit,'" *Frankfurter Allgemeine Zeitschrift* (March 3, 1977): 19.

65. See Knoll, *Glaube und Kultur,* 408–10; Gerhard Krüger, "Unsere geschichtliche Zukunft," in C. Münster et al., *Zukunft Geschichtliche Zukunft,* 82–89.

66. See Ruster, *Die verlorene Nützlichkeit,* 183–90.

67. See Dulles, *Models of the Church,* 95–108.

Chapter Nine. An Interpreter of Truth

1. *Berichte,* 109.
2. *Wahrheit,* 85.
3. Ibid., 47.
4. This image of Guardini is corroborated by others' views of him. Eva Maria Faber holds that "Guardini's deepest desire was the reciprocal illumination of the faith and the world in the service of the truth and the meaning of personal existence"; see E. M. Faber, "Guardini," in LThK3 4: 1087–88. Arno Schilson's book has the title "Conservative with the view to the future"; see Schilson, *Konservativ mit Blick nach vorn.* Alfons Knoll has also chosen a title that conveys Guardini's twofold commitment: "faith and culture"; see Knoll, *Glaube und Kultur.* Hanna Barbara Gerl has observed that the center point of Guardini's life and thought was his longing for God; see Gerl, *Anfechtung,* 9. According to Hans Mercker, Guardini's "deepest intention" was his "attempt to propose a new conception of theology in the attire of the 'Christian worldview,' which takes seriously the world as a genuine theological fact which is anchored in God's innermost life"; see Mercker, *Christliche Weltanschauung,* 77. In Ingeborg Klimmer's judgment, Guardini was "a Socratic teacher" who was called "to awaken the truth in others"—"the truth that determined and sustained his own life"; see I. Klimmer, "Vorbemerkung," in RGL, 10. Finally, Hans Urs von Balthasar has given his book on Guardini the subtitle "reform on the basis of the source"; see Balthasar, *Romano Guardini: Reform aus dem Ursprung.*
5. See Thomas F. O'Meara, "Romano Guardini's *Akademische Feier* in 1964," in RoGu, 98–103.
6. Helmut Kuhn, Heinrich Kahlefeld, and Karl Forster, eds., *Interpretation der Welt* (Würzburg: Echter, 1965), 9. On his fiftieth birthday Guardini received a *Festschrift:* Schmidthüs, ed., *Christliche Verwirklichung.* Its twenty-nine essays include contributions by Josef Bernhart, Anton Bruckner, Ildefons Herwegen, Jacques Maritain, Hermann Platz, Vera Sussmann, and Josef Weiger.
7. For part of the letter, see Edmund Szydzik, "Romano Guardini (1885–1968)," in Knauft, ed., *Miterbauer des Bistums Berlin,* 77–91, 77; Gerl, *Romano Guardini,* 60.
8. *Wahrheit,* 84.
9. See Gerl, *Romano Guardini,* 360–63.
10. *Wahrheit,* 74, 77, 82, 124, 132. According to Bishop Ernst Tewes, Guardini was increasingly burdened by his ailments during the postwar years; see E. Tewes, "Romano Guardini."
11. "Der angefochtene Glaube" (1961), in RGL, 86–96.
12. *Wahrheit,* 120, 134.
13. Quoted in Karl Rahner, "Why Does God Allow Us To Suffer?" in idem, *Theological Investigations,* 19: *Faith and Ministry,* trans. Edward Quinn (New York: Crossroad, 1983), 194–208, 207–8. Walter Dirks made this conversation public shortly after Guardini's death; see W. Dirks, "Ein angefochtener sehr treuer Christ," *Die Zeit* (October 13, 1968).

14. *The Virtues*, 40.

15. See Félix-Alejandro Pastor, "Secularization," and Solange Lefebvre, "Secularity," in DicFTh, 971–75, 976–86.

16. "The Stages of Life and Philosophy" (1955), trans. Edwin G. Kaiser, *Philosophy Today* I (1957): 75–79, 78; see *Faith and the Modern Man*, trans. Charlotte E. Forsyth (New York: Pantheon Books, 1952 [1944]). Unless otherwise noted, Guardini's statements on life's phases are quoted from "The Stages of Life and Philosophy."

17. See Knoll, *Glaube und Kultur*, 493; Mercker, *Christliche Weltanschauung*, 70.

18. *Briefe*, 55; see "Mickymaus & Co." (1962), in *Sorge um Welt*, 1, pp. 235–37. Unless otherwise noted, Guardini's statements in these letters are quoted from *Briefe*.

19. See ibid., 13, 17, 26, 44, 56.

20. See *Freedom, Grace and Destiny*, 219. A fresco of the last judgment fills the sanctuary wall at Munich's St. Ludwig Church where Guardini preached for fifteen years. See Hanna Barbara Gerl, "Romano Guardini (1885–1968)," in Helmut Hempfer and Peter Pfister, eds., *St. Ludwig in München* (Weissenhorn: Anton H. Konrad, 1995), 93–108; Frank Büttner, "Unzeitgemässe Größ," *Das Münster* (1993): 293–304.

21. See Mercker, *Christliche Weltanschauung*, 42. The original text reads: "Im Glauben an Jesus Christus und seine Kirche. Im Vertrauen auf sein gnädiges Gericht." In the cemetery at St. Laurence Church the Oratorians who are buried beside Romano Guardini are: Philipp Dessauer (1898–1966), Joseph Jammers (1906–1987), Heinrich Kahlefeld (1903–1980), Franz Schreibmayr (1907–1985), Klemen Tilmann (1904–1984), and Jan Wiggers (1907–1961).

22. "Wahrheit und Ironie," in Karl Forster, ed., *Akademische Feier zum 80. Geburtstag von Romano Guardini* (Würzburg: Echter, 1965), 36–41, 37. The address also appears in *Stationen und Rückblicke* (Würzburg: Werkbund, 1965), 41–50. Unless otherwise noted, Guardini's statements in this address are quoted from *Akademische Feier*. The melancholy of Guardini's last years may have influenced him in this address; see Schlette, "Romano Guardini—Versuch einer Würdigung," 281–83.

23. Plato, *Republic*, trans. Paul Shorey, in Edith Hamilton and Huntington Cairns, eds., *The Collected Dialogues of Plato* (Princeton: Princeton University Press, 1971), 744.

24. Edward Schillebeeckx, *Jesus*, trans. Hubert Hoskins (New York: Seabury, 1979), 44.

25. See *Wahrheit*, 59, 39.

26. Peter Hebblethwaite, *Paul VI* (New York: Paulist Press, 1993), 182.

27. See Williams, *The Mind of John Paul II*, 115–40.

28. John Paul II, "Ansprache bei der Begegnung mit Theologieprofessoren im Kapuzinerkloster St. Konrad in Altötting am 18. November 1980," in Sekretariat der Deutschen Bischofskonferenz, ed., *Predigten und Ansprachen von Papst Johannes Paul II. bei seinem Pastoralbesuch in Deutschland*, 3d rev. ed. (Bonn: Sekretariat der Deutschen Bischofskonferenz, 1981), 169.

29. See M. Farrugia, "Romano Guardini," in DicFTh, 403–6; A. Babolin, *Romano Guardini: Filosofo dell'Alterita*, 2 vols. (Bologna: Zanichelli, 1968, 1969); H. Engelmann and F. Ferrier, *Romano Guardini: Le Dieu vivant et l'Existence chrétienne* (Paris: Editions

Fleurus, 1966); A. Lopez Quintas, *Romano Guardini y la dialéctica de lo viviente* (Madrid: Talleres Gráficos de Ediciones Castilla, 1966).

30. Obituaries in English appeared in the *New York Times* (October 2, 1968): 39; *The Tablet* 222 (October 12, 1968): 1021; *Time* 92 (October 11, 1968): 102. Earlier articles in English on Guardini include: "Faith is the Center," *Time* 75 (March 14, 1960): 51; "Candid Monsignor," *Newsweek* 45 (January 10, 1955): 50. See Robert A. Krieg, "North American Catholics' Reception of Romano Guardini's Writings," in RoGu, 43–59.

31. Sophia Institute Press has reprinted *Meditations Before Mass; Prayer in Practice,* under the new title *The Art of Praying;* and *The Rosary of Our Lady.* Regnery has reprinted *The Lord.*

32. See RoGu, whose contributors are L. Cunningham, K. Hughes, R. Krieg, H. Kuehn, R. Kuehn, G. Mueller Nelson, T. O'Meara, A. Schilson, and A. Wimmer. The anthology is: Heinz R. Kuehn, ed., *The Essential Guardini* (Chicago: Liturgy Training Publications, 1997). Also, soon available in English will be Hans Urs von Balthasar, *Romano Guardini,* trans. Albert Wimmer (San Francisco: Ignatius Press, forthcoming [1970]).

33. See Massimo Borghesi, "Reflection: A New Beginning," *30 Days* 12 (1992): 62–68; Roland Hill, "Spiritual Liberator," *The Catholic World Report* 1 (June 1992): 52–55.

34. Walter J. Ong, S.J., on the other hand, appealed to *The End of the Modern World* in his proposal that Catholics participate more fully in American culture; W. Ong, *Frontiers in American Catholicism* (New York: Macmillan, 1957), 9. See Krieg, "North American Catholics' Reception of Romano Guardini's Writings."

35. See Brigid Merriman O'Shea, *Searching for Christ* (Notre Dame: University of Notre Dame Press, 1994), 78.

36. George N. Shuster, "The Several Humanists," *Commonweal* 40 (April 2, 1930): 613–15. See Thomas E. Blantz, *George Shuster* (Notre Dame: University of Notre Dame Press, 1993), 64, 89, 90, 202.

37. See Dorothy Day, *The Long Loneliness* (New York: Curtis Books, 1952), 98; William D. Miller, *Dorothy Day* (San Francisco: Harper and Row, 1982), 198, 234, 413.

38. See Joseph B. Gremillion, "Interview with Romano Guardini," *America* 100 (November 15, 1958): 194–95.

39. See Linda Gray Sexton and Lois Ames, eds., *Anne Sexton* (Boston: Houghton Mifflin, 1975), 125.

40. Monika K. Hellwig, "A Catholic Scholar's Journey through the Twentieth Century," in James L. Heft, ed., *Faith and the Intellectual Life* (Notre Dame: University of Notre Dame Press, 1996), 71–85, 81.

41. See Avery Dulles, *The Assurance of Things Hoped For* (New York: Oxford University Press, 1994), 130–32, 134, 137, 142, 247; idem, *The Craft of Theology* (New York: Crossroad, 1995), 120; idem, *Revelation Theology,* 145–46.

42. In 1954, impressed by Merton's *The Sign of Jonah* (1953), Guardini revised his previously negative view of the American spirit; see *Wahrheit,* 98. Guardini also intuited that Merton might have written "a truly great book for our age" if he had taken a break from writing for a few years; see Gremillion, "Interview with Romano Guardini," 194.

43. See Thomas Merton, *A Search for Solitude,* ed. Lawrence S. Cunningham (San Francisco: HarperCollins, 1996), 246, 248.

44. Thomas Merton, *The Courage for Truth,* ed. Christine M. Bochen (New York: Farrar, Straus, and Giroux, 1933), 56.

45. Thomas Merton, *Conjectures of a Guilty Bystander* (Garden City: Doubleday, 1966), 284–85.

46. See John Howard Griffin, *Follow the Ecstasy* (Fort Worth, Texas: JHG Editions, 1983), 135–36.

47. Thomas Merton, *The Road to Joy,* ed. Robert E. Daggy (New York: Farrar, Straus, and Giroux, 1989), 97.

48. See Rose Bowen, "Christology in the Works of Flannery O'Connor," *Horizons* 14 (1987): 7–23.

49. Flannery O'Connor, *The Habit of Being: Letters of Flannery O'Connor,* ed. Sally Fitzgerald (New York: Farrar, Straus, and Giroux, 1979), 74.

50. Ibid., 131, 150.

51. Flannery O'Connor, *The Presence of Grace and Other Book Reviews,* compiled by Leo J. Zuber, ed. Carter W. Martin (Athens, Ga.: University of Georgia Press, 1983), 16.

52. See O'Connor, *The Habit of Being,* 191. In the autumn of 1956 O'Connor read Guardini's "Dostoyevsky's Idiot: A Symbol of Christ" (1939), trans. Francis X. Quinn, *Cross Currents* 6 (1956): 359–82.

53. O'Connor, *The Habit of Being,* 99.

54. Ibid., 304.

55. O'Connor, *Presence of Grace,* 55.

56. O'Connor, *The Habit of Being,* 230–31.

57. Ibid., 169.

58. *Der Spiegel* 22 (October 7, 1968): 224.

59. See Schilson, "Romano Guardini und die Theologie der Gegenwart"; Gerl, *Anfechtung.*

60. Karl Rahner, "Festvortrag," in Forster, ed., *Akademische Feier,* 17–35. Reprinted: K. Rahner, "Ansprache zum 80. Geburtstag von Romano Guardini," in idem, *Gnade als Freiheit* (Freiburg: Herder, 1968), 253–65. An abbreviated version is Karl Rahner, "Thinker and Christian," in idem, *Opportunities for Faith,* trans. Edward Quinn (New York: Seabury, 1975), 127–31. See Karl Rahner, *I Remember,* 73–75.

61. See Elio Guerriero, *Hans Urs von Balthasar* (Milan: Paoline, 1991); Eicher, *Offenbarung,* 292. Guardini and Balthasar remained in contact throughout their lives; see *Wahrheit,* 59, 115. Interestingly, while Guardini declined Paul VI's invitation to become a cardinal, Balthasar accepted John Paul II's invitation but died before receiving the red hat.

62. Balthasar, *Romano Guardini,* 21.

63. Ibid., 108.

64. Ibid., 11, 108.

65. Ratzinger, "Von der Liturgie zur Christologie."

66. See Joseph Ratzinger, *A New Song for the Lord,* trans. Martha M. Matesich (New

York: Crossroad, 1996 [1995]), 25, 42–44, 49, 73, 117–18; idem, "Guardini on Christ in Our Century"; idem, "God and Freedom: Jesus, the Way, the Truth and the Life," *Origins* 19 (February 8, 1990): 591–96; esp. 595; idem, "The Church and the Theologian," *Origins* 15 (May 8, 1986): 761–70; esp. 763, 766; Aidan Nichols, *The Theology of Joseph Ratzinger* (Edinburgh: T. & T. Clark, 1988), 29, 114, 137, 215, 288–89.

67. On the ahistorical tendency in Ratzinger's thought, see Robert A. Krieg, "Cardinal Ratzinger, Max Scheler and Christology," ITQ 47 (1981): 205–19.

68. See Gerl, *Romano Guardini*, 335–36.

69. On Guardini's influence, see Gunda Böning, "Theologie des Existenz: Zum 25. Todestag Romano Guardinis am 1. Oktober 1993," *Münchener Theologische Zeitschrift* 44 (1993): 359–63; Winfried Böhm, "Über das geistige Erbe Romano Guardinis," in Josef Schreiner and Klaus Wittstadt, eds., *Communio Sanctorum* (Würzburg: Echter, 1988), 610–23; Heinz Robert Schlette, "Guardini-Literatur im Jubiläumsjahr," *Theologische Revue* 81 (1985): 441–50; Hans Maier, "Romano Guardini: Erinnerungen am 10. Todestag," *zur debatte: Themen der Katholischen Akademie in Bayern* 8 (November-December, 1978): 1–3.

70. See *Wahrheit*, 49–50, 71, 77, 81, 86, 111–12; Gerl, *Romano Guardini*, 64, 87, 134, 144, 331, 359, 360; Hugo Ott, "Um die Nachfolge Martin Heideggers nach 1945," in Annemarie Gethmann-Siefert, ed., *Philosophie und Poesie*, 2 (Stuttgart: Frommann-Holzboog, 1988), 37–59.

71. See *Wahrheit*, 50, 108; Gerl, *Romano Guardini*, 80, 122, 132–34, 254, 298, 348, 354.

72. See Friedman, *Martin Buber's Life and Work: The Later Years, 1945–1965*, 111, 118, 397. On June 17, 1953, Buber was awarded the Peace Prize of the German Book Association at Frankfurt's Church of St. Paul and was joined by Guardini, who had received this award in the previous year; see Gerl, *Romano Guardini*, 354. In 1963 Guardini donated funds for the Martin Buber Forest in Israel's Kibbutz Hazorea; see Nahum N. Glatzer and Paul Mendes-Flohr, eds., *The Letters of Martin Buber*, trans. Richard and Clara Winston and Harry Zahn (New York: Schocken Books, 1991), 657.

73. See Friedrich Georg Friedmann, *Hannah Arendt* (Munich: Piper, 1985), 16; Elisabeth Young-Bruehl, *Hannah Arendt* (New Haven: Yale University Press, 1982), 34, 36, 45, 283.

74. See *Der Spiegel* 47 (May 31, 1993): 260.

75. See Bernard Häring, *My Witness for the Church*, trans. Leonard Swidler (New York: Paulist Press, 1992), 27.

76. See *Berichte*, 116; *Wahrheit*, 58.

77. See Kasper, *Theology and Church*, 45–46, 55, 129–32, 149; idem, *The God of Jesus Christ*, trans. Matthew J. O'Connell (New York: Crossroad, 1984), 53, 347; idem, *Jesus the Christ*, 33, 188.

78. According to Avery Dulles (*The Assurance of Things Hoped For*, 134), Jean Daniélou "builds consciously on the work of Guardini." Also, Guardini is frequently cited in HanFTh. Further, he receives a chapter in Fritz März, *Klassiker christlicher Erziehung* (Munich: Kösel, 1988), 373–420. Also, he is described as one of the "contemporary church fathers" by Thomas Kampermann, *Das Geheimnis des Alten Testaments*

(Munich: Hueber, 1962). See Joseph Bernhart, *Leben und Werk in Selbstzeugnissen*, ed. Lorenz Wachinger (Weissenhorn: Anton H. Konrad, 1981), 11, 37, 39, 42, 45, 47, 78, 214, 253, 286, 289, 298, 355, 379.

79. See Paul Fechter, *An der Wende der Zeit* (Gütersloh: E. Bertelsmann, 1949), 159–67; Gerhard von Rad, *Reden und Denkworte*, 9 (Heidelberg, 1969), 147–52; Helmut Thielicke, *Notes from a Wayfarer*, trans. David R. Law (New York: Paragon House, 1995), 207–9, 330–31; Pöhlmann, *Gottes Denker*, 169–90.

80. See German Bishops' Conference, *The Church's Confession of Faith*, trans. Stephen Wentworth Arndt, ed. Mark Jordan (San Francisco: Ignatius Press, 1987 [1985]), 28.

81. Dirks, "Romano Guardini," 249.

82. *Berichte*, 86.

83. Kasper, *Theology and Church*, 5; see idem, *Jesus the Christ*, 15.

84. Kasper, *Theology and Church*, 7.

85. "'Europa,'" 20–21.

86. "Wahrheit und Ironie," 43.

87. *The Life of Faith*, 89.

88. *Wahrheit*, 125. Cf. Karl Rahner's statement: "Theology consists in conscious reflection upon the message of the gospel in a quite specific situation in terms of the history of the human spirit"; see Karl Rahner, "Ecumenical Theology in the Future" (1971), in idem, *Theological Investigations*, 14, trans. D. Bourke (New York: Seabury, 1976), 254–69, 256.

89. *Berichte*, 109–10. On this statement's context, see Heinz R. Kuehn, "Fires in the Night," in RoGu, 1–14.

BIBLIOGRAPHY

1. A Chronological List of Selected Writings by Romano Guardini

This list gives in chronological order the original publication information and English translations of selected writings by Romano Guardini. Most of this information is taken from Merker, ed., *Bibliographie*.

Michelangelo: Gedichte und Briefe. Berlin: Pan, 1907.

Gegensatz und Gegensätze. Freiburg: Caritas, 1914.

Vom Geist der Liturgie. Freiburg: Herder, 1918. *The Church and the Catholic, and The Spirit of the Liturgy.* Translated by Ada Lane. New York: Sheed and Ward, 1935.

Der Kreuzweg unseres Herrn und Heilandes. Mainz: Matthias Grünewald, 1919. *The Way of the Cross of Our Lord and Saviour Jesus Christ.* Translated by Ada Lane. London: Sheed and Ward, 1932.

"Thule oder Hellas? Klassische oder deutsche Bildung," *Der Wächter* 3 (1920): 2–16, 66–79. Pseudonym: Anton Wächter. A portion of the text is available in RGL, pp. 206–11.

Die Lehre des heiligen Bonaventura von der Erlösung. Düsseldorf: Schwann, 1921.

"Anselm von Canterbury und das Wesen der Theologie," 1921. In *Auf dem Wege* (1923), pp. 33–65.

Gottes Werkleute: Briefe über Selbstbildung. Burg Rothenfels am Main: Deutsches Quickbornhaus, 1921.

"Das Objecktive im Gebetsleben," *Das Jahrbuch für Liturgiewissenschaft* 1 (1921): 117–25.

"Die Lehre vom lumen mentis, von der gradatio entium und von der influentia sensus et motus und ihre Bedeutung für den Aufbau des Systems Bonaventuras." Bonn: unpublished *Habilitationsschrift*, 1922. Published text: *Systembildende Elemente in der Theologie Bonaventuras.* Leiden: Brill, 1964.

Vom Sinn der Kirche. Mainz: Matthias Grünewald, 1922. *The Church and the Catholic, and the Spirit of the Liturgy.* Translated by Ada Lane. New York: Sheed and Ward, 1935.

"Ein Gespräch vom Reichtum Christi," 1923. In *Auf dem Wege* (1923), pp. 151–65.

Auf dem Wege. Mainz: Matthias Grünewald, 1923.

Liturgische Bildung. Burg Rothenfels am Main: Deutsches Quickbornhaus, 1923.

"Vom Wesen katholischer Weltanschauung," Sch 4 (1923): 66–79. Reprinted in *Unterscheidung des Christlichen* (1963), pp. 1–22.

Der Gegensatz. Mainz: Matthias Grünewald, 1925.

"Gedanken über das Verhältnis von Christentum und Kultur," Sch 6 (1926): 281–315.

"Gedanken über politische Bildung" (1926), Sch 13 (1933–34): 177–82.

"Karl Neundörfer zum Gedächtnis," Sch 6 (1926): 385–91.

"Über Sozialwissenschaft und Ordnung unter Personen" (1926), in *Unterscheidung des Christlichen* (1963), pp. 34–63.

Briefe vom Comersee. Mainz: Matthias Grünewald, 1927. *Letters from Lake Como.* Translated by Geoffrey W. Bromiley. Grand Rapids: William B. Eerdmans, 1994.

"Der Ausgangspunkt der Denkbewegung Sören Kierkegaards," H 24 (1927): 12–33. Reprinted in *Unterscheidung des Christlichen* (1963), pp. 471–501.

"Der heilige Franziskus: Zum Gedächtnis," Sch 7 (1927): 3–18. "St. Francis and Self-Achievement." In *The Focus of Freedom.* Translated by Gregory Roettger. Pp. 7–30. Baltimore: Helicon, 1966.

"Madeleine Sémer," Sch 7 (1927): 161–83.

"Heilige Schrift und Glaubenswissenschaft," Sch 8 (1928): 24–57.

"Vom Sinn der Schwermut," Sch 8 (1928): 103–25. "The Meaning of Melancholy." In *The Focus of Freedom.* Translated by Gregory Roettger. Pp. 55–90. Baltimore: Helicon, 1966.

"Das Wesen des Christentums," Sch 9 (1929): 129–52.

Von heiligen Zeichen. Mainz: Matthias Grünewald, 1929. *Sacred Signs.* Translated by Grace Branham. St. Louis: Pio Decimo, 1956.

Vom lebendigen Gott. Mainz: Matthias Grünewald, 1930. *The Living God.* Translated by Stanley Godman. New York: Pantheon Books, 1957.

"Die Religiöse Existenz in Dostojewskijs grossen Romanen," Sch 11 (1931): 98–130, 193–228, 316–51, 420–51.

Das Gebet des Herrn. Mainz: Matthias Grünewald, 1932. *The Lord's Prayer.* Translated by Isabel McHugh. New York: Pantheon Books, 1958.

Der Mensch und der Glaube: Versuche über die religiöse Existenz in Dostjewkijs grossen Romanen. Leipzig: Hegner, 1932.

In Spiegel und Gleichnis. Mainz: Matthias Grünewald, 1932.

"Die religiöse Entscheidung im Leben Pascals," H 30 (1932–33): 23–34, 167–75.

"Religiöse Erfahrung und Glaube," Sch 13 (1934): 283–306. Reprinted in *Unterscheidung des Christlichen* (1963), pp. 307–39.

Christliches Bewusstsein. Leipzig: Hegner, 1935. *Pascal for Our Time.* Translated by Brian Thompson. New York: Herder and Herder, 1966.

Die Bekehrung des Aurelius Augustinus. Leipzig: Hegner, 1935. *The Conversion of St. Augustine.* Translated by Elinor Briefs. Westminster, Md.: Newman Press, 1960.

Vom Leben des Glaubens. Mainz: Matthias Grünewald, 1935. *The Life of Faith.* Translated by John Chapin. Westminster, Md.: Newman, 1961.

"Der Heiland," Sch 14 (1935): 97–116. Reprinted in *Unterscheidung des Christlichen* (1935), pp. 362–88.

Unterscheidung des Christlichen. Mainz: Matthias Grünewald, 1935.

Das Bild von Jesus dem Christus im Neuen Testament. Würzburg: Werkbund, 1936.

Der Engel in Dantes Göttlicher Komödie. Leipzig: Hegner, 1937.

Der Herr: Betrachtung über die Person und das Leben Jesu Christi. Würzburg: Werkbund, 1937. *The Lord.* Translated by Elinor Castendyk Briefs. Chicago: Henry Regnery, 1954.

Das Wesen des Christentums. Würzburg: Werkbund, 1938.

"Zu Rainer Maria Rilkes Erster Elegie," Sch 17 (1938): 170.

Besinnung vor der Feier der heiligen Messe. Düsseldorf: Schwann, 1939. *Meditations before Mass.* Translated by Elinor Castendyk Briefs. Westminster, Md.: Newman, 1955. Reprinted: Mansfield, N.H.: Sophia Institute Press, 1993.

Hölderlin: Weltbild und Frömmigkeit. Leizig: Hegner, 1939.

Welt und Person. Würzburg: Werkbund, 1939. *The World and the Person.* Translated by Stella Lange. Chicago: Henry Regnery, 1965.

Religiöse Gestalt in Dostojewskijs Werk. Leipzig: Hegner, 1939. "The Legend of the Grand Inquisitor," *Cross Currents* 3 (1952): 58–86. Translated by Sally S. Cunneen. "Dostoyevsky's Idiot: A Symbol of Christ," *Cross Currents* 6 (1956): 359–82. Translated by Francis X. Quinn.

Das Herrentum Christi. Würzburg: Werkbund, 1939.

Der Rosenkranz Unserer Lieben Frau. Würzburg: Werkbund, 1940. *The Rosary of Our Lady.* Translated by Hans von Schuecking. New York: Kenedy, 1955. Reprinted: Mansfield, N.H.: Sophia Institute Press, 1994.

Die letzten Dingen. Würzburg: Werkbund, 1940. *The Last Things.* Translated by Charlotte E. Forsyth and Grace Branham. New York: Pantheon, 1954. Reprinted: Notre Dame: University of Notre Dame Press, 1966.

Die Offenbarung: Ihre Wesen und ihre Formen. Würzburg: Werkbund, 1940.

Jesus Christus: Sein Bild in den Schriften des Neuen Testaments. Part One: *Das Christusbild der Paulinischen Schriften.* Würzburg: Werkbund, 1940.

Jesus Christus: Sein Bild in den Schriften des Neuen Testaments. Part Two: *Das Christusbild der Johanneischen Schriften.* Würzburg: Werkbund, 1940.

Ein Wort zur liturgischen Frage. Mainz: Grünewald, 1940. Reprinted in *Liturgie und liturgische Bildung* (1966), pp. 193–213. "Some Dangers of the Liturgical Movement." In Alfons Kirchengässner, ed., *Unto the Altar.* Translated by Rosaleen Brennan. Pp. 13–22. New York: Herder and Herder, 1963.

"Einführung." In *Jean Pierre de Caussade.* Edited by Wolfgang Rüttenauer. Pp. 1–20. Freiburg: Herder, 1940. French edition: "Introduction à Jean-Pierre de Caussade," translated by Claire C. Lossey, *Dieu Vivant* 13 (1949): 83–96.

"Die Grundgestalt von Jesu Dasein," Sch 20 (1941): 1–6.

Zu Rainer Maria Rilkes Deutung des Daseins. Berlin: Küpper, 1941.

Der Tod von Sokrates. Berlin: Küpper, 1943. *The Death of Socrates.* Translated by Basil Wrighton. New York: Sheed and Ward, 1948.

Vorschule des Betens. Einsiedeln: Benziger, 1943. *Prayer in Practice.* Translated by Prince Leopold Loewenstein-Wertheim, 1963. Reprinted: *The Art of Praying.* Mansfield, N.H.: Sophia Institute Press, 1994.

Glaubenserkenntnis. Basel: Hess, 1944. *Faith and the Modern Man.* Translated by Charlotte E. Forsyth. New York: Pantheon Books, 1952.

Das Jahr des Herrn. Augsburg: Weber, 1946.

Der Heilbringer in Mythos, Offenbarung und Politik. Stuttgart: Deutsche Verlagsanstalt, 1946. Reprinted in *Unterscheidung des Christlichen* (1963), pp. 411–58.

Die Waage des Daseins. Stuttgart: Wunderlich, 1946. Reprinted in *Deutsche Stimmen. 1945–1946.* Edited by Carl Georg Heise et al. Hamburg: Maximilian-Gesellschaft, 1948.

Vision und Dichtung. Tübingen: Wunderlich, 1946.

Freiheit, Gnade, Schicksal. Munich: Kösel, 1948. *Freedom, Grace and Destiny.* Translated by John Murray. New York: Pantheon Books, 1961.

Theologische Gebet. Frankfurt am Main: Knecht, 1948. *Prayers From Theology.* Translated by Richard Newnham. New York: Herder and Herder, 1956.

"Auf der Suche nach dem Frieden," H 41 (1948–49): 105–22.

A la Recherche de la Paix. Strasbourg: Éditions F.-X. LeRoux, 1948.

"De Zin van de Universiteit," *Universitas. Tijdschrift voor Universitair Katholiek Leven,* 11 (1949): 9–17. Translated by P. Leemans from the German text: "Vom Sinn der Universität."

Drei Schriftauslegung. Würzburg: Werkbund, 1949. *The Word of God on Faith, Hope and Charity.* Translated by Stella Lange. Chicago: Henry Regnery, 1963.

Vom Sinn der Schwermut. Zürich: Verlag der Arche, 1949. "The Meaning of Melancholy." In *The Focus of Freedom.* Translated by Gregory Roettger. Pp. 55–90. Baltimore: Helicon, 1966.

Das Ende der Neuzeit. Mainz: Matthias Grünewald, 1950. *The End of the Modern World.* Translated by Joseph Theman and Herbert Burke. New York: Sheed and Ward, 1956.

Deutscher Psalter. Munich: Kösel, 1950.

Die Sinne und der religiöse Erkenntnis. Zurich: Verlag der Arche, 1950.

"Der Mythos und die Wahrheit des Offenbarung," *Frankfurter Hefte* 5 (1950): 712–23. "Myth and the Truth of Revelation," *Cross Currents* 1 (1951): 3–12. Translated by Marie Christine Hellin and Sally S. Cunneen.

Die Macht. Mainz: Matthias Grünewald, 1951. *Power and Responsibility.* Translated by Elinor C. Briefs. Chicago: Henry Regnery, 1961.

Lob des Buches. Olten: Schweizerisches Vereinssortiment, 1951. *In Praise of the Book.* Translated by Maria H. Arndt. New York: St. Paul Publications, 1966.

"Die Liturgie und der geistige Situation unserer Zeit," in *Eucharistiefeier am Sonntag. Reden und Verhandlungen des Ersten deustchen Liturgischen Kongresses.* Edited by Johannes Wagner and Damascus Zähringer. Trier: Paulinus, 1951.

Nur wer Gott kennt, kennt den Menschen. Würzburg: Werkbund, 1952. Reprinted in *Religiöse Erfahrung und Glaube* (1974), pp. 102–17.

Verantwortung: Gedanken zur jüdischen Frage. Munich: Kösel, 1952. Also printed in H 44 (1952): 481–93.

Rainer Maria Rilkes Deutung des Daseins. Munich: Kösel, 1953. *Rilke's Duino Elegies.* Translated by K. G. Knight. Chicago: Henry Regnery, 1961.

"Überlegungen zum Problem des Films," H 45 (1952–1953): 389–405. Reprinted in: *Sorge um den Menschen,* volume 2 (1966). "Thoughts on the Problem of the Film," *Cross Currents* 6 (1956): 189–99. Translated by Patricia Greene.

"Die Begegnung," H 47 (1954–55): 224–34.

"'Europa' und 'Christliche Weltanschauung'" (1955), in *Stationen und Rückblicke* (1965), pp. 9–22.

"Warum so viele Bücher?" (1955), in *Stationen und Rückblicke* (1965), pp. 23–34.

Die Lebensalter und die Philosophie. Würzburg: Werkbund, 1955. "The Stages of Life and Philosophy," *Philosophy Today* 1 (1957): 2–4. Translated by Edward E. Kaiser.

Über ein Gedicht von Eduard Mörike. Würzburg: Werkbund, 1956.

Der Heilige in unserer Welt. Würzburg: Werkbund, 1956. *The Saints in Daily Christian Life*. Philadelphia: Chilton, 1966.

Wahrheit und Ordnung. Universitätspredigten. Würzburg: Werkbund, 1956–59.

"Philosophische Anmerkungen zu Sigmund Freuds Psychologie." In *Sigmund Freud*. Edited by Werner Leibbrand and Paul Matussek. Pp. 25–37. Munich: Hueber, 1956. "Some Reflections on Freudian Psychology," *Philosophy Today* 1 (1956): 274–82. Translated by William J. Kramer.

"Das religiöse Bild und der unsichtbare," in *Arte liturgica in Germania. 1945–1955*. Pp. 13–25. Munich: Schnell und Steiner, 1956. "Sacred Images and the Invisible God," *The Furrow* 8 (1957): 350–63. Reprinted in *Cross Currents* 10 (1960): 211–20.

"Wer ist ein Gentleman? Ein Brief." In *Vom stilleren Leben*. Edited by Felix Messerschmid and Hans Waldmann. Pp. 49–56. Würzburg: Werkbund, 1956.

"Das Unendlich-Absolute und das Religiös-Christliche," *Philosophisches Jahrbuch der Görresgesellschaft* 65 (1957): 12–23. "The Absolute and the Christian Religion," *Philosophy Today* 2 (1958): 211–20. Translated by Marcellus Dreiling.

Jesus Christus, Geistliches Wort. Würzburg: Werkbund, 1957. *Jesus Christus: Meditations*. Translated by Peter White. Chicago: Henry Regnery, 1959.

Die menschliche Wirklichkeit des Herrn. Mainz: Matthias Grünewald, 1958. *The Humanity of Christ*. Translated by Ronald Walls. New York: Pantheon Books, 1964.

Landschaft der Ewigkeit. Der menschliche Existenzraum in der Göttlichen Komödie. Munich: Kösel, 1958.

Religion und Offenbarung, volume 1. Mainz: Matthias Grünewald, 1958.

"Evangelisches Christentum in katholischer Sichte heute," *Una Sancta Rundbriefe* 13 (1958), 225–33.

Nähe des Herrn. Würzburg: Werkbund, 1960.

"Das Phänomen der religiöse Erfahrung." In *Il problema dell' esperienza religiosa*. Pp. 39–50. Brescia: Morcelliana, 1961. "The Phenomenon of Religious Experience," *Philosophy Today* 6 (1962): 2–4, 88–92.

"Zur Theologie der Welt," *Der katholische Gedanke* 16 (1960): 76–85.

Das Christusbild der paulinischen und johanneischen Schriften. Würzburg: Werkbund, 1962.

Johanneische Botschaft. Würzburg: Werkbund, 1962.

Sorge um den Menschen, volume 1. Würzburg: Werkbund, 1962.

Sprache, Dichtung, Deutung. Würzburg: Werkbund, 1962.

"Europe: Réalité et mission." In *Praemium Erasmianum* (1962), pp. 43–48. Translated from "Europa: Wirklichkeit und Aufgabe." Reprinted in: *Sorge um Menschen*, volume 1 (1962), pp. 238–53. "Europe: Reality and Mission," in *Charactère et culture de l'Europe* (1962), pp. 143–47.

Tugenden: Meditationen über Gestalten sittlichen Lebens. Würzburg: Werkbund, 1963. *The Virtues.* Translated by Stella Lange. Chicago: Henry Regnery, 1967.

"Die Bäume von Isola Vicentina" (1963). In *Stationen und Rückblicke* (1965), pp. 35–40.

Unterscheidung des Christlichen: Gesammelte Studien. 1923–1963. Second Edition. Edited by Hans Waltmann. Mainz: Matthias Grünewald, 1963.

Weisheit der Psalmen. Würzburg: Werkbund, 1963. *The Wisdom of the Psalms.* Translated by Stella Lange. Chicago: Henry Regnery, 1968.

"Der Kultakt und die gegenwärtige Aufgabe der liturgischen Bildung: Ein Brief," LitJb 14 (1964): 101–6. "A Letter from Romano Guardini," *Herder Correspondence* (Special Issue, 1964): 24–26.

Die Kirche des Herrn. Mainz: Matthias Grünewald, 1965. *The Church of the Lord.* Translated by Stella Lange. Chicago: Henry Regnery, 1966.

"Wahrheit und Ironie" (1965). In *Akademische Feier zum 80. Geburtstag von Romano Guardini.* Edited by Karl Forster. Pp. 36–41. Würzburg: Echter, 1965. Also printed in *Stationen und Rückblicke* (1965), pp. 41–50.

Stationen und Rückblicke. Würzburg: Werkbund, 1965.

Liturgie und liturgische Bildung. Enlarged edition. Würzburg: Werkbund, 1966.

Sorge um den Menschen, volume 2. Würzburg: Werkbund, 1966.

"Abraham," H 61 (1969): 193–95.

"Gebet in der währenden Stunde," H 61 (1969): 195–96. Reprinted in *Theologische Briefe an einen Freund* (1976), pp. 65–66.

"Zum Problem des Demokratie" (1946); "Zur Kritik der historischen Begriffe" (1952); "Verantwortung und Urteilsmöglichkeit in politischen Frage" (1953); "Über Loyalität" (1954); "Zum ethischen Problem unserer kulturellen Situation" (1957); "Gesichtspunkte für ein Gespräch über Freiheit, Demokratie und humanistische Bildung" (1959); "Das Phänomenon der religiösen Erfahrung" (1960); "Zur Frage der Wiedereinführung des Todesstrafe" (1961); "Wille zur Macht oder Wille zur Wahrheit: Zur Frage der Universität" (1965). Edited by Felix Messerschmid. In *Geschichte in Wissenschaft und Unterricht* 21 (1970): 711–59.

Die Existenz des Christen. Paderborn: Ferdinand Schöningh, 1976.

Theologische Briefe an einen Freund. Paderborn: Ferdinand Schöningh, 1976.

Wahrheit des Denkens und Wahrheit des Tuns. Notizen und Texte 1942–1964. Edited by Felix Messerschmid. Paderborn: Ferdinand Schöningh, 1980.

Berichte über mein Leben. Autobiographische Aufzeichnungen. Edited by Franz Henrich. Düsseldorf: Patmos, 1984.

Ethik. Vorlesung an der Universität München. Edited by Hans Mercker, Martin Marschall, and the Katholische Akademie in Bayern. 2 volumes. Mainz: Matthias Grünewald, 1993.

2. Selected Books on Romano Guardini

Babolin, Albino. *Romano Guardini-Filosofo dell'alterità.* Volume 1: *Realta e persona.* Bologna: Zanichelli, 1968.

———. *Romano Guardini-Filosofo dell'alterità.* Volume 2: *Situazione umana ed esperienza religiosa.* Bologna: Zanchelli, 1969.

Balthasar, Hans Urs von. *Romano Guardini. Reform aus dem Ursprung.* Munich: Kösel, 1970. Idem., *Romano Guardini.* Translated by Albert Wimmer. San Francisco: Ignatius Press, forthcoming.

Berning-Baldeaux, Ursula. *Person und Bildung im Denken Romano Guardini.* Würzburg: Echter, 1968.

Binkowski, Johannes. *Jugend als Wegbereiter.* Stuttgart: Konrad Theiss, 1981.

Biser, Eugen. *Interpretation und Veränderung.* Paderborn: Ferdinand Schöningh, 1979.

Börsig-Hover, Lina. *Das personale Antlitz des Menschen. Eine Untersuchung zum Personbegriff bei Romano Guardini.* Mainz: Matthias Grünewald, 1987.

Faber, Eva-Maria. *Kirche zwischen Identität und Differenz.* Würzburg: Echter, 1993.

Fischer, Dorothee. *Wort und Welt. Die Pneuma-Theologie Romano Guardinis als Beitrag zur Glaubensentdeckung und Glaubensbegleitung.* Stuttgart: W. Kohlhammer, 1993.

Forster, Karl, ed. *Akademische Feier zum 80. Geburtstag von Romano Guardini.* Würzburg: Echter, 1965.

Gerl, Hanna Barbara. *Anfechtung und Treue: Romano Guardinis geistige Gestalt in ihrer heutigen Bedeutung.* Donauwörth: Ludwig Auer, 1989.

———. *Begegnungen in Mooshausen.* Weissenhorn: Anton H. Konrad, 1990.

———. *Romano Guardini 1885–1968.* Mainz: Matthias Grünewald, 1985.

Halda, Bernard. *Christianisme et humanisme chez Romano Guardini.* Paris: Editions Fleurus, 1978.

Haubenthaler, Reinhard. *Askese und Freiheit bei Romano Guardini.* Paderborn: Ferdinand Schöningh, 1995.

Henrich, Franz. *Die Bünde der katholischen Jugendbewegung.* Munich: Kösel, 1968.

Honnefelder, Ludger, and Matthias Lutz-Bachmann, eds. *Auslegungen des Glaubens. Zur Hermeneutik christlicher Existenz.* Berlin: Morus, 1987.

Kleiber, Hansruedi. *Glaube und religiöse Erfahrung bei Romano Guardini.* Freiburg: Herder, 1985.

Knoll, Alfons. *Glaube und Kultur bei Romano Guardini.* Paderborn: Ferdinand Schöningh, 1993.

Krieg, Robert, ed. *Romano Guardini: Proclaiming the Sacred in a Modern World.* Chicago: Liturgy Training Publications, 1995.

Kuhn, Helmut. *Romano Guardini.* Munich: Kösel, 1961.

———. *Romano Guardini, Philosoph der Sorge.* St. Ottilien: EOS, 1987.

Lopez Quintas, Alfonso. *Romano Guardini y la Dielectica de lo Viviente.* Madrid: Los Libros del Monograma, 1966.

Marschall, Martin. *In Wahrheit beten.* St. Ottilien: EOS, 1986.

Mercker, Hans. *Christliche Weltanschauung als Problem: Untersuchungen zur Grundstruktur im Werk Romano Guardinis.* Paderborn: Ferdinand Schöningh, 1988.

Mercker, Hans, and the Katholische Akademie in Bayern, eds. *Bibliographie Romano Guardini (1885–1968).* Paderborn: Ferdinand Schöningh, 1978.

Negri, Luigi. *La antropologia di Romano Guardini.* Milan: Jaca, 1989.

Ratzinger, Joseph, ed. *Wege zur Wahrheit.* Düsseldorf: Patmos, 1985.

Richter, Klemens, and Arno Schilson, eds. *Den Glauben feiern* Mainz: Matthias Grünewald, 1989.

Ruster, Thomas. *Die verlorene Nützlichkeit der Religion* Paderborn: Ferdinand Schöningh, 1994.

Schilson, Arno, ed. *Konservative mit Blick nach Vorn: Versuche zu Romano Guardini.* Würzburg: Echter, 1994.

———. *Perspektiven theologischer Erneuerung.* Düsseldorf: Patmos, 1986.

Schlette, Heinz Robert. *Romano Guardini. Werk und Wirkung.* Bonn: Bouvier, 1985.

Schmucker von Koch, Joseph F. *Autonomie und Transzendenz: Untersuchungen zur Religionsphilosophie Romano Guardinis.* Mainz: Matthias Grünewald, 1985.

Schuster, Hermann Josef, ed. *Guardini Weiterdenken.* Berlin: Guardini Stiftung, 1993.

Seidel, Walter, ed. *"Christliche Weltanschauung". Wiederbegegnung mit Romano Guardini.* Würzburg: Echter, 1985.

Watzal, Ludwig. *Das Politische bei Romano Guardini.* Percha am Starnberger See: R. S. Schulz, 1987.

Wechsler, Fridolin. *Romano Guardini als Kerygmatiker.* Paderborn: Ferdinand Schöningh, 1973.

Wucherer-Huldenfeld, Karl. *Die Gegensatzphilosophie Romano Guardinis in ihren Grundlagen und Folgerungen.* Vienna: Verlag Notring, 1968.

INDEX

Adam, Karl, 13, 50, 120, 124, 144, 159, 196
Adenauer, Konrad, 132
Adorno, Theodor, 177
Aeschylus, 130
Albert the Great, St., 193
Algermissen, Konrad, 120
Altizer, Thomas, 187
Alypius, 28
Andersen, Friedrich, 122
Anselm, St., 9, 13, 18–19, 144
Arendt, Hannah, 9, 201
Aubert, Roger, 59
Augustine, St., 9, 13, 18–19, 26–29, 35, 41, 44, 46, 91, 130, 152, 169, 171, 195, 198–201
Aussem, Josef, 9, 62, 208

Bach, Johann Sebastian, 130
Balthasar, Hans Urs von, 2, 9, 14, 22, 97, 184, 197–201, 210, 221n.94, 235n.30, 251n.4, 254n.61
Bares, Nikolaus (bishop of Hildesheim), 118
Barth, Karl, 26, 138, 144, 165, 177
Baumgartner, Alexander, 95–96
Baumstark, Anton, 73
Bea, Augustin, 141
Beauduin, Lambert, 73, 87
Becker, Carl, 8
Beethoven, Ludwig van, 48
Beinert, Wolfgang, 42
Belser, Johannes Evangelist, 5
Bendix, Ludwig, 63, 228n.65
Benedict XV, 1
Benjamin, Walter, 177
Berger, Karl, 98
Bergson, Henri, 13, 48
Bernanos, Georges, 196
Bernhard of the Netherlands (Prince), 11, 184
Bernhart, Josef, 251n.6
Berning, Wilhelm (bishop of Osnabrück), 119
Bertram, Adolf (archbishop of Breslau), 84, 119

Beyle, Marie Henri, 4, 99
Bismarck, Otto von, 164
Bloy, Léon, 4, 94, 98, 196
Böll, Heinrich, 97
Bonaventure, St., 6, 7, 13, 16–19, 144, 152, 166, 192, 198, 219n.74, 243n.13
Bonhoeffer, Dietrich, 162
Boniface, St., 3, 122
Bouyer, Louis, 195
Braig, Carl, 5–6
Brauer, Theodore, 120
Brentano, Lujo, 4
Brown, Raymond E., 157
Bruckner, Anton, 251n.6
Brunner, Emil, 26, 144
Bruno, Giordano, 172
Buber, Martin, 7, 26, 30, 33–38, 201, 223n.37, 255n.72
Büchner, Fritz, 118
Buddha. See Gautama Buddha
Bultmann, Rudolf, 138, 141, 165
Butler, Eliza Marian, 110

Cajetan, 17
Calvin, John, 171
Camus, Albert, 186
Cano, Melchior, 17
Casel, Odo, 73, 82, 86, 231n.49
Cassier, Ernst, 13
Caussade, Jean Pierre de, 136
Cavour, Benso di, 3
Cézanne, Paul, 187
Chamberlain, Houston Stuart, 27–28, 121–22, 239n.28
Charlemagne, 122
Christine, Lucie, 99
Clemen, Paul, 7
Collaltino di Collalto, Count, 103
Congar, Yves M.-J., 12, 17
Cox, Harvey, 187

Cunningham, Lawrence S., 248n.29
Cyril of Alexandria, 152

Daniélou, Jean, 184, 195, 255n.78
Dante Alighieri, 3, 4, 13, 91, 98–99, 102, 108, 127, 130, 142, 166, 198, 208, 236n.50
Day, Dorothy, 194
Descartes, René, 79
Dessauer, Philipp, 252n.21
Dibelius, Martin, 141
Dibelius, Otto, 66
Dieckmann, Hermann, 17
Dilthey, Wilhelm, 13, 30, 32–33, 35, 44
Dinter, Artur, 121
Dirks, Walter, 10, 81, 159, 186, 190, 201, 251n.13
Döpfner, Julius (archbishop of Munich-Freising), 11
Doré, Paul Gustave, 98
Dörner, August, 84
Dostoyevsky, Fyodor, 9, 13, 29, 91, 99, 108, 114, 196, 198
Dulles, Avery, 194, 224n.49, 255n.78

Ebert, Friedrich, 49
Ebner, Franz, 26
Eckart, Dietrich, 121
Ehlen, Nikolaus, 226n.34
Ehrhard, Albert, 94
Eichendorff, Joseph von, 98
Eicher, Peter, 229n.88
Einstein, Albert, 116
Eisner, Kurt, 118
Erzberger, Matthias, 49
Eschweiler, Karl, 120, 124
Esser, Gerhard, 7

Faber, Eva Maria, 251n.4
Faulhaber, Michael (archbishop of Munich-Freising), 64, 117–19
Fechter, Paul, 92, 201
Federer, Heinrich, 94
Fetcher, Iring, 236n.62
Feuerbach, Ludwig, 37, 163, 170, 186
Fichte, Johann Gottlieb, 78
Fischer, Balthasar, 86
Francis I, Emperor, 164
Francis of Assisi, St., 18, 82
Freud, Sigmund, 37, 91, 115, 170, 186, 188–90
Frings, Josef (archbishop of Cologne), 6
Fritsch, Theodor, 121

Frühwirth, Andreas (archbishop), 97
Funk, Franz Xavier, 5

Gadamer, Hans Georg, 92, 108–112
Galen, Clemens August Graf von (bishop of Münster), 117
Galileo, 180
Garrigou-Lagrange, Reginald, 17
Gautama Buddha, 91, 146, 149, 159
Gerl, Hanna Barbara, 250n.55, 251n.4
Gerlich, Fritz, 120
Gide, André, 115
Gilson, Étienne, 196
Goebbels, Joseph, 115
Goethe, Johann Wolfgang von, 15, 48, 78, 94, 111–12, 130, 149, 173, 185, 190
Goettsberger, J. B., 140
Gogarten, Friedrich, 34, 165, 177
Görres, Guido, 93
Görres, Joseph, 93
Gottron, Adam, 54
Grassi, Ernesto, 100
Green, Martin B., 92, 108, 110
Gremillion, Joseph B., 194
Grimm, Jacob, 130
Grimm, Wilhelm, 130
Gröber, Conrad (archbishop of Freiburg im Breisgau), 65, 82–84, 117–19, 232n.55
Gropius, Walter, 50
Guardini, Aleardo, 3, 8, 207
Guardini, Gino, 3, 8, 207
Guardini, Mario, 3, 8, 207
Guardini, Romano Michele Antonio Maria. As a Benedictine oblate: Odilo, 5. Pseudonyms: Anton Wächter and A. Wacht, 216n.13.
Guardini, Romano Tullo (father), 3, 6, 207, 236n.50
Guardini, Paola Maria (mother, née Bernardinella), 3, 6, 8, 73, 166–167, 207, 209, 236n.50
Guéranger, Prosper Louis Pascal, 72, 85, 87
Gundlach, Gustav, 120, 239n.26
Gunkel, Hermann, 141
Gurian, Waldemar, 120
Gutenberg, Johann, 3

Habermas, Jürgen, 177
Hamilton, William, 187
Hammenstede, Albert, 73
Handel-Mazzetti, Enrica von, 95

Häring, Bernard, 201
Harnack, Adolf von, 8, 25–26, 143–44, 152, 165
Harth, Philipp, 98
Hartmann, Nicolai, 13, 78
Hatzfeld, Countess, 100
Hauer, Jakob Wilhelm, 121–22, 126
Hegel, Georg Wilhelm Friedrich, 15, 25, 31,
    110, 163–64, 186
Heidegger, Martin, 6, 10, 13, 165, 201
Heiler, Friedrich, 58, 184
Heine, Heinrich, 115
Heisenberg, Werner, 210
Hello, Ernst, 94
Hellwig, Monika, 159, 194, 245n.51
Helmholtz, Hermann L. F. von, 130
Henrich, Franz, 80
Heraclitus, 130
Herder, Johann Gottfried von, 162
Hertling, Georg Freiherr von, 93–94
Herwegen, Ildefons (abbot of Maria Laach
    Abbey), 73, 75, 86, 230n.24, 251n.6
Hesse, Hermann, 15, 50
Hildebrand, Dietrich von, 50, 120
Himmler, Heinrich, 9
Hindenberg, Paul von, 119
Hitler, Adolf, 9, 79, 110, 115–35, 151, 160, 169,
    177–78
Hoffmann, Hermann, 50, 226n.34
Hohoff, Carl, 92, 108
Hölderlin, Friedrich, 13, 91, 100, 102, 108–9,
    130, 142, 198, 208
Holtzmann, Heinrich Julius, 140
Homer, 131
Horst, Ulrich, 243n.15
Hügel, Friedrich von, 111
Hughes, Kathleen, 80
Hugo, Ludwig Maria (bishop of Mainz), 119
Husserl, Edmund, 13
Huysmans, Joris Karl, 4, 98

Ihering, Rudolf von, 74
Innitzer, Theodor (archbishop of Vienna), 84
Irenaeus, St., 46

Jammers, Joseph, 252n.21
Jaspers, Karl, 32, 44, 165, 177, 201
Jens, Walter, 92
John XXIII, 1, 12, 22, 68, 85, 97, 182, 216n.8,
    238n.13, 254n.61
John Paul II, 14, 193

Jung, Carl G., 15, 128, 148, 190
Jünger, Ernst, 177
Jungmann, Josef, 20, 86

Kaas, Ludwig (monsignor), 119–20,
Kahlefeld, Heinrich, 85, 200, 246n.67, 252n.21
Kähler, Martin, 144
Kampermann, Thomas, 255n.78
Kandinsky, Wassily, 50
Kant, Immanuel, 13, 24, 78–79, 169, 172, 199
Kasper, Walter (bishop of Rottenburg-
    Stuttgart), 67, 97, 151, 159, 201–3, 224n.42,
    245n.44, 249n.33
Kassiepe, Max, 82–84
Keller, Helen, 115
Ketteler, Wilhelm Emmanuel von (bishop of
    Mainz), 59, 164, 181, 227n.41
Kierkegaard, Søren, 9, 13, 26, 30–32, 35, 40, 91,
    99, 108, 222n.22
Kirstein, Georg Heinrich (bishop of Mainz),
    6–7
Klages, Ludwig, 13
Klausner, Erich, 120
Klimmer, Ingeborg, 251n.4
Knies, Richard, 97, 243n.14
Knoll, Alfons, 251n.4
Koch, Wilhelm, 5–6, 12, 21, 26, 43, 52, 216n.22,
    220n.86
Kolping, Adolf (d. 1895), 227n.42
Kolping, Adolf (b. 1909), 221n.93
Kralik, Richard von, 95–96, 99,
Kraus, Franz Xavier, 94
Krebs, Engelbert, 6, 144, 226n.34
Kreiten, Wilhelm, 95
Kuehn, Heinz R., 71, 80
Kuehn, Regina, 71, 80, 89
Kunisch, Hermann, 92, 108, 111–12, 185
Küng, Hans, 92, 97, 159, 235n.30

LaFarge, John, 239n.26
Lagarde, Paul de, 49, 121
Lagrange, Marie Joseph, 20, 139
Lakner, Franz, 144
Landersdorfer, Simon Konrad (bishop of
    Passau), 83
Langbehn, Julius, 94, 121
Langgässer, Elisabeth, 97
Lao-Tzu, 146, 149, 159
Laros, Matthias, 226n.34
Leeuw, Gerardus van der, 124

Le Fort, Gertrud von, 97
Lehmann, Karl, 220n.86
Leibnitz, Gottfried Wilhelm von, 130
Leinhard, Friedrich, 94
Leo XIII, 1, 59, 93, 139–40, 144, 164, 182, 238n.13
Lessing, Gotthold Ephraim, 24, 162
Lichtenberg, Bernhard, 134
Lippert, Peter, 50, 144
Loisy, Alfred, 25
London, Jack, 115
Lortz, Joseph, 120, 124
Lubac, Henri de, 20, 195
Ludendorf, Erich, 122
Ludwig III (king of Bavaria), 49
Luther, Martin, 171

Maglione, Luigi (archbishop), 84
Maier, Hans, 79–80
Mann, Heinrich, 115
Mann, Thomas, 15, 50, 115
Manser, Anselm, 230n.24
Marc, Franz, 50, 55
Marcel, Gabriel, 184, 196
Maréchal, Joseph, 20
Maritain, Jacques, 182, 196, 251n.6
Martius, Konrad, 218n.47
Marx, Karl, 163–64, 170
Mauriac, Francois, 196
May, Karl, 98
Meinecke, Friedrich, 49, 177
Mercker, Hans, 42, 179, 251n.4
Mersch, Emile, 47
Merton, Thomas, 195–96, 253n.42
Metz, Johannes Baptist, 178, 187, 235n.30
Michel, Ernst, 61–62
Michel, Virgil, 194
Michelangelo, 5, 98–99, 166
Milosz, Czeslaw, 195
Mirgeler, Albert, 118
Misner, Paul, 2
Moenius, Georg, 120
Mohlberg, Kunibert, 73, 75
Möhler, Johann Adam, 52–54, 59, 66, 193, 226n.28
Molina, Louis de, 171
Mommsen, Theodor, 130
Montaigne, Michel, 91
Montini, Giovanni Battista. See Paul VI
Mörike, Eduard, 10, 13, 91, 100
Moser, Johannes, 5, 26

Moses, 159
Mozart, Wolfgang Amadeus, 130
Muckermann, Friedrich, 239n.20
Muhammad, 146, 149, 159
Müller, Joseph, 234n.17
Mumbauer, Johannes, 96
Münster, Clemens, 10
Mussolini, Benito, 127, 178
Muth, Carl, 4, 94–99, 108, 235n.31

Nabb, Ingbart, 120
Napoleon I, 162
Nell-Breuning, Oswald, 210
Neumann, Klemens, 50, 62
Neundörfer, Karl, 4–6, 12, 27–28, 51, 67, 74–75, 208, 218n.52
Neunheuser, Burkhard, 89, 231n.42
Newman, John Henry (cardinal), 4, 98
Nicholas of Cusa, 13, 193
Nietzsche, Friedrich, 13, 48, 78, 91, 121, 163, 169–70, 178, 185–88, 190

O'Collins, Gerald, 151
O'Connor, Flannery, 195–96, 200
Odilio. See Guardini, Romano
Ong, Walter, 253n.34
Otto I, King, 164
Otto, Rudolf, 30, 35–37, 177
Otto, Walter F., 93

Pacelli, Eugenio. See Pius XII
Pannenberg, Wolfhart, 135
Papen, Franz von, 164
Parmenides, 171
Parsch, Pius, 73, 86–87, 230n.16
Pascal, Blaise, 9, 13, 29, 91, 99, 130, 144, 169, 171, 195, 198, 243n.13, 249n.33
Pasternak, Boris, 110
Paul, St., 35, 40–41, 65, 153, 170–71
Paul VI, 11, 63, 65, 68, 69, 184, 193, 209, 254n.61
Paulus, Friedrich von, 137
Percy, Walker, 249n.38
Pesch, Christian, 17, 143
Pesch, Otto, 66
Petavius, Dionysius, 17
Pfeilschifter, Franz, 5
Pflumm, Placidus, 230n.24
Picard, Max, 196
Pieper, Josef, 9, 61–62, 177, 184, 237n.3
Pinsk, Johannes, 82

Pius IX, 1, 22, 46, 95, 97, 164, 180, 238n.13
Pius X, 1, 42, 72–73, 81, 95–97, 140, 152, 180, 230n.12
Pius XI, 59, 121, 239n.26
Pius XII, 11, 21, 42, 47, 63, 67, 71, 84–85, 120, 153, 157–58, 193, 200, 209, 238n.13
Planck, Max, 130
Plato, 12–13, 37–38, 78, 91, 130, 191–92, 230n.24
Platz, Hermann, 120, 226n.34, 251n.6
Plotinus, 13
Pöhlmann, Horst Georg, 159
Porphyry, 13
Preuss, Hugo, 49, 114
Preysing, Konrad Graf von (bishop of Berlin), 65, 118, 134
Probst, Adalbert, 120
Proust, Marcel, 115
Przywara, Erich, 59, 97, 159, 193, 221n.93
Ptolemy, 172

Raabe, Wilhelm, 13, 91, 100
Rad, Gerhard von, 201
Rahner, Anna, 61
Rahner, Hugo, 144
Rahner, Karl, 2, 11–12, 61–62, 84, 97, 151, 157–58, 184, 197–200, 210, 220n.86, 256n.88
Raphael, 98, 130
Rathenau, Walter, 115
Ratzinger, Joseph (archbishop), 2, 14, 22, 97, 158, 197–201, 219n.69, 221n.94, 249n.30, 255n.67
Reimarus, Hermann Samuel, 143, 162
Reinhold, Hans Anscar, 241n.64
Remarque, Erich Maria, 115
Remigius, St., 122
Renan, Ernst, 143
Reuter, Fritz, 98
Reventlow, Ernst zu, 123
Ricoeur, Paul, 184
Rilke, Rainer Maria, 10, 13, 48, 91–92, 99–112, 142, 154, 198, 200, 209
Rösch, Konstantin, 140
Rosenberg, Alfred, 121–24
Rouault, Georges, 139
Ruster, Thomas, 159
Ruysbroeck, Jan von, 81

Sartre, Jean Paul, 185
Saul of Tarsus. *See* St. Paul
Schaezler, Karl, 235n.31

Scheeben, Matthias, 193
Scheffczyk, Leo, 245n.51
Scheler, Max, 7, 12, 14, 32, 47–51, 78, 91–92, 98, 101, 114, 146, 177, 179, 193, 199, 226n.34, 230n.24
Schell, Hermann, 5, 26, 94, 234n.17
Schelling, Friedrich Wilhelm Joseph von, 223n.42, 245n.44
Schillebeeckx, Edward, 151, 192, 235n.30
Schilson, Arno, 66, 86, 159, 251n.4
Schlegel, Friedrich, 48
Schleiermacher, Friedrich, 8
Schlette, Heinz Robert, 22, 249n.30
Schleussner, Renate Josephine, 4, 53–54, 98, 166
Schleussner, Wilhelm, 4, 53–54, 98, 166
Schlüter-Hermkes, Maria, 217n.27
Schmaus, Michael, 120–24, 184, 201
Schmid, Carlo, 10
Schmidt, Karl Ludwig, 141
Schmitt, Carl, 164, 239n.22
Schnackenburg, Rudolf, 157
Scholl, Hans, 241n.62
Scholl, Sophie, 241n.62
Schopenhauer, Arthur, 78
Schott, Anselm, 72, 80–81
Schreibmayr, Franz, 252n.21
Schulte, Carl Joseph (archbishop of Cologne), 119
Schwartz, Rudolf, 80, 166, 231n.41
Scott, Nathan A., 92
Seneca, 153
Sexton, Anne, 194
Shakespeare, William, 4, 60, 100
Sheen, Fulton J., 196
Shuster, George, 194
Silone, Ignazio, 248n.29
Simson, Otto von, 201
Sinclair, Upton, 115
Socrates, 9, 13, 31, 91, 100, 146, 149, 191, 198
Soergel, Albert, 92, 108
Sonnenschein, Carl, 59, 65, 78, 182
Spengler, Oswald, 73, 165
Spörl, Johannes, 217
Spranger, Eduard, 44
Stalin, Joseph, 118, 178
Stallmann, Martin, 186
Stampa, Gaspara, 103–4
Stein, Edith, 50, 218n47.
Steinbach, Erwin von, 130

Stendahl. *See* Beyle, Marie Henri
Stohr, Albert (bishop of Mainz), 64–65, 83, 219n.69
Strassburg, Gottfried von, 130
Stratmann, Franziskus, 120
Strauss, David Friedrich, 143
Streeter, Burnett Hillman, 140
Strehler, Bernhard, 50, 62
Suárez, Francisco de, 17
Sussmann, Vera, 251n.6

Tanquerey, Adolphe, 17, 25, 57, 143
Teilhard de Chardin, Pierre, 189
Tewes, Ernst (bishop), 88, 251n.10
Theobald, Michael, 245n.50
Thielicke, Helmut, 201
Thomas Aquinas, St., 6, 93, 111, 144, 171
Thucydides, 153
Tillmann, Fritz, 7, 120, 140
Tilmann, Klemen, 252n.21
Toller, Ernst, 97
Tönnies, Ferdinand, 48
Troeltsch, Ernst, 8, 32, 93, 146, 165
Tromp, Sebastian, 47

Vahanian, Gabriel, 186
Veuillot, Louis, 94
Vogels, Heinrich J., 140

Vorgrimler, Herbert, 158

Wagner, Johannes, 85, 87
Wagner, Richard, 95, 121, 124
Weber, Alfred, 177
Weber, Max, 146
Weiger, Josef, 5, 10–12, 74, 75, 89, 128, 167, 188–90, 208, 222n.15, 240n.48, 251n.6
Wellek, René, 102
Wellhausen, Julius, 140–41
Wells, Herbert George, 115
Westhoff, Clara, 107
Wiggers, Jan, 252n.21
Wilhelm II (Kaiser), 49, 53, 93
Wittelsbach, 97
Wojtyla, Karol. *See* John Paul II
Wolff, Odilo, 74, 230n.24
Wolter, Maurus, 72
Wolter, Placidus, 72
Wust, Peter, 218n.47

Yeats, William Butler, 110–11

Ziolkowski, Theodore, 92
Zola, Emile, 115
Zweig, Arnold, 115
Zweig, Stefan, 115